Throughout the fall of 1941, the diplomatic situation in the Pacific became critical. So much so, in fact, that an attack upon the United States was deemed Japan's only hope by her military leadership. On December 7, 1941, the United States Naval Base at Pearl Harbor was suddenly attacked by Japan's carrier force. Four days later Germany and Italy, fulfilling their obligation to their Axis ally, declared war on the United States. The undeclared war was no more.

On November 23, 1941, Adm. Ernest J. King celebrated his sixty-third birthday. He now had one more year to go before reaching mandatory retirement age.

The day after Pearl Harbor, King went to Washington to confer with the top brass. There he found a stunned leadership.

On December 15, he was back in Washington for a meeting with Secretary of the Navy Knox. The secretary had just returned from Pearl Harbor where he had personally assessed the extent of the damage. Knox told King that it had been decided to send Nimitz to the Pacific as the new Commander in Chief, Pacific Fleet. Then he told King that it also had been decided that he, King, be appointed Commander in Chief, U.S. Fleet. King wondered when he would retire . . . .

NEW ADVENTURES FROM ZEBRA

THE BLACK EAGLES:
HANOI HELLGROUND   (1249, $2.95)
by John Lansing
They're the best jungle fighters the United States has to offer, and no matter where Charlie is hiding, they'll find him. They're the greatest unsung heroes of the dirtiest, most challenging war of all time. They're THE BLACK EAGLES.

THE BLACK EAGLES #2:
MEKONG MASSACRE   (1294, $2.50)
by John Lansing
Falconi and his Black Eagle combat team are about to stake a claim on Colonel Nguyen Chi Roi—and give the Commie his due. But American intelligence wants the colonel alive, making this the Black Eagles' toughest assignment ever!

MCLEANE'S RANGER #2:
TARGET RABAUL   (1271, $2.50)
by John Darby
Rabaul—it was one of the keys to the control of the Pacific and the Japanese had a lock on it. When nothing else worked, the Allies called on their most formidable weapon—McLeane's Rangers, the jungle fighters who don't know the meaning of the word quit!

SWEET VIETNAM   (1423, $3.50)
by Richard Parque
Every American flier hoped to blast "The Dragonman," the ace North Vietnamese pilot, to pieces. Major Vic Benedetti was no different. Sending "The Dragonman" down in a spiral of smoke and flames was what he lived for, worked for, prayed for—and might die for . . .

Available wherever paperbacks are sold, or order direct from the Publisher. Send cover price plus 50¢ per copy for mailing and handling to Zebra Books, Dept. 1755, 475 Park Avenue South, New York, N.Y. 10016. DO NOT SEND CASH.

THE
GREAT ADMIRALS
OF
WORLD WAR II
VOLUME I: THE AMERICANS

BY CHARLES E. PFANNES AND
VICTOR A. SALAMONE

ZEBRA BOOKS
KENSINGTON PUBLISHING CORP.

FOR LILLIAN
Wife, Lover, Mother, Friend, Companion, Inspiration

ZEBRA BOOKS

are published by

KENSINGTON PUBLISHING CORP.
475 Park Avenue South
New York, N.Y. 10016

Third printing: August 1985

Printed in the United States of America

TABLE OF CONTENTS

It has been more than forty years since the attack on Pearl Harbor which initiated America's greatest challenge. Luckily, talented individuals paved the way for victory during the grueling four years of war. The war in the Pacific has sometimes been called a navy's war, Though this statement is inaccurate, since many army forces were involved throughout the entire Pacific war, nevertheless the admirals who helped bring victory are readily recalled: Nimitz, Halsey, Spruance, and Turner. This first volume of *The Great Admirals of World War II* is going to focus on six admirals who helped bring victory to America in World War II.

In the introduction we focus on the great achievement of the cryptographers who broke the Japanese secret code. In chapter one, Admiral King, our wartime Chief of Naval Operations is studied. We next study Admiral Nimitz. After Pearl Harbor, Nimitz came to the Pacific and thereafter guided America's forces until the end of the war. Admiral Spruance is the subject of our next chapter. His quietness covered a great naval mind, an asset needed at Midway and as commander of the Fifth Fleet. Landing forces on a hostile shore is perhaps one of the military's hardest jobs. Admiral Turner, chapter four's subject, reduced amphibious assaults to a fine science. "Bull" Halsey, perhaps America's most famous fighting admiral is the subject of chapter five. Lastly, Admiral Kinkaid, who performed superbly in the Aleutian campaign and at Leyte Gulf is the subject of our final chapter.

We would like to thank our reading public for faithfully following our Great Commanders' series. We would again like to mention our wives, Susanne and Lillian, and our children, Charles, Victor, Thomas, Jennifer, and John. Thank you for your love, patience, and support, for without it our achievement would mean nothing.

Charles E. Pfannes
Cold Spring, New York
Victor A Salamone
Poughkeepsie, New York
November, 1982

The fact that the Japanese code was broken by American cryptographers is by now a well-known fact. This brief introduction is designed to tell how Magic and Ultra aided the Americans during the war in the Pacific. Since it is but an introduction to a book about American admirals, this chapter will only attempt to give the briefest summary. The text of the book that follows will elucidate the greater story. The overriding purpose of this introduction is merely to inform the reader about this all-important weapon in America's arsenal.

General Marshall perhaps said it best in a letter to New York Governor Thomas Dewey during the 1944 presidential campaign:

> The battle of the Coral Sea was based on deciphered messages and therefore our few ships were in the right place at the right time. Further, we were able to concentrate our limited forces to meet their naval advance on Midway.
>
> Operations in the Pacific are largely guided by the information we obtain of Japanese deployments. We know their strength in various garrisons. . . . We check their fleet movements and the movements of their convoys. . . . We know the sailing dates and routes . . . and can notify our submarines to be in wait at the proper points.[1]

Therefore, the fact that the code was compromised was of extreme importance.

Magic refers to all the information gathered from the encipherment of the Japanese diplomatic signals, while Ultra (not to be confused with the German Enigma encipherments) was the name given to the intelligence gathered by the code breakers of the Japanese naval and army signals. Combined with Magic, Ultra provided the American high command with an excellent insight into Japanese intentions and plans.

The story of the breaking of the Japanese code is a lengthy circuitous one. Certain personalities stand out above all others. Code-breaking has been accomplished for as long as man has attempted to deceive his fellow man by the use of cryptic statements. Even during the American Civil War codes predominated. Perhaps the most celebrated of the American code-breaking organizations was the American Black Chamber made famous by Herbert Yardley. In 1921, Yardley's Black Chamber broke the then-existing Japanese code. This effort had a great bearing on the Washington naval conference that settled the issue of a 5:5:3 ratio of capital ships between the United States, Great Britain, and Japan respectively.

The man most celebrated as the one who broke the Japanese diplomatic code, however, was William F. Friedman. By the fall of 1940, Friedman and his group of cryptanalysts had solved some of the highest grade cryptographic systems of the Japanese Foreign Office. The Signal Intelligence Service constructed four machines—called Purple—to decipher the secret Japanese diplomatic traffic. At that time, the military codes remained undecipherable.

The U.S. Government quickly reaped the benefit of these intercepts. When the new Japanese Ambassador to the United States, Admiral Nomura, presented himself to Cordell Hull, the United States Secretary of State, his pacific attitude was welcomed as a sign of a positive prospect for peace. Through the intercepts, however, the government was able to establish the true intent of the Japanese Government, which hardly reflected Nomura's pacific manner. It helped Hull and Roosevelt to better estimate the actual Japanese intention which was hidden by the cosmetics of the well-meaning Nomura.

An immediate question poses itself here. Since the code breakers had broken the diplomatic code, why was the attack on Pearl Harbor a surprise? Two recent books have been published, each taking a different side of the question. John Toland, in *Infamy*, states emphatically that President Roosevelt had advance notification of the approach of the Japanese Task Force and that, prior to this notification, vital Japanese intercepts were not handled properly or sent to the necessary people.

In Ronald Lewin's book, *The American Magic*, he presents an excellent case of exonerating the President and the military chiefs in Washington. Both eminent scholars have convincingly argued their point and both portray what might be the "truth." The authors of this chronicle merely direct the readers to these two outstanding books and will let them draw their own conclusions. Will the truth ever be known?

After Pearl Harbor the Japanese war machine spread its mighty tentacles throughout the Pacific and southeast Asia. In time their victories swelled the Japanese with a deep sense of pride which was later translated into "victory disease." Having conquered an empire with so little loss, the Japanese were hesitant to swing over to the defensive. Australia, a potential base for an Allied counterattack, had to be eliminated. In addition, the American aircraft carriers which, fortunately for the Americans, had escaped destruction at Pearl Harbor, had to be dealt with. This gave rise to two possible Japanese offensives: one toward Port Moresby and the other toward Midway.

It was up to Commander Joseph Rochefort of the Fleet Radio Unit, Pacific (FRUPac as it was called), to piece together the many enemy intercepts in an attempt to determine the Japanese intentions.

The Japanese naval code, JN 25, was attacked by Rochefort and his men more extensively than earlier codes. JN 25 presented them with a host of problems. Naval Intelligence in Washington, OP-20-G, also put its expertise to work attempting to crack the Japanese naval code.

Aiding the code breakers was the fact that the Japanese were fattened by their easy victories and by the vast multiplication of their bases throughout the Pacific. The latter situation created an intelligence problem for them. To maintain a code's integrity it must be changed frequently. To overuse a code might easily expose it to decipherment. The extent of the Japanese Empire, however, mitigated against rapid dispersement of new code books. This resulted in the retention of their old codes for dangerously long periods of time. Therefore, thanks to the vastness of their newly conquered empire, the Japanese were forced to extend the use of the JN 25 code. This allowed the American intelligence teams the time to crack the code. Because of the latter's success, both the Port Moresby operation and, more importantly, the Midway offensive were disclosed to Admiral Nimitz.

With the knowledge provided by Ultra, Nimitz was able to position Fletcher's carriers at the right place in the Coral Sea. So, too, at Midway, the intelligence allowed Nimitz to stay one step ahead of the Japanese.

Shapes and patterns gradually emerged to be confirmed in the end by intercepts so specific in detail and so conclusive in their significance that Nimitz, on the eve of his next great battle (Midway), had a more intimate knowledge of his enemy's strength and intentions than any other admiral in the whole previous history of sea warfare.[2]

Midway was as much a victory for the cryptographers as it was for the brave pilots who risked their lives to sink the Japanese carriers.

In June 1942, just prior to Midway but too late to foil the

Americans, the Japanese changed the JN 25 code system. Not because they suspected its integrity, but simply as part of the normal routine. This necessitated the code breakers' beginning their efforts anew. W. J. Holmes of FRUPac commented on the plight of a code breaker.

Progress on the five-digit code that the Japanese had been using since 1 June, 1942 was slow. It was August before any light began to dawn. That same month the code, having been in effect only a little more than two months, was changed again.[3]

It was unfortunate for Nimitz that the change occurred just as the invasion of Guadalcanal (August 7, 1942) was about to commence. Though cryptanalysis was temporarily blind, radio intercepts (traffic analysis) were still functional. Through this, Nimitz discovered in June that the Japanese were constructing an airfield on the jungle-clad island of Guadalcanal in the Solomons. This news impelled the admiral to quickly schedule Operation Watchtower before the Japanese could make the airfield operational. Holmes comments again:

Until the Battle of Midway, communications intelligence completely dominated combat intelligence, but when the action shifted to the Solomons there was also a change in the nature of combat intelligence. The Japanese, being now on the defensive and having their forces concentrated in Rabaul, no longer needed to transmit their plans by radio and this, together with the change in their code made it impossible for radio intelligence to determine specific details of their dispositions and timing. We could still read some minor codes. . . . With this information and traffic analysis, it was frequently possible to detect a build-up of Japanese naval strength.[4]

Thus, until the code breakers could open that elusive window again, traffic analysis, aerial reconnaissance, and the daring and brave coastwatchers had to supply the necessary eyes and ears for the Americans.

The debacle at Savo Island could have been linked to the fact that the Japanese code could not be read at that time. During most of the campaign, only low-grade codes were penetrated. However, through these low-grade codes, combined with the aforementioned traditional methods of intelligence-gathering, the job was done. In part, eventual victory was as much aided by these advance warnings as by the blood of the army, navy, and marine forces.

When the new year of 1943 dawned, FRUPac was again reading the Japanese code.

Meanwhile, in the southwest Pacific, through traffic analysis, MacArthur received advance warning of the Japanese attack on Port Moresby. This valuable information disclosed the Japanese intention to utilize the Kokoda Trail across the Owen Stanley Mountains, the spiny backbone of Papua, New Guinea. Thanks also to Ultra, in March, 1943, during what would later be called the Battle of the Bismarck Sea, Army Air Force planes of the Fifth Air Force flew four hundred sorties with a loss of but five aircraft. The Japanese, on the other hand, lost an entire convoy loaded with reinforcements and supplies destined for New Guinea. Ultra told the American pilots where to be and what time to be there in the Bismarck Sea.

The next coup credited to Ultra intelligence was none other than the assassination of Admiral Yamamoto. His itinerary, showing just where the admiral would be on April 18, was intercepted and deciphered four days prior to the trip. The Americans prepared a trap and the brilliant designer of the Pearl Harbor attack was killed.*

*The Great Commanders of World War II, Volume IV: The Japanese, chapter 2.

Ultra also provided Admiral Nimitz with a fairly accurate estimate of Japanese forces on the many islands invaded in the central Pacific. However, it could not make the job any easier for the combat troops.

Decoded signals translated into Ultra could provide and often provided abundantly precise information concerning the enemy's capability on an island about to be assaulted. The name, the strength, and the location of individual units, the amount of ammunition or rations available . . . all these and many other invaluable details came to the Americans from the fountain of Ultra. But what signal intelligence could not do was to provide topographical knowledge, nor could it penetrate the camouflage of those defensive positions so secretly and so skillfully devised by the Japanese.[5]

Ultra could only provide so much. It had its limitations which the assault forces dramatically discovered on their bloody trail across the central Pacific.

As the reader will discover in the forthcoming chapters on Nimitz, Spruance, and Turner, Ultra intelligence convinced Nimitz that Kwajalein Atoll in the Marshalls should be invaded directly, even though his principal commander opposed that move. From intercepts Nimitz knew that the Japanese expected an attack on the perimeter islands in the Marshalls and were deploying their forces to meet just such a threat. They ignored Kwajalein.

By the spring of 1943, the Japanese Army code, which had eluded the code breakers, was finally broken. From then until the end of the war, the wealth of Japanese intelligence compromised to the Americans was enormous. The Maru* code was also broken in 1943. Thus, through Ultra,

*Merchantman cipher

15

the Japanese homeland was quickly cut off from the natural resources of its empire. With the knowledge provided, American submarines found the Japanese merchant ships and sent them to Davy Jones's locker. As Holmes explains:

> There were nights when nearly every American submarine on patrol in the central Pacific was working on the basis of information derived from cryptanalysis.[6]

With the aide of Ultra, by the middle of 1943, the submarines had doubled their kill ratio. The information was so accurate that not only were the names of all Japanese ships known, but also their numbers, cargoes, and routes. Even the precise noontime positions for every day of their voyages was disclosed. The tonnage of Japanese losses was astounding. Over seventy percent of all Japan's shipping losses was the result of U.S. submarine attacks, an awesome achievement when the size of the Pacific Ocean is considered. Thanks to Ultra, the submarines were at the right spot at the right time.

Though the Japanese military cipher eluded the code breakers for the early months of the war until the major breakthrough in 1943, and excepting the periods prior to the Coral Sea and Midway battles, the Japanese diplomatic code, Purple, continued to supply Washington with a clear insight into the Japanese political scene throughout the war. In fact, it even gave the code breakers an insight into the German situation as Japanese diplomats diligently reported Germany's military and economic situation to their home. This added bonus filled many gaps in the knowledge already gained from the breaking of the German Enigma code.*

*See introduction to *The Great Commanders of World War II, Volume II: The British*.

For example, on December 10, 1943, the Japanese ambassador in Germany, Baron Oshima, described the Atlantic Wall for his superiors in Japan. He gave an accurate description of the German defensive systems, placements of divisions, and much additional useful information.

Thanks to the efforts of the code breakers, the daily policies of the Japanese Government were known in Washington. This was of inestimable value during the final months of the war as Japan attempted to bring about a favorable settlement of the war. Their policy toward Russia was made clear to the Washington planners. In addition, Washington also received insight into the Soviet positions on the Japanese overtures.

Truly, Magic and Ultra were America's greatest allies in the Pacific war. However, the final outcome still boiled down to bitter fighting against a determined foe, fighting which Allied combat troops were forced to endure. But without Ultra, that enemy would have been better fortified. Their supply ships would have reached their destinations unscathed.

The authors would like to recommend the books listed in the bibliography of this introduction for the serious reader who would like to pursue this topic in depth.

Legend holds that Adm. Ernest King was so tough that he shaved with a blowtorch. While this might seem to be a highly unorthodox method of removing facial hair, the symbolism is not lacking. Never in American history has one man held so much power over the navy. Attaining the rank of Fleet Admiral, he was both Commander in Chief of the Fleet and Chief of Naval Operations as well as being a member of both the Joint and Combined Chiefs of Staff. By 1945, King commanded the world's largest navy, made up of more than eight thousand ships, twenty-four thousand aircraft, and over three million officers and enlisted men.

Admiral King was not known for his tact. Winston Churchill considered him "tough, blunt, rude, intolerant, and suspicious of all things British."[1]

Admiral of the Fleet Sir Andrew Cunningham, another member of the Combined Chiefs of Staff, thought King "ill-mannered, ruthless, and arrogant."[2]

Well might the British harbor these feelings, for King was a man of candor. He said what he wanted to, regardless of whom he hurt, providing it was the truth as he viewed it. During the many high-level conferences he participated in during the Second World War, King championed a strategy contrary to that of many of his colleagues. Convinced of the correctness of his course, he caused his co-belligerents many a sleepless night. One can easily understand then, why it was rumored he shaved with a blowtorch. His toughness and resolve were unshakable. Yet it was this hard-as-rock determination that steered the

United States Navy through its greatest challenge.

Spawned from mixed Scottish-English ancestry, Ernest Joseph King was born on November 23, 1878, in Cleveland, Ohio. Young Ernest's father was a great influence on the future admiral. Relatives were able to observe the young boy's truthfulness and candor at a very early age. More than once his bluntness caused them to take note. As a high-school student Ernest excelled and was named valedictorian of his graduating class. Even before graduation, he had been entertaining the possibility of entering the naval academy. His father was amenable to that desire and sought a congressional appointment for his son. Discovering that he would have to pass a competitive exam, Ernest crammed during his final months of high school. Competing against thirty other hopefuls, Ernest was apprehensive, but his competency was noted and he far surpassed the others. King received the coveted appointment.

On August 15, 1897, Ernest King arrived at Annapolis. The academy he entered was fifty-two years old and was in a dreadful state. Neglected by Congressional financing, the buildings were decrepit. In fact, the barracks which housed the cadets were called the new quarters, even though they had been erected during the Civil War and were in dire need of renovation. Yet, the young midwesterner was full of excitement as he "smelled the aromas of salty air" for the first time.

Life at the academy was hard and the attrition rate high. Discipline bordered on the sadistic, but King adapted himself to the rigors of his new life. He found the academic studies easy and was well-liked by his classmates and by the administration who recognized his ability.

In April of his plebe year America embarked on its first imperial venture by declaring war against Spain. The naval academy rocked with excitement as all looked forward to action. Junior officers, who for the most part made up the faculty, were ordered to the fleet immediately. The first classmen were graduated prematurely, commissioned, and sent off to war. King and the rest of his class were ordered to go home, but he yearned for action. During his enforced leave, King and a classmate discovered how another class-mate had wangled orders for sea. Finagling similar orders, he and four other classmates boarded the cruiser *San Francisco* at Provincetown, Massachusetts. After serving for a while protecting the New England coast against an illusionary threat of attack, the *San Francisco* was finally ordered south to Cuba where it joined the American block-ade force. On August 12, the cruiser was fired on by shore batteries near Havana. Soon afterward, hostilities in America's "splendid little war" ceased and, since there was no further need for the cadets, on the return trip the com-mander of the cruiser left King and company off at Key West, Florida, where they were each forced to reach home by train. For King, the entire experience was exhilarating and years later he would note that he "had been at sea and had been shot at."[3]

In June, 1901, Ernest King became a passed midship-man; his academic days were behind him. During the four years that he was at Annapolis, great changes had come to the sleepy little village. The Spanish-American War had awakened the country to the need for a strong military. One of the beneficiaries of this new attitude was the naval academy. When the class of 1901 graduated, they left behind a new bustling academy. America, the naval academy, and Passed Midshipman King were on their way.

Along with the Spanish-American War, Teddy Roosevelt was responsible for the new outlook. After the assassination of President William McKinley, Roosevelt became Presi-dent. Greatly influenced by the sea-power advocate, Alfred Thayer Mahan, Roosevelt was determined to transform the United States into a great naval power. It was auspicious that King graduated at this opportune time.

During the next four years, the U.S. Congress, under the

President's prodding, authorized the construction of ten battleships, four cruisers, and seven other ships. The navy and the country were in a state of transition.

Following graduation, King was sent to the Naval Torpedo Station at Newport, Rhode Island, to study the design and operation of the torpedo. He was then assigned to a survey ship, the USS *Eagle* as navigator. The *Eagle* was a small ship, not a very prestigious post for one of the top graduates of the class of 1901. Deftly, King navigated the ship down the east coast, past the Florida Keys, then down to Cuba. The job of surveying was not very exciting and King often suffered from boredom. While on duty in the tropics, the bright sunlight caused him to develop eye trouble and resulted in his transfer to the Brooklyn Naval Hospital.

After his eyes healed, King sought a new, more exciting assignment. His wishes were granted. He was ordered to the new battleship, *Illinois*. For King, the opportunity to serve on the *Illinois* was a challenge. The battleship was given the task of showing the colors in the ports of northern Europe and the Mediterranean. Basically, the voyage was for prestige purposes, but in a sense, the ship was sent to show off the might of the New World to the Old World.

King was ambitious; he strove constantly to be the best. He was reaching for the top and wanted to learn all there was to know in order to achieve that goal. Service on the *Illinois*, he reasoned, was ideal for that purpose. However, he was disappointed with his job, referring to himself as the errand boy for Rear Admiral A. S. Crowninshield, so he sought another assignment.

The new assignment was as a division and watch officer on the cruiser *Cincinnati*. King readily accepted the assignment since it was a unique position for a man who was not as yet a commissioned officer.

The new job had King responsible for forty sailors. This was his first experience of command over men. He quickly proved an excellent leader with the ability to strike enthusiasm in his subordinates. King set out to form a top-rated division and worked hard to achieve this goal. In the process, he gained the admiration and respect of both his subordinates and superiors.

While serving on the *Cincinnati*, King took the examination for ensign in the spring of 1903. The questions were prepared by the academic board of the naval academy and sent under seal to King's commanding officer, who then administered the examination and returned the papers to Annapolis for grading. King passed and received his commission.

The *Cincinnati* now set sail on an Asiatic cruise. The long voyage was not without problems for young Ensign King. At this early stage in his life an alcoholic problem was detected. Once in Singapore and again in Shanghai, he was out drinking with his companions and returned to the ship late, drunk and disorderly. King was reprimanded and restricted to quarters. He repeated the offense and was once more confined to quarters, only this time the incident was noted in his fitness report. That was the last time he was late. King had learned his lesson the hard way.

In addition to his drinking, King also exhibited a stubbornness sometimes described by his superiors as arrogant insubordination. He preferred to call it forthrightness, however. When he felt he was right, King would argue his case with venom. His superiors viewed this as insubordinate conduct and arrogance. Unfortunately, these negative statements also went into his fitness reports. For a man striving for flag rank, King's service record was amassing far too many negative statements.

When in the Far East, the Russo-Japanese war was fought, though it was a ship of a neutral country, the *Cincinnati* did steam through the battle zone to deliver foo to the Russian refugees at Port Arthur. The young ensi formed some early favorable impressions of the Imperi

Japanese Navy.

By the spring of 1905, having been away from the United States for more than two years, King found himself longing to return home. Requesting reassignment to the States, he eventually received orders to return home several months later.

On October 10, 1905, King married Martha Egerton. Following their honeymoon, he reported to Hampton Roads, Virginia where he was ordered to duty on the battleship *Alabama*.

The typical career of a naval officer was one spent alternating between sea duty and shore assignments. King's career was no exception. After a short tour on the *Alabama*, he was reassigned to the naval academy as an instructor of ordnance, gunnery, and seamanship. In addition, he was battalion drillmaster with the added duty of teaching marching and infantry maneuvers. Vigorously, he drove the cadets through forced marches, amphibious landings, and rifle exercises. King was a hard taskmaster. Two years later, he was transferred to the executive department as officer in charge of enforcing discipline in Bancroft Hall, the cadet dormitory. During his three years at the academy, King drove himself hard. In fact, he did not even take one day of leave. He was rapidly becoming a workaholic.

In 1909, King returned to sea as flag secretary to his former commanding officer on the *Cincinnati*, Hugo Osterhaus. After a year on the admiral's staff, King transferred to the battleship *New Hampshire* as a member of the ship's engineering department. In a month's time, he became engineering officer. King brought the same dedication and determination to this position as he had to his former jobs.

When Admiral Osterhaus became Commander in Chief, Atlantic Fleet, King accepted an offer to serve once more as flag secretary. He proved to be a valuable and proficient secretary.

In May, 1912, King returned to Annapolis as the executive officer of the Naval Engineering Experimental Station. There he tested materials and equipment for future engineering use. During this time he made his first contact with a young aviator who was most zealous in proving that aircraft were the weapons of the future. The officer's name was Lt. John H. Towers. To King, aircraft simply did not seem to present the great threat to battleships that Towers claimed. Later on, however, King changed his mind.

By the late winter of 1913, King was itching once more for sea duty. There was a threat of war with Mexico and he wanted to be in on it. Although he was a thirty-five-year-old lieutenant commander, he as yet had not experienced independent command. King wanted command of a destroyer.

In the early spring of 1914, his aspirations were rewarded with orders to report to Galveston, Texas to take command of the destroyer *Terry*. After a successful tour of duty with the *Terry*, he was moved up to the larger destroyer *Cassin*. He also doubled as aide to Capt. William Sims. The latter was probably one of the most influential naval officers of the time, and service with him could not help but benefit an aspiring young officer. King's candor, however, caused Sims to explode at him on one occasion when the young officer imprudently spoke out against a Sims decision that King thought absurd. He was relieved as Sims's aide shortly afterward and was elevated to command of a four-ship division in addition to retaining his duties as captain of the *Cassin*.

With Europe engulfed in war, the American Navy stirred with excitement. King, as commander of the division, was amassing a good efficiency report. So much so in fact, that he earned the attention of Adm. Henry Mayo, Commander of the Battleship Force, Atlantic Fleet. Mayo asked King to join his staff. After careful consideration, King agreed. It was a fortunate decision. Mayo soon became the

Commander in Chief, Atlantic Fleet.

King reported for duty on Mayo's staff in December, 1915, as staff engineer. He was impressed by Mayo's ability and worked himself to his usual optimum. In April, 1917, when the United States finally went to war against the Central Powers, King was ready but the navy was not.

The President's injunction against any war talk during the presidential campaign of 1916 placed an obstacle in the way of any war preparation. When war was finally declared, the navy was not prepared; nor, for that matter, was the army.

Mayo and his staff, including King, arrived in England in August, 1917. From there they moved on to the war-torn continent. King and William Pye, another aspiring flag officer, were frequent guests of the Royal Navy. Occasionally, King even accompanied the Grand Fleet into the North Sea for war games. He met Adm. David Beatty, the famed battle-cruiser commander, at Jutland and Admiral Jellicoe, the First Sea Lord. It was with Jellicoe, aboard the destroyer *Broke* which was escorting a British raiding party, that King came under German fire from land fortifications. Though it was not the first time he had been under fire, the event impressed King. Jellicoe remarked to him at the time:

"That'll be something to tell your grandchildren," to which King replied, "Yes, Admiral, and the more years that intervene, the closer the shells are likely to get."[4]

King was in Europe again when the war ended on November 11, 1918.

During the war, King had learned much about commanding a navy at war. While a member of Mayo's staff, he found himself dealing with the Navy Department and Washington politicians. King also attended many conferences with civilian and military leaders during this period. He learned the how and the why and the what to do while at war. He had been appropriately educated. In his autobiography, King vented his anger on the state of naval leadership at that time, which he said was pursuing backward policies that were stifling naval progress. As a firm believer in Mahan's naval theories, King was appalled at the navy's poor performance. He had no patience for ineptitude and did not attempt to conceal this contempt.

He showed it, hostile, arrogant, sometimes disrespectful and even insubordinate.[5]

With the exception of Mayo, King held the current leadership in contempt.

At war's end, he was forty, a captain, and holder of the Navy Cross in recognition of his brilliant staff work. His first postwar assignment was back at Annapolis where he was directed to reopen the Naval Postgraduate School.

King was determined to apply the latest naval theories to the postgraduate school. Things went along fine until Rear Admiral Henry B. Wilson was named superintendent of the naval academy. King was appalled at the choice, since he considered Wilson very backward-looking. When Wilson's appointment was announced, King suddenly became anxious to move on, so he applied for a transfer.

In July, 1921, King was appointed captain of the supply ship, USS *Bridge*. Command of a supply ship was certainly no reward. The work was boring and primarily consisted of carrying supplies up and down the east coast for the Atlantic Fleet. King remained with the *Bridge* for a year before seeking transfer to a destroyer. There were no positions open, however, so he was asked if he would be interested in submarines, since possibilities for command existed in this branch once an aspirant attended submarine school at New London, Connecticut. King jumped at the chance.

Upon completion of submarine school, King was assigned to command of a four-submarine division. In January, 1923, King hoisted his pennant on the submarine *S-20* and led his division south for the annual Caribbean cruise. Soon, mechanical problems began to plague the division. Although he wished to ultilize the submarines in the maneuvers, King found that postwar economizing coupled with low fuel allotments, prevented his participation.

In September, 1923, he was assigned command of the submarine base at New London. While there, the submarine *S-51* was rammed and sunk near Block Island, just south of Rhode Island. King was handed the hazardous job of salvaging the stricken submarine and its thirty-four entombed crewmen. After months of near-impossible weather conditions which caused a four-month hiatus until the spring, the task was successfully accomplished and the *S-51* was towed to New York. The epic raising gave King national prominence. His reputation soared. In fact, King had placed his reputation on the line. If he had failed to raise the *S-51,* it might have spelled the end of any aspirations for flag rank. But he gambled and won.

With that job completed, King sought new fields. He was hoping for command of a cruiser, but his involvement with the *S-51* had caused him to miss some fine opportunities for sea command. At this point he was sent for by Rear Admiral William Moffett. The latter, foreseeing the need for qualified senior officers for aviation command, was naturally anxious to persuade a certain number of captains to come over into the aviation field.

Just at that time, King was pondering what future course to take; so after mulling over Moffett's invitation, King accepted. Having had experience on the sea and below, he now turned his attention to the air. His attitude had changed from the days prior to World War I when he had debated with John Towers over the potential of naval aviation.

King's first aviation command was with the seaplane tender USS *Wright*. Since it was required that he become a qualified pilot, early in 1927 King was ordered to report to Pensacola, Florida to begin formal flying lessons. He completed all the requirements necessary to earn his wings and, nearing fifty years of age, finally soloed. After five months at Pensacola, he was awarded the prized breast insignia of a naval aviator on May 26, 1927. King then returned to the *Wright*.

On June 18, 1928, with his reputation growing, Admiral Moffett recommended King for command of the new aircraft carrier *Lexington*. At the last moment, however, the orders were changed and King was ordered to become the assistant to the Aeronautics Bureau under Moffett. His stubbornness, however, soon caused a falling out between him and Moffett. Eager for a more active command, he sought release from the assignment. Moffett happily sent King to command the air base at Norfolk, Virginia. Then finally came the assignment King had originally wanted, command of the *Lexington*.

In June, 1930, Ernie King took command of the "Lady Lex." He immediately set to work enforcing the letter of the law on what was considered up to that time to be a loose-running ship. The *Lexington*'s new captain laid down exacting standards for his officers, always demanding the best. If they failed to measure up, King had them transferred.

Although King was an exacting taskmaster, his browbeating paid off. The *Lexington* became a model ship, "a clean, smart, glistening man-o'-war."[6]

He proved a man of great stamina, but his caustic personality more than once caused him to irritate subordinates and superiors.

King was an enigma. Aboard ship he was unapproachable, aloof, stern, and austere. Once ashore, however, he was one of the boys. He loved parties and in the process of party-hopping picked up a nickname, Uncle Ernie. He still retained his disposition for liquor and developed a reputation as a womanizer. King had once told a friend:

"You ought to be suspicious of anyone who won't take a drink or doesn't like women."[7]

He liked both. King's reputation as a ladies' man was at times downright lecherous. Whether his wife knew of the extent of his chasing women is unknown, but within the service he had a notorious reputation.

Though the United States was in an economic depression and military appropriations were at their lowest, King, nevertheless, wholeheartedly worked his crews as if nothing else mattered. He conducted training exercises just as if America were at war. He never allowed the excuse of little appropriations to hinder preparations.

Meanwhile, in 1931, Japan invaded Manchuria. The *Lexington* was sent to San Francisco, then to Hawaii as a show of force to the Japanese.

After two years at the helm of the *Lexington*, King relinquished command. His superiors had rated his overall performance excellent. He had passed the final test on the road to flag rank.

King was recommended for promotion to rear admiral with only one final rung on the ladder to be climbed, attendance at the Naval War College. While there, in August 1932, he was selected by the promotion board for elevation to the rank of rear admiral.

King's first assignment after his promotion was as chief of the Bureau of Aeronautics. Obtaining that appointment was no mean chore and he had to use all his powers of persuasion to land the prestigious appointment. He thus became only the second chief since the bureau's conception twelve years earlier. Reporting to the chief of the bureau were fifty naval officers and a hundred civilians. The hardships of the Great Depression, reaching into every level of the military, caused the naval aviators to tighten their purse. Hindered by Congress, King found his first and most important job to be convincing the lawmakers not to economize further at the expense of naval aviation. For the three years he was the bureau's chief, King cajoled, compromised, and debated with Congress over naval aviation appropriations. Though initially a novice in the methods of dealing with Congress, King learned quickly and managed to steer the bureau through the heart of the depression. In the process he kept aviation alive despite the nation's woes.

After three years as chief of the bureau, King realized that if he was going to reach the top of his profession, he would have to fly his flag at sea. He thus sought a sea-going command. Shortly afterward, he was appointed Commander, Scouting Force, which gave him command of a dozen or so squadrons of land- and sea-based patrol planes totaling more than a hundred aircraft located at such widely divergent places as San Diego, Honolulu, and Panama.

King was convinced that war was inevitable. Though his opinion was in the minority, he nevertheless approached the new command with the determination of a zealot. He established three priorities. The first was the training of pilots under wartime conditions. Second was the establishment of patrol seaplanes to protect the coast in the event of an attack. The new PBY or Catalina (a plane he fostered during his tenure as chief of the Aeronautics Bureau) played a vital role in these patrols. Finally, King wanted to establish bases throughout the Pacific from which these seaplanes could operate.

Just as he had been during previous assignments, King was an exacting boss. He was ruthless to subordinates, particularly those he felt were incompetent. Adm. J. J. "Jocko" Clark said this of King:

"If a man knew his business, it was easy enough to get along with Ernie King. But God help him if he were wrong; King would crucify him."[8]

On another occasion, Clark noted:

"King was the only naval officer I ever knew who would actually curse his subordinates."[9]

Even though he could be ruthless, at times King was kind. He was truly a paradox.

After the China incident which precipitated the Sino-Japanese War in July, 1937, King's command was placed on alert. Nothing came of the situation, but his forces moved one step closer to the real thing.

After two years as commander of the Scouting Force, King was advanced to Commander Aircraft, Base Forces, in January, 1938. Along with this new command came promotion to vice admiral.

Included in King's newest command were the large fleet carriers, *Saratoga, Lexington,* and *Ranger.* Later on, two more carriers were added: the *Yorktown* and *Enterprise.* Upon assuming command King presented a plan to the chief of the Bureau of Navigation which in essence stated that the carriers, with their faster speed of thirty-three knots, should be detached from the slower moving battleships that were only capable of attaining twenty-one knots. The carriers would patrol with the faster sailing cruisers and destroyers. The conservative-minded commanders at the Navigation Bureau, however, nixed the idea, feeling that the carriers would be vulnerable to attack without the battleships covering them. Undeterred, King filed his plan for use at another time.

Vice Admiral King made the *Saratoga* his flagship. Later in 1938, he shifted his flag to the *Lexington.* For most of that year, he was involved in fleet exercises as he honed the fleet to peak efficiency.

King harbored ambitious hopes that his next assignment would be that of Chief of Naval Operations (CNO), the top naval position. He felt that he was the best qualified of all those of appropriate rank, since he had served in all three branches of the naval service: surface ships, submarines, and aviation. In addition, he had extensive staff experience and had held a bureau job in Washington. When the position of CNO came open in 1939, King sought the position.

His hopes were soon dashed as the laurels instead went to Rear Admiral Harold Stark. Why had King been passed over? He pondered the reasons. Was it his drinking? Was it his caustic nature which had netted him too many enemies? Was it that he was not intimate with Roosevelt? Or was it the fact that he was a naval aviator, which placed him in the minority of those holding flag rank? Perhaps it was for all these reasons. Anyhow, King was ordered to the General Board, an honorary position usually given to flag officers who were nearing retirement and had nowhere else to go. For all intents and purposes, King's career was as good as over. Over sixty, and thoroughly discouraged, King left for Washington in July, 1939.

The General Board was established in 1900 as an advisory body. Reverting to his permanent rank of rear admiral, King, along with nine other rear admirals and a small staff of officers, secretaries, and recorders, took up what was supposed to be an honorable conclusion to a career which, for a naval officer, ended when he reached the age of sixty-four.

Not long after King arrived in Washington, Hitler's blitzkrieg was unleashed against Poland. Most members of the General Board worked only a few hours a day. Not King, however. Sensing the world crisis, he toiled long hours, studied issues, and wrote recommendations. He could not, he would not, accept the fact that his career was nearly over.

In March, 1940, King's chance came. The new Secretary of the Navy, Charles Edison, son of the famous inventor, Thomas Edison, invited King to tour the fleet with him on a fact-finding mission. When the trip was over King returned to the General Board.

Meanwhile, Hitler had invaded the Low Countries, France was drowning in defeat, and England stood defiantly alone. With war seeming ever closer, Edison began to rely on King more and more. He gave King an important assignment to increase the fleet's antiaircraft armament. Allowing King carte blanche, Edison made a three-hundred-million-dollar appropriation recommendation.

King approached the job with the enthusiasm of a crusader. He studied the plans of every ship, noting what type of antiaircraft guns should be installed. His authority was total and his ability was not unnoticed by Edison who said so in a memorandum to the President just prior to leaving the cabinet post.

> I take the liberty of bringing to your attention the need for shaking the service out of peacetime psychology. . . . I believe that Rear Admiral E. J. King, USN, is outstandingly of this type (leadership) and that his appointment as commander in chief of the United States Fleet would do wonders for the fleet and the service. I earnestly recommend his appointment.[10]

King's new command was vast, encompassing the entire Atlantic Ocean. Since he could not be everywhere, he did something he rarely did. He relied on the initiative of his subordinates. He even went so far as to issue an order in late April, 1941, entitled, "Exercise of Command — Correct Use of Initiative."

In early January, the Secretary of the Navy restructured the naval command. He abolished the position of Commander in Chief, U.S. Fleet, and in its place named three separate fleets: Atlantic, Pacific, and Asiatic. King, naturally, fell easily into the position of Commander, Atlantic Fleet. With that position came the rank of full admiral. On February 1, 1941, Adm. Ernest J. King assumed the title, Commander in Chief, Atlantic Fleet.

While King settled into his new assignment, the beleaguered British stood bravely alone. Roosevelt, however, was broadening the United States's commitment to the hapless British as each day passed. Admiral Stark felt that it was necessary for the United States and Britain to begin planning jointly in order to avoid the chaos of 1917. Since the U.S. Atlantic Fleet was the nearest force available to aid the British, King was put on the spot.

King knew that the fleet was not ready to meet the challenge ahead. Too many of the ships still needed repairs, overhauls, and alterations, in order to bring them up to combat efficiency. In addition, the fleet suffered from shortages of men, materiel, and ships. He nevertheless refused to be pessimistic, but instead issued a fleet order in March entitled "Making the Best of What We Have."

With the passage of the Lend-Lease Act, more and more supplies of war were dispatched to the British. Concurrently, German U-boats were wreaking havoc with the British merchant fleet, sending thousands of tons of shipping to Davy Jones's locker each month. In late March, British and American planners agreed that the Atlantic Fleet would help escort the Royal Navy across the submarine-infested Atlantic. This presented King with some unanswered questions. What if a confrontation occurred between American and German vessels? What should the policy be? Roosevelt could provide no clear-cut answers to these questions.

Lacking any definitive guidance, King developed his own plans for deploying the fleet. He ordered a force of battleships, cruisers, and destroyers to be stationed off Maine and

Canada to escort North Atlantic convoys. A smaller group of old cruisers and destroyers were sent to patrol off South America. King also established a reserve force and stationed it off the Atlantic Coast ready to rush to wherever it was needed.

As far as King was concerned, the United States was at war in the Atlantic. His position was made more plausible when Roosevelt proclaimed an unlimited national emergency on May 27, 1941. The navy was thus empowered to take such steps as it deemed necessary to combat the German threat. Still, however, the issue of what to do if an enemy ship was spotted remained unanswered. Do you fire or do you wait to be fired upon?

On July 8, Stark ordered King to escort a brigade of marines to Iceland to relieve the British garrison there so that those troops could be sent to North Africa where Sir Claude Auchinleck was preparing an offensive against Rommel in the fall.

On August 2, King ordered the captain of the cruiser *Augusta* to leave port in Newport and make for New York City. When the cruiser arrived, dignitaries began boarding the ship. These included General Marshall, Army Chief of Staff, and Admiral Stark. Two days later, at an anchorage off Martha's Vineyard, the *Augusta* picked up its most precious cargo, President Roosevelt. The President was on his way to a secret meeting with Winston Churchill in Argentia, Newfoundland.

King had known of the meeting since earlier in the year when he had been summoned to Hyde Park by the President to discuss the possibilities of a meeting with Churchill. Sworn to secrecy, King began to make plans in the event the meeting became a reality. On July 25, Roosevelt once more sent for King. When the Admiral arrived at Hyde Park, he was told that the meeting was definitely on. Roosevelt then explained the details of the proposed conference. King was informed that security was all-important.

In order to maintain the strictness of security, he issued only the barest minimum of orders necessary.

With Roosevelt on board the *Augusta,* King ordered the courses and speed for the rendezvous with the British. He drove the force at twenty-knots though the fog was thick and visibility poor. Luckily, the journey was without incident. The *Augusta* and her escorts arrived at Argentia on August 7.

While the ship swung at anchor at Placentia Bay, the Americans bided their time awaiting the arrival of the British. Two days later, the new British battleship, *Prince of Wales,* which only three months earlier had been with HMS *Hood* when the salvos from the mighty *Bismarck* sent the famous *Hood* to the bottom, arrived at Placentia with Mr. Churchill and the British delegation aboard. King acted as host for the illustrious body of dignitaries as they came aboard the *Augusta.*

Although for years he had mistrusted British motives, King was highly impressed by the negotiating skills of the British. He was a novice when it came to high-level negotiating, but was willing to make the Atlantic Fleet available to the Royal Navy and to help escort British shipping between North America and Iceland. He did, however, embarrass General Marshall in front of the British by asking him if and when the army would relieve the recently installed marines in Iceland. Marshall as yet had no troops available and resented what he considered implied criticism. This was not the last time these two principals were involved in a verbal debate.

The result of the meeting was the famed Atlantic Charter which stated the common interests of the Americans and the British. The statements were forthright and idealistic and laid the groundwork for a peaceful world after the war was over.

With King accepting a more involved role in escorting British ships, it was inevitable that American ships would be forced to fight. On September 4, the destroyer *Greer* found herself in just that position. Returning from Iceland, the destroyer located a U-boat. The *Greer* tracked the submarine on sonar and reported its position to a British aircraft which arrived on the scene and dropped a few bombs. The captain of the U-boat realized that his only hope of escape was the elimination of the threat from the *Greer.* Accordingly, he fired on the American ship. The *Greer* answered by counterattacking with depth charges. The incident could have precipitated war, but it didn't. Most Americans were completely oblivious to what was happening in the Atlantic.

In mid-October, the Atlantic Fleet suffered its first damage in the undeclared war. The destroyer *Kearny* was hit by a German torpedo that killed eleven men. Though badly damaged, the *Kearny* managed to reach Iceland. On October 30, the naval tanker *Salinas* took two torpedoes in its side. The following day, the destroyer *Reuben James* was struck amidships. The destroyer quickly broke in two and sank with the loss of about a hundred lives. This was true war and King knew that more incidents were yet to come.

I am sure that you realize that the *Kearny* incident is but the first of many that, in the nature of things, are bound to occur. It is likely that repetition will lead to open assumption of a war status.[11]

King wrote to a friend.

In the midst of this undeclared war, King gave up drinking, not a very easy chore for a man who, according to definition, could have been considered an alcoholic.

Although Americans remained ignorant of the loss of life suffered by the navy, nevertheless, King's reputation soared. On November 24, 1941, he appeared on the cover of *Life* magazine with the caption, "King of the Atlantic." The article depicted him as a rough and tough sailor in whom the American people could place their confidence. Not one word was uttered about the casualties sustained in the undeclared war in the Atlantic.

On November 23, King celebrated his sixty-third birthday. He now had one more year to go before reaching mandatory retirement age.

Throughout the fall of 1941, the diplomatic situation in the Pacific became critical. So much so, in fact, that an attack upon the United States was deemed Japan's only hope by her military leadership.* On December 7, 1941, the United States Naval Base at Pearl Harbor was suddenly attacked by Japan's carrier force. Four days later Germany and Italy, fulfilling their obligation to their Axis ally, declared war on the United States. The undeclared war was no more.

The day after Pearl Harbor, King went to Washington to confer with the top brass. There he found a stunned leadership. After completing his business, he returned to Newport.

On December 15, he was back in Washington for a meeting with Secretary of the Navy Knox. The secretary had just returned from Pearl Harbor where he had personally assessed the extent of the damage. Knox told King that it had been decided to send Nimitz to the Pacific as the new Commander in Chief, Pacific Fleet, replacing Adm. Husband Kimmel. Then he told King that it also had been decided that he, King, be appointed Commander in Chief, U.S. Fleet (COMINCH).

King wasn't sure if he should have the job, feeling that perhaps it should go to Admiral Stark, the current CNO. Knox, however, insisted that King was the right choice. King accepted, but requested that his headquarters be in Washington, in close proximity to the White House and the

*See *The Great Commanders of World War II, Volume IV: The Japanese.*

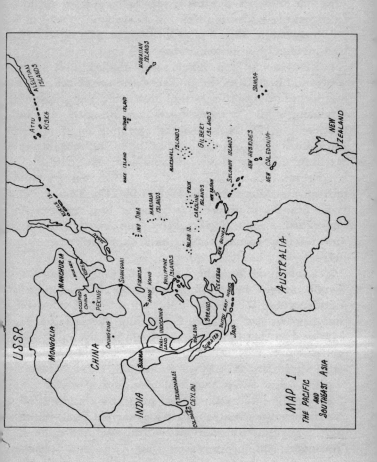

MAP 1

THE PACIFIC
AND
SOUTHEAST ASIA

Navy Department. He then went on to state that he did not want to hold press conferences or be bothered with appearances before Congress. King also insisted on command over all the bureaus in the Navy Department. President Roosevelt said that it would require a federal law to change the system to meet this last demand, but he did tell King that he could replace any bureau chief he wanted to if he found him uncooperative.

On December 17, Roosevelt signed the executive order appointing King COMINCH. There were two key elements in the order. The first stated that King had supreme command of the operating forces comprising the various fleets of the U.S. Navy and the operating forces of the Naval Coastal Frontier Command. The second element was that King would be directly responsible to the President.

King now set about organizing his staff, bringing into it such men as Rear Admirals Richmond Kelly Turner and Willis Lee. Soon his headquarters began to take shape. A car, airplane, and a flagship were made available to King who officially assumed his command on December 30, 1941.

Meanwhile, on December 22, Winston Churchill and his advisors arrived in Washington for the first high-level Allied meeting, the Arcadia Conference. The British were glad that they now had a full-fledged ally, but were exceedingly worried that their new ally would not live up to the prewar agreement, called the ABC-1 Staff Agreement, which stated that if America found itself in a two-ocean war, the defeat of Germany would have first priority.

Though they had little time to prepare a platform, the Americans sat down to negotiate with the politically astute British. The American delegates to the conference were the President's personal advisor, Harry Hopkins; Henry Stimson, Secretary of War; Frank Knox, General Marshall, Lt. General Henry Arnold of the Army Air Force; and for the navy, Admirals Stark and King.

King said little, but listened intently to what the British had to say. Churchill was lively and optimistic. He was well-prepared. En route to Washington, the prime minister had composed three papers regarding the future conduct of the war. The first paper dealt with the Atlantic front, the second with the Pacific, and the final one with the proposed campaign in 1943.

In the first paper Churchill spoke at length, expostulating that the main offensive effort should be in north and west Africa in 1942 with the whole of the northern African shore from Tunis to Egypt under Allied control.

The second document spoke of further Japanese successes, but not of a total British collapse in southeast Asia. Singapore would be held, Churchill boasted. The burden of the Pacific war, he went on, would be upon the Anglo-American Navy, but for the time being, the Far Eastern war should not absorb an unduly large proportion of U.S. forces.

In the third paper, Churchill talked about the victorious Allies' exploiting their superiority in the Mediterranean via attacks into Sicily, Italy, and the Balkans. As for a cross-channel attack, that should come only as a *coup de grâce* against an already defeated German Army which would be brought to its knees through the sheer weight of keeping it fighting on so many different fronts.

Churchill had expertly expounded his views. Now the Americans responded to the proposals. As spokesman, General Marshall affirmed the Germany-first strategy. However, the immediate crisis in the Pacific could not be ignored. Even while Marshall spoke, the Japanese juggernaut was overpowering the U.S. garrison at Wake Island, the British in Hong Kong, and the American-Filipino forces in the Philippines. Australia's lifeline was being threatened and the danger of isolation was real.

Thus the inital talks proved inconclusive. Nevertheless,

all present admitted the Japanese threat. What was needed to halt the Japanese was unity of command, i.e., one commander who could pull the divergent forces in the southwest Pacific together under a unified command. Marshall suggested that the British General, Sir Archibald Wavell, be nominated as supreme commander. King concurred. Though reluctant, Churchill agreed to send the American proposal to his government, urging approval.

King's backing of the concept of unified command, however, was qualified. He stated to a friend:

"I have no intention whatever of acceding to any unity-of-command proposals that are not premised on a particular situation in a particular area, at a particular time, for a more or less particular period."[12]

The crux of the issue was determining who would direct strategy in a coalition command. If the Arcadia conference accomplished anything at all, it was answering this question. The British proposed that a Combined Chiefs of Staff committee be formed, made up of the British and American Chiefs of Staff. This committee alone, they stated, would determine Allied strategy and direct the Allied Supreme Command.

Roosevelt asked King what he thought of the British proposal. King replied that with so many participants in the war, the decision-making process would be extremely slow if each warring nation were asked its opinion. Under the circumstances, the British idea made sense. Then, since the United States and Great Britain were providing the lion's share of men and materiel, they should be allowed to run the war and make the final decisions.

Roosevelt accepted the British plan. King carried the President's consent back to the chiefs. This marked the beginning of the Combined Chiefs of Staff organization.

The American members were King, Marshall, Stark, and Arnold. This all-important creation, which forged what was to become the most successful coalition in military history, made the Arcadia conference worthwhile.

Almost from the beginning of the meetings of the Combined Chiefs, a sharp difference of opinion was evident. The British, concerned over Hitler's attempts to defeat them in 1942 before the U.S power could be brought to bear, were inclined to steer discussions toward the defeat of Germany. For King and Stark, however, Japan held a prominent position. They had bombed Pearl Harbor and humiliated the American Navy. It was the Japanese who had to be dealt with.

After a short break, the Combined Chiefs' talks resumed on January 10. King brought up the topic of the defense of the island bases between Hawaii and Australia. The chiefs were unanimous in their view that Australia had to be held and that the lines of communication to that country had to be safeguarded. To insure this, New Caledonia, Fiji, and American Samoa had to be reinforced with air and naval forces. King asked the British to reinforce New Caledonia, but the latter were not eager to commit troops. However, since the Japanese octopus was grabbing more and more of the Pacific, King was more and more convinced that Japan had to be dealt with. He could visualize the Japanese seizing Hawaii, the Aleutians, even Alaska, unless they were stopped immediately.

King was disturbed over the British lack of support for his Pacific plans and their continued emphasis on the European-African theaters. Despite this, he stuck to his guns regarding the importance of New Caledonia. Marshall recommended sending ten thousand American troops, aircraft, gasoline, and war materiel. The war materiel would not come from the British supplies, but rather would have to come at the expense of reducing Russian lend-lease aid. That decision, though, needed presidential approval.

Would Roosevelt agree? The President asked King if New Caledonia was really as important as he said. When King replied, yes, Roosevelt consented to the reinforcement of the island.

The Arcadia conference passed into history on January 14, 1942. Besides being the first wartime meeting that allowed each side to size up the other, it had accomplished much. The establishment of the Combined Chiefs of Staff committee was by far its most significant and lasting achievement. The creation of the combined Australian, British, Dutch, American command (ABDA), under General Wavell, was another. Though Japanese victories would later devour Wavell's command, the concept of unified command was unique and daring.

The Arcadia conference did leave a number of loose ends, however. Churchill's African strategy was not totally acceptable to the Americans. Marshall wanted a cross-channel assault as soon as possible. Future meetings would have to clear up that question. Another loose end was King's preoccupation with the Pacific. The British lack of enthusiasm for the Pacific galled him and would form the basis for much future debate.

King's future was about to begin. The war was in its infancy and so was his role as a war leader. King received his baptism of fire at Arcadia and would be ready for the British the next time.

Eisenhower, who at the time of Arcadia was in the War Plans Division, observed and noted his impressions of the differences between both sides.

The struggle to secure the adoption by all concerned of a common concept of strategical objectives is wearing me down. Everybody is too much engaged with small things of his own. We've got to go to Europe and fight and we've got to quit wasting resources all over the world and still worse—wasting time. . . . We've got to begin slugging with air at West Europe to be followed by a land attack as soon as possible.[13]

Eisenhower's opinion also left the question of the Pacific unanswered.

With Arcadia concluded, King could now devote his efforts to directing the navy at war. His first directive was to Nimitz, ordering him to keep the lines of communication from the United States to Hawaii and Midway safeguarded, as well as the line between Hawaii and Australia. King also reviewed strategy with Nimitz, especially regarding the use of the carriers.

Meanwhile, the Japanese war machine continued its magnificent string of victories. Malaya, Singapore, the Dutch East Indies, and the Bismarck Archipelago all fell. With Australia obviously in peril, King proposed the formation of an Australian-New Zealand command (ANZAC) under an American flag officer, to deal with the crisis.

King ordered continued action in the Pacific. He wanted the carriers to hit the Japanese with nuisance raids. Hit them, run, and hit them again. Basically, these nuisance raids accomplished very little and were dangerous in light of Japanese superiority. But they also demonstrated King's aggressiveness and his desire to hit and hit again.

One difficulty King found in accomplishing his job as COMINCH was the presence of Admiral Stark as CNO. The trouble wasn't so much with Stark as it was with the overlapping responsibilities and authority between the two commands. There was only one solution and Roosevelt elected to take it. King was appointed CNO in addition to his duties as COMINCH and Stark was sent to London as the Commander in Chief, U.S. Naval Forces in Europe. On March 12, 1942, the executive order was signed making King the most powerful naval officer in the history of the

U.S. Navy. He had complete military control over naval affairs.

By the end of February, 1942, the ABDA forces were nearing defeat. Wavell had returned to India. The first attempt at unified command had ended in failure although many of the problems of joint command had been ironed out and precedents had been established.

With ABDA ready to fold, King knew that it was time to reorganize the areas of responsibility in the Pacific. On February 17, he recommended that Great Britain take responsibility for everything west of Sumatra including the China-Burma-India theater. Nimitz, he said, would be responsible for the Australian-New Zealand and Pacific Ocean areas.

On February 22, Roosevelt summoned King, Marshall, and Harry Hopkins to an important conference for the purpose of reviewing the situation in the Philippines and the fate of General MacArthur. The President stressed the importance of getting MacArthur out of the Philippines safely. He cut an order telling the general that he was to proceed to Australia.

Also under discussion at the meeting was the importance of safeguarding the lines of communication between Hawaii and Australia, and the protection of the latter.

Two days later, Marshall sent King a memorandum asking him for details on how he intended to keep those communication lines open. King received the memo on March 2 and promptly replied by stating a bold and aggressive policy. The communications would be kept open, he said, by establishing strong points on the various islands astride the trade routes. These strong points would become potential staging areas for an offensive through the New Hebrides, up the Solomons, and into the Bismarcks. King's aggressive stance was remarkable in the face of the sensational Japanese string of victories. He also stated that he intended to use the marines in order to seize and occupy the strong points, but went on to say that he wanted army troops for garrison duty—at least three divisions—along with eight groups of assorted Army Air Force units. King's reply to Marshall contrasted with the Germany-first strategy agreed upon at Arcadia and before that, in the prewar staff meetings.

Roosevelt, meanwhile, had received a gloomy message from Churchill relating the details of the loss of Singapore. In the letter the prime minister appeared extremely pessimistic. So much so, in fact, that Roosevelt quickly conferred with the Joint Chiefs about what could be done in the Pacific. King responded with a written memorandum which he gave to the President on March 5. In it he said that America's role in the war against Germany should be that of supplying the necessary materiel to fight the war: the munitions, fuel, food, and vehicles. In the Pacific, however, he repeated the same arguments presented in the memo to Marshall, urging the reinforcement of bases on the Hawaii-Australia line of communication. King also urged an eventual American offensive into the Solomons, New Guinea, and the Bismarcks.

Roosevelt passed King's proposals along to Churchill who, though he had hoped simply for the containment of Japan until Germany was defeated, grudgingly agreed in light of Roosevelt's consent to the plan.

With a positive plan of action adopted for the Pacific, areas of responsibility became a hotly debated issue. Marshall wanted General MacArthur to have overall command. King was vehemently opposed to that idea. For the previous twenty years, the navy had been preparing for just the type of war they were now involved in. To be subordinated to the army now was unthinkable. The Pacific Fleet would never be under MacArthur's operational control, King said, particularly since he was convinced that MacArthur knew next to nothing about sea power. On the other hand, MacArthur would never agree to serve under naval leaders. Some sort of division of command had to be found.

The Army came up with one such plan while King came up with another. The latter's plan called for dividing the Pacific into two spheres, with Australia, New Guinea, the Netherland East Indies, and the Solomon Islands (later the Philippines were added) falling into MacArthur's Southwest Pacific Theater. The Navy would get the rest of the Pacific and would be under Admiral Nimitz's operational control. King's plan was accepted by the Joint Chiefs. MacArthur's boss would be Marshall; Nimitz's, King. Thus, a uniform command structure in the Pacific was not adopted. Roosevelt formally approved the plan on March 31.

Nimitz's official title was Commander in Chief, Pacific Ocean Areas (CINCPOA). His command had unified control over all naval, Marine Corps, and U.S. Army ground and air forces. He also held the position of Commander in Chief, Pacific Fleet, giving him authority over all naval forces in the Pacific except for those directly under MacArthur.

King's primary concern, related to Nimitz, was the protection and holding of what the U.S. already had and the preparation for major amphibious attacks in the Solomons. In the interim, King directed Nimitz to keep the Australian lines of communication open and to hit the Japanese at every opportunity.

King had gotten his wish. General Eisenhower, who had come to know the admiral during the early years of the war, made this comment on Admiral King.

> He is an arbitrary stubborn type, with not too much brains and a tendency toward bullying his juniors. One thing that might help win this war is to shoot King. He's the antithesis of cooperation, a deliberately rude person, which means he's a mental bully.[14]

It is descriptive and sums up the army's opinion of him. Of course one must remember that Eisenhower, as an army man and Marshall's protégé, was firmly behind the Europe-first policy which King opposed. Although Eisenhower and the army might have felt that way toward King, history can only speculate what the consequences for the navy would have been had someone less formidable than King been at the helm. The navy might have been reduced to a branch of the army and the Pacific offensive might not have begun where and when it did.

Meantime, King's staff developed a scheme to raise American morale and to partially avenge the attack on Pearl Harbor. It took the form of a bombing raid on Tokyo. The admiral was enthusiastic about the plan and obtained approval from both Roosevelt and the Joint Chiefs, Arnold and Marshall. It was a daring and unique plan calling for a force of Army B-25 bombers, under the command of Lt. Col. James Doolittle, to be flown off the decks of carriers. After weeks of practice, the operation took place in April.

While the naval task force, led by Adm. William Halsey, made its way to Japan carrying Doolittle's raiders, American code breakers discovered that a major Japanese offensive aimed at Port Moresby, was in the offing. If the Japanese captured this port, on the southeast coast of New Guinea, it would threaten the line of communication that Nimitz was under orders to protect. King issued orders to stop the Japanese.

King must have had a few misgivings about the operation. Having been informed by the code breakers that the Japanese attack on Port Moresby would take place in early May, he knew that he would have to rely on a commander in whom he had little confidence. Since Halsey was tied up with the Doolittle raid, there were only two carriers left in the Pacific to halt the Japanese offensive. This task force was commanded by Rear Admiral Frank

Jack Fletcher, an officer whom King felt lacked aggressiveness. However, there was little choice.

King was also faced with a jurisdictional problem. Port Moresby lay in MacArthur's southwest Pacific area and according to a Joint Chiefs directive, the general was to take on any Japanese force within his designated zone, whether on land or on the sea. That might be all well and good, but King was determined to stop the Japanese and there was no way he was going to allow MacArthur to command the aircraft carriers of the fleet. Therefore, King simply decided to ignore the boundary lines.

King and Nimitz met in San Francisco on April 25 to discuss the plans to defend Port Moresby. The Coral Sea was selected as the site for the battle. King hoped that the Japanese would delay their advance long enough to allow Halsey time to bring his carriers into the area. If not, then the Americans would have to rely on Fletcher. King reviewed Nimitz's battle plan and found it to be sound. He specifically liked its aggressive tone. King was a great believer in the old adage that the best defense was an active offense.

Before Nimitz returned to Pearl Harbor, he and King made one structural change in the Pacific command. Nimitz's area of responsibility was so vast that it was decided to split the command into a north, central, and south Pacific area. For the South Pacific, it was decided to appoint a commander who would be directly responsible to Nimitz but would maintain his headquarters in that region so that he could be readily available for on-the-spot decisions. The South Pacific area boundaries extended south of the equator and east of the 159° parallel. King's and Nimitz's choice of commander was Vice Admiral Robert E. Ghormley, a man they both felt was capable of the job. They would both regret their choice later on.

Before Ghormley left for the Pacific, King made it clear to him that his new task was both important and difficult, since the resources to carry it out as wished were not available. King said that Ghormley should establish his headquarters in Aukland, New Zealand, with an advance at Tongatabu. He also stated that in the autumn, an offensive from the South Pacific would probably get under way. With that, Ghormley left Washington on May 1, and went to Pearl Harbor for a round of meetings with Nimitz. Finally, at the end of the month, he established his headquarters at Aukland.

The Battle of the Coral Sea blunted the Japanese attempt to take Port Moresby, but the loss of the carrier *Lexington* deeply affected its former skipper, Ernie King. While the battle raged in the blue waters of the Coral Sea, King, as usual, waited and hoped. He had a policy of not interfering with a commander once a battle was in progress.

Meanwhile, the American code breakers again uncorked pertinent messages pertaining to another major Japanese offensive. Nimitz was certain the Japanese target was Midway Island and wanted to deploy his striking force of three carriers to protect against just such a move. King, however, was unsure at first. He still suspected that the enemy would strike in the South Pacific against the Hawaii-Australia line of communication. Both admirals were receiving the same data, yet both came to different conclusions. King even wanted Halsey to remain in the South Pacific, but Nimitz used his powers of persuasion to get King to reconsider and allow Halsey and his task force to return to Pearl. King procrastinated, still believing that the South Pacific was the Japanese target, but Nimitz stuck to his guns, took the bull by the horns, and ordered Halsey back from the South Pacific after telling his staff that if King disagreed, he could always cancel the order. King was slow to respond. Finally, after additional analysis by his own intelligence staff, he concluded that Nimitz's appreciation was probably correct and on May 17, sent word that he approved of Halsey's movements.

This set a precedent that would be followed until the conclusion of hostilities. King would try at all costs not to give Nimitz direct orders. Instead, he preferred to make suggestions in the hope that Nimitz would pick up on them. At times their dialogue became very heated with King using very persuasive language. On the whole, however, the King-Nimitz team proved itself by its results. In the long run, that was what counted.

Luckily, Nimitz was correct regarding Midway. The United States won a great victory there, sinking four Japanese carriers. Midway was the turning point of the war.

The great victory at Midway overjoyed King, but also presented him with a dilemma. How could he report to the news media the fact that our carriers just happened to be at the right place at the right time without compromising the fact that the Japanese code was broken. On June 7 he held a news conference during which he issued a contrived report saying that the U.S. took a calculated risk in guessing the intentions of the enemy. Luckily, he said, it guessed right. He was so ambiguous and general that nothing confidential was revealed.

While the Navy was winning a stunning victory in the Pacific, King was preparing himself for another round of debates with the Joint and Combined Chiefs. To Marshall, King's overpreoccupation with the Pacific would only serve to drag the war out longer. Marshall was firmly convinced that the war could only be won by an early invasion of the European continent. The Pacific was secondary. King, although he supported a Germany-first policy in principle, resented the fact that the Pacific would be neglected. He did not repudiate the general concept of concentrating large American forces against Germany, only the idea of doing so while the issue in the Pacific remained in doubt. King held that the needs of the Pacific were more urgent in point of time. Therefore, he advocated reinforcing that theater. Basically it boiled down to two different interpretations of the statement: to hold in the Pacific. For Marshall it meant to defend, to King it meant to make secure.

In June, Churchill arrived in Washington for another round of talks. Accompanying him were the British Chiefs and Lord Louis Mountbatten, the dashing cousin of King George VI. Mountbatten had come to talk to King, navy man to navy man. During their discussions, Mountbatten recommended that King assign an American to work along with the British on the development of plans for amphibious training. King agreed and appointed Rear Admiral H. Kent Hewitt to the post. In Marshall's eyes, King appeared to have finally committed himself to the full support of the war against Germany.

During the Washington conference, Gen. Sir Alan Brooke, Chief of the Imperial General Staff, once more raised the question of a North African invasion as opposed to an invasion of Europe across the English Channel. King objected violently. Such a move would require naval support—ships and men which America did not have. In fact, at that very time King was attempting to amass enough shipping for a campaign in the Solomons against the little-known island of Guadalcanal which was scheduled for August. Besides that, King said, the U-boats were wreaking havoc on Atlantic shipping and any convoys sailing for North Africa would be vulnerable to attack. Therefore, he opposed Gymnast, the proposed Anglo-American invasion of North Africa.

Neither did he back Marshall in his bid for an early cross-channel invasion, for many of the same reasons. With the British pushing the Mediterranean and King the Pacific, Marshall was like a voice crying in the wilderness. Alan Brooke too was distraught. In his private notes he said of King:

Adm. Ernest King, a tough sixty-three-year-old salt of strong views and uncompromising temper.[15]

The second Washington conference thus ended inconclusively. Churchill returned home and reported to his War Cabinet. They were vehemently opposed to a cross-channel landing (Sledgehammer), but wholeheartedly behind Gymnast. Churchill cabled Roosevelt on July 8, informing the President of the British position.

Marshall was fit to be tied. In an amazing about-face he cast his lot with King and advocated a deeper Pacific commitment.

> If the British persist in advocating North Africa rather than Europe, we are definitely of the opinion that we should turn to the Pacific and strike decisively against Japan.[16]

Later on, Marshall would claim that this was only a bluff. Nevertheless, King exploited the inter-Allied squabble to the limit.

When Roosevelt received the memorandum along with a hastily prepared plan of action for the Pacific, he was piqued and rejected the plan with the comment that it was just what Germany would want America to do and that a full effort in the Pacific would not affect the world situation; nor would it help Russia and the Near East. King and Marshall were naïve to think that the President would turn his back on Britain or the Soviet Union. Since 1942 was a congressional election year, if the Democrats expected to win, American troops would have to be involved in the fighting against Germany by November. If it had to be in North Africa, Roosevelt reasoned, then let it be so.

The President ordered King and Marshall to London to finalize the plans for action against the Germans. They arrived on July 17 and immediately received an invitation from Churchill to join him at Chequers, his weekend retreat. The American officers declined, saying that business demanded they meet first with General Eisenhower who himself had arrived in London only a few weeks earlier.

All weekend King, Marshall, Eisenhower, and their advisors pondered strategic alternatives. They wished to form a consensus before meeting with the British on Monday. The awesome responsibility weighed heavily on King and Marshall. Thus far, the war had gone badly. With the exception of Midway, there had been one setback after another. The U-boats were menacing the Atlantic sea lanes, the Russians were on the verge of defeat, the Japanese had yet to be halted and there was a very real possibility that Rommel might soon be in Cairo. The Americans knew that any strategy they adopted would have an enormous impact on the world's future. The fate of the free world was at stake.

Marshall stuck to his guns regarding a cross-channel attack in 1942 rather than a North African diversion. King, who still desired more emphasis in the Pacific, fell in line behind Marshall, perhaps as a concession for the general's good will in giving his approval to the Guadalcanal plan. If reinforcements were going to be sent to the South Pacific, King knew that he would have to rely on Marshall's further good will.

At their first meeting with the British on Monday, July 20, the Americans presented a prepared memorandum stating their opinion of the importance and practicability of a cross-channel attack. Churchill and the British Chiefs veered the discussion away from the American plan toward the prime minister's pet project, the North African operation. Marshall and King continued their attempt to steer the discussion toward a cross-channel attack for 1942, but the talks got nowhere.

The British rejected the American plan. Roosevelt finally cabled Marshall to forget about a cross-channel attack in 1942 and ordered him to join the British in planning some kind of operation, preferably an Anglo-American invasion of French North Africa. Secretary of War Henry Stimson said of the Presidential action:

> The Torch (formerly Gymnast) decision was the result of two absolutely definite and final rulings, one by the British, and the other by the President. Mr. Churchill and his advisers categorically refused to accept the notion of a cross-channel invasion in 1942. Mr. Roosevelt categorically insisted that there be some operation in 1942. The only operation that satisfied both of these conditions was Torch.[17]

The Joint Chiefs were thus coerced into settling on an invasion of Northwest Africa. With that, the conference came to a close. Before returning to the United States, King met with the haughty French leader, Charles de Gaulle, who attempted to press his claims for American recognition of his French leadership on the admiral. King also met with King George VI. These amenities completed, the Joint Chiefs returned home.

During the next few months, the planning for Torch continued. Both Marshall's and King's hearts were not in it, Marshall because of his obvious dislike for what he felt was a diversion, King because of his preoccupation with the Pacific. Torch, however, proved immensely successful, thanks to Eisenhower and his staff, and Rear Admiral Hewitt, who proved a true master of amphibious action. On November 8, 1942, the Allies were in French Northwest Africa.

King continued to focus his gaze on the Pacific. After the Japanese losses at Midway were digested, he felt that the best thing was to hit them quickly while they were temporarily stunned. Even before the Joint Chiefs left for London in July, a major debate had taken place. The June debate centered upon two divergent strategies, one proposed by Admiral King, the other by General

MacArthur. Quite naturally, the latter proposal was endorsed by Marshall.

MacArthur, whose headquarters was in Australia, proposed an operation aimed at the immediate seizure of Rabaul. King reviewed the general's plan and found it to be much too ambitious. Rabaul was too heavily defended. Besides, King said, any amphibious assault in the South Pacific would have to be a naval one and he continued to be adamantly opposed to MacArthur's commanding naval forces. Instead, the naval planners proposed an indirect approach toward Rabaul through the eastern Solomons where it was felt the Japanese were weaker. A naval officer—under Nimitz, not MacArthur—would command the amphibious assault.

As the debate continued, King took the bull by the horns and ordered Nimitz to prepare to seize Tulagi, even though it was west of the 159° line, placing it in MacArthur's Southwest Pacific Area. On June 25, King presented the Joint Chiefs with a prepared plan. Having already promised MacArthur the command, Marshall found himself in a bind. Ironically, MacArthur himself backed down from his direct-approach plan and accepted the indirect plan which King's planners had drawn up.

The question of command, however, remained unresolved. This subject was debated for days. Finally, the controversy reached a climax on June 29, when King and Marshall agreed to meet face-to-face. The next day a compromise was reached. The Southwest Pacific boundary line was shifted westward, thus placing the islands of Guadalcanal and Tulagi in Nimitz's sphere. MacArthur could no longer claim that he should command all naval forces in his area since Guadalcanal no longer lay there. Instead, Vice Admiral Robert Ghormley, Nimitz's deputy in the South Pacific, would command the assault.

Three tasks were laid down for the Pacific strategy. Task I was the assault on Guadalcanal and Tulagi. This would be handled by Nimitz's forces. Tasks II and III involved the capture of the western Solomons, eastern New Guinea, and the Bismarck Archipelago with the seizure of Rabaul. These last two tasks would be under MacArthur. King and Marshall agreed to this strategy on July 2, with the proposed landings on Guadalcanal and Tulagi scheduled for August 1, 1942. (It was later changed to August 7.)

On July 4, Nimitz and King met in San Francisco to discuss the forthcoming offensive. Rear Admiral Richmond Kelly Turner was also present at the meetings. Turner was to command the amphibious phase of the operation. On the fifth, it was learned that the Japanese were constructing an airfield on Guadalcanal. This news emphasized the necessity for promptness if the communications line between Hawaii and Australia was to be safeguarded. Thus, Operation Watchtower, the assault on Guadalcanal and Tulagi, took shape.

Along with Marshall, King then went to London. Upon his return from England, King pleaded for more men, guns, and aircraft to support Ghormley. His plea fell on deaf ears. Marshall's gaze was firmly focused on the North African landings while MacArthur, piqued at having no control over the Guadalcanal operation, concentrated all of his forces on New Guinea. The U.S. Navy and Marine Corps were on their own.

After a week's postponement, the landings on Guadalcanal and Tulagi took place on August 7. For the first few days hardly any definitive reports came through to King. On the twelfth, however, the boom was lowered as King's duty officer woke the admiral from his sleep and handed him the report of the battle of Savo Island during which four Allied cruisers were sunk, another severely damaged, and two destroyers were lost. King was utterly crushed.

That, as far as I am concerned, was the blackest day of the war.[18]

King wanted answers and wanted them fast. Since he had stuck his neck out by pushing for the Guadalcanal operation, he was afraid of a negative reaction from Washington. Therefore, he kept the news of the debacle at Savo from the press.

The struggle for Guadalcanal was a long and bitter one. Throughout the campaign the shortage of supplies was critical. In reality, Guadalcanal became a sacrifice to Torch. During the long campaign the United States would lose twenty-four ships, including two carriers. At one point, there was only one operational aircraft carrier left in the entire Pacific. Thanks to Japanese blunders and American determination and bravery, however, Guadalcanal was held, albeit by a shoestring.

Ghormley proved himself the wrong man for the task at hand. Critics have faulted King for choosing Ghormley in the first place. King atoned for his error in October when he replaced Ghormley with the firebrand, Adm. William "Bull" Halsey.

By the end of January, 1943, Guadalcanal was in American hands. In the end King's efforts had justified themselves as that jungle-covered island became a staging area for an offensive aimed at the reduction of Japan's South Pacific bastion, Rabaul.

By late 1942, with the Guadalcanal campaign still hanging in the balance and the Allies stalemated after the Axis beat them to Tunisia, King and the Joint Chiefs pondered future moves. For the Pacific, the next move depended on when Guadalcanal would be secured. As for Europe, King had no choice but to accept the Germany-first strategy, but with the standing reservation that the Pacific would not be neglected. When pressed as to whether Sicily should be assaulted after the Axis defeat in North Africa, King said yes. It would give the Allies control of the Mediterranean and secure the vital line of communications from Gibraltar to the Suez Canal. However, when the subject of invading the Italian mainland was broached, King emphatically said no. He believed that an assault into Italy would not defeat the Germans. They would just keep on fighting, falling backward until they reached the Alps whose peaks would be utilized to block any Allied entrance into central Europe. The cross-channel invasion, therefore, was a must, King said. When, was still a question mark. As for Russia, King believed that she should receive as much lend-lease aid as possible since she was in the best physical position to eventually defeat Germany.

In regard to China, King wanted that country equipped so that its vast population could be used against the Japanese. In order to keep China in the war he sided with General Stilwell and those who advocated action in Burma in order to facilitate the movement of war materiel to China.

In December, Roosevelt and Churchill decided that it was again time for a face-to-face meeting in order to review strategy for the prosecution of the war. A conference was scheduled in Casablanca, Morocco, for the middle of January, 1943.

On January 7, Roosevelt met with the Joint Chiefs of Staff in order to define the American position. The chiefs had already met the previous month to resolve some difficulties. They had agreed to adopt a stance whereby the special interests of Marshall, King, and Arnold of the Army Air Forces were reflected; i.e., a continuance of the Pacific offensive, a cross-channel invasion in 1943, and a strategic air offensive against Germany. Meanwhile, the British were developing their own strategy reflecting their particular interests. The Casablanca conference was expected to raise many heated controversies.

On January 9, 1943, King and the Joint Chiefs left for Casablanca. They arrived four days later and were pleased with the warmth of Morocco which contrasted sharply with the dreary winter cold of Washington. The site of the conference was a luxury hotel in Anfa, a suburb of Casablanca.

The Joint Chiefs had planned their arrivals for several days prior to that of the President in order to allow for preliminary meetings with the British chiefs. King was ready to insist on a revision of the allocation of men and materiel between Europe and the Pacific theaters. Unfortunately, he found himself up against the politically adept British who had anticipated just such a maneuver.

The first meeting began on January 14. Marshall opened the gathering by stating that the Allied resources should be allocated between the two theaters by a 70:30 ratio instead of the current 85:15. When the British turn to speak came, they did not respond to Marshall's opening statement, but instead reviewed their appraisals of the war thus far. Air Marshal Charles Portal remarked that the defeat of the German U-boats should have the first priority. The meeting ended with King sniping at the RAF for its lack of aggression in bombing the submarine construction yards and installations. If these were destroyed, he said, U-boat activities would be drastically curtailed.

That afternoon, Brooke invited King to discuss the progress of the Pacific war. The admiral reviewed the course of the war and went on to emphasize the importance of seizing the Marianas. The British responded negatively to this proposal saying that there were not enough resources available to sustain simultaneous offensives. King was convinced that the British took this position because they lacked a desire to participate in the war against Japan. He completely mistrusted their motives believing that the British were more concerned with preserving their empire. Brooke responded that the British had every intention of prosecuting the war against the Japanese as well as the Germans. The afternoon session also ended with nothing resolved.

The British, however, had formed impressions about King. Sir Ian Jacob, secretary to the British Chiefs of

Staff, said of the admiral:

> well over sixty, but active, tall, and spare, with an
> alert and self-confident bearing. He seems to wear a
> protective covering of horn which it is hard to
> penetrate. He gives the impression of being exceed-
> ingly narrow-minded and to be always on the lookout
> for slights or attempts to put something over on him.[19]

General Sir Hastings Ismay called King:

> tough as nails and carried himself as stiffly as a poker.
> He was blunt and stand-offish, almost to the point of
> rudeness. At the start, he was intolerant and
> suspicious of all things British, especially the Royal
> Navy, but he was almost equally intolerant and sus-
> picious of the American Army. War against Japan
> was the problem to which he had devoted the study of
> a lifetime, and he resented the idea of American
> resources being used for any other purpose than to
> destroy the Japanese. He mistrusted Churchill's
> powers.[20]

King, too, had formed impressions of his British counterparts. He liked Portal and Admiral Pound, but disliked
Alan Brooke, the Chief of the Imperial General Staff. King
felt that Brooke was too arrogant and inflexible.

For the next few days the talks progressed. The participants unanimously decided that priority should be given to
the Battle of the Atlantic. They also agreed to the British
plan for an invasion of Sicily, feeling that this island's
capture would allow them virtually free passage through
the Mediterranean and so effect an important economy of
shipping. That in turn would increase the possibility of
knocking Italy out of the war and thus force the Germans to
assume the Italian commitments. To satisfy Marshall, the

chiefs also agreed that the strongest possible force be assembled in Great Britain in readiness to reenter the continent just as soon as German resistance was weakened to the required extent. The British agreed to make concessions in the Pacific, but only after more days of intense debate.

For the next two days Churchill informally tried to dissuade King from his Pacific persistence. In the end, however, thanks to the combined weight of Roosevelt and King who both were concerned with China, the prime minister was persuaded to launch a campaign in Burma. Churchill had very little faith in Chiang Kai-shek, but faced with the unified pressure of the President and the admiral, he was forced into agreeing to a greater effort in Burma.

At the formal meeting on the eighteenth, Brooke and King again went at each other over priorities. Brooke did not want the Pacific to prejudice the effort against Germany in the slightest. King was exasperated. In his diary, Brooke lambasted King for his obsession with the Pacific. Finally, after long debate, the British chiefs drafted a position paper in which they laid down future strategies. There were three statements regarding the Pacific and they were just what King had hoped for; although no real overall plan for the defeat of Japan emerged from Casablanca.

The upshot of the discussion on the Pacific-Far East operations at Casablanca was a series of limited and contingent agreements. The United States was to conduct a two-way advance in the Pacific through the central and Southwest Pacific. Plans and preparation were to be made for the recapture of Burma in 1943, but final decision on the operation was to be postponed until the summer of 1943. Increased aid to China in the way of air forces and transports would be provided by the United States. The delegates agreed that the Pacific-Far East operations for 1943 were to be aimed at maintaining pressure on Japan, holding the initiative, and attaining positions of readiness for a full-scale offensive against Japan immediately upon the defeat of Germany.[21]

Though not detailing a specific strategy, a significant keynote was sounded at Casablanca. The British would have to pay more attention to the Pacific; King would see to that.

With the Casablanca conference concluded, the Allied chiefs left with a firm commitment to invade Sicily, to use all means to win the Battle of the Atlantic, to intensify the bombing offensive in Germany, and of course to move ahead in the Pacific. Only Marshall was disappointed that no firm date was selected for a cross-channel attack. The conference ended with Roosevelt making the controversial statement that committed the Allies to a policy of unconditional surrender.

The Joint Chiefs returned to Washington. King now had to deal with the problem of the U-boats. The Battle of the Atlantic had been a running sore for the Allies. The U-boats had been wreaking havoc on Atlantic and Arctic convoys, and the losses were staggering. American efforts during 1942 to thwart the enemy submarines were futile. The U-boats were destroying merchant shipping at a faster rate than American shipyards were turning them out. Before any further action could be launched against Germany, therefore, the Battle of the Atlantic had to be won. In order to heal the running sore, King secretly convened a conference known as the Washington Convoy Conference, on March 1, 1943. Present were naval and air force representatives from the United States, Great Britain, and Canada.

At the opening session of the conference, King stressed the urgency of keeping supplies flowing to Russia and Great Britain. He charged the delegates with finding a method of escorting convoys that would allow them to reach their destinations safely. After twelve days, the conference ended with most of King's concepts accepted. The ocean would be divided into zones of responsibility with the British and Canadians retaining control of the North Atlantic convoys. The United States would be responsible for the central Atlantic and the Interlocking Convoy System. King also decided that one central authority was required in order to organize, route, and protect the convoys; coordinate all intelligence, research, and development; and to administer all antisubmarine activities. He designated this organization the Tenth Fleet. King kept the Tenth Fleet under his control, but in reality delegated its operation to Rear Admiral Francis S. Low. The fleet was staffed by fifty hand-picked men and women who monitored every merchantman that moved into the areas under American responsibility.

Through code-breaking and Tenth Fleet efforts, by the middle of 1943, the tide had turned in the Atlantic battle. In May alone, the Germans lost forty-one U-boats. The head of the German Navy, Admiral Doenitz, was forced to withdraw his submarines from the central Atlantic. By July, merchant-ship production began to exceed losses and the convoys were beginning to reach their destinations relatively unscathed.

Meanwhile, King continued planning in the Pacific. The problem of Rabaul held a prominent position in this planning. According to an earlier Joint Chiefs decision, Rabaul was to be assaulted by MacArthur's forces. King had reservations about this because MacArthur would require naval forces, and the admiral's views on allowing Mac-Arthur to command naval forces were well-known.

The Joint Chiefs called a conference in March, 1943, known as the Pacific Military Conference. Once again differences in strategical thinking made it necessary to clarify Pacific strategy. King was thinking in terms of naval forces from Hawaii and the United States mainland directly across the central Pacific. MacArthur, with a return to the Philippines uppermost in his mind, was planning the capture of New Guinea and the reduction of the enemy base at Rabaul, to be followed by a movement northwestward toward the Philippines.

Present at the conference were General Sutherland, MacArthur's chief of staff, Adm. Raymond Spruance and Capt. Miles Browning, chief of staff to Admiral Halsey. The final outcome of the meeting was an acceptance of MacArthur's plan for the reduction of Rabaul with the full cooperation of Halsey's naval forces.

By the spring of 1943, signs of victory were evident in North Africa and the Solomons. The Allies were also getting ready to invade Sicily. However, as for operations after the fall of Sicily, things remained very much in the air. The war in Burma was going nowhere. The American theater commander, Lt. General Stilwell,* wanted to build up a strong ground force for the eventual reconquest of Burma while Major General Chennault advocated an increase in air power. The British, on the other hand, wanted a diminution of activity in Burma in order to concentrate everything into further Mediterranean operations. Since so many questions were unanswered, another major conference of the Combined Chiefs of Staff was deemed necessary. Roosevelt and Churchill arranged for just such a meeting to take place in Washington during May. It was given the name Trident.

Both the American chiefs and the British chiefs quickly drafted position papers arguing their respective positions. According to his diary, Brooke dreaded the anticipated haggling with the Americans, especially with King. He was convinced that King was sending shipping to the Pacific,

*See *The Great Commanders of World War II, Volume III: The Americans.*

shipping that was supposed to be used against Germany, and he was determined to have it out with the admiral.

The opening session of the Trident conference took place on May 12. Each side was divided by its own position. On the thirteenth, Adm. William Leahy presided over the meeting. According to him, General Brooke

> gave a talk on global strategy which indicated that the British would decline to engage in 1943 in any major military undertaking outside the Mediterranean area. This did not meet with the approval of President Roosevelt, who had directed me to press for a British-American invasion of Europe at the earliest possible date.[22]

The Joint Chiefs then presented their strategic concept for defeating the Axis. The British listened intently and said that they needed time to study it and would respond the next day. When they did respond it was to disagree with the statement dealing with the war against Japan which read:

> Simultaneously, in cooperation with our allies to maintain and extend unremitting pressure against Japan in the Pacific and from China.[23]

Brooke maintained that that kind of pressure would weaken the total effort against Germany. Leahy responded by repeating the earlier statement in even stronger language. Two days later, the delegates were still at an impasse.

King felt one of the major objectives of Trident should be the development of a master plan for the conduct of the war. He was determined to have the British sign a long-range plan, firmly committing them in writing to a course of action. He spoke to the assembled dignitaries saying that basic fundamentals should be agreed upon by all. Once this was accomplished, then a strategy could be designed within the framework of the agreement. Brooke agreed. Throughout the night the planners articulated those basic fundamentals. Immediately, however, a roadblock was reached, for the Americans and British were unable to agree upon a strategy for the defeat of Japan. All they could do was define their basic differences of opinion. They did agree on a cross-channel invasion and even future Mediterranean ventures, but when it came to the Pacific, an impasse was reached.

After a weekend's respite, the chiefs convened again on Monday, May 17. The British proposed invading Italy after the conclusion of hostilities in Sicily. They called Italy the soft underbelly of Europe. King opposed the invasion of Italy by saying that it would require scarce shipping while providing few dividends. In fact, King said, Italy was more a liability to Germany than an asset, thus making it better to leave it alone. After endless debate, the chiefs reached a compromise. The British could continue limited operations in Italy and could postpone their offensive in Burma. In return they had to commit themselves to a May 1, 1944 date for the invasion of France.

For King the British now appeared ready to agree to an intensification of the Pacific offensive. On Friday, May 21, he had his chance to explain his Pacific strategy to the British. The admiral reviewed past studies on Pacific war strategy showing the importance of the Philippines and how it dominated American strategy. He then went on to discuss three possible avenues of approach toward recovering the Philippines, one from the north, another from the south, and a third across the central Pacific. King emphasized the importance of capturing the Marianas which he called the key to victory. Possession of these islands, he claimed, would sever the enemy's sea lines of communication to the Carolines. The Americans could then strike westward to the

Philippines, China, or even toward Japan itself. An invasion of the Philippines, he went on, would probably serve to draw out the Japanese Fleet for an all-out naval battle. From that point on Japan would suffer strangulation and eventual defeat by the combined use of bombing, blockade, and assault. The admiral concluded his presentation by emphasizing the need to accelerate the Pacific war.

The British were duly impressed by King's presentation, but still refused to allow him carte blanche in the Pacific. They wanted some restrictions placed on the Pacific effort in order to give first priority to the defeat of Germany. Thus the debate over wording of the official statement continued.

The American chiefs held firm and were willing to appeal to Roosevelt if necessary in order to uphold their position. Finally, thanks to Adm. Sir Dudley Pound, a compromise was reached. The paragraph that had given the British so much trouble was amended to read that the Combined Chiefs of Staff would give consideration to any major Pacific offensive before it was actually begun.

Though the results of Trident were not startling in themselves as regards the Pacific war, they did indicate a positive growth of the realization that attention would henceforth have to be given to long-range planning on the combined level. The nebulous Pacific strategy set forth at the Casablanca conference had been replaced by the adoption of new short-range objectives and an effort to analyze the future course and requirements of the war in the Pacific. King was satisfied. On May 25, Roosevelt and Churchill approved the final version of the Combined Chiefs' master plan.

Soon after Trident, King flew to San Francisco to meet with Nimitz and discuss future operations. King was particularly interested in gathering any information about the campaign then taking place on the Aleutian island of Attu which had been assaulted while the Trident conference was in session. Unfortunately, little information was as yet available. Nevertheless, he and Nimitz forged ahead with plans for a central Pacific offensive. King told Nimitz that the Marshall Islands would be the initial objective. The two also discussed candidates to command the Central Pacific Forces. Nimitz nominated Rear Admiral Raymond Spruance. King agreed. For the amphibious force commander, Richmond Kelly Turner, the amphibious commander at Guadalcanal, was chosen. To command the land force, Marine Maj. Gen. Holland M. Smith was selected.

After the meeting King returned to Washington. He was impatient to initiate the central Pacific drive fearing British ambivalence. King did not want to give them the opportunity to renege on their Trident agreement. He submitted his proposals to the Joint Chiefs on June 11. These proposals were not acceptable to the army, however, for they slighted MacArthur. King had gone so far as to recommend that there should be only one supreme commander for the Pacific and that the central Pacific drive be given priority over MacArthur's.

Meanwhile, MacArthur was clamoring for more resources in order to facilitate the capture of Rabaul. A real interservice battle was in the making and a compromise was needed.

One was found. MacArthur would not assault Rabaul, but merely surround and bypass it before continuing along the north coast of New Guinea toward the Philippines while at the same time releasing the Second Marine Division to Nimitz. For tactical reasons, Nimitz would take the Gilberts before the Marshalls.

Thanks to American industrial output, the Joint Chiefs did not have to choose between MacArthur and Nimitz. Instead, Japan was to be approached on two fronts, two giant pincers, each mutually supportive of the other and aimed at a common goal: the total destruction of the

Japanese war machine.

The Joint Chiefs approved the recommendations of the Joint Staff planners on July 20. King made one change by shifting the Gilberts invasion from November 1 to November 15. Finally, his long-sought-after central Pacific offensive was about to begin.

When the Trident conference ended in May, many important issues were left unresolved. For example, there was still the question of what course to take after Sicily was invaded. Should Italy be attacked or should the Allied effort be concentrated on the cross-channel invasion? There was also the question of the China-Burma-India theater. The Americans feared that the British were stalling. In addition, further clarification was needed regarding long-term Pacific objectives. Therefore, another conference was deemed imperative. This one convened in Quebec in August, 1943, at the beautiful Château Frontenac overlooking the St. Lawrence River. Code name for the conference was Quadrant.

The British came to Quebec prepared to do battle with the Americans. They wanted an invasion of Italy. King was appalled. He was of the opinion that such an operation would prove more a liability than an asset. Foremost in his mind was still the Pacific and he was unhappy with the resource allocation for that theater. Only fifteen percent of available resources were still being sent to the Pacific. King wanted that number doubled. As such, he was prepared to use the Quadrant conference to stage a showdown with the British. The admiral was insistent that the British live up to their Trident promises regarding their support in opening up the Burma Road. Keeping China in the war was vital, for if she collapsed, millions of Japanese troops would be free to defend those Pacific islands which were to be shortly assaulted by Nimitz's forces. As a sign of good faith, therefore, King wanted the British to designate a supreme commander for Burma.

The Joint Chiefs met with the President on August 10 to firm up the American position. It was universally agreed that the cross-channel operation, Overlord, must be finally agreed upon as the major operation for 1944. No more British delays would be tolerated. The Joint Chiefs also urged Roosevelt to push the British into fulfilling their promises for the China-Burma-India (CBI) theater.

To the British, King and his "damned Pacific policy" was an obstacle.

> Admiral King was determined not to have a single additional warship, so badly needed in the Pacific operations, diverted to any extra operations in that area so favored by our British allies. British insistence on expanding the Italian operations provoked King to very undiplomatic language, to use a mild term.[24]

The Quadrant conference convened on August 14 with the British reviewing the European war. They expressed their desire to move from Sicily to Italy, stating that this would give the Allies a foothold on the continent and an approach into central Europe. Hoping to make their arguments more attractive, the British said that a campaign in Italy would serve to drain German troops from the Overlord assault area since Hitler would have to defend Italy.

In his diary, Admiral Leahy stated:

> A difference of opinion was apparent from the outset as to the value of the Italian campaign toward our common war effort against Germany.[25]

After lunch, the Americans presented their view. King gave his usual scenario about the inadequate means to fight Japan and the neglect of the CBI theater. The British were on the defensive, but did not respond to King at that time. The next day, European strategy was discussed with

Overlord holding center stage. The British said that for Overlord to be successful, German strength had to be dissipated. As a prerequisite for Overlord then, they urged an invasion of Italy. King argued against the proposal and no compromise was reached.

Two more days of meetings finally brought about an agreement. A target date for Overlord was firmly established for May 1, 1944. The cross-channel attack would have priority of resources over the Mediterranean. As for Italy, the Allies would maintain "unremitting pressure" on the German forces there. Regarding the Pacific and the Far East, there was still problems, primarily over Burma. The British did, however, nominate Admiral Mountbatten to be Supreme Commander, Southeast Asia. King quickly endorsed the selection.

The Combined Staff planners took all the various ideas and plans expressed during the conference and put together a paper expressing the various positions. The outcome was a masterpiece of compromise.

In summary, Quadrant affirmed giving first priority to Overlord and reducing the Mediterranean to a secondary theater. An invasion of southern France simultaneous to Overlord was agreed to. Regarding the Pacific, King could expect additional resources. In addition, the Combined Chiefs agreed to the seizure of the Gilberts, Marshalls, Carolines, Palaus, and the Marianas. MacArthur's bypassing of Rabaul and his drive along northwest New Guinea was approved. Lastly, Mountbatten would take command of the Burma campaign whose objective was to open the Burma Road. King could feel satisfied with the results of Quadrant.

On September 25, the admiral flew to Pearl Harbor to talk with Nimitz. With the central Pacific offensive about to begin, King wanted to review strategy on Operation Galvanic, the seizure of the Gilbert Islands. During a meeting with Nimitz and Spruance, discussions centered on which islands in the Gilberts should be invaded and which should be bypassed. Tarawa and Makin were selected for assault. Originally, King had wanted Nauru Island, but Spruance talked him out of it because of its distance from Tarawa. Instead, Spruance suggested Makin because, he felt, it was closer to the Marshalls, large enough for an airfield, and close enough to Tarawa so that the fleet could support both assaults at the same time. King agreed that the arguments made sense.

As 1943 drew to a close, the need for a major conference, this time involving the Russians, was deemed necessary. It was felt that if the cross-channel operation was to be a success, Russian cooperation was necessary. There was also the question of whether or not the Soviets would become involved in the Far Eastern war. It was agreed to hold a Big Three meeting in Teheran before the end of the year.

Since Roosevelt's health was not the best, it was decided that the President would travel across the Atlantic in the newly commissioned battleship, USS *Iowa*. It was hoped that the sea voyage might improve his health. On November 12, Roosevelt and the Joint Chiefs boarded the *Iowa* for the precarious journey across the Atlantic.

Though not nearly as hazardous as a year previously, the Atlantic still harbored enemy U-boats seeking prey. Strict secrecy cloaked the *Iowa*'s precious cargo. Incredibly, during the journey, an American destroyer decided to use the *Iowa* as a target for torpedo practice. A torpedo was accidently fired and exploded in the wake of the battleship with such a thud that many thought the ship had been hit.

That it did not run hot and straight saved the United States Navy the embarrassment of having torpedoed their commander in chief and the Joint Chiefs of Staff.[26]

King wanted to relieve the commanding officer of the

destroyer at once, but to his amazement, the President told him to forget it.

During the voyage, King and his fellow chiefs joined Roosevelt and Harry Hopkins for planning sessions. The President announced that before proceeding to Teheran, the Combined Chiefs would meet in Cairo to iron out any last minute differences prior to facing the Russians. It seemed that the Americans were more concerned with the attitude of the British than that of the Russians. Topics such as who should command Overlord, whether or not all of Europe should be unified under one command, or if there should be separate commanders for Europe and the Mediterranean, were deliberated. They also discussed postwar Germany.

Landing at Oran, Algeria, the delegation boarded cars for the fifty-mile journey to La Serva airfield from where they flew on to Tunis. They spent the night in Tunis and proceeded to Cairo the following day. After landing in Cairo the party was taken to Mena House, a hotel on the outskirts of the city near the great pyramids. There, amid the splendors of the ancient world, the Combined Chiefs and the two political leaders argued, discussed, and attempted to forge a united front before proceeding to Teheran and their meeting with Stalin and the Russians.

The Cairo meeting lasted ten days, during which discussions centered upon two areas, Europe and the Far East. The Far East topic monopolized much of the time for one of the participants was Generalissimo Chiang Kai-shek. Along with the Chinese leader came his very attractive wife and General Stilwell.

The meetings became rather heated. At one session, Alan Brooke provoked a storm when he suggested canceling amphibious operations in Burma so that more landing craft could be made available for use in the Mediterranean. King became enraged at what he considered to be typical British double-dealing. In his candid papers, Stilwell paints an eloquent picture of the scene.

> Brooke got nasty and King got good and sore. King
> almost climbed over the table at Brooke. God, he was
> mad. I wish he had socked him.[27]

Stilwell liked the British even less than King.

The British and Americans were unable to reach any agreement on the Far East. At the last meeting of the chiefs on November 26 before their departure for Teheran, Brooke once more suggested canceling amphibious operations in Burma. King closed his ears to the thought of that. The chiefs could not even come to an agreement regarding Overlord and the Anvil (invasion of southern France) operations.

The first Cairo Conference thus ended in Allied disunity with each side waiting to make its appeals to Stalin.

On November 27, King and Arnold flew from Cairo to Teheran. In the Persian capital they found themselves billeted at an American base outside of the city along with Marshall. Neither King nor anyone else had any idea what Stalin was going to say.

King was primarily a spectator at the first meeting. Roosevelt, Churchill, and Stalin dominated the session as each presented his own views, ideas, and opinions. After a lengthy review of the war, Roosevelt asked Stalin how the Allies could best assist the Soviet Union. To King's happy surprise, Stalin began talking about the Pacific, promising Soviet participation after Germany had been defeated. As for the war in Europe, the Soviet leader urged a cross-channel attack combined with a simultaneous assault into southern France. Then, to Churchill's dismay, Stalin went on to say that any operation in Italy or the eastern Mediterranean were of little or no consequence. The prime minister did all he could to swing Stalin over to his own point of view, but to no avail.

During the second meeting, King was once more a passive spectator. At this session, Stalin wanted to know the name of the person who was to direct Overlord. Meanwhile, Churchill attempted to once more revive his Mediterranean plans, but Stalin turned a deaf ear.

On the third day, the Combined Chiefs met in session to decide on the date for Overlord. The availability of landing craft would decide the schedule. King promised to make available all possible landing craft short of diverting them from the Pacific. The actual date however, was the biggest question. The Americans wanted it to be in May, 1944, while the British wanted it delayed until July. Nothing definitive was agreed upon.

Finally, after hours of endless meetings, the Combined Chiefs agreed on a schedule. The Allied advance in Italy would proceed to the Pisa-Rimini Line, Overlord and Anvil would land simultaneously, and both would be launched in May, 1944. At the official meeting, Roosevelt read the Combined Chiefs' recommendations. Stalin seemed satisfied. The historic meeting ended on a cordial note with Stalin pledging a massive offensive in conjunction with the landings in France.

The next day King started back to Cairo after a brief stopover in Jerusalem. When he returned to Egypt the Combined Chiefs began the second Cairo conference on the afternoon of December 3. The main issue was the size and scope of Operation Anvil. If it was up to the British, the operation would not take place at all, but if it were to be, they wanted it limited to a two-division assault. King said that at Teheran it was agreed that the size of Anvil would be limited to the availability of landing craft. For the next five days the size of the invasion of southern France was debated.

Where could landing craft be found? The British suggested the abandonment of Buccaneer (code name for the proposed amphibious assault in Burma). Ironically, though the British disliked the concept of Anvil, they viewed it as a means of lessening their commitment in Burma by dangling the landing craft as bait. King, on the other hand, wanted Buccaneer salvaged. He was prepared to make concessions, but remained unmoved. The prime minister reasoned that with Stalin's promise to enter the war against Japan, the need for China's support was not as critical, so an offensive to open the supply line through Burma was no longer necessary. Finally, on December 6, Roosevelt yielded on the issue even if it meant discarding earlier promises to Chiang Kai-shek.

King returned to the United States on December 12. During the month that he was away, Nimitz's central Pacific offensive commenced with an assault of Tarawa and Makin on November 20. The battle for Tarawa was bloody with the marines suffering heavy casualties. Meanwhile, the Army's 27th Division, which had assaulted Makin, was criticized for proceeding too slowly against relatively light opposition. Friction between the services was inevitable.

On January 3, 1944, King flew to San Francisco to meet with Nimitz and Halsey and review with them the implications of the Cairo-Teheran conferences. King emphasized the importance of the Mariana Islands. Capture of these, he said, would pierce Japan's inner defensive circle, block the line of communications between the homeland and her major naval base at Truk in the Carolines, and open the Chinese coast for exploitation. King was determined to exploit the vast manpower resources of China and to use that country as a staging area for a final assault on Japan itself. He left, assured that Nimitz and his staff realized the importance of the Marianas.

Quite the contrary, however, was the case. MacArthur's staff, represented by General Sutherland, argued for the pooling of all Pacific resources for a drive to the Philippines which could then be used as a staging area for an assault on China. Nimitz and his staff seemed more sympathetic to

Sutherland's proposals than to King's enthusiasm for the Marianas. When he saw the minutes of the January 27-28 Pearl Harbor meeting where Sutherland had presented his case, King was furious at Nimitz and said so in a scathing letter whose contents again emphasized the importance of the Marianas. Besides reiterating his previous reasons, King stated, in hopes that he could obtain Army Air Force support, that the islands could be used as a staging area for the B-29 bombing offensive of the Japanese home islands.

MacArthur's and King's strategy thus seemed to fly in each other's faces. In a February 2 dispatch to Marshall, MacArthur emphasized the importance of his approach to the exclusion of the central Pacific. The general argued that one strong thrust was infinitely preferable to two weak ones.

King quickly responded to MacArthur's note with one of his own stating that apparently

> General MacArthur had not accepted the Combined Chiefs of Staff decisions at Cairo that there would be a dual drive across the Pacific and that the central Pacific took priority in scheduling and resources.[28]

King concluded by asking Marshall to tell MacArthur to stick to the rules.

In mid-February, King was still unhappy with Nimitz. The latter wanted to capture Truk while King wanted this island bypassed. In addition, Nimitz procrastinated about making a firm commitment on the Marianas. Meanwhile, the Marshall Islands were successfully assaulted during February and March. In Washington, however, the struggle to determine Pacific strategy continued. The Joint Chiefs favored the already agreed upon dual thrust, but MacArthur was not satisfied and continued to harass Marshall.

Nimitz arrived in Washington in early March to meet with the Joint Chiefs in the hope of pinning down Pacific strategy. MacArthur was also invited, but as usual declined, saying that he could not leave his headquarters while his forces were engaged in action. Sutherland attended instead. MacArthur's chief of staff could not withstand the arguments of the Joint Chiefs. King's theories dominated.

The admiral found a ready ally in Arnold who wanted the Marianas for a different reason from King's. Nevertheless, Arnold's support swayed Marshall and Leahy. The final decision was that MacArthur could complete the isolation of Rabaul and proceed westward along the New Guinea coast before jumping to Mindanao in the Philippines on November 15. Nimitz would bypass Truk, seize the southern Marianas on June 15—thereby isolating the Carolines, and seize the Palaus on September 15 in order to provide a fleet base for support of MacArthur's attack in the Philippines. Following that, Nimitz was to seize Formosa on February 15, 1945, while MacArthur took Luzon. After Formosa would come the China coast. Finally, after months of haggling, the American commanders had a blueprint to follow.

In the meantime, King began to give serious thought to the Japanese Fleet which had remained inactive for over a year. Would this fleet finally make an all-out attack when the Marianas were invaded? He hoped so. As the months slipped by, it appeared that the Japanese would do just that. King was apprehensive about the ability of Spruance's Fifth Fleet to stop the enemy fleet. Nimitz reassured him that Spruance was capable and ready. Spruance, however, understood his primary concern to be the protection of the Saipan beachhead, not the destruction of the Japanese Fleet. This accounted for the subsequent escape of the Japanese Fleet despite heavy losses. King had done all he could do; the rest was up to Nimitz and Spruance. With that, his attention turned to Europe where Overlord was about to begin.

Since the Cairo conference, the British had been agitating against the Anvil landings. They wanted the operation abandoned completely. The Americans were dead set against that proposal. By April, however, the simultaneous landing of Anvil and Overlord was postponed and the former's future was left open to further debate. Scarcity of landing craft settled that issue.

As June rolled around, King's attention was divided between the Marianas and the Normandy shore. Since all planning for these operations was by and large complete, he became a mere spectator and could only hope for the best.

The Normandy landings began on June 6. Two days later, King, Marshall and Arnold flew to England in the event any major decisions from the Combined Chiefs were needed. Within a few days, they accompanied the British chiefs on a visit to Normandy. They were met by General Eisenhower at Portsmouth where the British boarded a Royal Navy destroyer while the Americans went aboard an American ship. They landed amid the carnage of Omaha Beach where only a few days earlier Gen. Omar Bradley had pondered evacuating his forces from the beach and shifting them to the other beaches. Bradley guided the visitors inland a few miles where they had lunch. This was followed by more sightseeing.

After the tour, which proved most satisfying, the Combined Chiefs settled down to three days of meetings. They discussed the Marianas, future Pacific ventures, the CBI, and of course the fate of the postponed Anvil. The British continued to cling to the belief that resources for Anvil could be better put to use in Italy. King, however, remained unconvinced that the Italian campaign was anything but a dead end and saw no reason to delay Anvil any longer. After all, the Allies had promised the Russians at Teheran that Anvil would be launched. Churchill relented and the invasion of southern France was rescheduled for August 15.

When King returned to the United States he immediately

ordered shipping sent to the Mediterranean for use in Anvil, shipping that was already engaged in the Normandy operation. This caused a storm of protest. Churchill hit the roof, angry that King could unilaterally remove shipping from Overlord without first consulting the Combined Chiefs, the Supreme Commander, or even the Joint Chiefs. This was the last straw as far as Churchill was concerned. For months he had felt that King manipulated American shipping to suit his own purposes. The prime minister was determined to do something about it if at all possible. Luckily, the showdown never occurred.

With the Americans fighting in the Marianas, and Mac-Arthur soon to complete the conquest of New Guinea, subsequent operations needed clarification. The Combined Chiefs had already authorized the invasion of the Philippines, Formosa, and the Palau Islands. Still, some question remained as to operations. Should Luzon and Formosa be invaded? Each target offered equal benefits as far as severing Japanese lines of communication to its southern empire. Each could also serve as a base for a later assault on the mainland of China. Limitation of resources, however, mitigated against attacking both islands. It had to be either one or the other.

King wanted Formosa since he felt it was closer both to Japan and to China and its seizure would eliminate the need to invade the island of Luzon whose massive Japanese garrison could be left to wither on the vine. In addition, Formosa was in Nimitz's area, which would make it a Navy show, while Luzon was in MacArthur's.

MacArthur obviously was dead set against King's proposal. His promise to return to the Philippines had to be fulfilled. He said that it was the moral obligation of the U.S. to liberate the Filipinos who were subjected to Japanese control. The general did not want to see his theater become secondary as it surely would if the Philippines were bypassed. Besides, he said, any assault on

Formosa would need land-based air protection from Luzon, thus necessitating the need for the Philippines.

To argue his point, King went to Pearl Harbor in mid-July for a meeting with Nimitz. After some preliminary discussions, King and Nimitz flew to Saipan for a close-up view of the hard-won island. King toured Saipan despite the proximity of Japanese snipers.

During discussions regarding the Formosa plan, King found Spruance and Turner cool to the concept. Both felt that Luzon should be assaulted first. Besides creating air bases, they argued, Luzon would also provide an anchorage for future operations. King then asked Spruance what he wanted to take. Spruance answered that Iwo Jima and Okinawa should be attacked. King saw the wisdom of those two objectives, but was not persuaded to change his mind about Formosa.

When they returned to Pearl Harbor, King received word that Roosevelt was on his way to Hawaii to discuss the divergent strategies with both Nimitz and MacArthur. King used all his powers of persuasion in an effort to sway Nimitz to the Formosa plan. He knew that he could order Nimitz to agree, but felt that it would be better if the latter could be convinced of the advantages involved instead. Before leaving Hawaii, King also mentioned the possibility of carrying out carrier raids against Japan.

King left Hawaii before Roosevelt arrived. At the Roosevelt-Nimitz-MacArthur meeting, the general's arguments about the Philippines won out. King was disappointed in Nimitz. Nothing, however, was solved regarding Formosa. The Joint Chiefs debated into September when they finally gave MacArthur approval to invade Leyte in December and Luzon early the following year. With that issue resolved, the Joint Chiefs left Washington for yet another conference with the British, the second Quebec conference, code name, Octagon.

Churchill was the driving force at this conference. With

the Allies victorious on all fronts, the prime minister's main concern was the postwar world. Allied boundary lines and occupation zones needed clarifying. Churchill was also prepared to finally commit the British to an all-out campaign in the Pacific. This gave rise to one of the bitterest confrontations of the war.

The prime minister wanted to commit the Royal Navy to fight alongside the American Fleet in the Pacific. As the British had not yet developed mobile logistical support, King felt that would be more of a liability than an asset. Roosevelt, however, accepted the offer, but King demurred until it became a matter of personal pride and prestige for the British. For King to refuse to accept the Royal Navy would be to publicly embarrass and insult an ally. A compromise was finally reached that would allow the British Fleet to participate in the main operations against Japan, but only if it could become self-supporting. The American Navy, King said, would not provide any logistical support to the Royal Navy. The British Fleet lived up to its proud tradition and proved a tremendous asset during the remaining months of the war.

On September 13, while the Third Fleet was involved in neutralizing central Philippine air bases, its commander, Admiral Halsey, found the Japanese defenses to be weak. He immediately recommended to the Joint Chiefs that the Palau Islands and Mindanao be bypassed and Leyte be invaded at once. The proposal was accepted, but it was too late to call off the Palaus operation. However, the invasion of Yap was canceled and the forces dedicated to this operation were offered to MacArthur for his use at Leyte. The invasion of this island was therefore advanced to October 20, two months ahead of schedule.

The Octagon conference ended on September 16. On the twenty-ninth, King met with Nimitz in San Francisco. There Nimitz finally convinced King to abandon his Formosan plans by telling him that there would not be enough Army troops available for an invasion of that island. There would, however, be enough for an invasion of Okinawa and enough marines available for an attack on Iwo Jima. On October 2, King yielded. The Joint Chiefs then ordered MacArthur to seize Luzon after Leyte and Nimitz was given orders to attack Iwo Jima and Okinawa.

During the invasion of Leyte and the related Battle of Leyte Gulf, King closely monitored the dispatches regarding the battle. The controversy over Halsey's leaving his position during the battle was in many ways as much King's fault as Halsey's, thanks to his repeated advocacy of a divided command. From the very beginning King had refused to allow MacArthur control of the Navy. Unity of command might have avoided the misunderstanding. Halsey was under orders from Nimitz that in case the opportunity for the destruction of the enemy fleet presented itself, such destruction would become the primary objective. King knew Nimitz's directive, and he was familiar with Halsey's impetuous nature. By not countermanding or amending that order therefore, King, by default, allowed Halsey to abandon the beachhead resulting in a near disaster. In his own autobiography, Halsey said:

> The fact that it was not coordinated under any single authority was an invitation which disaster nearly accepted.[29]

After the battle, King could not, or would not, criticize America's most popular admiral. To publicly condemn Halsey would imply that the Battle of Leyte Gulf was not the great victory that the press claimed. Besides, it would also criticize a policy advocated by King and might yet force the Joint Chiefs to insist on unity of command thereby placing the navy under MacArthur's control and creating a situation that was anathema to King. Yes, Halsey had erred, but he could not be criticized for it since the fault was not his alone. Unfairly, King therefore attempted to shift the blame to the commander of the Seventh Fleet, Adm. Thomas Kinkaid.

The U.S. Navy had had a close call, but the Japanese Navy was finished once and for all. In December, King, along with Nimitz and Leahy were awarded a fifth star and named fleet admirals. On the 20th of January, 1945, Roosevelt was inaugurated for an unprecedented fourth term. A few days after the inaugural festivities, the President and the Joint Chiefs found themselves on their way to yet another meeting of the Big Three, this time at Yalta in the Crimea. King flew across the Atlantic with stopovers in Bermuda and Casablanca. On the twenty-ninth he was in Malta where the Americans began preliminary talks with their British counterparts. The agenda was limited to one military item: when would Eisenhower's forces cross the Rhine? After this meeting, the group moved on to Yalta where the postwar division of Europe was discussed.

King had little to say regarding the political settlement; that was left to the politicians. Since political decisions predominated, the Joint Chiefs were rarely consulted. King's primary interest centered on where and to what extent the Russians would fulfill their commitment and come into the war against Japan. After days of merely observing, King heard Stalin commit the Red Army to fight against Japan three months after the conclusion of hostilities in Europe. With that, the admiral returned to the United States.

On February 19, Iwo Jima was invaded, followed in April by an attack on Okinawa. On April 12, Roosevelt died suddenly. King was no close friend of the President and was not overly upset by his passing. The new President, Harry S Truman, King knew, could not affect the future course of the war.

On May 7, Germany surrendered. Now King and the Joint Chiefs discussed methods for transferring forces from Europe to the Pacific and what to do about the fate of Japan—invade it or starve it?

In early May, the Joint Staff planners recommended that Japan be invaded. Even though high casualties were expected, the chiefs accepted the planners' recommendations. They also agreed to make MacArthur and Nimitz jointly responsible for the operation.

In July, the final wartime conference was scheduled. This time it was to be held in defeated Germany. King left for the meeting on July 12. After a stop-off in Paris, he arrived in war-torn Berlin. King could feel the tension in the atmosphere, a tension that would shortly escalate into the Cold War. The admiral considered himself a spectator again rather than a participant in the conference. Before returning home though, he did manage to make a visit to the remains of Hitler's mountain villa at Berchtesgaden.

On July 17, General Marshall cleared the room where the Joint Chiefs were meeting at Potsdam and reported the successful detonation, in New Mexico, of a new type of weapon, an atomic bomb. King had known of the secret Manhattan Project as far back as 1943 when Marshall had reviewed it with him. Now it was a reality, a new type of bomb with an enormous killing potential. The next day, Marshall told the chiefs that Truman had made the decision to use the bomb against the Japanese.

Two bombs were dropped; on August 6 at Hiroshima and on the 9th at Nagasaki. On the fourteenth, the Japanese surrendered. King immediately sent a message to Nimitz ordering the suspension of all air attacks. The Second World War was over.

With war's end, King's career also came to a close. He formally retired on December 15, 1945, when Admiral Nimitz relieved him and became the first postwar Chief of Naval Operations. Honor after honor was presented to King.

Following his retirement, the admiral began work on his memoirs in collaboration with Walter Muir Whitehill. In 1947, King was felled by the first of a series of strokes. Others soon followed. Although his mind remained alert, his speech and dexterity were affected. In a short time he became an invalid, but lived until June 25, 1956, when he passed away at the age of seventy-eight. Admiral King was buried at Annapolis.

Ernest King was by far America's most powerful naval commander. Never in American history had one commander ever wielded such power over naval forces. By 1945, he controlled the world's largest navy and his influence was world-wide.

King's career was long and eventful. He served in three wars and had experiences in all three branches of the service: submarines, surface ships, and the air. He became one of the prime movers and supporters of naval aviation and in that proved most perceptive.

King was not known for his tact and his dealing with the British was not always cordial to say the least. He was tough, so much so that the rumor that he shaved with a blowtorch was common knowledge and probably even believed in some quarters. Yet he was important to America, for he served the country through its greatest crisis and helped steer it to ultimate victory. King advocated a strategy contrary to that of his cobelligerents and stuck to his guns no matter how much he was criticized. Truly, Adm. Ernest King was one of a kind, the likes of which the United States Navy will never again see.

Chapter Two

The English vocabulary contains many adjectives suitable for describing the Commander in Chief of the Pacific Fleet and Pacific Ocean Areas during World War II. Among them are modest, quiet, compassionate, humane, courteous, loyal, competent, and efficient, to name but a few. He assumed command when American morale was at its lowest, arriving at Pearl Harbor amid the destruction of the Pacific Fleet. Shortly thereafter he was able to launch raids against the victorious enemy and give America's sagging morale a lift. From the dark days of defeat to final victory, Chester W. Nimitz led his country's forces from the jungles of the Solomons, through the coral atolls of the central Pacific, to the caves of Okinawa. The confidence he engendered, the competence he demonstrated, encouraged America. In conjunction with the indomitable MacArthur, he gave America hope when all seemed hopeless, courage to move ahead, and a leader to admire and of whom to be proud.

The Nimitz name stems from an ancient Saxon-German family whose family crest depicts the fact that his ancestors were an order of Teutonic knights. During the Thirty Years' War the Nimitzes fought on the side of the great Swedish king, Gustavus Adolphus, against the Catholic Hapsburgs. The family prospered until Chester's great grandfather, Karl Heinrich, squandered the family wealth on loose living, bringing the family to bankruptcy. In 1840, Karl Heinrich's three oldest children immigrated to America settling in Charleston, South Carolina. One son,

Karl Heinrich, Jr., being more adventurous than the others, went to sea and wound up in Texas where he joined a group of German immigrants. From the Gulf Coast the fledgling pioneers trekked through the wilderness, suffering endless hardships on their way westward. In May, 1846, the survivors reached their destination, a tract of land previously purchased by the group. There they founded a town and settled down. Karl Heinrich Anglicized his name to Charles Henry Nimitz. He founded an inn and prospered. During the Civil War such dignitaries as Robert E. Lee, Philip Sheridan, and later, O. Henry, were guests at the Nimitz Inn. It was this illustrious innkeeper who would keep his grandchildren enthralled with stories of his youth, especially tales of the sea acquired during his short time as a seaman. One of the grandchildren whom he thrilled with these tales was Chester W. Nimitz.

A son had been born to Chester Bernard, one of Charles Henry's sons, on February 24, 1885 — a blond-haired boy, who was named Chester William. The baby's father, however, was sickly and did not live to see his son born. So the grandfather immediately stepped forth and took his daughter-in-law and infant child under his wing.

As a youngster, Chester was popular and made friends easily. His mother taught him the importance of physical fitness, perhaps because of her fear that the young boy had inherited some of his father's physical weaknesses. At an early age he resolved to remain physically fit, a determination he maintained until his death.

As a student, he achieved excellent grades. When he wasn't attending school, Chester worked around the inn which his mother and stepfather (his father's brother) managed at Kerriville, Texas.

During the summer of 1900, he met two recent graduates of the military academy at West Point. Nimitz was quickly fascinated by their relative youth, bearing, and self-confidence — since they were only five years older than himself. He became enthralled with the possibility of a life of adventure and travel. Thus, Nimitz enthusiastically applied to his congressman for an appointment to West Point. His hopes were dashed when the congressman replied that all the appointments were filled and would be for the next few years. However, the congressman added, he still had one opening left for the naval academy. Lack of knowledge about Annapolis failed to flag Nimitz's enthusiasm and the young hopeful immediately set about disciplining himself to study long hours in preparation for the entrance exam. With aid from his stepfather, teachers, and his high-school principal, he took and passed the exam in April, 1901. On September 7 of that year, Chester W. Nimitz was sworn in as a naval cadet.

Entering the academy the same year that Ernest King graduated, Nimitz found a new feeling of resurgence. After years of neglect, in response to the recent Spanish-American War, Congress finally surged ahead with new naval appropriations. Spurred on by the newly elected President, Theodore Roosevelt, the naval academy and the navy were feeling the new breezes.

In response to the needs of an expanding navy and short-ages of naval officers revealed by the recent conflict, Nimitz's class was the largest one to enter Annapolis since its founding in 1845.

Chester was a model cadet. He worked diligently and studied hard. Halfway through his first semester, however, he was felled by pneumonia. So Chester had to work even harder to make up for the time he had missed while ill.

Attending the academy at the same time as Nimitz were William Halsey, Harold Stark, Frank Jack Fletcher, Husband Kimmel, Royal Ingersoll, Robert Ghormley, Raymond Spruance, John Towers, John McCain, Thomas Kinkaid, H. Kent Hewitt, and R. Kelly Turner. The June before Nimitz's entry saw Ernest King and William Pye graduate. Though all the aforementioned were not in the same class, during those early years of the twentieth century, Annapolis was the breeding ground of America's World War II naval leaders. Thankfully, foresighted leadership prodded congressional interest in naval growth. Without that leadership, the United States would have been caught woefully short in the 1940s.

Nimitz learned much during his academy days. One lesson that remained with him for the rest of his life was the disgraceful debate between Admirals Sampson and Schley. Both claimed to be the victor at Santiago, but during the campaign, Schley was branded a coward. This shameful affair troubled the young cadet who vowed that if he ever rose to high command, he would never wash the navy's dirty laundry in public. That was a vow he steadfastly kept.

Nimitz was graduated as a passed midshipman on January 30, 1905, five months ahead of schedule, thanks to the need for junior officers in the rapidly expanding fleet. As a passed midshipman he was eligible for commission as an ensign after the satisfactory completion of two years of naval service.

After graduation, Nimitz returned home on leave to Texas. From there he traveled to San Francisco for his first assignment aboard the battleship USS *Ohio* which had been ordered to the Orient to serve as flagship of the U.S. Asiatic Fleet.

At that time Japan was at war with Russia and the famed Admiral Togo had recently annihilated the Russian Fleet at the Battle of Tsushima. One of the high points of the American visit occurred for Nimitz shortly after the conclusion of hostilities. In order to mark the return to peace, the Emperor of Japan gave a large garden party to honor his victorious army and navy commanders. Invitations went out to the *Ohio* which was then at anchor in Tokyo Bay. Nimitz was one of the guests. Toward the end of the party, as the hero of Tsushima was being whisked away, he passed the table where the Americans were sitting. Nimitz was delegated to invite Admiral Togo to the table. This gave rise to an event that the future American admiral would never forget, the moment when he shook hands and spoke with the legendary Japanese admiral. Shortly afterward, the *Ohio* was ordered home, but Nimitz opted to remain in the Far East. Accordingly, he transferred to the cruiser *Baltimore*. While on board this ship, he took the exam for his commission as ensign.

Nimitz received his commission on January 31, 1907. A short time later he assumed command of a gunboat in the Philippines, the USS *Panay*. He was thrilled with this command for he saw it as a welcome chance to practice his piloting and navigation. Essentially, his job was to show the flag to the recently pacified Filipinos and Moros in the Sulu Archipelago and to assist wherever he was needed to settle any troubles.

In addition to commanding the *Panay*, Nimitz was also in charge of a naval station containing twenty-two marines. Soon, however, the international scene grew tense as the once-cordial relationship between the United States and Japan deteriorated. The threat of war brought Nimitz at the age of twenty-one to the command of the destroyer *Decatur* which at that time was undergoing repairs. In record time he had the ship repaired, seaworthy, and ready for action. Eventually the war scare abated and Japan, extending its hand of friendship, formally invited the Great White Fleet to visit its shores. This fleet was comprised of sixteen battleships which President Roosevelt had sent on a world-wide tour with the intention of showing off American naval strength. In advance of the fleet went Secretary of War William Howard Taft as Roosevelt's ambassador of peace and good will.

Ensign Nimitz was assigned the task of escorting the Taft party from Olongapo back to Manila aboard the *Decatur*. With the departure of Taft, the *Decatur* proceeded south to Mindanao where Nimitz continued to perform duties similiar to those of his previous term with the *Panay*.

On July 7, 1908, an event happened that might have spelled the end of Nimitz's promising career. On that date he grounded the *Decatur*. Grounding a ship is perhaps one of the worst offenses a naval officer can be guilty of. Nimitz was immediately transferred to the cruiser *Denver* to stand court-martial. Taking his spotless record into consideration as well as the poor state of charts for the area of the grounding and impressed by Nimitz's honesty in relating the event, the charge was reduced to neglect of duty and the sentence was a public reprimand. The court-martial had no effect on his subsequent career. In fact, within eighteen months he was promoted to lieutenant, skipping the lower rank of lieutenant, J.G.

After the court-martial, Nimitz returned to the U.S. Following a brief visit to his home he reported to his new duty station with the First Submarine Flotilla. At that time the submarine force was considered a backwater branch of the navy. Nimitz could justifiably look upon this assignment as punishment for having grounded the *Decatur*. However, in time he came to appreciate the potential of the submarine.

Shortly afterward he was sent to sea in command of the submarine *Narwhal*. This was followed by duty with a succession of other boats. In November, 1911, he met the woman with whom he was to share the rest of his life, Catherine Freeman. They would have a long and happy life together despite the frequent and extended absences typical of a military career. Their marriage was a model one and the old cliché that said "they were made for each other" aptly fit the Nimitzes.

In the spring of 1912 he was invited to address the Naval War College on the topic of submarines, a unique honor for a twenty-seven-year-old lieutenant. The success of the lecture launched Nimitz on a secondary career as a lecturer and writer.

Chester and Catherine Nimitz were married in April, 1913, and departed for Europe the following month. Chester was given orders to study the performance of the German submarines.

In June of 1913, Germany was in the throes of Kaiser Wilhelm II's silver jubilee. Nimitz's specific assignment was to study diesel engines, particularly the working drawings of those engines manufactured at the Blohm and Voss shipbuilding yard in Hamburg. While studying the performance of the diesel engine, Nimitz witnessed the launching of a new giant battleship to the strains of "Deutschland Über Alles." He was awed by the colorful uniforms, bright spiked and plumed helmets, and forceful-looking soldiers who paraded before him.

Following a month of study and travel the Nimitzes returned to the States. Lieutenant Nimitz reported to a new assignment in the machinery division of New York's Brooklyn Navy Yard, where he was directed to supervise the construction and installation of a diesel engine in the new oiler, *Maumee*. In time Nimitz became the foremost naval expert in diesel engines. Offers were received from numerous civilian firms that would have dazzled a less dedicated officer, but Nimitz ignored them. By the middle of 1916, the *Maumee*'s engines were completed and installed and Nimitz was assigned to the ship as both executive officer and chief engineer.

While work proceeded on the *Maumee*, Europe became engulfed in flames. By 1916 the Germans resumed unrestricted submarine warfare causing the United States to respond with a declaration of war on April 6, 1917. The *Maumee* was ordered to the mid-Atlantic with the task of refueling destroyers en route to Ireland. In August, Nimitz, promoted to lieutenant commander, was transferred to the Submarine Forces, Atlantic Fleet as aide to the commander of the submarine force, Samuel S. Robison.

In February of the following year Robison, along with

his aide, left for Europe where they toured British naval bases and shipyards. They then moved on to the continent where they had an opportunity to inspect French antisubmarine devices along the Mediterranean Coast. Most of their time, however, was spent at Scapa Flow where the great British Fleet lay at anchor. While the two American officers were there studying submarine techniques, the guns fell silent in Europe.

Upon his return home, Nimitz reported to the Norfolk Navy Yard, but his stay was brief as he was ordered to Pearl Harbor in June of 1920 with orders to construct a submarine base. This was a most formidable task for a thirty-five-year-old lieutenant commander.

The Pearl Harbor of those days was a primitive-looking naval base and certainly not an encouraging sight for the energetic engineer. Nimitz had full command responsibility for building the submarine facility. After a busy year, the job was completed and Nimitz, by now a full commander, remained on as commanding officer.

In the late spring of 1922 he was ordered to report for instruction at the Naval War College. Nimitz was elated since any officer aspiring for flag rank knew that attendance at the War College was the pathway to high command. He spent the next few months attending classes or participating in war games. He would later reflect upon his War College days as most formative in helping to prepare him for command during World War II. Since the hypothetical enemy during the war games was Japan, the various strategies devised were many of the same ones later used in a real war waged against a genuine enemy. Nimitz experimented with the use of a new circular ship formation as opposed to the traditional line of battle. He also participated in the controversy over the respective worth of the battleship in light of the newly developed aircraft carrier. The latter had the ability to lengthen the battle radius by over two hundred miles.

No longer would ships have to be in view of each other to initiate combat. There were many orthodox naval leaders who clung to the belief that the battleship was queen of the seas despite Gen. Billy Mitchell's demonstration of bombers sinking a battleship in 1921. From all evidence, Nimitz was neutral at the time, but later action as CinCPac (Commander in Chief, Pacific) made his disposition toward carriers obvious.

Toward the end of his tour of duty at the War College he was directed to proceed to San Pedro, California, where he was ordered to report for duty with the battleship *California*, flagship of the battle fleet. Once more he found himself working with his former superior, Admiral Robison, as the latter's aide, assistant Chief of Staff, and tactical officer. He participated in the fleet's tactical exercises, advocating what he had introduced at the War College; i.e., the circular formation for capital ships. The tactic was tried and proved successful. As Potter, Nimitz's official biographer has said:

> The tactical innovations introduced into the United States Fleet by Chester Nimitz are as epochal as the column formation that Oliver Cromwell's generals imposed on the English sailing fleet in the seventeenth century.[1]

Soon thereafter Admiral Robison became Commander in Chief of the fleet. Nimitz went along as assistant Chief of Staff. After a year in that role he was one of six naval officers selected to establish the first Naval Reserve Officer's Training Corps (NROTC) in American universities. Nimitz was assigned to the University of California at Berkeley, where he remained for the next three years. In June of 1927, he received the coveted promotion to the rank of captain.

As a teacher the recently promoted captain proved to be

excellent and inspired. He thoroughly enjoyed those years at Berkeley.

> My chief satisfaction came in getting in touch with up and going young men—working with young and extremely independent young men with untrammeled minds.[2]

In June, 1929, Captain Nimitz was reassigned as Commander, Submarine Division at San Diego. He remained there for two years, at the end of which time he became commander of destroyers at the same base. In the late summer of 1933 he was ordered to the new cruiser *Augusta* as the ship's captain. The *Augusta* was shortly designated flagship of the Asiatic Fleet and Nimitz received orders to take her to Shanghai. The new skipper transformed the *Augusta* into a model ship. Expecting the most from his crew, he transferred anyone who failed to measure up. Though anticipating the best and utilizing discipline to obtain it, Nimitz earned the respect of his men. Accordingly, they performed at their peak for him. Years later one admiral commented on Nimitz's performance:

> I think one can safely say that the *Augusta* had reached an absolutely unheard level of high morale, high pride, and competence at every level, down to the lowliest mess cook.[3]

Nimitz's tour of duty on the *Augusta* ended in the spring of 1935, when he was ordered to report to Washington and assume the post of Assistant to the Chief of the Bureau of Navigation (later changed to the Bureau of Personnel).

Three years later, in 1938, Nimitz reached flag rank and was given a new command, Commander of Cruiser Division Two in San Diego. Just as he was about to take command however, he developed a hernia and was required to undergo surgery. Since he would be laid up for over a month, the cruiser command went to someone else. Fully recovered, Nimitz was instead assigned to the more prestigious post of Commander of Battleship Division One with his flag on the USS *Arizona*.

In January of the following year he was given command of Task Force Seven consisting of the *Arizona*, a carrier, cruiser, seven destroyers and auxiliaries, and a tanker. His enthusiasm with his new command was infectious and officers who served with him recalled how hard the admiral worked and how competently he led the Task Force in maneuvers.

Due to the shortage of seagoing billets for flag officers his command of the battleship division did not last more than a year and by late spring of 1939 he found himself ordered to Washington once more, this time as Chief of the Bureau of Navigation. As bureau chief it was Nimitz's responsibility to procure and train the sailors required for the expanding fleet and assign them to duty. These responsibilities often brought him before the House Naval Affairs Committee where he quickly learned the methods of politicians and made important friends in Congress.

Lack of aviation experience, however, brought him into conflict with Rear Admiral John Towers, head of the Bureau of Aeronautics. Towers wanted to assign all senior aviation commands, but Nimitz had no intention of relinquishing the authority that rightfully belonged to the Bureau of Navigation.

With war in Europe approaching, the American armed forces were in dire need of expansion. Nimitz had to utilize many techniques to attract more people into the navy. With the outbreak of war in September of 1939, followed by the fall of France the following June, the ranks of the navy swelled, particularly after all reservists were recalled to active duty. Then the Japanese attacked Pearl Harbor.

The events leading up to the Japanese attack are

examined in depth in *Volume IV: The Japanese,* of our Great Commander series. In it we point out the critical situation in which Japan found itself in 1941. Cut off from U.S. oil, squeezed by the British and Dutch, Japan felt that its only option, other than complete capitulation, was war. Without foreign oil Japan was forced to seize its own oil resources in the Dutch East Indies. To insure the success of her move into southeast Asia, Admiral Yamamoto designed the Pearl Harbor raid in order to neutralize American naval strength. December 7, 1941, was the day the Japanese unleashed their blitzkrieg.

On that fateful day, Rear Admiral Nimitz was in his Washington apartment. He turned on the radio at 3:00 P.M. to listen to music when the dramatic news of the bombing of Pearl Harbor was frantically reported by an overexcited broadcaster. Nimitz immediately called for his aide and proceeded to his office. There he conferred first with his staff before attending a conference with Secretary of the Navy Frank Knox and Chief of Naval Operations Harold Stark. During this meeting he was apprised of the extent of the damage.

Nimitz's job immediately assumed vast proportions. He had to man a wartime navy. Thanks to his foresight, however, the chore was made easier since he had already prepared for such an eventuality.

Secretary Knox left Washington on the ninth to personally inspect the damage at Pearl Harbor. Upon his return he recommended that Admiral Kimmel, whose name now became irrevocably associated with the disaster, be immediately relieved of duty. On December 16, one day after his return, Knox recommended to President Roosevelt that Nimitz become Commander in Chief, Pacific. Roosevelt endorsed Knox's decision. Edwin Hoyt says of the choice:

The qualities of the Nimitz character were apparent

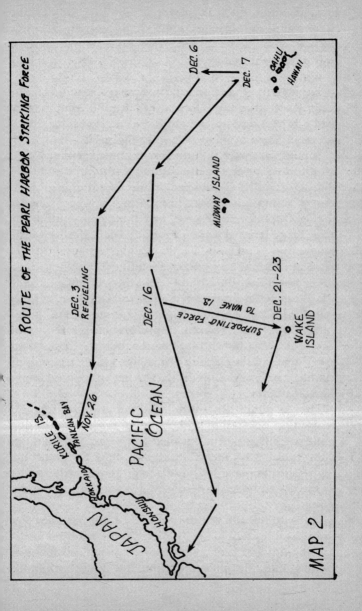

ROUTE OF THE PEARL HARBOR STRIKING FORCE

JAPAN

HOKKAIDO

HONSHU

KURILE IS.

TANKAN BAY

NOV. 26

PACIFIC OCEAN

DEC. 3
REFUELING

DEC. 16

SUPPORTING FORCE
TO WAKE IS.

DEC. 21~23

WAKE ISLAND

MIDWAY ISLAND

DEC. 6

DEC. 7

OAHU

HAWAII

MAP 2

in his face, in his career, and in his heritage; combined, these factors made him precisely the man he was and placed him in this particular situation at this moment in history.[4]

For his part, Nimitz was startled when Knox told him the news. Later that afternoon, he, Knox, and Admiral King had a brief interview with the President. After that Nimitz returned home to inform his wife, Catherine.

Nimitz was aware that he was assuming command at an inauspicious time. The battleship force was heavily damaged and Hawaii's air power was all but destroyed. All that remained there was the striking power of the fast carriers *Saratoga, Enterprise,* and *Lexington.* Fortunately, these ships had not been present at Pearl Harbor on the fateful day. In addition, Nimitz would be relieving Admiral Husband Kimmel, a personal friend.

On December 19, disguised as a Mr. Freeman, Nimitz left Washington by rail for California. On the long cross-country journey he studied reports, wrote letters, played cards, and simply relaxed in preparation for the ordeal ahead. Arriving in San Diego on the twenty-second, he was eager to board the Catalina flying boat for the trip to Pearl Harbor, but heavy winds delayed his departure until late on Christmas Eve.

The admiral's first view of Pearl Harbor was disheartening. Some ships lay bottom-up, others on their side, while still others sat sunk at their berth with only their topsides visible. Black fuel oil covered much of the anchorage. As he left the plane his nostrils were immediately assailed by the horrid stench of disaster which permeated the naval base.

En route to his new headquarters he was informed that the relief force sent to fortify Wake Island had been turned back by Admiral Pye, the interim commander. Nimitz said nothing about the aborted mission, but deep down he was disappointed.

Presently he was greeted by Pye who escorted him to his office. There he ate breakfast and was joined shortly afterward by Admiral Kimmel. Nimitz was shocked by the appearance of his old friend and felt a great deal of sympathy for the unfortunate officer. He told Kimmel that it could have happened to anyone.

Nimitz quickly plunged into his new task, ably assisted by Pye and whenever possible, Kimmel. He learned all he could about the new command. He inspected offices, communication facilities, and even the damaged ships and salvage operations. After the extensive inspection tour he reached two major conclusions.

First, as Commander in Chief, Pacific, he would not be allowed to go to sea. The responsibilities of the position were too far-flung and the contacts too numerous to allow him to leave the communications center at Pearl Harbor and move with the fleet as was traditional. Secondly, the damage at Pearl Harbor was not as bad as it might have been, thanks to the Japanese Commander, Admiral Nagumo's decision not to press for a third wave. Thankfully, the oil-tank farm with over four and a half million barrels of fuel remained intact. So, too, did the repair facilities and the submarine base. Then there was also the carrier force.

Nimitz's next step was the selection of a staff. Anticipating relief, most of Kimmel's former staff were preparing to leave. Nimitz surprised them all by stating that he had confidence in them and did not blame them for what had happened. He wished them to remain at their posts.

As Chief of Staff, Nimitz chose Admiral Draemel. For war plans officer, Capt. Charles H. McMorris; for intelligence officer he retained Kimmel's man, Lt. Com. Edwin Layton. If anyone had expected to be cashiered, it was Layton.

On the last day of 1941, Adm. Chester W. Nimitz

officially became CinCPac.

Admiral King's first orders to Nimitz were to guard the Hawaiian Islands along with Midway and to protect the lines of communication between Hawaii and the U.S., and Hawaii and Australia. King wanted immediate action, but left it to Nimitz to decide upon what action was appropriate. He did, however, recommend raids against Japanese-held islands in the central Pacific in hopes that these raids might divert Japanese drives on the Dutch East Indies and Singapore. Additionally, King hoped, such action would raise the morale of the depressed American forces.

Nimitz reviewed various plans submitted by his staff and examined them all thoroughly. Though personally favoring raids against enemy bases, he wanted his staff to discuss every plan so that he could listen to all their opinions and advice. Opinion was divided. The aggressive McMorris favored carrier raids, whereas Admiral Block, Commandant of the 14th Naval District at Pearl Harbor, opposed them for fear of losing the carriers which were America's last mobile line of defense.

The debate ended abruptly on January 7 when the fire-eating commander of the *Enterprise* force, Vice Admiral William Halsey, barged into Nimitz's office and forcefully backed the plan to raid the enemy. Halsey was appalled at the defeatism he found and soundly backed Nimitz, a fact the latter never forgot.

Three days later, Halsey was summoned to CinCPac headquarters. There Nimitz gave him the order to implement a plan calling for a two-carrier raid against the Japanese-held Marshall Islands. Halsey, aware of the burden thrust upon him, took up the order and the following day, steamed out of Pearl Harbor on board the *Enterprise* with an escort of three heavy cruisers, six destroyers, and one oiler. This left the Hawaiian Islands guarded by only the *Saratoga* and *Lexington*, but on the very day Halsey sailed, the *Saratoga*, patrolling four hundred and fifty miles southwest of Oahu, was holed by an enemy torpedo. The damage was extensive, necessitating at least three months of repair.

By January 20, Halsey's force arrived off Samoa where he waited for Admiral Fletcher to join up with the *Yorktown* force. Five days later the two forces were on their way to the Gilberts and Marshalls.

Through radio detection and reconnoitering submarines, Nimitz learned that the Marshalls were not as developed as originally anticipated and ordered Halsey to strike more than the assigned targets. He ordered the force to Kwajalein. Go for the heart, he said.

The raids commenced on January 31. Halsey's pilots reported extensive enemy damage including the destruction of two subs, one light cruiser, and one small carrier; four auxiliaries sunk, and many other types of ships destroyed. In fact, the pilots had exaggerated. Inexperienced in recognizing types of ships and assessing damage, they had greatly overestimated their achievements. They had actually destroyed one transport, sunk two smaller vessels, and damaged eight other ships while inflicting minor damage to shore installations. Fletcher's *Yorktown* force had achieved even less.

American newsmen at Pearl Harbor, eager to report good news, accepted the exaggerated claims and added to them. When overzealous editors in the states received the dispatches from their field reporters, even more was added with the result that some newspapers, in banner headlines, proclaimed, "Pearl Harbor avenged." Though fallacious, it did boost morale and help shore up sagging spirits.

Although the American press reported a resounding victory, in reality Halsey's raid hardly dented the Japanese steamroller which at that very time was making mincemeat out of General Wavell's ABDA command and General Percival's forces in Singapore. Its all-conquering forces continued to stretch their hold across New Guinea, the Bismarck Archipelago, and the Solomon Islands. Australia was being threatened with total isolation.

In response to that threat Admiral King and the Joint Chiefs rushed forces to garrison New Caledonia in the South Pacific, establishing a new defensive zone, the ANZAC, encompassing Australia, New Zealand, British New Guinea, New Caledonia, the Loyalties, New Hebrides, Fiji and Solomon Islands. King ordered Nimitz to send the *Lexington* force to the ANZAC zone along with whatever army and navy aircraft he could spare. It was essential that Nimitz keep Australia from becoming isolated.

King also ordered raids against enemy positions to be stepped up. Nimitz responded that because of the markedly inferior Pacific fleet, aggressive action could not be conducted except for hit-and-run operations. These operations, he told King, were not likely to relieve the pressure in the southwest Pacific. King was unhappy with Nimitz's wording and retorted:

Pacific Fleet not, repeat not, markedly inferior in all types of forces enemy can bring to bear within operating radius of Hawaii while he is committed to extensive operations in southwest Pacific. Your forces will, however, be markedly inferior from Australia to Alaska when the enemy has gained objectives in southwest Pacific unless every effort is continuously made to damage his ships and bases.[5]

The Commander in Chief was ordering action.

Nimitz and his staff reviewed various options and finally decided to send the *Enterprise* and *Yorktown* forces on a combined raid against Wake, Eniwetok, and Marcus islands.

On February 14, Halsey left for the central Pacific, raiding Wake ten days later and Marcus on March 4. Nimitz learned an important lesson during these early operations. During the first raid into the Marshalls, he had done a lot of coaching from the sidelines, a fact which Halsey apparently resented. Consequently, during the next raid the latter maintained complete radio silence. Nimitz got the point and from that time forward made it a practice not to interfere once a commander left on a mission with an approved plan.

Meanwhile, in February, General MacArthur was ordered out of the Philippines. He failed to leave until March. Then, after a daring escape, the general and his family made it safely to Australia. With MacArthur now in Australia, the Joint Chiefs divided the Pacific between him and Nimitz. MacArthur was made Supreme Commander, Allied Forces in the Southwest Pacific Area which included Australia, the Solomons, Bismarcks, New Guinea, and the Philippines. Nimitz was appointed Commander in Chief, Pacific Ocean Area. This made him commander of all land, sea, and air forces in that area. The Pacific Fleet, however, was to remain under the admiral even though it was required to enter MacArthur's area. Because Nimitz's command area was so vast, it was subdivided into three zones: north Pacific, central, and south. Since the South Pacific was deemed the most active area, it was decided that a commander be chosen who would be directly responsible to Nimitz while at the same time maintaining his headquarters in the South Pacific. To command this area Vice Admiral Robert Ghormley was chosen, an appointment Nimitz would later regret.

As previously mentioned, Nimitz had retained Kimmel's intelligence officer, Commander Layton. It was a wise decision. Under Layton was Lieutenant Commander Rochefort, a man of exceptional intelligence. Layton kept Nimitz completely informed of the location and movements of the Japanese naval forces. Thanks to that superior intelligence garnered from code-breaking, the inferior United States Fleet was able to counter and eventually stop the superior Japanese Fleet.

On April 9, 1942, Layton handed Nimitz word that the Japanese were planning an offensive against eastern New Guinea during the latter part of the month. Nimitz was disturbed since he had already dispatched Halsey on a secret mission. The latter was escorting the carrier *Hornet* carrying Lt. Col. James Doolittle's small band of flyers. Doolittle's pilots were to fly B-25 Army bombers from the carrier's deck on a bombing mission against the Japanese homeland. Partly to raise morale while also striking a blow against the perpetrators of Pearl Harbor, this Task Force sailed from Hawaii on April 8.

Utilizing information received from Rochefort and Layton, Nimitz and his staff concluded that if Japan desired to control eastern New Guinea, they would have to seize the Australian base at Port Moresby on the southeastern portion of Papua. This port sat on the Coral Sea. Additional intelligence reports pointed to a major Japanese move into the central Pacific either toward Midway or Hawaii itself. Nimitz placed his bet on Midway.

By the middle of the month additional radio intercepts convinced Nimitz that Port Moresby was the target. Intelligence reports indicated that the Japanese transports would enter the Coral Sea escorted by the light carrier *Shoho* and that two large carriers would be included in the strike force. Tulagi and Guadalcanal would also have to be taken. The Japanese had to be stopped.

Assembling his forces, Nimitz ordered Fletcher's *Yorktown* force, then operating in the Coral Sea, to retire to Tongatabu for replenishment and there join with the *Lexington* force under Rear Admiral Aubrey Fitch. The combined force would then return to the Coral Sea in an effort to halt the Japanese advance. Nimitz now had cause to regret sending Halsey on the Tokyo raid. The latter's aggressiveness would have been greatly appreciated in the Coral Sea.

On April 21, Nimitz flew to San Francisco to confer with

King. There they discussed the forthcoming Japanese move. Both admirals expressed apprehension that Fletcher had total control of the American force. King was particularly disturbed for he feared Fletcher's lack of aggressiveness. Both officers hoped that the Japanese would fall behind schedule thus allowing Halsey time to return from the Tokyo raid and bring his forces into the Coral Sea.

While Nimitz and King conferred, Halsey's force did indeed arrive in Hawaii, jubilant over the apparent success of their mission. The Task Force was looking forward to a well-deserved rest, but to their regret was ordered to refit immediately and make for the Coral Sea as soon as possible.

Nimitz returned on the twenty-eighth to Pearl where he conferred with Halsey and informed him that as soon as the situation stabilized in the Coral Sea, he must return to Pearl Harbor to meet the anticipated Japanese thrust in the central Pacific.

On May 3, the Japanese seized Tulagi and Guadalcanal. While those islands were being occupied Nimitz flew to Midway to inspect the defenses there. He was certain that this base was the next intended Japanese target.

The initial blow in the Battle of the Coral Sea was struck by the American force. On May 4, Fletcher dispatched carrier planes to bombard the Japanese positions on Tulagi. He then fired off an optimistic report to Nimitz. Unfortunately, what he had actually achieved was minute in comparison to what was reported. Nimitz later said. "The Tulagi operation was certainly disappointing in terms of ammunition expended to results obtained."[6]

What Fletcher did accomplish, however, was to alert the Japanese to the American presence. This caused them to send the large carriers *Zuikaku* and *Shokaku* searching for the American force.

Throughout the sixth the two fleets searched for each other. Then, on the seventh, the Japanese light carrier *Shoho* was located, attacked, and sunk by American carrier

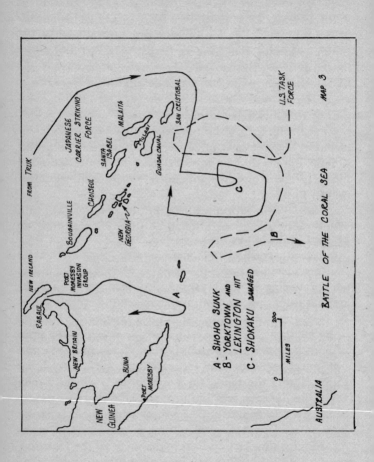

FROM TRUK

JAPANESE CARRIER STRIKING FORCE

NEW IRELAND

KABAUL

NEW BRITAIN

BUNA

PORT MORESBY

NEW GUINEA

BOUGAINVILLE

PORT MORESBY INVASION GROUP

CHOISEUL

NEW GEORGIA

SANTA ISABEL

MALAITA

TULAGI

GUADALCANAL

SAN CRISTOBAL

U.S. TASK FORCE

A

B

C

A - SHOHO SUNK
B - YORKTOWN AND LEXINGTON HIT
C - SHOKAKU DAMAGED

0   200
MILES

AUSTRALIA

BATTLE OF THE CORAL SEA   MAP 3

planes. Meanwhile, Japanese planes located what they thought was a carrier, but what was in fact the oil tanker *Neosho* and the destroyer *Sims*. The latter was quickly sunk and the *Neosho* was left burning. Though Nimitz was concerned over the loss of the tanker and destroyer, at the same time he was grateful that these two ships had unwittingly drawn off the strike aimed at the American carrier force. Nevertheless, by nightfall both sides were well aware of the proximity of each other and looked forward to the morning when each hoped for a decision in their favor.

In the early-morning mist, carriers from both fleets turned into the wind and launched scout planes. At 8:24 A.M. a Japanese scout sent the electrifying message, "Two American carriers 235 miles away." Almost simultaneously came reports from American scout planes who had located the Japanese fleet. Both sides scrambled to launch their attack.

The first Japanese wave concentrated on the *Yorktown* before turning their attention to the *Lexington*. The placid idyllic Coral Sea was turned into a churning inferno. Both American carriers were badly hit. However, even while Fletcher's force was undergoing its ordeal, American planes were pouncing on the Japanese carriers. *Shokaku* was hit, but her sister ship, *Zuikaku* managed to elude the attackers by hiding under a nearby rain squall.

By midday, the first naval battle during which the ships of both sides never came into contact with each other, was over and the planes were en route home to their burning ships. During the battle the Japanese had lost the *Shoho* while the *Shokaku* was burning so badly that her planes were forced to detour to the *Zuikaku*. Additional Japanese planes were lost because there simply wasn't enough room on the remaining flattop to accommodate all the returning planes. Consequently, many Japanese pilots were forced to ditch at sea.

Meanwhile, on board the American carriers, fires raged,

but damage-control parties felt that they had the situation under control. It seemed as if the Japanese had come off second best since the *Shoho* was gone and the *Shokaku* badly mauled. The returning Japanese aviators, however, reported that both American carriers had been sunk and jubilantly claimed a victory.

On the *Lexington* the fires that were originally thought to be under control reached vital sections of the ship, causing a series of severe explosions which ripped out the ship's innards and doomed her. *Yorktown*, also heavily damaged, was ordered back to Pearl Harbor where it was estimated that months of repair would be required.

Meanwhile, back at Pearl Harbor, while the Coral Sea debacle raged, Nimitz and his staff monitored the radio traffic hoping for information about the battle. Initially, there was a happy air of excitement in Hawaii, but as news of the *Lexington* disaster began to filter in, the jubilation was replaced by a quiet gloom. Nimitz was appalled. He did manage, however, to take some comfort from the fact that the Japanese had in fact suffered a strategic setback albeit a tactical victory. Unfortunately, the Japanese losses were not as severe as had been originally thought. Yes, the *Shokaku* was damaged, but not as severely as reports had indicated. Nevertheless, the main Japanese objective, the capture of Port Moresby, had been thwarted. Once the Japanese realized that American carriers were in the Coral Sea they recalled their transports to Rabaul. Thus, for the first time in the war a Japanese advance had been turned back. In addition, neither of the large Japanese carriers involved would be ready for the next operation.

While Fletcher was engaged in the Coral Sea, Halsey was making full steam toward his colleague's position hoping to merge the two forces. Though tempted to allow Halsey to proceed, Nimitz eventually decided against it because of the impending enemy threat in the central Pacific. Therefore, he ordered all carriers back to Pearl, but not until Halsey had trailed his coat for Japanese search planes based on Tulagi to see. Nimitz wanted to deceive the enemy into thinking he was reinforcing the South Pacific forces. Perhaps the Japanese might retain forces there to protect against just such an eventuality. If they did, then their next operation would be watered down to a degree. Nimitz was certain that this next operation would be directed against Midway.

Thanks to the efforts of his code breakers, Rochefort, too, was convinced that Midway was the Japanese target. His suspicions merely confirmed what Nimitz's instinct had already told him. The problem was how to convince others who had reached different conclusions.

MacArthur and King felt that the next Japanese move would be in the New Guinea-Solomon Islands area. No, Nimitz told Rochefort, concrete evidence was required— evidence that proved without a shadow of a doubt that Midway was on the Japanese agenda.

Rochefort's staff had been picking up repeated Japanese references to something called AF. The cryptologists were certain that AF was Midway. If the skeptics were to be silenced they would have to prove it beyond a shadow of a doubt. Accordingly, Rochefort suggested to Nimitz that he order Midway to send a radio message in the clear stating that its water distillation had broken down. Nimitz agreed to the ruse and ordered Midway to send the message. Two days later a Japanese intercept was decrypted stating that AF had a shortage of fresh water. At last, hard evidence.

Hard evidence notwithstanding, there were some individuals who remained unconvinced. There was always the possibility that the Japanese were practicing a deception game of their own. Despite the critics, however, Nimitz knew that he had to act with speed. Aware that he would be confronted by a superior force, he would nevertheless have to make do with whatever forces were available.

There was no margin for error. If the American forces

were scattered to cover all potential targets, there would be no single force left that was sufficiently strong to halt a Japanese attack. Nimitz would have to gamble on Midway.

At that time the backbone of the American forces was the three fleet carriers, *Enterprise, Yorktown,* and *Hornet.* But the *Yorktown* was in urgent need of at least three months' worth of repairs thanks to the damage incurred in the Coral Sea.

On the other side of the coin, the Japanese had a potential of ten carriers, twenty-three cruisers to Nimitz's eight, and the enemy battleships outnumbered the Americans by a score of eleven to six.

Meanwhile, the cryptographers also discovered that the Japanese planned to assault the Aleutians as well. Originally, Nimitz had not planned to defend these islands, but later had second thoughts since the Aleutians were U.S. territory. To allow the Japanese to conquer the islands by default would constitute a severe blow to American morale. Consequently, Nimitz formed a North Pacific force under Admiral Theobold to deal with the potential threat.

Rochefort and Layton continued to feed Nimitz every bit of intelligence gathered. From this information Nimitz was able to form an excellent picture of just what he was up against. The data was uncannily accurate. Thanks to it, Nimitz was able to develop a defensive plan. The brilliant code breakers even managed to pinpoint the actual dates of the Japanese attacks: June 3 for the Aleutians and June 4 for Midway.

In developing his strategy, Nimitz concentrated on what he considered were the key Japanese forces: Admiral Nagumo's four large carriers. Eliminate them and the Japanese plan would fall apart. So these ships became the focal point of the American plans.

On May 26, Halsey's task force returned to Pearl Harbor. When Nimitz met face-to-face with Halsey he was shocked at the latter's haggard and sickly appearance. In addition, the fire-breathing admiral was suffering from severe skin disorder. There was no question but what the nervous strain of the previous weeks was causing Halsey to suffer and that he obviously required immediate hospitalization. Unfortunately, this would make him unavailable for the forthcoming battle. After a brief argument, Halsey conceded he was too ill for command. He did, however, recommend that Rear Admiral Raymond Spruance be given his command. Nimitz concurred readily for he knew Spruance was a deep thinker who reacted coolly in combat. Nevertheless, the loss of Halsey continued to nag at Nimitz.

Spruance and Nimitz quickly set to the urgent tasks at hand. The former added some of his own theories to the plan that was already in place. Together, the two admirals forged the plan which would ultimately bring victory to the American forces.

On May 27, Fletcher's Task Force Seventeen arrived back at Pearl. Immediately the battered *Yorktown* was sent into drydock. Nimitz met with the dockyard workers and told the that the ninety-day estimate for repairs to the ship was unrealistic. He then proceeded to shock them with the pronouncement that he wanted the *Yorktown* ready for sea within three days. Work commenced around the clock and the impossible was achieved. The repair teams rose to the occasion magnificently and three days after the *Yorktown* was docked, the huge carrier was ready to raise steam. Nimitz's judgment had proved correct.

In the interim, Nimitz briefed the exhausted Fletcher on the plans for the Midway operation even though he was under pressure from King to relieve Fletcher due to the latter's apparent lack of aggressiveness. Nevertheless, Nimitz elected to make the decision on his own. Accordingly, he requested Fletcher to commit his conduct of operations at the Coral Sea to writing. Nimitz would then use that document to determine if indeed Fletcher was fit to remain in command.

The following day Fletcher submitted a superbly written report. After reading it, there was little doubt in Nimitz's mind that Fletcher simply was not suited to command an offensive operation. Nevertheless, with Halsey on the sidelines, this was no time to relieve his only other senior commander. Fletcher would have to remain on until the conclusion of the forthcoming battle at Midway.

During the planning sessions, the Americans emphasized that surprise would be their greatest weapon.

> The guiding principles were that the Americans, with inferior forces but presumably better information concerning the opposition, must get the jump on the enemy and must catch the enemy carriers in a vulnerable state.[7]

Accordingly, the American planners hoped that they could catch Nagumo's carriers while they were in the process of recovering the Midway attack force.

On the twenty-eighth, Spruance, in command of Task Force Sixteen, comprising the *Enterprise* and *Hornet* groups, steamed out of Pearl Harbor. Fletcher, temporarily reprieved, followed the next day with Task Force Seventeen centered around the miraculously repaired *Yorktown*. The two Task Forces were to rendezvous at a point approximately three hundred and fifty miles north of Midway, designated Point Luck.

Meanwhile, far to the west in the Coral Sea, an American cruiser began broadcasting on a frequency normally reserved for carrier air groups. It was hoped that this ruse would convince the Japanese that American carriers were still operating off the Solomons.

At the same time, in Japan, the Commander in Chief of the Combined Fleet, Admiral Yamamoto was taking steps that would keep him informed of the exact location of the American forces. He instituted plans for an aerial recon-

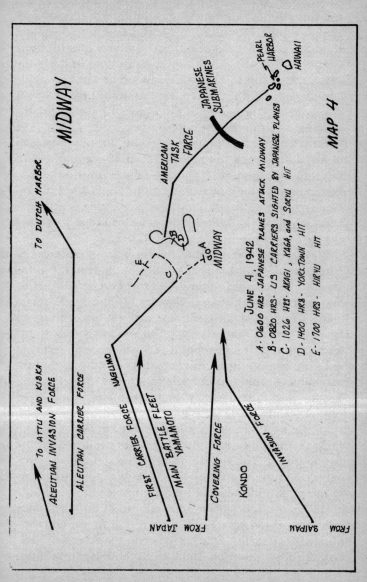

MAP 4

MIDWAY

TO DUTCH HARBOR

TO ATTU AND KISKA

ALEUTIAN INVASION FORCE

ALEUTIAN CARRIER FORCE

NAGUMO

FIRST CARRIER FORCE

MAIN BATTLE FLEET
YAMAMOTO

COVERING FORCE

KONDO
INVASION FORCE

FROM JAPAN

FROM SAIPAN

AMERICAN TASK FORCE

JAPANESE SUBMARINES

PEARL HARBOR

HAWAII

MIDWAY

JUNE 4, 1942
A - 0600 HRS - JAPANESE PLANES ATTACK MIDWAY
B - 0820 HRS - US CARRIERS SIGHTED BY JAPANESE PLANES
C - 1026 HRS - AKAGI, KAGA, and SORYU HIT
D - 1400 HRS - YORKTOWN HIT
E - 1700 HRS - HIRYU HIT

naissance of Pearl Harbor. Operation K, as this plan was known, called for a seaplane to refuel from a submarine at French Frigate Shoals, a small atoll between Midway and Hawaii. The plane would then continue on to Pearl Harbor and report if the American carriers had left the base or were still in harbor. Nimitz's code breakers made him aware of the plan, however, and the admiral dispatched a ship to French Frigate Shoals and forced the Japanese to scrub the entire operation.

Yamamoto had also ordered a picket line of submarines to patrol the seas between Midway and Hawaii. It would be their job to report the approach of the American Fleet. Fortunately for the Americans, Nimitz also learned of that plan and by the time the picket line was finally established, both American Task Forces had already sailed past their assigned position en route to Point Luck.

With all preparations final and the wheels in motion, all Nimitz could do now was sit idly by and wait for the Japanese to make their move. Control of events now passed to Spruance and Fletcher. However, Nimitz could retain tactical control of all land, sea, and air forces from his headquarters at Pearl Harbor. This was in contrast to the course adopted by his opponent, Yamamoto, who elected to sail with the fleet. Reduced to impotence by the necessity of maintaining radio silence while at sea, the great Japanese admiral was forced to rely on subordinates to make the crucial life-and-death decisions.

Precisely on schedule the Japanese forces bore down on Midway where they were promptly discovered by a Catalina patrol plane. To Nimitz's intense relief, Layton's intelligence had been correct. Two events bore grim testimony to the validity of the American intelligence.

On June 3, The Japanese Second Carrier Striking Force consisting of the light carriers *Ryujo* and *Junyo*, launched an air strike against Dutch Harbor in the Aleutians. T second event was the sighting of the Japanese for approaching Midway. Nimitz now knew that an air strike against Midway itself on the fourth was imminent.

At dawn on June 4, Nimitz and his staff were already at their stations. Around 6:00 A.M. an urgent message was received from Midway indicating that the location of the Japanese carriers was known. Meanwhile, Nagumo had already launched a strike toward the island. However, had he known that three American carriers were sitting on his flank he would have undoubtedly changed his strategy. Half an hour after the initial message from Midway, another was received stating that the base was being bombed. For the next two hours all was quiet at Nimitz's headquarters until 8:30 when word was received that only three fighters remained undamaged at Midway.

In the meantime, the diligent intelligence staff intercepted a message from one of the Japanese Fleet's scout planes stating that ten enemy surface ships had been sighted approximately two hundred forty miles from Midway. Layton immediately took the message to Nimitz who was quick to note that the intercept contained no mention of carriers. He therefore correctly concluded that Nagumo had no knowledge of the presence of the three American carriers. If the Japanese were contemplating a second strike against Midway, the time was ripe for an American strike.

Laboring under the impression that the American force did not contain a carrier, Nagumo did just what Nimitz hoped he would do. He ordered his planes armed for another attack against the installations on Midway. An attack by Army bombers based on the island merely served to convince the Japanese commander that his decision was correct.

While the Japanese planes were rearming, an additional message was received from one of the scout planes that had been delayed in its launch due to technical difficulties. This report contained the electrifying words that the American forces did indeed contain a carrier. Impossible, thought Nagumo. Nevertheless, he ordered the armaments changed to torpedos while the hastily unloaded bombs were carelessly stacked like cords of wood on the Japanese carriers. There was simply not enough time for the overworked deck crews to store them safely below.

Precisely at this critical time, with the American fleet finally discovered by the enemy, Pearl Harbor suffered an information blackout. Though outwardly remaining calm, inwardly Nimitz was deeply troubled. Small blurts of information did manage to come through, but nothing significant.

With Nimitz in the dark and Nagumo rearming his planes, the American planes hit the Japanese carriers. Though the first attack was successfully beaten off, more and more American planes arrived on the scene and swarmed over and around the astonished Japanese force. Within minutes raging fires were consuming three of Nagumo's proud carriers; the *Akagi, Kaga,* and *Soryu.*

Bit by bit Nimitz was able to fit the pieces of the battle together. Sadly, amid the jubilation, word was received that the *Yorktown* was on fire. Nimitz followed the heroic salvage efforts as fire teams fought valiantly to save the gallant ship. Then came word that the *Yorktown* had been hit again by the Japanese who had mistaken her for another of the American carriers. However, thanks to intrepid damage control, the *Yorktown* remained afloat. Nimitz ordered no effort spared to save the carrier and tow it back to Pearl. Shortly after the disheartening news about *Yorktown,* word came through that a fourth enemy carrier, the *Hiryu,* was on fire.

By evening Nimitz's face was beaming. Four Japanese carriers had been destroyed. Victory was assured. He took time to send a message to his victorious fleet.

You who participated in the Battle of Midway today

have written a glorious page in our history. I am proud to be associated with you. I estimate that another day of all-out effort on your part will complete the defeat of the enemy.[8]

At 4:00 A.M. on June 5 Spruance's position was well to the east of the Japanese. Some members of the CinCPac staff wondered aloud why Spruance was so far east if the Japanese were retreating westward. Why wasn't he in hot pursuit? Nimitz ignored their comments and refused to intervene, feeling that Spruance was the commander on the spot and knew just what he was doing. Nimitz trusted his subordinate's good sense. Nevertheless, many of the staff continued to grumble at what seemed to be a lost opportunity.

In fact, Spruance was being cagey. He had turned eastward rather than toward the Japanese Fleet because it appeared that the enemy was seeking a night action — an action in which Spruance knew the Japanese would have the edge.

In the interim Midway reported that it was being shelled. Actually, the bombardment was being conducted by one lone Japanese submarine, the *I-168*. However, steaming full speed ahead to relieve the submarine were four heavy cruisers under Admiral Kurita.

When Spruance was handed the report of Kurita's approach he ordered all American submarines in the area to converge on Midway. Shortly thereafter Kurita reversed course unaware that the submarine USS *Tambor* was lying in wait. When the sub's periscope was sighted two of the Japanese cruisers collided in their frantic efforts to avoid torpedo wakes. The bow of the *Mogami* was staved in and one of the *Mikuma*'s fuel tanks was so badly ruptured that it caused oil to leak out leaving an easy trail to follow.

Having reversed his course also, Spruance ordered an air strike against the retiring enemy cruisers. Within a few hours the *Mikuma* was battered to the bottom by the stalking American planes. The *Mogami*'s upper decks were obliterated, but she managed to make good her escape.

Spruance continued to pursue the retreating Japanese throughout the fifth. Yamamoto hoped for one last shot at revenge as his fleet moved closer to the protection of Japanese land-based planes on Wake Island. Cannily, Spruance refused to push his luck any further and called off the pursuit on the sixth.

Champagne corks popped during the subsequent victory celebration at CinCPac headquarters. Nimitz was visibly relieved that the battle was finally over and heartily endorsed Spruance's decision to abandon the pursuit. One bit of sad news did mar the celebration, though. While being towed to Pearl Harbor, the *Yorktown* was torpedoed by a Japanese submarine on June 6. The gallant veteran sank the next morning. She had served her country well. Lost with the carrier was the destroyer *Hammann*.

Accolades descended upon Nimitz from Allied headquarters around the world. The Japanese offensive drive had finally been halted. Midway was the turning point of the Pacific war. Even though they would win more victories in the future, after Midway never again would the Japanese win a campaign.

Nimitz was on hand to personally welcome Fletcher and Spruance upon their return to Hawaii on June 13. But Midway had not been a cheap victory. The *Yorktown* and *Hammann* were lost, three hundred seven men were killed, and one hundred forty-seven aircraft destroyed. This in addition to extensive damage to the installations at Midway and moderate damage to those at Dutch Harbor. Attu and Kiska in the Aleutians were lost when the Japanese invaded them on June 7.

As far as the Japanese were concerned, however, the Battle of Midway was catastrophic. Four carriers were sunk along with one heavy cruiser. Another heavy cruiser was wrecked, a battleship, an oiler, and three destroyers were damaged. Three hundred twenty-two aircraft would never fly again; nor would their experienced pilots. All told, the Japanese Navy had lost two thousand five hundred men. A phase of the Pacific war had passed. Nimitz was now ready to surge forward.

On the last day of June the admiral set off once more for San Francisco and an important meeting with Admiral King. The purpose of this conference was to discuss the possibility of an offensive in the South Pacific. King, however, was delayed in Washington, locked in a fierce debate with General Marshall over future Pacific strategy.

The debate centered around two divergent strategies, one proposed by King himself and the other by General MacArthur. The latter, whose headquarters was in Australia, proposed the immediate seizure of Rabaul. After a careful study of this plan, King concluded that MacArthur's proposal was much too ambitious. Furthermore, it would require the use of extensive naval forces and King was dead set against letting MacArthur command any naval forces.

As an alternative, King proposed an approach to Rabaul through the eastern Solomons with a naval officer under Nimitz, not MacArthur, in command.

On the day Nimitz left for San Francisco a compromise was finally reached which shifted the southwest Pacific boundary westward so that Guadalcanal and Tulagi in the Solomons now fell into Nimitz's sphere. King and Marshall laid down three tasks with Nimitz given the first one, the assault of Guadalcanal and Tulagi.

That issue settled, King set out for San Francisco and his meeting with Nimitz now scheduled for July 4. During the conference the two admirals reviewed the compromise reached five days earlier in Washington. High on the agenda also was the forthcoming campaign to capture Guadalcanal. The urgency of this operation was reinforced

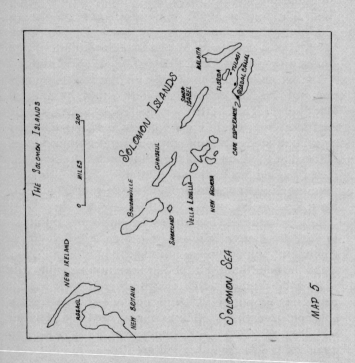

THE SOLOMON ISLANDS

SOLOMON ISLANDS

NEW IRELAND

RABAUL

NEW BRITAIN

BOUGAINVILLE

SHORTLAND

CHOISEUL

VELLA LAVELLA

NEW GEORGIA

SANTA ISABEL

MALAITA

FLORIDA

TULAGI

CAPE ESPERANCE

GUADALCANAL

SOLOMON SEA

MILES

0   200

MAP 5

the following day when Nimitz was given evidence that the Japanese were in the process of constructing an airfield on the island. Therefore, time now became a factor. The Americans had to seize Guadalcanal before the air base became operational. If they hesitated, Japanese aircraft would be one step closer to Australia. Armed with King's directives, Nimitz quickly returned to Hawaii.

Following the Battle of Midway, Spruance was appointed Chief of Staff to CinCPac. Most of the staff Nimitz had inherited from Kimmel were now transferred to other commands. This created vacancies on the staff which Nimitz filled with officers of his own choosing.

In many ways Spruance resembled his chief. He was easygoing and shared many of Nimitz's likes and dislikes. Accordingly, they formed an excellent team and as time progressed Nimitz increased his reliance on Spruance's talents and expertise. He was grateful for the fact that he now had someone whom he could use as a sounding board for his own ideas.

The immediate concern facing the reconstituted staff was the invasion of Guadalcanal and Tulagi. The choice to command the operation fell upon Adm. Robert L. Ghormley, Nimitz's South Pacific subordinate. The latter intended to give Ghormley as much assistance as possible short of direct interference. Accordingly he directed Fletcher to provide heavy air support with the carriers *Enterprise, Saratoga,* and *Wasp.* Rear Admiral Richmond Kelly Turner was brought in to command the amphibious force. Finally, Gen. Archer Vandergrift's first Marine Division was assigned to carry out the actual invasion.

Operation Watchtower, as the campaign was officially christened, was more commonly referred to as Operation Shoestring because of the relatively meager forces available to carry it out. It seemed that eighty-five percent of all war supplies were being funneled into the European theater, leaving very little left over for the Pacific.

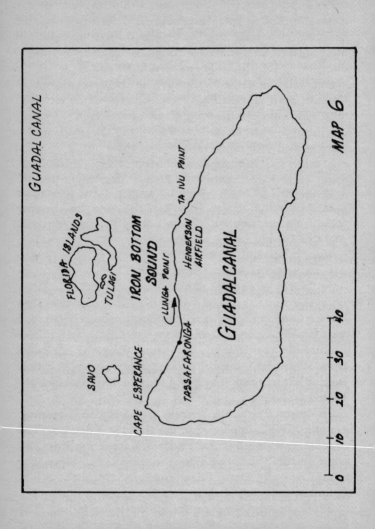

GUADAL CANAL

SAVO

CAPE ESPERANCE

FLORIDA ISLANDS

TULAGI

IRON BOTTOM SOUND

LUNGA POINT

TASSAFARONGA

HENDERSON AIRFIELD

TA IVU POINT

GUADALCANAL

0   10   20   30   40

MAP 6

The original schedule for Watchtower called for it to commence on August 1. However, this was postponed for a week to allow Ghormley additional time to scrape together more forces. But August 7 was firmly established as the latest possible date since the Americans were determined to prevent the Japanese from completing the airfield.

On the seventh, Nimitz waited anxiously at his headquarters for word from the invasion forces. Ironically, it was not American sources, but broken Japanese radio transmissions emanating from Tulagi that informed Nimitz that the invasion was on. Nimitz promptly informed King.

Lacking reports to the contrary, Nimitz had every right to assume that all was going well in the Solomons until he received word that a Japanese naval force was making for Guadalcanal. In the meantime, Fletcher, using the excuse that his carriers needed refueling, withdrew his covering force from the area leaving the vulnerable transports and marines devoid of air protection.

Since information from the battlefront was sketchy it was not until August 11 that Nimitz learned of the debacle at Savo Island. During that battle the Allies lost the heavy cruisers *Astoria*, *Quincy*, *Vincennes*, and the Australian cruiser *Canberra*. The cruiser *Chicago* and two destroyers were heavily damaged. Only the reluctance of the Japanese commander to follow up his victory saved the transports from destruction and the marines from being totally isolated without supplies. It was a first-rate disaster for the United States Navy.

Following the battle, Turner withdrew his transports crammed with supplies that had not been landed. The marines were forced to make do with what few supplies had come ashore. This action made the unhappy marines sitting ducks for an enemy counter-attack. Nimitz's earlier optimism was badly shaken.

The loss of the warships was a severe blow indeed. The campaign was already operating on a shoestring. Admiral

King demanded answers immediately, but as yet Nimitz had none to give. Ghormley himself was still in the dark regarding the entire picture so he was hardly able to give Nimitz any information.

On August 13, Turner arrived at Moumea and filled Ghormley in on the details. The latter in turn informed Nimitz who forwarded the gruesome details on to King. Fatigue, inexperience, and faulty deployment of forces were the culprits, Ghormley claimed.

Nimitz refused to accept Ghormley's appreciation of the disaster. He was puzzled as to how ships equipped with radar could be taken by surprise. No, Ghormley's reasons simply would not do. Nimitz still wanted answers.

In the meantime the long struggle for Guadalcanal continued. Fortunately the Japanese repeatedly underestimated American troop strength on the island and continued to dispatch reinforcements in a piecemeal fashion. American code breakers, however, discovered the presence of a Japanese carrier force at Truk, Japan's Pacific base approximately seven hundred miles north of Rabaul. Fletcher's carriers, unfortunately, were southeast of Guadalcanal protecting the line of communication.

The Japanese brought a portion of their carrier force south from Truk to protect their latest reinforcement effort. Fletcher was ordered to intercept the enemy force. The resulting carrier battle, known as the Battle of the Eastern Solomons, saw Fletcher attack Admiral Nagumo's force on August 24. During this engagement the light carrier *Ryujo* was lost.

Then Nagumo retaliated with aircraft from the Pearl Harbor and Coral Sea veterans, *Shokaku* and *Zuikaku*. The Japanese planes managed to hit the *Enterprise,* knocking out her elevators and extensively damaging the ship's compartments, forcing the ship to break off the action and head for Pearl Harbor and repairs. The reduction of his force by one carrier rattled Fletcher.

THE NAVAL BATTLES
FOR
GUADALCANAL

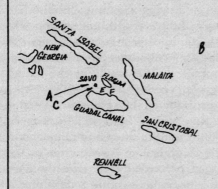

A- BATTLE OF SAVO ISLAND - AUG. 9 1942
B- BATTLE OF THE EASTERN SOLOMONS, AUG. 23-25
C- BATTLE OF CAPE ESPERANCE , OCT. 11-12, 1942
D- BATTLE OF THE SANTA CRUZ ISLANDS, OCT. 26
E- NAVAL BATTLE OF GUADALCANAL, NOV. 13-15,1942
F. BATTLE OF TASSAFARONGA, NOV. 30. 1942

```
0    40   80   120
```
MILES

MAP 7

Later in the month the *Saratoga* was hit by a torpedo which necessitated this ship's return to Pearl Harbor also. Fletcher himself was wounded during the action and was finally sent home, never to return, King had had enough.

The temporary loss of the *Enterprise* and *Saratoga* left only two operational carriers in the South Pacific: *Hornet* and *Wasp*. Nimitz sent a letter to King urging that during subsequent operations in the Solomons, Bismarcks, and New Guinea, carriers not be used to provide protection since they seemed too vulnerable to attacks from land-based aircraft. Instead, he requested that additional aircraft be dispatched to the South Pacific.

In September Nimitz found himself once more in San Francisco for yet another meeting with King. Present this time was Undersecretary of the Navy James Forrestal, who had just returned with Nimitz after a fact-finding tour of Pearl Harbor. In addition to Forrestal, Admiral Halsey, cured of his skin disorder and chomping at the bit for action, attended the conference.

The main topic of discussion on the agenda was the issue of personnel changes. King wanted Admiral Towers out of the Bureau of Aeronautics and transferred to command of the Air Forces, Pacific Fleet. Halsey was to return to the Pacific. The group then proceeded to analyze the Savo Island Battle. The result was criticism of the state of intelligence, alertness, and the night deployment maintained by the cruiser force. King also brought up the subject of Ghormley's ability to continue as Commander, South Pacific. Nimitz promised that he would check on the latter's physical condition and report back.

On the eleventh, Nimitz and Halsey returned to Hawaii. Meanwhile, on Guadalcanal, the situation continued in doubt as the Japanese obstinately poured reinforcements into the island. At sea a Japanese submarine torpedoed and sank the *Wasp,* leaving the *Hornet* as the only operational carrier left in the theater. Despite all, Nimitz remained convinced that Guadalcanal could be held.

Gen. Henry "Hap" Arnold, Commander of the Army Air Forces and a member of the Joint Chiefs of Staff along with General Emmons, Army Commander at Pearl Harbor, went to the South Pacific on a fact-finding mission. They found Ghormley to be pessimistic and some of the pessimism seemed to rub off on Emmons. After hearing Arnold's comments Nimitz decided that it was high time he reviewed the situation in person. On September 25, he went to Ghormley's headquarters at Noumea, New Caledonia. One glance at the haggard appearance of Ghormley was all that was needed to convince Nimitz that fatigue and anxiety had overcome his unfortunate subordinate.

A conference was held aboard Ghormley's flagship. Present in addition to Nimitz, Ghormley, and Arnold, were Admiral Turner and Major General Harmon, South Pacific Army Commander. MacArthur's command was represented by Maj. Gen. Richard Sutherland and Lt. Gen. George Kenny. Nimitz opened by expressing his desire to be made aware of any problems. Ghormley described the current situation and reviewed his future plans. Then Sutherland presented MacArthur's proposals.

Then it was Turner's turn before the floor was taken by Arnold who discussed global strategy and the demands of the same. He compared the South Pacific to other theaters and attempted to convince the assembly that it was not as important as some of the other areas, such as North Africa.

During the question-and-answer session, Nimitz raised some pointed questions. Why weren't army troops being sent to reinforce the marines on Guadalcanal? Could New Zealand troops be used there? What was the navy doing to stop the nightly run of the Tokyo Express?*

After presenting some decorations he once more paused to take stock of Ghormley's mental and physical condition.

*Japanese reinforcement effort of Guadalcanal.

Then he prepared to visit Guadalcanal.

During a heavy rainstorm the admiral's plane landed on the jungle-clad island. There he and his party were met by General Vandergrift despite the horrid weather. Nimitz requested to inspect all facilities: flight headquarters, hospitals, even Bloody Ridge and other points in the defensive perimeter.

In the intense heat and stifling air Nimitz absorbed the sights and sounds of the jungle where wild orchids flourished, cockatoos screeched, insects thrived, and men struggled to exist. The ninety menacing miles of this island teeming with malaria, rot, and corruption held the entire fate of the Pacific war.

After his visit with Ghormley, Nimitz was pleased and surprised by Vandergrift's optimism. The marine general spoke bluntly and pulled no punches. He said he needed more men to hold the perimeter and additional fighter planes to beat off the incessant enemy air attacks. The key to the campaign was to hold the airfield, now named Henderson Field. To do that Vandergrift urgently needed reinforcements. Nimitz was noncommittal, but privately agreed with Vandergrift's strategy and needs.

After a contemplative and precarious flight back to Noumea, Nimitz resumed talks with Ghormley. Foremost on the list of topics were the problems of reinforcing Guadalcanal and what methods to use to derail the Tokyo Express. The outcome of the conference was the decision to dispatch the Americal Division, then based on New Caledonia, to Vandergrift's aid.

Twelve days after his return to Pearl Harbor, Nimitz's directive to halt the Tokyo Express began to bear fruit. Though the Americans did not sink any Japanese transports during the night time Battle of Cape Esperance on October 11-12, they did manage to sink a cruiser and destroyer for the loss of one destroyer of their own. The Japanese ships had been ambushed during an attempt to bombard Henderson Field. Unfortunately, the American commander, Adm. Norman Scott, erroneously reported sinking a large number of enemy ships. Though the claims were exaggerated, they did prove a boost to American morale, albeit temporarily.

The first segments of the Americal Division began arriving on Guadalcanal on October 13. Despite their attempts to stop the Tokyo Express though, within a few days of the Battle of Cape Esperance, Japanese vessels were once more landing men and supplies after their nightly runs down the Slot with relative impunity. Events began to reach the critical point. The concerted effort of the Japanese to reinforce their garrison indicated a major counteroffensive, and soon.

On October 15, Nimitz summoned his staff together for an extraordinary meeting. The main topic of discussion was the forthcoming American effort on Guadalcanal and Ghormley's ability to deal with the Japanese threat. Was he tough enough to meet the enemy challenge? Did he have the ability to inspire his subordinates? Most of those present responded negatively. Pointing to each one in turn Nimitz then asked whether Ghormley should be relieved. Each response was affirmative. There could be no question in Nimitz's mind now. Ghormley had to go.

That presented another problem. Who could take Ghormley's place? Turner? No. Though a brilliant leader, Turner's character and his recent dispute with Vandergrift precluded his being selected. Someone senior was needed. Halsey perhaps?

Nimitz decided to delay making a decision until he had had an opportunity to study the issue further. He only needed one day to make up his mind. The day after the staff conference he sought permission from King to relieve Ghormley with Halsey.

King wasted little time in signaling his concurrence. Nimitz immediately drew up the necessary orders. Then he wrote a dispatch to Ghormley in which he attempted to announce Halsey's appointment as diplomatically as possible. Justifying his action to his wife, Nimitz wrote:

> Ghormley was too immersed in detail and not sufficiently bold and aggressive at the right time.[9]

Word of Halsey's appointment spread like wildfire through the South Pacific and was greeted with jubilant enthusiasm. He responded by vigorously attacking the problems confronting him immediately.

Meanwhile, when Ghormley arrived at Pearl Harbor en route back to the United States, he insisted on knowing the reason why he had been relieved. Always the master diplomat, Nimitz responded:

> "Bob," he said, "I had to pick from the whole Navy the man best fitted to handle that situation. Were you that man?"
> "No," replied Ghormley. "If you put it that way I guess I wasn't."[10]

The next few months were difficult ones. The waters around Guadalcanal raged with major battles: the Battle of Santa Cruz on October 26, the Naval Battles of Guadalcanal from November 12 through 15, and the Battle of Tassafaronga on November 30. On land the marines and GIs fought grimly against a determined and fanatical foe. At Santa Cruz the veteran *Hornet* was lost and *Enterprise* damaged once more. But so, too, were many skilled Japanese pilots killed.

As November arrived the Japanese began making preparations to accomplish what they had previously failed to achieve in October. Radio intercepts pointed to the middle of the month as the time for the next major Japanese push. Nimitz promptly notified Halsey.

Combining this welcome information with intelligence gathered from coastwatchers and aerial reconnaissance, Halsey prepared to meet the onslaught.

At the conclusion to the three-day Naval Battle of Guadalcanal, Nimitz, after digesting all the reports, expressed an opinion that the critical phase of the campaign was past. Perhaps, but on November 30 the Japanese proved him wrong by striking a mighty blow at the American naval forces. Unquestionably much hard fighting remained ahead.

The second week in December found Nimitz back in San Francisco for yet another meeting with King. The latter wished to accelerate the war in the South Pacific and suggested that this might best be accomplished via bypassing the rest of the Solomons and the Bismarcks. Nimitz objected, stating that the advance had to be step by step in order to insure adequate land-based fighter protection. The next move, he said, should be to New Georgia where the Japanese were in the process of building an airfield at Munda Point, a mere one hundred eighty miles from Guadalcanal.

King relented and agreed to Nimitz's proposal. He promised to make every effort to supply the ships, men, and materiel necessary for a successful prosecution of the advance. He also told Nimitz that he would soon be traveling to Casablanca, Morocco, for a major meeting with the Combined Chiefs of Staff. When he got there, he stated, he would forcefully argue for the doubling of the supply allotment for the Pacific theater.

Before parting, King and Nimitz discussed the situation in the Aleutians. It was decided to send a new commander to that area as well. Adm. Thomas Kinkaid replaced Admiral Theobold. They also discussed future Pacific plans and the possibility of reviving the old "Orange Plan" envisioning a drive along the central Pacific islands to the Philippines and China coast. The possibility of Halsey having to operate in MacArthur's area was also reviewed.

Both admirals were adamant in their opposition to having MacArthur command major naval forces. Therefore a compromise was settled on. Strategically Halsey would be subject to MacArthur's directives, but tactically he was on his own. All issues resolved to their satisfaction, the two admirals parted; Nimitz for the return trip to Hawaii, and King for North Africa.

In January Nimitz decided that another tour of the South Pacific was called for. This time he was accompanied by Secretary of the Navy Frank Knox. On the fourteenth of January the party took off for Midway. Engine problems caused the plane to return almost immediately, but a short time afterward they were airborne again. After stopovers at Midway and Espiritu Santo the entourage moved on to Guadalcanal on the twenty-first. Following a brief visit, Nimitz and his party left for Noumea.

En route to Noumea Nimitz had time to reflect on the contrast between his earlier visit to Guadalcanal and the recently concluded one. The entire atmosphere had improved. Upon arrival at Noumea, Nimitz and Knox joined Halsey at the latter's headquarters for a review of the entire South Pacific picture.

Since the Americans had secured the upper hand on Guadalcanal the discussion at Halsey's headquarters centered around the next objective. Nimitz asked when Halsey would be ready to move against Munda. Halsey's staff reported that April 1 was a reasonable date if the amphibious troops were ready. Despite further discussions nothing definite was decided at Noumea.

Shortly after his return to Hawaii on January 28, Nimitz came down with malaria and he was laid up for a few weeks. The one bright note during his illness was the news that the Japanese had evacuated Guadalcanal. The bitter six-month struggle was over.

Once Guadalcanal was secured a period of relative

inactivity settled over the South Pacific, the exception being aerial attacks against Japanese-held positions. At Pearl Harbor, however, there was no lull. Planning for future operations continued full tilt.

After regaining his strength Nimitz made another of his frequent visits to San Francisco for a meeting with King. The Commander in Chief recommended an attack against the Gilberts in order to forestall any possibility of a Japanese advance from those islands in the direction of the Ellice Islands and Samoa. Nimitz, however, urged patience until enough forces had been built up to adequately launch a massive drive with a reasonable chance of success. On the bright side King reported that the new *Essex*-class carriers would soon be available. They would be just the weapon needed to sustain a strong drive across the central Pacific.

A month later the Joint Chiefs invited Nimitz, Halsey, and MacArthur to send representatives to Washington for a conference on the Pacific. The main topics of discussion were the division of American forces between Europe and the Pacific, moves against Rabaul and the Aleutians, and the possibility of opening a central Pacific drive. The feasibility of bypassing Rabaul completely was also reviewed.

Spruance had been entrusted by Nimitz with securing approval from the Joint Chiefs for an operation aimed at recapturing Kiska and Attu in the Aleutians. When the proposal was made King seized the opportunity to put forth a recommendation that a central Pacific offensive be considered also. In the end the Joint Chiefs approved the Aleutians plan, but delayed a decision on the central Pacific proposal until such time as they could discuss the matter with their British counterparts. Nevertheless, when Spruance returned to Pearl Harbor he and Nimitz began planning a central Pacific offensive.

With the increase of the size of the fleet the problem of a suitable commander was taken into consideration.

Command of what would be designated the Fifth Fleet would naturally be one of the most prestigious commands of the entire war and there would be bitter competition for the position. Nimitz, however, wasted little time in proposing his trusted Chief of Staff, Spruance.

On April 14, 1943, intelligence sources handed Nimitz a decoded Japanese transmission detailing the itinerary for Admiral Yamamoto who was making a tour of the front and would visit bases in the Bougainville area on the eighteenth. Although he was not overjoyed at setting out to kill one individual Nimitz forwarded the information to Halsey with instructions to prepare an ambush. The subsequent operation was a complete success. Over Bougainville, Yamamoto's plane was intercepted by a flight of American P-38 fighters and shot down. The architect of the Pearl Harbor attack was dead.

Nearly a month later, on May 11, following two postponements, the U.S. Seventh Division slammed ashore at Attu. In less than three weeks the division secured the island on May 29. A final Japanese suicide attack merely insured the elimination of the last defenders.

On June 1, Nimitz was again on the west coast awaiting the arrival of King. The latter came directly from a Combined Chiefs of Staff conference (Trident) in Washington and was interested in hearing the post-mortem on the battle for Attu. He then reviewed the summaries of the Trident conference. The Commander in Chief was happy to report that after a long debate with the British a compromise had finally been reached. The Allies were persuaded to accept the concept of a two-pronged approach toward Japan, one through the southwest Pacific by MacArthur and another across the central Pacific by Nimitz. With the authorization for creation of a Central Pacific Force, King accepted the nominations of Spruance for Fifth Fleet commander and Turner for the command of the amphibious forces.

One week later Nimitz was back in Pearl Harbor where, to his joy, was the first of the new twenty-seven thousand-ton *Essex*-class carriers, the ship that would spearhead the central Pacific offensive.

Returning to Hawaii with Nimitz was Marine Maj. Gen. Holland M. Smith. Spruance had requested Smith as amphibious corps commander. Nimitz was not as eager as Spruance to have Smith as part of the team, but nevertheless he welcomed the opportunity to get to know the general better.

Smith managed to make a favorable impression. After he and Nimitz traveled to the South Pacific for a discussion with Halsey about the invasion plans for New Georgia, on the return trip Nimitz informed Smith that he was being given command of all the marines in the central Pacific.

When Nimitz returned from his visit to Halsey he was greeted with formal orders from the Joint Chiefs directing him to plan for an invasion of the Marshall Islands on or about November 15. On hearing of the directive, MacArthur immediately protested, fearing a diminution of his forces in deference to the central Pacific. The general questioned the logic of attacking strongly fortified islands. As an alternative he proposed bypassing strong points claiming that it was more economical and would save lives.

Despite MacArthur's protest, however, the central Pacific drive became a reality. The question facing Nimitz was which islands to assault. His staff proposed five simultaneous landings on Kwajalein, Maloelap, Wotje, Mili, and Jaluit atolls. Spruance objected to this plan stating that attacking five heavily defended points at the same time would be impractical because there simply were not enough troops to go around. Furthermore, he said, the fleet could not support all five landings at the same time. To split the fleet would be to invite its piecemeal destruction at the hands of the enemy. In addition, Spruance insisted that land-based air protection was a prerequisite. But this

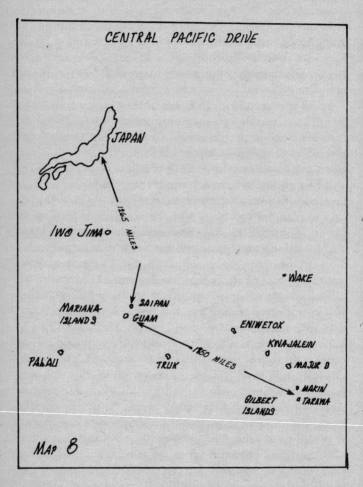

CENTRAL PACIFIC DRIVE

JAPAN

1265 MILES

IWO JIMA

WAKE

MARIANA ISLANDS

SAIPAN

GUAM

ENIWETOK

KWAJALEIN

PALAU

TRUK

1850 MILES

MAJUR D

MAKIN

TARAWA

GILBERT ISLANDS

MAP 8

requirement meant eliminating the Marshalls completely.

Various other proposals were submitted, but the planners kept returning to the seizure of the Gilberts first. From there, land-based air forces could support the Marshalls' invasion.

Early in July Nimitz accepted the proposal to invade the Gilberts first with tiny Betio in Tarawa atoll the primary target.

Late summer saw the American forces on the move. Halsey jumped from New Georgia to Vella Lavella on August 15. The north Pacific forces assaulted Kiska in the Aleutians only to find that the Japanese had evacuated it.

On August 5, the Central Pacific Force, the Fifth Fleet, was formally established with Spruance as its commander. The commander of the Fast Carrier Force was Rear Admiral Charles Pownall and the Fifth Amphibious Force was given to Admiral Turner. The amphibious troops, designated the V Amphibious Corps, had for their commander Gen. Holland Smith. Command of the land-based air forces with responsibility for pre-invasion photoreconnaissance and raids against the target was given to Rear Admiral John Hoover.

Critics immediately cried out against the command setup. The aviators felt they were not fully represented. Spruance himself had no previous aviation experience and only two members of his staff had earned their wings. The army protested loudly that no army general was assigned any position of responsibility even though its Twenty-seventh Division was one of the primary attack forces. The chief army commander at Pearl Harbor, Lt. Gen. Robert Richardson was upset that a naval officer was commanding U.S. Army Air Forces and a marine general was commanding army ground units. As a sop Nimitz appointed an army officer to command a task group of air units under Hoover.

While Spruance was engrossed in preparations for the

launching of Operation Galvanic, the invasion of the Gilberts, Nimitz maneuvered behind the scenes smoothing the ruffled feathers of the army and navy aviators. Service rivalry gave him one long headache, one that never would subside. Questions of command and interservice rivalry became a time bomb ready to explode at any time.

During the planning stage for Galvanic, Smith and Turner approached Spruance with a proposal relative to exchanging one of the targeted islands for another. The original island, Nauru, they said, should be substituted with Makin. The latter was nearer to Tarawa and easier for the fleet to support. Nimitz agreed with Turner and Smith and gave his assurances that he would take the issue up with King at their next meeting, scheduled for Pearl Harbor during the last week in September.

As the date for Galvanic approached, raids against the targets were stepped up by air forces operating from Canton and Funafute islands. On the fifth and sixth of October a six-carrier force attacked Wake. Nimitz and his staff were impressed with the power demonstrated by the carrier raids and their ability to destroy enemy bases. The aviators on Nimitz's staff urged that the carriers be unshackled and free to cruise about to hit the Japanese air bases and carrier forces at will. Spruance and Turner, both nonaviators, held a contrary view feeling that the American carriers had to remain at the beaches to protect the landing and the transports.

After a twenty-four-hour postponement, Galvanic slammed ashore on November 20, 1943. Nimitz kept abreast of the assault by monitoring radio transmissions. Quickly he realized that Tarawa was proving more difficult than anticipated. The landing on Betio proved more difficult than expected because prior intelligence regarding the tides and reefs around the atoll was erroneous. This caused the landing barges full of marines to become hung up on the reefs. The unfortunate marines were forced to wade ashore under the deadly raking fire of Japanese machine guns. Early in the afternoon Nimitz was shocked by a message from Admiral Hill stating, "Issue in Doubt."

The battle raged for four days, but on the afternoon of the twenty-third, Spruance reported that enemy resistance had ended on Makin and Tarawa. The campaign had been longer than expected and the butcher's bill was excessive.

The naval aviators were also upset over the length of the battle. Towers complained that Spruance kept the carrier groups too close to the beachhead enabling the Japanese to locate them easily. The carriers, he stated, should not be confined to supporting the troops ashore. Instead, Towers went on, they should be free to roam widely, hitting ships, planes, and bases that might threaten the overall success of the entire operation. Damage to the light carrier *Independence* by Japanese air attack and the torpedoing of the carrier *Liscombe Bay* by an enemy submarine were cited as proof positive that amphibious assaults had to be swift so the carriers could be set free to roam. Being tied to a beachhead invited retaliation.

For his part, Nimitz was markedly upset over the high amount of casualties at Tarawa. He decided to visit the atoll himself to view firsthand the strong defenses constructed by the Japanese. Before leaving he took pains to memorize the names of the principal officers he would meet for the first time, wishing to establish an immediate rapport.

From the air Betio resembled a scene from Dante's description of hell. The seared and blasted landscape was one large scar on the beautiful blue Pacific. As Nimitz descended from his plane the pungent odor of burned and rotting flesh assailed his nostrils. He could still see pieces of bodies lying where they had fallen during the four days of murderous fighting. Nimitz met with Spruance and Gen. Julian Smith, Commander of the second Marine Division. The horror witnessed on his visit left a permanent mark on him.

Back at Pearl Harbor Nimitz met a furious Holland Smith, ranting over the ordeal of Tarawa and the poor performance of the army's Twenty-seventh Division at Makin. This division had taken three days to mop up the islet which contained only twenty-five percent of the strength of Betio. Smith felt the Twenty-seventh had performed poorly under fire. In fact, he bluntly stated, they were totally inept. Now that he was warmed up the marine general went on to state that the whole operation was useless. The Gilberts should have been bypassed completely. After the war the volatile Smith authored a book, *Coral and Brass,* in which he vented his anger, giving reasons why the Gilberts should have been left alone. Whether they should have been bypassed or not was an academic question as far as Nimitz was concerned. The big question now was what lessons could be learned from the operation and how these lessons could be applied to the forthcoming Marshalls campaign.

Turner forwarded his recommendations to Nimitz who readily absorbed them. Such suggestions as increased photoreconnaissance, additional landing barges including Amtracs, more bombardment vessels, more ammunition, and a longer aerial bombing period prior to the assault were accepted and incorporated into plans for future operations.

Meanwhile, when word of the excessive casualties during the recently concluded campaign hit the newspapers in America, Nimitz came in for a great deal of criticism. He was flooded with letters, some of them blaming him personally for the death of loved ones. He was deeply hurt and attempted to answer the accusations by saying that the Gilberts had not cost as many lives as had Guadalcanal, yet the advantages accrued in their capture were equal. Furthermore, he reasoned, the lessons learned during the battle would be invaluable for future campaigns. Nevertheless, critics outside of and from within the service persisted.

Army general Richardson blamed the high losses on the marine command pointing to their inexperience in directing such large operations.

Despite the controversy, plans for the Marshalls campaign, Operation Flintlock, continued unabated. After a great deal of consideration the target finally settled on was the island of Kwajalein, thanks to its twin airfields and fine anchorage. Kwajalein would prove, the planners argued, invaluable to the capture or neutralization of the rest of the islands in the Marshalls chain.

Spruance, however, was not convinced that Kwajalein was the most suitable target. Instead he believed that Wotje and Maloelap astride the Kwajalein to Pearl Harbor line of supply offered reasons for being considered. Turner and Smith supported Spruance, but Nimitz stuck to his guns. Radio intelligence had corroborative evidence that the Japanese were strengthening the outer islands at the expense of Kwajalein. The Japanese, Nimitz argued, were expecting the Americans to attack the outer islands and were making dispositions accordingly.

At a meeting on December 14, Nimitz polled his fleet commanders as to which island should be assaulted, the outer islands of Wotje and Maloelap or Kwajalein. Spruance, Turner, and Smith emphatically said the outer islands. They were supported by virtually every member of the CinCPac staff. After polling everyone, Nimitz said quietly. "Well gentlemen, our next objective will be Kwajalein."[11]

Although arguments continued for the next few weeks, Nimitz remained unmoved.

Two days after New Year's, Nimitz and Halsey, who had flown in from the South Pacific, were in San Francisco for another of their many wartime conferences with Admiral King. One of the points on the agenda was the problem of command of the carrier force which was vastly increased in size. Admiral Pownall had come under criticism for being too cautious. Adm. Marc Mitscher was nominated to replace Pownall. King endorsed the change.

Another problem was the aviator-nonaviator conflict. To placate the former, Admiral Towers, an aviator, was named deputy CinCPac. King and Nimitz also adopted the principle that all major commanders in the Pacific who were nonaviators had to appoint aviators as Chief of Staff or second in command and vice versa. This meant that many commanders—such as Spruance who lost nonaviator Carl Moore—lost close friends as Chiefs of Staff.

Finally the admirals discussed future operations. It was then that King forcefully emphasized the importance of the Marianas.

Meanwhile, the plans for the assault on the Marshalls were taking their final shape. D-Day was set for January 31, 1944. Nimitz waited in anxious anticipation as the Fifth Fleet moved its way toward the Marshalls. Had they absorbed the lessons of Tarawa? Would the Marshalls be easier?

When the first reports of the assault began filtering in, Nimitz was gratified. The lessons from the previous campaign had indeed been learned. By the fourth of February Kwajalein was in the hands of the U.S. Army's Seventh Division while the marines had secured Roi-Namur in one day. The fact that the army took longer to secure their target did not reflect on their aggressiveness, but rather a difference in tactics. The Seventh Division was well-led and had been battle-tested the previous year at Attu.

Operation Flintlock was a model operation. Clearly the Gilberts had served as a training ground making for a successful assault on the Marshalls. Intelligence was improved, the pre-invasion bombardment was more precise, and the fleet operated like a well-oiled machine.

Even as the battle was in full sway Nimitz left his headquarters for the front. His first stop was Tarawa. Upon landing he was mildly surprised with the contrast from his previous visit. The Seabees had constructed a superb airstrip and air base which served the Marshalls campaign well.

Two days later Nimitz was at Kwajalein. He had nothing but praise for the commanders of the attack and was particularly pleased with the way Mitscher had handled Task Force 58, the carrier force. He talked with his commanders about the next objective in the Marshalls chain, Eniwetok. Also Task Force 58 was given the task of neutralizing the great Japanese naval base at Truk.

For two days between February 16 and 18, Truk was subjected to an intense bombardment resulting in the loss of fifteen Japanese vessels, including two light cruisers, four destroyers, and about two hundred aircraft. After Truk the carrier force hit the Marianas, causing some damage there, but more importantly, an outstanding group of photographs was taken of the Marianas. These would be put to good use for planning the future invasion of the islands.

Eniwetok was finally secured. On the whole the Marshalls campaign was a gratifying success as far as Nimitz was concerned.

By the end of 1943 it was already an established fact that a dual advance across the Pacific was the correct strategy. It had the blessings of the Combined Chiefs of Staff and the two political leaders, Roosevelt and Churchill. MacArthur was to advance from the southwest Pacific while Nimitz hopped across the islands of the central Pacific. The two would converge on the Luzon-Formosa-China triangle which, when accomplished, would effectively blockade Japan and place the Allied forces in an ideal position to invade the enemy's homeland if necessary.

King began maneuvering for the Marianas as the next objective. MacArthur, however, opposed that move, believing that any advance unsupported by land-based air would be costly in men and ships. Besides, MacArthur knew that an invasion of the Marianas would necessitate reallocating supplies that were needed in his own Southwest Pacific Theater. Furthermore, if successful, the Marianas campaign might render his own advance superfluous.

For those reasons MacArthur lobbied against the continuation of the central Pacific advance. He sent General Sutherland, his Chief of Staff, to Washington to argue the case. Tarawa and its heavy toll was his greatest evidence. Basically, what MacArthur desired was that once the Marshalls were secured, Nimitz's forces would be sent southwestward to support his own advance.

Fortunately, the Joint Chiefs rejected the proposal. MacArthur, however, was not yet finished and he continued to utilize all his wiles to derail the central Pacific advance. He wrote to Secretary of War Stimson in hopes that the secretary would use his influence on the President, but to no avail.

On January 27, a Pacific Theater conference was held at Pearl Harbor. Representing MacArthur and ready to argue his cause were the ubiquitous Sutherland, General Kenney, MacArthur's Air Force commander, and Admiral Kinkaid, his naval commander. Nimitz himself was leaning toward a single-thrust strategy by this time. He was harboring doubts about invading the Marianas, feeling that the operation would be costly since the target was beyond the range of land-based air support. His staff also felt the same way.

Admiral Towers recommended bypassing the Marianas completely while concentrating on the Admiralties, the Palaus, and the Philippines. He was concerned that an assault on the Marianas would be contested by Japanese air forces based on Iwo Jima. Nimitz compiled all the recommendations and forwarded them to King.

MacArthur was elated over the apparent unanimous acceptance of his ideas. He was confident that he would, of course, be named the overall Pacific commander. That was all well and good, but he forgot to consider one item. That item was Adm. Ernie King. The latter wanted the Marianas and had the backing of General Arnold, along with himself, a member of the Joint Chiefs of Staff. King responded to Nimitz and forcefully pushed for the Marianas. In a letter to Nimitz, King made no effort to mask his indignation at being betrayed.

When Nimitz received the stern letter from his Commander in Chief, he was already planning his next move, an advance on Truk, not the Marianas. King was furious and in a follow-up letter told Nimitz so. But in a more tactful manner this time.

Early in March the Joint Chiefs decided that it was high time to settle the issue of the Pacific commanders' command responsibilities once and for all. Nimitz and MacArthur were both invited to Washington. As usual the general sent his chief of staff, Sutherland in his stead. From this meeting came a clarification of strategy. Truk was to be bypassed, the Marianas were to be invaded, and MacArthur would invade Mindanao beginning on November 15. The decision to invade either Luzon or Formosa was left open.

When Nimitz returned to Hawaii from Washington he found a personal note from MacArthur inviting him to Brisbane, Australia, for a one-on-one conference. Nimitz was surprised. Here was MacArthur, who only a few months earlier wanted control of all Pacific operations, inviting his coequal commander for a high-level strategy meeting. The general obviously knew when he was licked.

On March 25, Nimitz and a few key members of his staff landed in Brisbane where MacArthur himself greeted the party. When the conference opened the next day they discussed Nimitz's pledge to support MacArthur's operation against Hollandia in New Guinea. The meeting proved profitable, but on the last day Nimitz managed to strike a sour note when he suggested the possibility of bypassing the Philippines.

MacArthur quickly pontificated on the impossibility of bypassing these islands. It was obvious that this issue was bound to create difficulties as the year progressed.

On March 29 the seasoned traveler returned to Pearl Harbor, but only temporarily. Ten days later he was in Majuro in the Marshalls to discuss the support his forces were to give to MacArthur's Hollandia operation scheduled for April 21. After a brief stay, Nimitz was back at Pearl Harbor ready to begin planning for the Marianas.

Two weeks later, on May 5, Nimitz was again in San Francisco for a meeting with King. The purpose was to discuss the forthcoming campaign. Another topic under discussion was the rotation of fleet commands. In effect, this meant that Spruance's Fifth Fleet would be placed under Halsey when an operation was pending in the latter's section. The fleet would then be designated the Third Fleet. During that period Spruance and his staff could plan their next operation. Then the Third Fleet would revert to Spruance's command and become the Fifth Fleet once more. Halsey made an analogy, likening the situation to that of a stagecoach system changing the driver but keeping the horses.

As planning for the Marianas campaign proceeded full tilt the problem of army troops being commanded by marines reared its ugly head once more. Since two army divisions were slated for use in the operation trouble was bound to occur.

Meanwhile, Nimitz's intelligence system intercepted and deciphered Japanese plans calling for an all-out naval counteroffensive should the Americans penetrate as far west as the Marianas-Carolines line. Originally called Operation Z, the Japanese plan was now code-named operation A-Go. It looked as if the long-awaited opportunity to confront the Japanese carrier fleet, which had remained inactive since late 1942, had arrived.

While the Fifth Fleet moved toward the Marianas und.

radio silence, Nimitz waited at headquarters. On June 15, marines began swarming ashore, initiating a bloody campaign.

When word of American landings on Saipan was received, the Japanese Fleet, anchored in the Philippines, began to move. U.S. submarines tracked its movement and reported the same to Spruance. The subsequent Battle of the Philippine Sea will be covered in detail in the chapter on Spruance. For the purpose of this chapter we are only concerned with its effects on Nimitz.

Nimitz knew that a major fleet engagement was imminent. He placed all his hopes and confidence in the Fifth Fleet's ability to deal the Japanese a decisive blow. The battle commenced on June 19 and Nimitz waited anxiously for information. By evening reports indicated that a large number of Japanese planes had been destroyed, but that the enemy carriers remained unscathed. Both joy and dismay were evident at Pearl Harbor. Apparently the Japanese Fleet was still intact albeit minus almost three hundred aircraft. Spruance kept his carriers tied to the beachhead just as he had at the Gilberts, possibly fearing that the Japanese might sideslip him and attack the beachhead. Because of that possibility, he would not allow the carriers to advance toward the Japanese Fleet.

Nimitz, however, refused to criticize Spruance without having all the information regarding the day's activity available, although everything did seem to point to over-cautiousness on the part of the Fifth Fleet commander.

On the evening of the nineteenth news reached Pearl Harbor that one Japanese carrier, the Pearl Harbor veteran *Shokaku,* had been hit by a torpedo fired by the submarine *Cavalla.* From Spruance came word that Task Force 58 was heading westward to attack the enemy fleet. All night and throughout most of the next day the American carriers proceeded westward without making contact. Finally, late in the afternoon of the twentieth, the enemy fleet was located.

Mitscher ordered the carriers to launch their planes. The resulting attack sank one Japanese carrier, two destroyers, two large oilers, and damaged two additional carriers. The American planes returned to their carriers in the dark, but large numbers of them ran out of gas and ditched in the water. To save the remaining planes Mitscher ordered the lights aboard the carriers switched on despite the threat of a Japanese aerial or submarine attack.

The next day the chase was abandoned and the Battle of the Philippine Sea was over. The remaining Japanese ships had eluded their pursuers. Immediately afterward came the anticipated criticism of Spruance's tactics. Should he have gone for the enemy fleet when it had first been spotted? Some said yes. These included Mitscher, Task Force 58's commander. King, however, defended Spruance's decision to protect the beachhead. This was his primary responsibility. Nimitz also sided with Spruance, but the aviators at Pearl Harbor once more decried the missed opportunity.

This is what comes of placing a nonaviator in command over aviators.[12]

Whatever the criticism it could not be denied that the Japanese air fleet had suffered terrible and irreplaceable losses. The elusive carriers were mere empty shells having been rendered offensively useless.

No sooner had the controversy over Spruance's actions abated than an entirely new problem was dumped into Nimitz's lap. Gen. Holland Smith relieved U.S. Army Gen. Ralph Smith, the commander of the Twenty-seventh Division. The fact that a marine general had relieved an army general caused the army brass, particularly General Richardson, to explode. Holland Smith had accused the Twenty-seventh Division of lack of aggressiveness. The division had been placed between the Second and Fourth Marine Divisions and its slower pace dangerously exposed the marines' flanks. Smith blamed their lack of aggressiveness on poor leadership and so, hoping to inspire the division, he changed leaders.

The ensuing fiery debate, fraught with charges and countercharges, fought in the service and the newspapers, did the service little good. Richardson went personally to Saipan where he confronted Holland Smith and stated point-blank that the marine general had discriminated against the army in favor of the marines. Richardson questioned Smith's ability and competence to lead army troops. He called the marines "a bunch of beach runners,"[13] who knew nothing about land warfare.

When Richardson returned to Pearl he forwarded a report to Nimitz complaining of Smith and Admiral Turner who had insulted Richardson by his unseemly disrespect. Nimitz chose to disregard the whole interservice dispute.

The Joint Chiefs finally eased the tension by transferring Ralph Smith to Europe while the navy gave Holland Smith a newly created position as Commander, Fleet Marine Force, Pacific. In that position Smith would no longer command army units. Thus the controversy died down until after the war when Smith published *Coral and Brass* and reopened the old wounds. One must wonder, however, why Smith had placed the Twenty-seventh Division in the center, on very difficult terrain, between two seasoned and battle-hardened marine divisions in the first place. Aware of the differences in tactics between the marines and army why did he not place them in a less critical area? It was as if he were inviting trouble.

Meanwhile, during the summer of 1944 the Joint Chiefs reevaluated strategy. Could the tempo be stepped up? Nimitz advocated advancing toward Japan by way of the Philippines, Formosa, and the Ryukus, before assaulting Japan itself. MacArthur also favored this plan and went one step farther by laying down a timetable as to when the various invasions should take place.

As in the past, King came up with an alternative. He called for an invasion of Formosa and the China coast while the southwest Pacific forces merely took Mindanao. From there they could keep the Japanese air forces pinned down on Luzon.

MacArthur of course, opposed any plan to bypass the Philippines. The issue was coming to a head when the President, who had already planned an inspection tour of the Pacific bases, suggested a conference with both MacArthur and Nimitz. The conference was scheduled for July in Oahu.

On the thirteenth of that month, two weeks before Roosevelt was due to arrive, King landed at Pearl Harbor to meet with Nimitz. The next day the two admirals left for Kwajalein and after a brief visit moved on to Saipan where they toured the recently conquered bastion of the Marianas.

At dinner aboard Spruance's flagship, the cruiser *Indianapolis*, future objectives were discussed. King asked Spruance what he thought. The Fifth Fleet commander immediately responded, Okinawa. King himself preferred that Luzon be bypassed stating that Formosa was strategically better situated for subsequent advance to both China and Japan.

By July 20, King and Nimitz were back in Hawaii where the debate continued. The Commander in Chief wanted Nimitz to back his plan. Two days later King left for Washington just as the President's cruiser was bearing down on Pearl Harbor.

On the twenty-sixth of the month the principals assembled. In typical bravado style, MacArthur was the last to arrive aboard the President's ship where the official greetings were held. After keeping Roosevelt and Nimitz waiting, the general made a grand entrance up the gangplank amid a loud ovation. Then he greeted the President.

Following two days of touring the base installations, the participants got down to the main order of business. After a delightful dinner in a beautiful mansion overlooking Waikiki Beach, Roosevelt pointed to a map of the Pacific and said to MacArthur, "Well Douglas, where do we go from here?"

MacArthur replied, "Mindanao, then Leyte and Luzon."

Nimitz then proceeded to argue his case which was not presented as professionally as MacArthur's.

The general then expounded on the political ramifications should the Philippines be bypassed. The Filipinos already felt betrayed. To overlook them now would constitute yet another betrayal and subject them to Japanese brutality. The reputation of the United States was at stake.

Roosevelt felt empathy for that line of reasoning, but was fearful that there would be a heavy toll of lives during any campaign on Luzon. MacArthur answered:

> Mr. President, my losses would not be heavy, any more than they have been in the past. The days of frontal attack should be over. Modern infantry weapons are too deadly, and frontal assault is only for mediocre commanders. Good commanders do not turn in heavy losses.[14]

Nimitz glared at the general. Roosevelt accepted MacArthur's appraisal. The Philippines would be next.

When Roosevelt left Hawaii, Nimitz, Halsey, and his staff began making preliminary plans for the conquest of the Palaus, Yap, and Ulithi, all deemed necessary for supporting the assault on the Philippines.

Halsey could see the value of taking Ulithi; it would provide an excellent anchorage. But as for Yap and the Palaus, he questioned the logic, feeling that they would be a waste of lives and time and should be bypassed. The waning strength of the Japanese in the Carolines following the Marianas campaign did not warrant a campaign in the Palaus, he said.

Meanwhile, in mid-August the Marianas campaign came to a successful conclusion with the recapture of Guam. The Japanese inner defensive ring had been penetrated.

Despite the July meeting with Roosevelt, King was unhappy with the shelving of the Formosa plan and did all he could to keep the concept alive. In September, Spruance returned to Pearl Harbor after having turned the Fifth Fleet over to Halsey. There Nimitz informed him that Formosa might yet be a target. Spruance reacted negatively to the suggestion. Instead, he suggested, Iwo Jima and Okinawa should be considered. Despite this, Formosa, Nimitz said, was still a viable target until King said otherwise.

Early in September Halsey conducted a series of carrier raids in the central Philippines and found them to be a hollow shell. Very little opposition from ground-based aircraft was met. In his own words the admiral said:

> I began to wonder whether I dared recommend that MacArthur shift to Leyte the invasion which he had planned for Mindanao, and advance the date well ahead of the scheduled November 15.[15]

After mulling it over in his brain, he radioed Nimitz in Hawaii recommending the cancellation of the preliminary assaults on Yap, Mindanao, and the Palaus.

Nimitz was unwilling to cancel the Palaus operation, feeling that the airfield on Peleliu and the anchorage at Kossol Passage would be needed for the Leyte operation. He did, however, forward Halsey's report to the Joint Chiefs who were meeting in Quebec at that moment. Nimitz even offered to give the forces designated for the invasion of Yap to MacArthur. General Marshall forwarded the new directive to MacArthur. It was received by Sutherland because at that time MacArthur was en route to Morotai and observing radio silence. Therefore, in his chief's name, Sutherland accepted the directive and forwarded the information to MacArthur.

The result was the movement of the Leyte invasion to October 20. On September 15, Peleliu in the Palaus was assaulted with heavy loss of life. It was unfortunate that this operation was not scrapped for the benefits obtained were not worth the toll of over ten thousand casualties.

However, from the perspective of early September, Peleliu's strategic location did seem to offer certain advantages. Unfortunately for the invaders, the ten thousand Japanese defenders had entrenched themselves in over five hundred caves dug into the hillsides of Peleliu. Each cave had to be reduced one by one until, after a brutal month of fighting, the island was finally taken.

With the invasion of the Philippines imminent the Joint Chiefs and Nimitz became concerned with coordination of the forces being hurled against Leyte. Both Kinkaid's Seventh and Halsey's Third Fleet would be utilized. There was no overall naval commander. Kinkaid was under MacArthur's command while Halsey took his orders from Nimitz. With this awkward situation the potential for unilateral action was present. In the Halsey and Kinkaid chapters the Battle of Leyte Gulf and its problems will be reviewed at length. Nimitz's reaction to the battle is the main point considered here.

Nimitz gave Halsey orders to cover and support the forces of the southwest Pacific and to assist them in the seizure of the central Philippines. But he also ordered the Third Fleet commander

to destroy enemy naval and air forces in or threatening the Philippine area.[16]

To destroy and to cover could be construed as meaning two entirely different things, particularly when the order read further:

> In case opportunity for destruction of major portion of the enemy fleet offers or can be created, such destruction becomes the primary task.[17]

Halsey thus found himself ordered not only to protect the beachhead, but to do what Spruance had failed to do the previous June: destroy the Japanese Fleet if the opportunity arose. A dangerous situation was in the making.

Late in September Nimitz was again on the west coast for talks with King. The central Pacific planners had finally scrapped the Formosa plan and although reluctant to do so, King accepted the decision. Along with Generals Harmon of the Air Force and Buckner of the Army, Nimitz agreed that Formosa was not a suitable target. Instead, Iwo Jima and Okinawa were proposed as alternatives and tentative dates for attacks against these two islands were established. Nimitz also requested permission to move his headquarters to Guam. King approved.

The conference ended on October 2, and Nimitz quickly returned to Hawaii. There he hovered over the radio in an effort to garner information regarding Halsey's actions. One of the first news items Nimitz heard was a disturbing report from Tokyo which insisted that the Third Fleet had been annihilated by the Japanese Fleet.

The propaganda was so convincing that Hitler and Mussolini even sent congratulatory messages to the emperor.

Halsey, too, had monitored the transmission. He countered with a dispatch of his own to Nimitz:

> The Third Fleet's sunken and damaged ships have been salvaged and are retiring at high speed toward the enemy.[18]

To counter the Japanese propaganda, Nimitz released a communiqué.

> Admiral Nimitz has received from Admiral Halsey the comforting assurance that he is now retiring toward the enemy following the salvage of all the Third Fleet ships recently reported sunk by Radio Tokyo.[19]

On the twentieth, MacArthur's forces slammed ashore on Leyte. The Japanese knew that they had to halt the American attack at all costs and initiated their grand plan for just such an eventuality, the Sho I Plan, designed to annihilate the American Fleet. A near-disaster almost resulted caused not by the Japanese, but by the divided command structure and Halsey's dual orders.

At Pearl Harbor Nimitz followed the course of the battle intently. Meanwhile, Halsey began to wonder where the enemy carriers were. Throughout the afternoon of October 24, Mitscher's aircraft pummeled the Japanese forces in the Sibuyan Sea. But where were the carriers?

Nimitz was aware that the last known position of the Japanese carriers was in the Inland Sea of Japan. Therefore, they were obviously planning to attack from the north. Apparently Halsey reached the same conclusion for when he radioed Mitscher at 1:34 P.M. on the twenty-fourth, he said:

> Enemy carrier strength not located. Keep area to the north under observation.[20]

When Halsey's scouts finally did locate the enemy carriers, Nimitz was appraised immediately thanks to radio intercepts. Halsey quickly radioed that he was proceeding north with three groups to attack the enemy carrier force. Nimitz assumed this to mean that three carrier groups, but not the surface force of battleships, were moving to intercept. He merely assumed that Halsey would leave the battleships behind to cover the San Bernardino Strait.

At Pearl no one seemed unduly surprised at Halsey's decision. With the suspected destruction of Admiral Kurita's Center Force in the Sibuyan Sea, there seemed little to fear from an attack out of the strait. So, everyone knew that, given the chance, Halsey would elect to engage the enemy carriers.

It was the next morning before Nimitz began to harbor doubts that Task Force 34, the battleship force, had been left behind to protect the northern approach to Leyte Gulf. Nimitz was in the dark. Did Halsey, or did he not, leave a covering force behind? Kurita's fleet soon answered that question with dramatic suddenness.

Barreling down on the few escort carriers of the Seventh Fleet lying off the coast of Samar came Kurita's powerful surface force of battleships and cruisers. It was a David-and-Goliath encounter.

Nimitz paced the floor at Pearl Harbor impatiently as reports of the one-sided battle began to filter in. Finally, in desperation, he had a message sent to Halsey inquiring as to the whereabouts of Task Force 34. As was customary the message was packed with padded words which preceded and ended it. This padding was used to confuse enemy cryptographers.

It was common practice. The beginning of a radio message made an easy target for code breakers seeking a pattern. So usually the Americans included nonsense phrases in their messages. The composition of these phrases was usually left to the discretion of the individual radio operators. The person who happened to send this particular message must have been either a history buff or an English professor for he recalled that the day was the anniversary of the Battle of Balaklava. He also recalled Tennyson's poem about the Light Brigade which included the phrase "all the world wondered." This was the phrase used as padding in the message sent to Halsey.

Now usually when a message was given to the recipient the padding was eliminated by the radio operator. In this case, however, the opening padding, "Turkey trots to water," was struck off. But the closing padding, "the world wonders," was left in because it appeared to the radio operator to be part of the message. Thus, when Halsey received the message it read, "Where is Task Force Thirty-Four? the world wonders."

Unaccustomed to seeing padding Halsey took it to be part of the original message and was furious over the obvious sarcasm. He felt insulted and even hurt at what he considered to be the flippant attitude of CinCPac.

Halsey immediately ordered Task Force 34 to reverse course and head for San Bernardino strait at full speed. Luckily for him, however, Kurita, with total victory in sight, turned fainthearted and retreated. The American escort carriers and the transports at Leyte Gulf were spared annihilation.

The Battle of Leyte Gulf was a disastrous defeat for the Japanese Navy. In a letter to King, Nimitz regretted Halsey's decision not to leave Task Force 34 off Samar to guard San Bernardino Strait. He was careful, however, not to criticize Halsey publically.

I will not be a party to anything that detracts from him and his reputation.[21]

Nimitz would not forget the dark days of early 1942. Then it was Halsey who had stood by him. In addition, Nimitz himself might have felt somewhat responsible for the debacle at Leyte Gulf. Had he not issued Halsey the dual orders? Wasn't he familiar with Halsey's impetuous nature? Nevertheless, though it was a close call, the Battle of Leyte Gulf broke the back of the Japanese Navy once and for all.

At the next meeting with King the main topic of discussion was the length of time the Third Fleet would be tied down supporting MacArthur. Due to the heavy and incessant rains at Leyte, airfield construction was delayed necessitating retaining the carriers to insure adequate air protection for the troops. This delay caused the postponement of the invasion of Luzon.

The delays in the Philippines also meant that the invasion of Iwo Jima had to be put off for a month along with the follow-up attack against Okinawa. King and Nimitz also discussed the possibility of blockading Japan rather than invading it. King also felt obligated to broach the subject of participation by the British Fleet in the Pacific war, an event with which he was not particularly in accord.

On December 11, King, Nimitz, and Admiral Leahy were rewarded the fifth star designating them fleet admirals.

On Christmas Day the new fleet admiral flew to Ulithi to inquire about the heavy damage sustained by Task Force 38 during a recent typhoon. Halsey was the recipient of most of the blame by the subsequent court of inquiry convened to review the facts. The court's chairman, Vice Admiral John Hoover, went so far as to recommend a court-martial. King and Nimitz quickly nixed that recommendation. Nevertheless, Nimitz drew up some hard-and-fast rules governing travel safety and awareness of changes in the weather.

From Ulithi, Nimitz flew to Leyte to confer with MacArthur regarding the forthcoming invasion of Luzon. Then he returned to Ulithi where he met once more with Halsey. The latter took the opportunity to broach the subject of the message which had so infuriated him during the battle of Leyte Gulf. Hearing about the misunderstanding for the first time, Nimitz was shocked and told Halsey that he would find out just who was responsible.

After supporting the invasion of Luzon, the Third Fleet again became the Fifth Fleet and reverted to Spruance's command. In the interim Nimitz had moved his headquarters to Guam where he could be closer to the front and away from the crowded and hectic conditions at Pearl Harbor.

During a meeting with Spruance regarding the Iwo Jima attack, the latter proposed a plan calling for a carrier raid against the Japanese mainland itself. If effective, the raid might prevent Japanese planes from interfering with the invasion. Although the actual assault was expected to be difficult, both Nimitz and Spruance felt that the strategic importance of Iwo Jima made the operation worthwhile.

Back at his headquarters Nimitz waited to hear reports regarding the success of Spruance's raid on Tokyo on February 16. The raid, the first since Doolittle's in April of 1942, proved a great success. Nimitz was also anxious to hear how the preliminary bombardment of Iwo Jima was progressing. Would the latter effectively eliminate enemy strong points?

On the nineteenth, the marines landed on Iwo. The blood bath was about to commence. Iwo Jima proved to be one of the bloodiest battles of the entire war. The Japanese had constructed one of the most elaborate underground tunnel systems yet seen in the entire Pacific war. It took the marines a full month to secure the five-by-three-mile-wide island.

Nimitz did not hear of the final cost of Iwo Jima until his arrival in Washington for another meeting with King. Upon arriving in the states, to his great dismay, he saw the news expressed in the headlines. The newspaper articles were highly critical of the central Pacific commanders and compared them unfavorably to MacArthur who usually had a low casualty rate during his campaigns. Once more Nimitz felt hurt.

At a meeting with the Joint Chiefs of Staff on March 5,

Nimitz was informed that the war in Europe was winding down and that they were going to pay closer attention to Pacific war strategy. The admiral then described the proposed Okinawa invasion and the role the navy would play during the invasion of Japan. Though he fervently hoped that Japan would surrender before an invasion became necessary, plans had to be developed nonetheless.

On March 8, Nimitz met with Roosevelt. The admiral noted how much the President's health had deteriorated since their meeting the previous summer. On March 15, Nimitz was back on Guam.

The day after his return to the Pacific, word was received that all organized resistance had ceased on Iwo Jima. The cost of the operation unnerved Nimitz and in the communiqué he sent announcing the fall of the island he closed by saying:

> Among the Americans who served on Iwo island, uncommon valor was a common virtue.[22]

Nimitz waited until the twenty-fourth of March before visiting Iwo Jima. With members of his staff he toured the volcanic island and was awed by the carnage and destruction that had cost over twenty-six thousand casualties. Six thousand eight hundred-twenty-one of these were killed.

Now attention focused on Okinawa. One of Nimitz's greatest concerns was Japanese air attacks. The enemy had as many as fifty-five airfields on Kyushu and sixty-five more on Formosa in addition to the many fields in the Ryukus themselves. Thousands of planes would be sent against the American fleet. Foremost of these would, of course, be the dreaded and deadly suicide pilots, the Kamikaze.

To reduce the danger, Spruance raided Kyushu's airfields. The Japanese fought back ferociously, damaging the carrier *Franklin* and killing over seven hundred men.

On April 1, the Tenth Army swarmed ashore on

Okinawa. Initial resistance was light, but as the troops moved inland and the days progressed, opposition became stiffer. On the sixth the first of nine Kamikaze attacks commenced. The effects of this effort were devastating. Thirty Allied ships were sunk and two hundred-thirty-three damaged in the deadly duel between gunners fighting to live and pilots fighting to die. The Japanese even sent their huge battleship, *Yamato* on a suicide mission to Okinawa. Mitscher's pilots located the ship and blasted the leviathan to the bottom of the sea.

On the twenty-second, Nimitz, accompanied by a few key staff members and the commandant of the Marine Corps, General Vandergrift, took off for Okinawa. They were on the island only a few minutes when they witnessed the horror of the dreaded kamikaze as a suicide plane crashed into a cargo ship.

The slow advance of the GIs concerned Nimitz. The quicker the campaign was over, the quicker the ships could be released from supporting the battle. Consequently he began to prod the army commander, Gen. Simon Bolivar Buckner to speed up the army's progress. Buckner retorted that the ground battle was none of Nimitz's business. With that, the normally patient admiral shot back:

> Yes, but ground though it may be, I'm losing a ship and a half a day. So if this line isn't moving within five days, we'll get someone here to move it, so we can all get out from under these stupid air attacks.[23]

There was a danger that interservice rivalry might mar the campaign. Nimitz, however, was intelligent enough not to allow that to happen. Soon after the disagreement with Buckner he held a news conference. Before seventy-six reporters, he diplomatically praised the army and its conduct of operations. The controversy vanished.

Nevertheless, the fighting on Okinawa continued into

June. It was the twenty-first before the island was finally declared secure. The cost was high: seven thousand six hundred-thirteen troops killed and thirty-nine thousand wounded. Added to this were the lives of over four thousand nine hundred sailors with an equal amount wounded. Among the dead were General Buckner himself and Ernie Pyle, the famed war correspondent. The Okinawa campaign proved to be one of the costliest of the entire Pacific war.

In American hands, however, the island was invaluable. It supported the intensification of the bombing campaign against the Japanese mainland, helped tighten the economic blockade, and was an excellent jumping-off point for the invasion of Kyushu.

The next major decision facing the Joint Chiefs was the matter of a commander for the invasion of Japan. Would it be MacArthur or Nimitz? Unable to decide, the chiefs came to a compromise. MacArthur would have command of all ground troops and air forces while Nimitz would lead the naval forces.

The thing that Nimitz had to be cautious of was allowing MacArthur to dominate the campaign and reduce the navy to a secondary role. Nimitz was determined never to allow MacArthur to gain a position where he could control the movements of the fast carrier force.

From April onward the staff of both commanders met frequently, reviewing plans for the proposed invasion. On May 15, Nimitz flew to Manila to meet MacArthur face-to-face. Together they endorsed the plans already developed and settled most of the remaining problems, forming the basis for cooperation during the forthcoming invasion.

Spruance was selected to command the fleet during Operation Olympic, the invasion of Kyushu. During operation Coronet, the invasion of Honshu, the fleet would revert to Halsey's command. Nimitz was determined to use the first team.

The invasion, as history has shown, never came to be. As early as February, 1945, Nimitz had received a top-secret letter from King which informed him of the atomic bomb for the first time. The bomb, a new type of weapon with fire potential equivalent to twenty thousand tons of TNT was awesome. The atomic bomb, King stated, would probably be available after August 1.

At the end of June, Nimitz flew to San Francisco for what would prove to be the final wartime meeting with King. The conference was a brief one. King stated that the Joint Chiefs of Staff had approved of Operation Olympic and had also directed that preparations begin for Coronet. However, both admirals knew that Japan was at the end of its tether and were relatively certain that the invasion would not be necessary.

On July 25, even while plans for the invasion continued, Nimitz, Spruance, and Gen. Curtis LeMay, commander of the Twentieth Air Force, were shown films of the atomic-bomb explosion in New Mexico. The very next day the cruiser *Indianapolis* arrived at Tinian with a cargo of uranium 235 for the atomic bomb. Privately, Nimitz hoped that the bomb would not have to be used. If only Japan would face the inevitable.

On August 6, the Enola Gay, a B-29 bomber piloted by Colonel Paul Tibbets, carried the first atomic bomb to Hiroshima. This was followed three days later by the dropping of a similar bomb on the city of Nagasaki. On the fourteenth, Nimitz received a message from King acknowledging Japan's capitulation. Accordingly, he ordered all commands to cease offensive operations, but to continue searches, patrols, and to maintain defenses and internal security measures.

On August 29, Nimitz arrived in Tokyo Bay and broke out his flag on the battleship *South Dakota*. At 8:03 on the morning of September 2, the admiral boarded the battleship *Missouri*. When MacArthur arrived, the formal surrender ceremony began. Peace was finally restored. Immediately afterward, Nimitz released a statement that was broadcast throughout the Pacific and the United States.

> On board all naval vessels at sea and in port, and at our many island bases in the Pacific, there is rejoicing and thanksgiving. The long and bitter struggle . . . is at an end. . . . Now we turn to the great tasks of reconstruction and restoration. I am confident that we will be able to apply the same skill, resourcefulness, and keen thinking to these problems as were applied to the problems of winning the victory.[24]

October 5, 1945, was designated Nimitz Day in Washington, D.C. A grateful nation turned out to welcome its conquering hero.

Nimitz wondered about his role in the postwar world. His wish was to be the next Chief of Naval Operations succeeding King. Secretary of the Navy James Forrestal, however, attempted to dissuade him from accepting that position. Forrestal wanted a more pliable personality in that office instead of a man of Nimitz's prestige. The admiral, however, was the unanimous choice of King and other prominent leaders. They forcefully argued Nimitz's cause. Thus he became the first postwar Chief of Naval Operations.

Even before assuming his new post the debate regarding merging all the services into one Department of the Armed Forces was being waged. Nimitz opposed such a merger.

On December 15, 1945, Nimitz was sworn in as Chief of Naval Operations (CNO). Thus he embarked on a most difficult job at a trying time. The work was nonstop, lasting seven days a week from early morning to late evening. There was much to be done including demobilization of the huge navy.

Nimitz remained as CNO for two years. During his term the future of the armed services was, after countless conferences and meetings, finally decided upon. There would be separate departments of the army, navy, and air force. Heading the establishment as a member of the President's cabinet, would be a Secretary of Defense. The Joint Chiefs of Staff were retained. Nimitz also had a hand in the development of the first nuclear-powered submarine.

After stepping down as CNO, Nimitz and his wife went to California where they hoped to live a long and happy life with their children and grandchildren. Shortly, though, the admiral became restless for something to do.

In March, 1949, Nimitz's retirement was happily disturbed when the United Nations requested him to become its good-will ambassador. He remained in that capacity until 1952 when he went back into retirement.

After a peaceful existence in sunny California, Nimitz was forced to undergo surgery in November, 1965. While in the hospital he contracted pneumonia. Though he appeared to be recovering, his health suddenly took a turn for the worse. Late in January, 1966, he lapsed into a coma and died on Sunday, February 20, 1966, at the age of eighty-one. His wish for a simple graveside ceremony and burial at the Golden Gate National Cemetery was granted.

This modest, quiet, compassionate man was by far one of America's greatest military leaders. His personality bred confidence, which caused America's leadership to turn to him in the aftermath of Pearl Harbor. He promptly picked up the pieces and brought his nation through to victory. Nimitz successfully conducted a war in the world's largest theater as he moved ships of fantastic might and handled subordinates who were frequently difficult to handle. Chester W. Nimitz, the blond-headed boy from Texas, served his country well and left America with a legacy of which it is proud.

Chapter Three

Raymond Ames Spruance commanded the greatest and most powerful fleet in the history of the world. He was in charge of the United States carrier force at Midway and successfully led the American forces in the capture of the Gilberts, Marshalls, Mariana Islands, Iwo Jima, and Okinawa. Yet his name does not readily come to mind when one thinks of American naval leaders. Nimitz and Halsey are quickly remembered, but not Ray Spruance.

The reason for this is remarkably simple. The man shunned publicity. He refused to accept any credit that he believed his subordinates had earned. In fact, he avoided the limelight, feeling that history itself would judge his performance. His peers and superiors, however, recognized his greatness. The wartime Chief of Naval Operations, Adm. Ernest King said that he

"was in intellectual ability unsurpassed among the flag officers of the United States Navy."[1]

Nimitz called him, "an admiral's admiral,"[2] and no less an authority than Samuel Eliot Morison said that

"Spruance's leading characteristics were attention to detail, poise, and power of intelligent decision."[3]

Despite the accolades, however, the man was not without his critics. There was much controversy over his use of the carriers during the Midway and Philippine Sea battles. The aviators of the fleet objected to the fact that, as a non-aviator, Spruance was allowed to lead carriers at all. Nevertheless, Admiral Nimitz felt that Ray Spruance was the right man for the job and never once had cause to regret his choice.

Raymond A. Spruance was born to Anne and Alexander Spruance on July 3, 1886. There was little warmth and affection in the Spruance family. His father was austere, undemonstrative. His mother was a career woman who preferred the professional world to the thankless chore of raising a child. Thus his earliest childhood was marked by feelings of loneliness. When two other sons were born to the Spruances, the youngest one was mentally retarded, so the mother abandoned all pursuits to care for the unfortunate youngster. Unable to care for all three boys, Anne turned Raymond over to the care of her parents and sisters, who spoiled the youngster as grandparents and aunts are wont to do. It was these years that Spruance later looked back upon as the happiest of his youth.

As a schoolboy, Spruance was shy and remained aloof from school activities although he maintained a high academic average. When his grandparents suffered a financial catastrophe, Raymond was forced to return to his parents in Indianapolis. Being by nature shy, he found life there miserable and the only recreation that afforded him comfort was hiking.

Lacking the funds for college tuition, Anne Spruance felt that her son should attend the naval academy. Not only could the academy provide him with a quality education and an honorable profession, it would not cost the family any money. After moving in with his aunt in South Orange, New Jersey, Spruance prepared himself for entry into the naval academy. In May, 1903, the local newspaper announced that a New Jersey congressman would sponsor a competitive examination in order to make his selection for Annapolis. Spruance studied hard and took the test. His high score netted him the nomination, but in the interim his mother had also been angling for a nomination from one of the local Indiana politicians. Spruance thus found himself with two nominations necessitating a choice. Preferring the New Jersey nomination since he had earned it on his own merit, he was about to accept when his aunts convinced him to accept the Indiana one because his mother had gone to such great lengths to obtain it.

As stated in both the King and Nimitz chapters, the academy at the turn of the century was in the midst of a renaissance. Spruance's class was one of the largest to be accepted at Annapolis. He was sworn into the navy as a midshipman on July 2, 1903, one day shy of his seventeenth birthday. Gradually, the civilian Spruance was transformed into a naval cadet. From the rigors of his plebe year to his graduation he mastered the traditions and customs of the navy, the discipline and obedience essential for a naval officer to survive on the open sea. Foremost, he learned duty, honor, and loyalty to the United States of America.

Spruance was an eager student who resented what he felt was a less than quality education offered by the academy. He disliked its very narrow curriculum and poor quality teachers who were themselves recent graduates of the same system. Though unhappy with many of the courses, he nevertheless managed to perform magnificently, ranking twenty-fifth in a class of two hundred and nine.

Though a member of the class of 1907, Spruance graduated on September 12, 1906, in order to enhance the flow of new officers into the fleet. The academy yearbook, the "Lucky Bag," had this to say of Passed Midshipman Spruance:

A shy young thing with a rather sober, earnest face and the innocent disposition of an ingénue—would never hurt anything or anybody except in line of duty.[4]

172

As a passed midshipman, Spruance's first duty was aboard the battleship USS *Iowa*, veteran of the recently concluded Spanish-American War. Aboard the *Iowa* he performed the many and varied duties designed to prepare young officers for future command. He supervised enlisted men, stood watches, and absorbed all there was to know regarding the operation of a capital ship. In June, 1907, Spruance was transferred to the newer battleship *Minnesota*. This ship was scheduled to leave shortly on President Theodore Roosevelt's propaganda tour aimed at showing off America's newly found naval strength. Dubbed the "Great White Fleet," this muscle-flexing was intended to impress the world with the great strength inherent in American democracy. Though many problems riddled the tour, for a young and impressionable officer like Spruance it was one great experience.

As the fleet paused at the world's most exotic ports of call, Midshipman Spruance found himself sought after to attend parties and special ceremonies. Unfortunately, not all of the experiences were pleasant. A raging typhoon off Luzon resulted in Spruance's becoming violently seasick. Then, as the fleet approached Japan, apprehension gripped the sailors, thanks to the recent strain of U.S.-Japanese relations. Happily, all went well during the visit and, at a garden tea party, Spruance had the honor of meeting the famous Admiral Togo of Tsushima fame.

In February, 1909, the Great White Fleet returned home. A lot had happened to Spruance during the two-year voyage. Departing as passed midshipman, he returned home an ensign, having passed the test for this rank the previous September. The experiences, the sights, and sounds of fabled ports, however, left an indelible mark on him. He felt a particularly deep respect and admiration for the Japanese, an admiration that would remain with him even through the darkest days of World War II.

After his return home, Ensign Spruance decided to

specialize in engineering. He applied for and was accepted for a course of advanced instruction in electricity at the General Electric Company in Schenectady, New York. There he gained invaluable knowledge and personal experiences with the intricacies of electricity.

The following year he was back at sea once more, this time on the battleship *Connecticut*, commanded by Capt. W. R. Rush, a harsh disciplinarian with a sour personality. Rush came down hard on the young ensign, making life barely bearable. Spruance applied for a transfer, but it failed to come through. Ironically, even though Rush seemed to lean heavily on Spruance, at the same time he was writing glowing fitness reports on the young officer. Finally, in October, 1911, Spruance was ordered to the cruiser *Cincinnati* in California as engineering officer.

For the next year and a half Spruance managed to keep the obsolete engines of the aged veteran operational as it steamed across the Pacific and up and down the China coast. As a member of the Asiatic Fleet, the *Cincinnati* had a dual responsibility: to protect American business interests in China and to preserve the open-door policy. While serving in this ship, Spruance received his promotion to the rank of lieutenant, junior grade.

Then, early in 1913, he was given his first command, the destroyer *Bainbridge*, which was moored at Olanpago in the Philippines. The ship was a creaky, rusty old bucket, but the undaunted young officer took the ship and turned it into a crack operating destroyer. Serving aboard the *Bainbridge* as engineering officer was Ens. Charles Moore, the man Spruance would select to serve as his Chief of Staff when he assumed command of the Central Pacific Forces in 1943.

Spruance relinquished command of the *Bainbridge* in May of the following year, leaving the ship in far better shape than when he had assumed command. Morale was high and each officer and enlisted man developed a deep and lasting respect for his young skipper. Having proven himself adept at independent command, Spruance was promoted to lieutenant and ordered back to the United States.

Soon after his return home he proposed to Margaret Dean. The two were married in November, 1914. Spruance was assigned as naval inspector of electrical machinery at Newport News, Virginia. Soon afterward, war broke out in Europe.

After their wedding the young couple settled down in an apartment. Although he had a reputation as a cold, feelingless person, the young bride quickly saw that "Old Stone Face" was not really like his reputation. He simply covered up his emotions and hardly showed them. She once said,

"His self-control was an enigma to me, Raymond was a stoic."

It was this ability to mask his emotions which gave rise to his very unflattering nickname.

Spruance was also a physical-fitness advocate. He exercised constantly. In this way he provided an outlet for his emotions. Much of this exercise consisted of endurance walking and swimming. He believed that a good diet and hard exercise kept the body attuned for maximum efficiency.

When the United States declared war on the Central Powers in April, 1917, Spruance was an electrical officer on the battleship *Pennsylvania*. He was looking forward to sea duty, but his hopes were soon dashed when to his great dismay his specialty earned him a shore assignment. Temporarily promoted to lieutenant commander, the chagrined Spruance reported to the Brooklyn Navy Yard. Though disappointed he would not let his feelings hinder his work. He plunged wholeheartedly into his important duties. Spruance was responsible for the installation and testing of a new gunnery control system. Eventually his expertise took him up and down the east coast and later to Europe. By war's end he had become the foremost expert on gunnery fire-control systems.

As peace settled over the world Spruance was appointed executive officer of the troop transport, *Agamemnon,* whose job it was to return America's fighting doughboys. He spent four months with the transport and made three transatlantic crossings. Late in 1918 he was elevated in rank to full commander.

In 1920, Spruance was given command of the destroyer *Aaron Ward.* After a brief European cruise he took the destroyer to the Pacific to join the Pacific Fleet. As part of this fleet Spruance's divisional commander was William F. Halsey.

Under Halsey's guidance the six destroyers comprising the division practiced hard perfecting their maneuvers. Both officers managed to make excellent impressions on their superiors. Spruance was considered a superb leader of men and an accomplished mariner. His proficiency reports were glowing. During this time Spruance and Halsey formed a close and lasting friendship.

In the summer of 1921, Spruance was again summoned to shore duty, this time to the Bureau of Engineering in Washington. Unhappy at having to leave San Diego and sea duty he nevertheless packed up his family and headed east. A short time later he was promoted head of the Electrical Division with responsibility for developing, testing, procuring, installing, and maintaining all shipboard electrical equipment for the U.S. Fleet.

In the spring of 1924, he was once again assigned sea duty as commander of the destroyer *Dale.* Just as he was about to take command of the *Dale,* however, his orders were abruptly changed and he was directed to report as Assistant Chief of Staff to Commander, Naval Forces,

Europe who at that time was Vice Admiral Philip Andrews. Andrews had a reputation for being a hard-liner and was immensely disliked by his subordinates.

Spruance took the *Dale* across the Atlantic and reported to Andrews at Cherbourg where the admiral's flagship, *Pittsburg,* was docked. As a representative of the United States Navy in Europe it was Andrews' job to steer the fleet into foreign ports, show the flag, and spread American good will.

Andrews lived up to his reputation and constantly made life miserable for Spruance. Yet in fitness reports the admiral usually wrote glowingly about Spruance's capability and his hard work. In time the relationship between the two improved as Andrews became captivated by Spruance's children.

By 1925, Andrews was back in the States and Spruance was in command of the destroyer *Osborne,* relieving his friend, Bill Halsey. The following summer he brought the *Osborne* back home. Awaiting him were orders to attend the Naval War College.

The War College had been founded in 1885 for the express purpose of training officers in the theories of war. Alfred Thayer Mahan, the famed naval exponent, was the driving force behind the college's founding and became its president in 1889. In the 1920s it was expected that any naval officer aspiring to flag rank attend the eleven-month course. As part of the curriculum, the students studied strategy, naval history, logistics, and international law. War games were also an essential part of the course. In these courses, budding admirals were able to put their theories into practice. Enemies were designated and given a specific color. Invariably the enemy most frequently fought in the war games was Japan, whose color was orange.

The studies of a war with Japan visualized a prolonged campaign fought across the broad expanses of the Pacific where the enemy, after initiating war with a surprise attack, would entrench themselves in a defensive ring. This would result in the U.S. overextending itself and becoming exhausted by attritional warfare. Eventually they would have to fight a decisive battleship duel which would either defeat the Japanese battle fleet or end in a stalemate. If the latter was the result, then a negotiated peace would be sought.

As was typical of this era the course of study usually glorified the battleship as the superior fighting machine. Aircraft carriers and submarines were not allowed their proper stations. It was in this orthodox college that the strategist of World War II developed. Luckily, many students later overcame the handicap of orthodoxy, Spruance among them.

Nevertheless, Spruance enjoyed the academic atmosphere at the War College and felt motivated to study the art of naval warfare deeply. The experiences gained at the college laid the foundation for his reputation as a sound professional thinker. The college taught him to analyze and solve problems. Eventually, his ability to do this became instinctive.

Upon completion of his term at the War College in the summer of 1927, Spruance was assigned to the Office of Naval Intelligence in Washington. Two years later he became executive officer of the battleship *Mississippi*. For an aspirant to flag rank, service as an executive officer on a battleship was essential. In this role he was responsible for the ship's administration. He was firm, stern, but always fair to the men under his command.

Spruance returned to the War College in the fall of 1931 as Officer in Charge of the Correspondence Courses Department. There were two basic courses in this department: strategy and tactics, and international law. Spruance was the instructor.

Late in 1931, he was promoted to the rank of captain. Another two years passed before he was given command of the USS *Vestal,* a repair ship. Just as he was about to assume command history repeated itself and he was ordered to report to Rear Admiral A. E. Watson, Commander Destroyers, Scouting Force, as Chief of Staff. Spruance diligently performed his tasks and earned Watson's admiration and praise. In a fitness report Watson said of his Chief of Staff that he was "fully qualified for command and promotion to admiral."[5]

March of 1935 found Spruance back at the War College again. He remained there for the next three years. Then, in 1938, he was given command of the battleship *Mississippi,* an assignment he eagerly accepted for he knew that to attain the coveted rank of rear admiral, a successful tour on a capital ship was a prerequisite.

As skipper of the *Mississippi* Spruance earned the respect of the crew who considered him a dignified gentleman, remote yet accessible. He maneuvered his ship through fleet exercises preparing it for future emergencies. During the yearly competition with other battleships, the *Mississippi's* crew excelled in gunnery and engineering. At the age of fifty-three with thirty-six years in the navy behind him, Spruance's outstanding record with the *Mississippi* earned him the rank of rear admiral.

On February 26, 1940, still a captain, Spruance reported to his next assignment, Commandant, Tenth Naval District with headquarters at San Juan, Puerto Rico. Though selected for promotion to rear admiral, a vacancy in that rank did not occur until October 1. Only then was he permitted to advance to that rank.

With war again raging in Europe, and the fall of France in June, 1940, the threat of German domination of French islands in the Caribbean via the puppet Vichy government resulted in a wave of fear in that corner of the globe. Spruance went to the French island of Martinique where he called on the senior French naval officer there. He received the Frenchman's assurances that he detested both the

Germans and the Vichy government and that French ships would not be used against the British.

While in the Caribbean, Spruance observed the U.S. Marines practicing amphibious landings. He was quickly impressed by one fiery brigadier general, Holland M. Smith. Spruance found Smith warlike, but at the same time brimming with technical knowledge about amphibious warfare. The admiral tucked Smith's name away for future reference.

As the danger of war intensified, Spruance's command was elevated to that of a sea frontier embracing all of the Caribbean. However, he yearned for a sea command. Eventually his hopes were realized when, on September 17, 1941, he was appointed Commander, Cruiser Division Five, Pacific Fleet. This cruiser division was part of Admiral Halsey's carrier force stationed at Pearl Harbor.

The Pearl Harbor at which Spruance arrived was in the midst of expansion. Up until 1939 the base had been primarily a submarine base and shipyard. Now, because of the international tension brought about by Japan's war with China, President Roosevelt ordered the Pacific Fleet to Pearl Harbor to act as a deterrent. Accordingly, Pearl Harbor was being enlarged to accommodate the fleet and the influx of sailors.

Breaking his flag out on the cruiser *Northampton*, Spruance found the division woefully unprepared for war. Unfortunately that went for the fleet in general. For political reasons Roosevelt had refused to ask Congress for additional appropriations that might have given the Pacific Fleet the tools it required for war. Underequipped and dreadfully understaffed, the Pacific Fleet was little more than a clay pigeon in a shooting gallery.

Spruance's highest priority was preparing his cruisers to fight a war. In his customary quiet way, the cool, remote admiral overhauled the division. Between September and November he took it out to sea no less than three times for periods of nine days at a time. During these maneuvers, he rode the division hard, honing it to a fine edge. As usual his staff ran everything. Spruance, meanwhile, spoke little but took everything in.

Day by day the tension between the United States and Japan worsened. Spruance was positive that war would come shortly. On November 28, as part of Halsey's Task Force, Cruiser Division Five set out from Pearl on what Spruance thought was simply another training exercise. They were scheduled to return on the fifth of December. Halsey, however, was under orders to reinforce Wake Island with aircraft. The Task Force, operating on a war footing with orders to attack any Japanese ships encountered, set course for Wake.

After debarking the planes at Wake, Halsey headed back for Pearl. Refueling at sea took longer than anticipated and caused Halsey to revise his estimated time of arrival to Sunday, December 7.

On that fateful morning Spruance and the *Northampton* were two hundred miles west of Honolulu. While eating breakfast Spruance received the extraordinary message: "Air Raid Pearl Harbor. This Is No Drill." The fleet immediately went to battle readiness. Spruance hurried to the bridge where he remained for the next twenty-four hours. With conflicting messages crowding the airwaves, Spruance took his cue from Halsey. Having received what he thought to be the whereabouts of the enemy, Halsey sent Spruance southwest to engage the Japanese Fleet. At that very time, however, the enemy was retiring to the northwest. A few hours later, Spruance's force began to run low on fuel and was forced to break off the chase and return to Pearl Harbor. Fortunately, the base's fuel-tanks had emerged unscathed from the attack.

On Monday, Spruance's flagship entered the burning harbor. For a man who pinned his hopes on the might of the battleship and had taught about their invincibility, the view was nerve-shattering. He was particularly taken aback at the sight of Admiral Kimmel, a man whom he respected highly. Though able to maintain his self-control, inwardly the attack affected Spruance deeply. At home he let his usually emotionless façade down and spoke candidly with his wife and daughter. To their amazement they spotted tears in his eyes for probably the first time.

By the next day he had recovered his composure and was ready for action. For the remainder of the month the cruisers and carriers conducted patrols seeking enemy ships. Spruance detested the indecisiveness of the interim commander and waited for the new Commander in Chief, Pacific, Adm. Chester W. Nimitz, to arrive and inject a fighting spirit into the fleet. Nimitz's arrival was a shot in the arm that helped dispel the gloom and doom prevalent at Pearl Harbor.

Now that the Hawaii-Australia line of communication was threatened, Halsey in the carrier *Enterprise* and Spruance in the *Northampton* set sail for Samoa on January 11, 1942. From there the Task Force was ordered to strike at the Marshall Islands in the hope of derailing the Japanese juggernaut. If unsuccessful, the raid could at least boost the badly shaken American morale.

On January 25, Halsey's Task Force arrived at Samoa and left behind a force of marines to guard against a Japanese invasion. From there Halsey joined Rear Admiral Frank Jack Fletcher's Task Force 17. Together they steamed toward the Marshalls.

Spruance's division of two cruisers and a destroyer was assigned Wotje Atoll as a target. For thirty-nine years Spruance had prepared himself for combat. Now he was about to see if he was truly ready. This was the real war, not a war game.

The Americans approached Wotje with caution. Surpri was deemed essential for Spruance knew that he w vulnerable to Japanese land-based air attack. Tl operation had to be conducted blindly. He had only obsolete charts and submarine reconnaissance reports to work with. Enemy ships rated the highest priority, followed by shore installations. Hopefully, Japanese air power would be neutralized by the American carriers.

Spruance's plan was far from innovative. He planned to bombard the shore installations just as he would engage an enemy ship, firing at high speed. Later in the war the method used by capital ships when attacking shore installations was to steam slowly back and forth, measure and aim their guns, then fire. At this early stage, however, Spruance lacked the luxury of prior experience.

On the night of January 31, Spruance's small force approached his target. The ships' navigators maneuvered their vessels through the darkness and the uncertain waters where hidden reefs could easily rip a ship's hull wide open. As the ships moved quietly into position, Spruance turned in to sleep.

When general quarters sounded the next morning, the *Northampton* was ready for combat. Halsey's planes began strafing Wotje while Spruance prepared for his first battle with a daring and foolhardy Japanese gunboat which closed on the small American squadron. The destroyer *Dunlap* made short work of the pesky intruder.

After reaching the required range, Spruance unleashed the cruiser's main batteries. The first targets selected were several small merchantmen lying in the anchorage. Most of the shells fell wide of their mark as the merchantmen frantically evaded the salvos.

Meanwhile, the *Northampton* reported a periscope on the port beam. Fearing the worst, Spruance immediately ordered a cease-fire and reversed course. His ideal plan began to come apart at the seams. After ascertaining that the submarine sighting was fictitious he brought his squadron about and resumed firing. For forty-five minutes no hits were made on the merchantmen. Therefore, the frustrated Spruance ordered fire shifted to the enemy shore installations that were hindering the American effort.

Then another submarine sighting resulted in a loss of discipline. Though this report was also erroneous, Spruance found it difficult to maintain order.

After a brief interval, order was restored to the formation and the ships closed on Wotje once more. But their lack of experience in firing at shore installations showed. Though some fires were started, they proved to be the exception rather than the rule.

Throughout the engagement Spruance remained on the open bridge instead of inside the armored conning tower. An hour and forty-five minutes after the start of the attack, he ordered his ships to break off and turn away from Wotje to rejoin Halsey.

On the return trip Spruance assessed the results. The air and sea attack had achieved some destruction of shore facilities including hangars, fuel storage tanks, a gasoline dump, shops, warehouses, barracks, and coastal defense batteries. Several ships in the lagoon were also sunk or damaged. As for his own forces, one cruiser had taken a bomb hit which caused little damage and no casualties. On the whole, however, the American attack had hardly dented the Japanese drive.

Upon their return to Pearl Harbor the Task Force was given a hero's welcome. Perhaps something had been achieved; an increase in morale, thought Spruance.

Personally, he was exhausted and disappointed with the results of the raid. Spruance felt that the cruisers had not performed as effectively as they should have in combat. Their antiaircraft fire was ineffective and the false submarine sightings resulted in a complete breakdown of discipline. He told his flag lieutenant, Robert J. Oliver, that

"The ships scattered in all directions, and no amount of signaling got them back. I had lost control."[6]

Nevertheless, the admiral felt that the Marshall raid had served a purpose. Having profited from his baptism of fire, he was ready to go out again. Nimitz awarded him the Navy Commendation Medal with this citation:

> For distinguished service in the line of his profession as Commander Cruiser Division Five and for his bold and effective handling of the bombardment group during the action of February 1, 1942. He pressed home his attack against the strong enemy positions in the face of enemy shore battery fire, silencing the enemy guns and inflicting heavy damage on enemy shipping and shore installations.[7]

Meanwhile, the Japanese winning streak continued uninhibited.

On February 11, Nimitz issued Halsey orders to conduct a raid on Wake Island. With his squadron, Spruance left harbor on the fourteenth to accompany Task Force 16.

Using reconnaissance photos of the target taken the day before the strike, Spruance and his staff studied the problem in depth and developed a bombardment plan. This plan called for an approach to Wake from the west at sunrise. The evening before the strike, Spruance's force of two cruisers and two destroyers separated from Halsey's main body and began their night approach. The attack was to commence just as Halsey's planes were preparing to attack the island.

Unfortunately, foul weather delayed the launching of Halsey's planes and because of the necessity of maintaining radio silence Spruance remained in the dark about Halsey's problem. While Halsey battled the elements, Spruance began his approach to Wake. The Japanese, however, had already discovered his force and a seaplane was shadowing Spruance. Undaunted, he continued toward the target expecting to attack in conjunction with Halsey's planes.

Eventually, Japanese seaplanes began to arrive and dived on the *Northampton*. Spruance refused to seek cover and needlessly exposed himself. A bomb narrowly missed the ship's bridge.

After shaking off the air attack the force was ready to strike back. Unfortunately, enemy shore batteries on Wake were just as ready to strike at the Americans. Each side opened fire. Spumes from near misses rose high around the small fleet while their own shells began to hit the island, causing slight damage. Seeing that he was simply wasting ammunition, Spruance ordered a cease-fire and withdrew.

After the action Spruance was in high spirits. Lieutenant Oliver thought that this was the ideal time to broach the subject of the admiral's refusal to protect himself under fire. Oliver's effort was in vain for Spruance believed that a naval commander should not hide from personal danger. In this attitude he was in good company. Admiral Nelson of Trafalgar fame and John Paul Jones shared Spruance's view.

En route to rejoin Halsey, Spruance was informed that the *Northampton*'s radar antenna was malfunctioning. Just then, Japanese planes which could not be detected thanks to the defective radar system, swooped out of the sky and narrowly missed the squadron. Spruance ordered the formation to seek the protection of a nearby fog bank. Without radar and sailing under radio silence, the task of locating Halsey would be formidable.

Fog persisted at the designated rendezvous point. Without radar Spruance could not know if Halsey was waiting. Someone suggested sending a signal by whistle. Spruance seized upon the suggestion and soon the electric whistle was tapping out a message. Gratefully, one of Halsey's ships responded in a like manner. Spruance was back with Task Force 16.

Anticipating a quick return to Pearl Harbor, Halsey was surprised when Nimitz ordered him to raid Marcus Island first. After a brief foray into this area, the Task Force returned to Pearl Harbor in mid-March after four weeks on the high seas.

A few days later Halsey and Spruance were at sea again, this time with orders to accompany Col. James Doolittle and his daring airmen. Doolittle's force was to fly B-25 Army bombers from the deck of the carrier *Hornet* on a bombing mission against Tokyo. Halsey and Spruance had the responsibility to escort the *Hornet* safely to within five hundred miles of Japan.

Spruance was of the opinion that these early raids, including Doolittle's, were doing little to stop the Japanese. The raids were accurately described as fleas on a dog's back. Unless America sank Japanese ships, destroyed Japanese planes, and killed Japanese soldiers, victory would never be a reality. The Doolittle raid inflicted little material damage. Psychologically, however, it boosted American morale.

But for the Japanese, the raid crystallized Admiral Yamamoto's plan to attack Midway Island. Yamamoto strongly believed that it was essential to continue an offensive strategy calculated to lure the U.S. Fleet to its destruction in an engagement with the markedly superior Japanese forces. He was convinced that if war continued, the balance of military power and the initiative would shift to the U.S. within a year to a year and a half. The Japanese admiral felt that the destruction of the American Fleet, coupled with a threat to Hawaii imposed by the occupation of Midway, would reduce the American will to fight and bring about a negotiated peace. The Japanese Naval General Staff, however, was reluctant to undertake an operation against Midway. Doolittle's raid changed their minds rapidly. Yamamoto had his way.

When Halsey's fleet arrived back at Pearl on April 25, they were soon out once more. Through code-breaking, Nimitz knew that Midway was threatened, but would not be attacked until June. The immediate concern was a threat in the Coral Sea. Consequently, Nimitz sent Halsey to aid Admiral Fletcher's attempt to thwart the Japanese effort to take Port Moresby on Papua, New Guinea. Sailing from Pearl on April 30, Halsey was too late to help Fletcher. In the Battle of the Coral Sea between May 6–8, the latter lost one carrier, the *Lexington,* and suffered grievous damage to the *Yorktown.* Nevertheless he had succeeded in turning back the Japanese attempt to take Port Moresby and had managed to sink one light carrier and damage a fleet carrier.

On May 16, Halsey was ordered to return to Hawaii immediately. Midway was the next Japanese target and Nimitz wanted to gather his forces and spring a surprise on the enemy.

As was customary, after arriving back at port, Spruance went to the *Enterprise* to discuss the just completed action with Halsey. He was delayed and by the time he reached the *Enterprise* he noted something radically wrong. Halsey was absent. The latter's flag lieutenant told Spruance that Halsey had been ordered to the hospital by Nimitz. The Task Force commander was ill with a skin rash, the severity of which necessitated his relief. Unbeknownst to Spruance, however, Halsey had urged Nimitz to make Spruance his successor. Nimitz agreed, with the stipulation that Spruance was to become his Chief of Staff following the Midway battle.

It was an ironic twist of fate. Spruance was a nonaviator. Now here he was suddenly placed in command of an air fleet. In fact, during his War College days, he had repeatedly expressed his faith in the battleship as the navy's decisive weapon. Yet this surface-ship advocate was now given command of two aircraft carriers for what could be a decisive fleet engagement.

The choice of Spruance caused many eyes to furrow. Granted, he could draw from the experience of Halsey's staff. Still, he was not an aviator. Halsey, however, had recommended him because, after years of close friendship, he knew Spruance to be an officer of great ability. In fact, he wrote:

> I consider him fully and superbly qualified to take command of a force comprising mixed types and to conduct protracted independent operations in the combat theater in wartime.[8]

Nevertheless, the aviators were skeptical.

Before leaving Pearl Harbor, Spruance received his orders from Nimitz who added this warning before finishing his conversation.

> "You will be governed by the principle of calculated risk, which you will interpret to mean avoidance of exposure of your force to attack by superior enemy forces without good prospect of inflicting, as a result of such exposure, greater damage on the enemy."[9]

Spruance boarded the *Enterprise* and set sail on May 28. Included in his Task Force 16 were two carriers; *Enterprise* and *Hornet,* six cruisers, and twelve destroyers. Fletcher's Task Force 17 would join him once the *Yorktown* was repaired. This force consisted of two cruisers and six destroyers in addition to the *Yorktown.* Furthermore, because he was senior to Spruance, Fletcher would exercise tactical command of the entire force.

Thanks to the code breakers' efforts, Spruance was informed of the Japanese order of battle. Heading for Midway were Vice Admiral Nagumo's Carrier Force built around four fleet carriers. Trailing three hundred miles behind was the main force of capital ships commanded by Yamamoto himself. There was also Admiral Kondo's Midway Invasion Force accompanied by a support group.

Added to the Japanese force was a fleet designated for the capture of the Aleutian Islands. This force included the Second Carrier Striking Force, an invasion force and a screening force all under the command of Admiral Hosagaya. From all points, west, northwest, and southwest, the huge enemy force was converging on tiny Midway. Spruance faced a David-Goliath situation, but hopefully, the breaking of the Japanese code would compensate somewhat for inferior numbers.

Spruance wanted to hit the Japanese before they hit him. He wisely considered the enemy carriers to be the primary target, followed by the battleships and cruisers. This was an ironic turn of events for one who held the battleship in deep respect. Now he was considering it a secondary target.

The greatest weapon in Spruance's arsenal was, of course, surprise. In order to insure that that surprise was thorough he ordered complete radio silence. On the thirty-first, he took station about three hundred-twenty-five miles northeast of Midway at a place designated Point Luck. On June 2, Fletcher with the hastily repaired *Yorktown,* arrived on station and assumed tactical command. However, he was wise enough to inform Spruance that during the heat of the battle he could feel free to operate independently.

Fletcher directed Spruance to take his force about ten miles distant from the *Yorktown.* The latter complied and readied his planes for immediate launching. On the morning of the third, search planes were airborne at first light looking for the enemy fleet. Both American commanders wondered if their intelligence was correct.

At midmorning the Japanese invasion force was sighted seven hundred miles southwest of Midway precisely where Nimitz had said they would be. American intelligence was correct. According to the intelligence in Spruance's possession then, the enemy carriers would be attacking Midway from the northwest early the next morning.

That night the three American carriers made ready. The

following morning the sun rose over a gentle sea. The sky was clear. It was a perfect day for war. American scout planes were up again searching for the enemy. At 5:34 A.M. a search plane from Midway located the Japanese carriers, but failed to give their position. Eleven minutes later the same plane reported a flight of enemy aircraft heading for Midway. Still there was no report of the exact location of the enemy fleet. The men aboard the American carriers were uneasy. Spruance wanted desperately to strike the Japanese carriers before they could launch a second attack against the island, but first they had to be found. Finally, a few minutes after 6:00, came the electrifying word that two enemy carriers and battleships heading for Midway were approximately one hundred eighty miles northwest of the island.

After studying the report, Spruance ordered his planes readied for launching. He did not care to wait, he was going for the enemy's jugular. Halsey's Chief of Staff, Capt. Miles Browning, was responsible for coordinating the launch. He recommended that it take place at 7:00. Spruance concurred.

Spruance's plan called for a coordinated attack by both the *Enterprise* and *Hornet* air groups flying in company. Then, when the enemy carriers were located, each group would attack independently. As current doctrine dictated, the dive bombers were to coordinate their attack with the torpedo planes skimming the surface of the waves. Both groups would be protected by a fighter escort.

In the midst of launching planes, Spruance was handed a message indicating a Japanese scout plane was on the horizon. Now more than ever he knew the enemy carriers had to be hit. The launching seemed to take an eternity. As the minutes ticked away, Spruance decided to send the dive bombers, already airborne, ahead of the torpedo planes. At 7:45 he gave Lt. Com. Wade McClusky the go-ahead to attack. So much for plans for a coordinated attack.

Nevertheless, he felt that to delay any longer would be too dangerous.

As the American planes winged their way toward the enemy, Spruance's formation remained alert to the possibility of a Japanese attack. Two hours passed and Spruance heard nothing from his pilots.

Meanwhile, Nagumo's planes had returned from attacking Midway. The admiral was still unaware that American carriers were in the vicinity. Consequently, he ordered the returning planes armed for another strike at the island. Shortly afterward, an attack by American B-17s from Midway firmed up his conviction that another attack on the target was essential. At that point a report from a tardy reconnaissance pilot announced the presence of American ships. Whether a carrier was present was not immediately ascertained. Then came word that an American carrier was indeed present.

Nagumo immediately ordered his aircrafts' armaments changed. High explosive and antipersonnel bombs were replaced by armor-piercing bombs. In their haste to complete the task the Japanese crews piled the off-loaded bombs carelessly around the decks of their ships. Precisely at that point, after hours of searching, American torpedo planes arrived on the scene.

The lumbering torpedo planes formed up for the attack. In small groups they picked out their targets and headed in. Between the Japanese combat air patrol and antiaircraft fire, the attack was a total failure. The *Hornet*'s Torpedo Eight was destroyed to a plane. The other planes fared almost as badly. After beating off the attack, Nagumo turned his fleet into the wind and prepared to launch. Then the American dive bombers arrived overhead.

The sacrifice of the torpedo planes had not been in vain. Their attack had lured the Japanese fighters down to the surface in defense of their ships. Consequently, when the American dive bombers arrived overhead, there was no combat air patrol to contest their attack.

Back aboard the *Enterprise*, Spruance waited agonizingly for results. He was able to monitor snatches of cryptic exchanges, but nothing definite. He would have to wait for his pilots to return before getting the full story. Meanwhile, what remained of the torpedo planes limped homeward. Many of the pilots were forced to ditch at sea. Some of the more fortunate ones managed to reach Midway. Spruance was disappointed with the early results.

Finally the dive bombers began to return. Little by little Spruance was able to piece together the facts of their attack. Three Japanese carriers were on fire. The brave assault by the torpedo planes had allowed McClusky's squadron to attack unimpeded even though they were low on fuel. Incredibly, the piecemeal American offensive had carried the day.

While Spruance was assessing this information, he received a frantic message from the *Yorktown* stating that she was under attack. Since he was in the midst of recovering aircraft, Spruance was unable to intercede. Sadly he watched as a large column of black smoke rose from the stricken *Yorktown*.

Spruance gathered himself and planned his next move. Obviously the remaining Japanese carrier had to be eliminated. But where was it? To avoid the pitfalls of the morning attack which saw his planes flying aimlessly in search of the enemy fleet, he decided to wait before sending out a new strike.

Browning urged Spruance to launch his planes immediately. The admiral, however, refused to be coerced into a wild-goose chase. The planes would not take off until confirmation was received of the location of that remaining enemy carrier.

In the meantime, the Japanese, thinking the *Yorktown* was a different carrier, attacked the luckless ship once more. Thanks to superb damage control the ship had remained operational after the first attack. This deluded the enemy into thinking that they were attacking an entirely different ship. Once more the *Yorktown* reeled under the incessant attack.

Even as the gallant carrier was undergoing the ordeal, her scout planes were searching for the ship's antagonist. Finally, the *Hiryu* was located. As soon as he received the sighting report Spruance sent his planes winging toward Nagumo's remaining carrier with orders to sink it.

Browning, however, dropped the ball. Although *Enterprise*'s planes were aloft immediately, the *Hornet* did not receive the launch order until half an hour later. Once more the attack would be uncoordinated. As far as Spruance was concerned, Halsey's staff had not passed the test.

A few hours later the *Hiryu* was a blazing wreck. Fletcher, meanwhile had been forced to abandon the *Yorktown* and turn tactical command over to Spruance. Therefore, it was up to the latter to determine the next move.

Midway still had to be protected. The Japanese surface force of battleships and cruisers remained intact. These ships could conceivably press on toward Midway. Spruance was faced with a dilemma. Should he proceed westward and intercept the enemy surface force or should he move out of harm's way?

Recalling Nimitz's injunction, Spruance decided not to risk a fleet encounter at night. Instead of intercepting the enemy he would position himself so that by morning he would be ideally situated to either oppose a landing on Midway or launch a strike against the remaining Japanese ships. Therefore he issued orders to move eastward until midnight, turn north for an hour, then move westward so that at first light he would be ready to meet any contingency. After issuing these orders, he retired for the night.

During the night Midway was subjected to a shelling from a Japanese submarine. In addition, four Japanese cruisers were reported to be approaching the island. An American submarine, the *Tambor* (Spruance's son Edward was aboard the *Tambor*), sent the enemy cruisers into a panic causing two of them, *Mikuma* and *Mogami,* to collide with each other. The undamaged ships made off at high speed leaving their two sisters to limp home on their own.

After breakfast the following morning an excited Browning urged Spruance to head full speed toward the enemy and attack them before they got away. The admiral hesitated. The weather was not ideal for flying and there was always the possibility that the Japanese still had one carrier left. (Actually they did have four small carriers which Yamamoto was recalling to join the main body of the fleet.) Before committing his own fleet, Spruance wanted to be sure. He did not launch any scout planes, preferring instead to rely on reports from submarines and Midway's patrol planes.

Nevertheless, by noon Spruance was on the move. He had finally decided to destroy the retreating enemy. In the interim Browning had developed an attack plan and circulated it among the squadron leaders. Upon receipt of the plan, Wade McClusky stormed onto the bridge and protested that Browning's plan was bad. He disputed the Chief of Staff's calculations.

McClusky claimed that the bombs his planes were to carry were much too heavy and the range was too far. His planes would not have enough fuel to accomplish the return trip to their carriers. A heated argument ensued during which Spruance sided with McClusky—to the dismay of Browning. Enraged, the Chief of Staff stormed from the bridge.

Despite the disagreement the American Fleet continued to close the gap on Yamamoto's retreating force. At 3:00 in the afternoon Spruance launched a strike toward the anticipated Japanese position. Unfortunately, the American planes were only able to locate two small ships which they attacked unsuccessfully. As the planes returned to their carriers darkness was beginning to settle over the fleet.

Fearing that many of the pilots would be lost due to lack of experience in landing on carrier decks in darkness, Spruance ordered the ships to illuminate their flight decks, a most controversial directive in light of the possibility that enemy submarines were lurking nearby. If this were true, the deck lights would make it easier for subs to discover the American carriers.

Another night of doubt as to the true Japanese intentions passed. On the sixth, search planes located the Japanese surface fleet approximately one hundred thirty miles southwest of the American position. Yamamoto was still retiring to the west. Spruance immediately ordered scout planes from his cruisers to maintain contact with the enemy.

At 8:00 A.M. the *Hornet* began launching planes. These were followed in short order by the *Enterprise*'s squadrons. The American planes attacked the unfortunate Japanese ships. Instead of the main body of Yamamoto's fleet, however, these ships proved to be the hapless *Mogami* and *Mikuma*. The Americans reported the sinking of one Japanese cruiser. This proved to be the *Mikuma*. *The Mogami,* her upper decks a twisted wreck, managed to limp away.

By evening Spruance knew that he would have to call off the pursuit. It was a painful decision, but his destroyers were low on fuel and the aviators were exhausted after three days of combat. Furthermore, he was acutely conscious that he would soon be in range of enemy aircraft based on Wake Island. Therefore, Spruance officially ended the battle.

Though criticized for terminating the pursuit, it was a wise move. Yamamoto still held one remaining trump card: a potential ambush by his surface force supported by land-based aircraft from Wake. Spruance refused to be lured into the trap. Instead, the American Fleet headed back to Pearl Harbor.

For his behavior during the battle, Spruance was awarded the Distinguished Service Medal. The accompanying citation read:

> For exceptionally meritorious service in a position of great responsibility as Task Force Commander, United States Pacific Fleet. During the Midway engagement, which resulted in the defeat of and heavy losses to the enemy fleet, his seamanship, endurance, and tenacity in handling his Task Force were of the highest quality.[10]

Magnanimously, Spruance remained silent about his reservations regarding Browning's performance. Ironically, the latter was also awarded the Distinguished Service Medal for his "brilliant execution and judicious planning."

Spruance was also unhappy with the performance of Rear Admiral Marc Mitscher who flew his flag on the *Hornet* during the battle. He blamed Mitscher for the carrier's uneven performance.

> Spruance's judgment of Mitscher was unfortunate because he would harbor a built-in prejudice for the wizened aviator.[11]

Indirectly, he blamed Mitscher for the loss of the *Yorktown* because the *Hornet* had failed to locate the Japanese carriers on June 4. Most of the carrier's planes flew aimlessly about without making contact with the enemy. Had they located the enemy force, Spruance maintained, they could have destroyed the enemy ship that later attacked the *Yorktown*. Fortunately, Mitscher was able to redeem himself later in the war.

What had Midway accomplished? It had halted Japanese expansion to the east, restored the balance of naval power in the Pacific, and removed the threat to Hawaii and the west coast of the United States. The Battle of Midway was truly a turning point in the war. Morison's comment on Spruance's handling of the battle was:

> Fletcher did well, but Spruance's performance was superb. Lord of himself yet receptive to advice, keeping in his mind the picture of widely disparate forces yet boldly seizing every opening—Raymond A. Spruance emerged from this battle one of the greatest fighting and thinking admirals in American naval history.[12]

On June 18, 1942, Spruance became the new Chief of Staff to CinCPac, Admiral Nimitz. He now found himself responsible for organizing the activities of a seventy-five-strong office staff in addition to being Nimitz's principal adviser.

Nimitz's responsibilities were awesome. His Chief of Staff's were no less. Nimitz had chosen Spruance because he believed the latter to be a clear thinker, an exceptional planner, and a brilliant strategist. The Battle of Midway reaffirmed this opinion.

Spruance moved into Nimitz's house at Makalapa, a compound located on the crater of an extinct volcano. The Commander in Chief and his Chief of Staff were totally compatible. They both enjoyed long walks and had similar tastes in music. Both admirals carried themselves with an air of confidence that placed most people at ease in their presence.

Spruance's efficiency made the machines at CinCPac headquarters run smoothly. He made wise and sound recommendations that greatly benefited the war effort. As an example: after personally witnessing the plight of the aviators he introduced a rotation system that sent new pilots to relieve those who had been at the front for long periods. The morale of the flyers soared. Heretofore, until the change was introduced, their only hope of relief was being wounded, captured, or killed.

During his term as Chief of Staff Spruance was called upon to answer those critics who felt he had been too conservative at Midway. Even afterward, when he assumed command of the Central Pacific Forces, his attackers continued to hurl their criticism at him. However, he answered his detractors by stating that his cautiousness was not timidity, but instead a deliberate weighing of the dangers in order to minimize risks. If lives could be saved, it was better to be cautious. Spruance was not a gambler. He preferred to know all the facts before acting. All the odds had to be stacked in his favor.

During the Guadalcanal campaign Spruance led, coordinated, and gave direction to the staff. This enabled Nimitz to provide broad direction and detailed support to the operation in progress.

In October, 1942, Nimitz dispatched Spruance to the South Pacific to personally observe the deteriorating war effort there. He was accompanied by Halsey who was preparing to assume command of the carrier forces. Upon arrival in the South Pacific, Halsey received orders from Nimitz to relieve Admiral Ghormley, Commander, South Pacific. Meanwhile Spruance visited Admiral Turner, commander of the amphibious forces at Guadalcanal. After visiting all commands he returned to Pearl Harbor and reported to Nimitz on the grim situation. Fortunately, thanks to Halsey's optimism and the determination and bravery of the naval, marine, and army forces, Guadalcanal was in American hands by February 1, 1943.

At the Casablanca conference in January, 1943, Admiral King lobbied for increased action against the Japanese. The prevailing strategy, however, opposed widening the Pacific war. The defeat of Nazi Germany had first priority. Nevertheless, King attempted to apply pressure on the British for their approval of a limited offensive in the Pacific. Reluctantly, the British agreed.

King then wired Nimitz on February 9, soliciting the latter's opinion about the prospect of seizing the Gilberts early in 1943. Nimitz responded negatively stating that he had neither sufficient ships nor troops.

Throughout 1943, however, plans took shape for a Central Pacific Offensive. It was not easy to convince the Joint Chiefs and the Combined Chiefs of Staff, or General MacArthur, Commander of the Southwest Pacific. King handled all the obstacles superbly and finally obtained the approval of all parties concerned, including the difficult MacArthur.

In March 1943, Nimitz sent Spruance to Washington to resolve future plans and in particular the problem of jurisdiction with MacArthur. Spruance distrusted the general and did all he could at the conference to counter any moves made by MacArthur's representatives who attempted to downgrade a Central Pacific Offensive in favor of handing MacArthur the dominant role.

On March 21, Spruance and King successfully submitted their proposals regarding the wisdom of the Central Pacific Strategy to the Joint Chiefs of Staff. Spruance argued for approval of an operation aimed at regaining the Japanese-occupied islands in the Aleutians. He went on to fight for a removal of any further threat to Hawaii by seizing the Marshalls and the Gilberts. Taking a unique approach, he argued that Pearl Harbor would be protected, not that it was a strategic approach to the defeat of Japan.

The Joint Chiefs absorbed all the information and gave Spruance approval for an advance against the Aleutians. The question of an advance across the Central Pacific remained unanswered.

Finally, in mid-June came word that the Joint Chiefs had

given their blessing to a two-pronged offensive against Japan via the Southwest Pacific and the Central Pacific. It was agreed that this twin offensive would apply continual pressure against the Japanese and keep them off balance. The offensives were scheduled to begin in the Marshalls with a target date of November 15, 1943.

Planning began immediately. The staff planners soon proposed a five-pronged attack against the Marshalls atolls of Wotje, Mili, Jaluit, Maleolap, and Kwajalein. Spruance objected to the plan saying that the seizure of five different targets was too ambitious. The fleet, he said, would be split and thus vulnerable to enemy counterattack. What was needed, he went on, was a suitable anchorage near the Marshalls that could serve as a fleet base and would provide logistical support for the attacking forces. Spruance also found the intelligence on the proposed targets to be nil. More air reconnaissance was necessary.

Spruance therefore recommended that the Gilbert Islands be taken first. The Gilberts, he argued, would provide bases which could be used to support the Marshalls attack. Airfields there would provide the means for both air reconnaissance and support. In addition, the lagoons in the Gilberts would provide excellent anchorages.

Initially Spruance's plan was rejected. Afterward, Nimitz changed his mind and agreed with his Chief of Staff's reasoning. The Joint Chiefs also approved the plan and on July 20 directed Nimitz to seize Tarawa Atoll and Nauru Island in the Gilberts during November. The operation was code-named Galvanic.

Meanwhile the subject of who would receive the coveted command of the operation was seriously debated by Nimitz. Obviously this command would be the most prestigious in the Pacific and competition for it would be fierce. Back in May, during a hike, Nimitz told Spruance that he would like to give him another chance at the Japanese, but his services as Chief of Staff were needed more. Though he was disappointed, Spruance had been brought up to accept orders. The following day, however, Nimitz told Spruance that he had thought things over and had decided to recommend him for the command pending Admiral King's approval.

On May 30, 1943, Spruance was promoted to vice admiral. Even before King's final approval was received he had already given thought to whom he wanted for Chief of Staff. He desired someone who was a hard worker, a good organizer, and an expert planner. Capt. Charles J. Moore, an old friend, had all these qualifications, so Spruance tabbed him for the position.

Early in June final approval of Spruance's appointment was given by King. He would lead the central Pacific offensive.

Spruance's assignment was to pierce the ring of Japanese defenses by assaulting the island bastions of the central Pacific. It was not an easy assignment. He knew that he needed an expert in amphibious warfare to command the operations and a marine general to lead the troops after they were ashore.

Spruance wasted little time in asking for Kelly Turner for the amphibs and Holland Smith of the marines. Turner was a brilliant tactician who had proven himself at Guadalcanal. Smith was a firebrand marine and expert on amphibious tactics and equipment. To command the carriers Spruance professed no preference. Nimitz appointed Rear Admiral Pownall to this position.

Planning for the Gilberts began in earnest. The Gilberts formally belonged to the British, but were seized by the Japanese shortly after the war began. Intelligence about the islands was scant. Betio Islet on Tarawa Atoll was selected as the primary target since it contained an airfield. Betio was approximately two miles long and about five hundred yards wide, approximately the size of Central Park in New York City.

Thanks to a Marine Raider attack on Makin Atoll in August, 1942, the Japanese made a determined effort to heavily fortify their islands. Tarawa was foremost among Japan's priorities and thus Betio was transformed into a veritable fortress. The Japanese commander on the island boasted that it would take a million marines a hundred years to conquer the fortress. In addition to hundreds of bunkers, beach obstacles, concrete fortifications, and a coconut-log wall around the entire islet, four thousand five hundred determined Japanese troops manned the defenses. In addition to these obstacles, the proximity of the Marshalls would allow the Japanese to mount bombing attacks against the fleet during the assault.

To offset this Spruance would have a vast array of ships, over two hundred of them in fact, including six fleet carriers, five light carriers, seven escort carriers, twelve battleships, fifteen cruisers, sixty-five destroyers, and a host of other vessels of lesser size. It was difficult to imagine that only one year previously the United States had but one carrier operational in the Pacific.

The two targets in the Gilberts were Tarawa and Nauru. While planning proceeded Spruance went to the South Pacific to meet with the various commanders who would be involved with Galvanic.

While in New Zealand he visited the Second Marine Division and its commander, Maj. Gen. Julian C. Smith. It was this division that would assault Tarawa. From New Zealand he traveled to Guadalcanal, Samoa, and Espiritu Santo in the New Hebrides where he conferred with Rear Admiral Harry Hill who was to command the ships supporting the amphibious troops. By August 22, Spruance was back at Pearl Harbor.

Later in the month Turner arrived at Pearl, followed a week later by Holland Smith. The first order of business was to clarify their respective fields of responsibility. Both were hard men to get along with and the two guarded their prerogatives with a passion. Carl Moore resolved the problem. Turner would be responsible for the men until they were established ashore where Smith would assume command. In addition to the differences between Smith and Turner, Spruance faced arguments from the army commanders. They resented a command structure that placed a marine general above them. There were also problems with the aviators who resented the fact that Spruance, a nonaviator, was given command of a fleet dominated by aircraft carriers.

On September 25, King arrived at Pearl Harbor to review Galvanic with Nimitz and Spruance. Originally, Tarawa and Nauru atolls were the designated targets. However, Turner and Smith both felt that Nauru Island should be scrapped in favor of Makin since the latter was closer to the Marshalls and large enough for construction of an airfield that could later be used during the Marshalls operation. Furthermore, Makin was close enough to Tarawa so that the fleet would be able to support both assaults simultaneously, whereas Nauru was too far removed from Tarawa. Assaulting Nauru would require splitting the fleet to support both landing points. Spruance agreed with his subordinates and argued the case before King who gave his approval for the substitution.

At the September conferences the Marshalls operation was also discussed. Nimitz wanted Kwajalein to be the primary target. Spruance, however, leaned toward Ujae Atoll, believing that it would provide an airfield that could be used to support a later invasion of Kwajalein.

Representing Spruance at that particular discussion was Carl Moore who argued his boss's case. Nimitz was peeved at Moore for bringing up the subject of Ujae Atoll in King's presence. He wanted to present a unified front to the Commander in Chief. Moore responded to Nimitz's anger by stating that he was only following orders.

While placing the finishing touches on the Galvanic

plan, Spruance became concerned about the Japanese Fleet and land-based enemy aircraft. He knew that once the assault began the Japanese Fleet would probably launch a counterattack. Tarawa and Makin must be taken quickly, he said, in order to free the fleet from having to provide close support to the vulnerable transports. As long as the transports remained in the vicinity, the fleet would have to protect them.

The naval aviators, particularly Admiral Towers, took exception to Spruance's decision to remain with the transports. Towers and his comrades believed that the carriers should be free to roam and use their offensive power to destroy Japanese air power at its source before the enemy could mount a counterattack against the American forces at Tarawa and Makin. Turner disagreed. After his experience at Guadalcanal during which the carriers were allowed to roam, he demanded a canopy of air protection. Thus he forcefully backed Spruance against the aviators.

Spruance compromised. He directed the carriers to hit Japanese air bases prior to the assault. Once the landings began, however, the carriers would have to provide air protection. The aviators were still upset at what they considered to be regressive strategy. With the power of the Pacific Fleet, it was foolish to wait for the enemy to make the first move. The criticism of Spruance and his almost universally nonaviator staff continued unabated.

After Spruance's final plan took shape it was submitted to Nimitz. It was detailed and precise in keeping with the personalities of both Spruance and Moore. In this respect Spruance differed greatly from Halsey who tended to operate less according to plan and more according to how the situation developed. In effect, Halsey was more flexible but less organized. Spruance, on the other hand, was super-organized with every point spelled out on paper and explained fully so that each subordinate knew at all times what was expected of him.

For Galvanic the carriers were to be divided. A Northern Attack Force, TF 52, would be under Turner and contain the Twenty-seventh Infantry Division, whose objective was the capture of Makin. A Southern Attack Force, TF 53, would be commanded by Admiral Hill and contain the Second Marine Division whose target was Tarawa.

As his flagship, Spruance chose the heavy cruiser *Indianapolis*. On November 5, 1943, his three-star flag broke out on the ship's mast. Five days later the *Indianapolis* and the rest of the ships of the Central Pacific Forces sailed from Pearl Harbor en route for the Gilberts to undergo a dangerous assault with mostly untried men.

Although the Second Marine Division had been in action at Guadalcanal, many recent recruits swelled its ranks. As for the Twenty-seventh Army Division, it was a New York State National Guard unit and as yet had not been subjected to hostile fire.

Spruance's flagship accompanied Turner's Northern Attack Force. He directed Turner to act as OTC (Officer in Tactical Command). This meant that the latter was responsible for courses, speeds, drills, exercises, and tactical dispositions of the force.

From Ellice Islands, Admiral Hoover's land-based aircraft began their pre-invasion bombardment and reconnaissance missions against the Gilberts. The carriers also began their pre-D-Day strikes against enemy land-based aircraft within range of the designated targets. Hill's Southern Attack Force moved up from the New Hebrides to rendezvous with Spruance and Turner. Spruance then joined Hill's force so as to be on hand at Tarawa.

On the eve of the assault, Spruance, as was his habit, demonstrated his calm by retiring to bed. Meanwhile, the fleet deployed for the next day's attack. All was quiet since the Japanese had not as yet detected the presence of the American Fleet.

Just before sunrise, red flares rose over Betio. The

astonished defenders scampered to their positions. Precisely at that time the large guns of the supporting ships commenced their D-Day bombardment and pounded the islet with their deadly heavy-caliber fire. The ships had the first crack at Betio. This was followed by an attack by the carrier planes. Then the ships took one last turn. Everyone felt that no one could possibly survive the devastating bombardment. Or could they?

From the *Indianapolis*, Spruance could see the marines moving toward Betio. His chief of staff recalled:

> Fires were burning everywhere, the coconut trees were blasted and burned, and it seemed that no living soul could be on the island. . . . The troops approached the beach, and it looked like the whole affair would be a walk-over.[13]

To Spruance's horror, the Japanese were very much alive. Moore's hope for a walkover failed to materialize. Quickly the battle degenerated into a bloody struggle. One thing after another went wrong. First the landing craft were unable to pass over the reefs; the expected depth of the water surrounding the islet proved erroneous. The marines, finding themselves hung up on the reef, had to disembark and wade to shore under a withering enemy fire. Landing craft burned and marine bodies littered the water. How could the Japanese have survived the pre-landing pounding?

The Japanese defenses were formidable. From Betio came the cryptic message "The issue is in doubt." It was at Wake Island in December of 1941 that the same issue-in-doubt statement was last used by the Marines. For a while it appeared as if the Central Pacific Drive would be ended before it even started.

Fierce fighting raged for the balance of the first day. It was four days before Betio was finally declared secure. The

Japanese commander's boast was exaggerated, it took less than a million marines and well short of a hundred years, but during the four-day battle one thousand marines lost their lives and another three thousand were wounded. The cost of one small hunk of coral and sand was excessive to say the least.

Spruance was upset at the length of time it had taken, but the slow progress at Tarawa could be excused by the heavy enemy fortifications. The situation at Makin was entirely different. The Twenty-seventh Division faced only eight hundred lightly armed Japanese troops and laborers. Spruance felt that sixty-five hundred GIs should have been able to take the island in one day allowing him to withdraw the fleet and avoid possible enemy attacks from the Marshalls. The army, however, took three days. During that time the supporting carrier, *Liscombe Bay,* was hit by a Japanese submarine resulting in a high toll of lives. If the army had taken Makin on the first day as anticipated, the *Liscombe Bay* would not have been sunk, Spruance felt. In a letter to Spruance, Turner lambasted the Twenty-seventh's lack of aggressiveness and poor leadership. Holland Smith made Turner's complaint sound mild.

The result of the army's poor performance and the scathing condemnation by Smith poisoned his relationship with the army forever and increased interservice rivalry to the detriment of the entire war effort.

By November 27, with both atolls secured, garrison troops and Seabees went to work turning the blasted, twisted islets into front-line military bases. H. Smith recalls what Betio looked like.

No words of mine can reproduce the picture I saw when the plane landed after circling that wracked and battered island. The sight of our dead floating in the waters of the lagoon and lying along the blood-soaked beaches is one I will never forget. Over the pitted, blasted island hung a miasma of coral dust and death, nauseating and horrifying.[14]

That same day, Spruance landed on Betio. After inspecting the island he understood why the prebombardment had failed to soften the island's defenses. Betio was a veritable fortress with concrete bunkers and pillboxes dotting the entire landscape. Each bunker was reinforced with logs and concrete. The only way they could have been eliminated was by a direct hit.

Nimitz also came to view the carnage. It was not a pretty sight that greeted him. For Spruance, this was his first direct encounter with the grotesqueness of war.

Spruance was anxious to get back to Pearl Harbor in order to begin planning for the Marshalls. After a two-week stopover in the Gilberts, the *Indianapolis* arrived at Pearl on December 11. No sooner had Spruance returned to Pearl than the controversy over Tarawa flared up. Was this island worth the price of a thousand lives?

Spruance defended the seizure of the Gilberts despite the high butcher's bill. Holland Smith grumbled that the Gilberts were not necessary and could have been bypassed. In retrospect, however, for want of experience and photographic intelligence, the Americans were in no position to bypass the islands and strike straight for the Marshalls. Tarawa provided the necessary experience and required air and naval bases. The success of further operations rested on the lessons learned at Tarawa. Betio became the textbook for further amphibious landings and assaults. Two most important lessons were learned: first, the need for prolonged air and surface bombardment; second, the need for more tracked vehicles.

With the seizure of the Gilberts behind him, Spruance continued to plan for the Marshalls. These islands are made up of thirty-two small island groups scattered over four hundred thousand square miles of ocean. The question facing the planners of the campaign, Operation Flintlock, was which islands to assault first. Nimitz preferred Kwajalein because of its twin airfields and excellent anchorage. Spruance disagreed. Instead, he leaned toward Wotje and Maloelap, astride the Kwajalein-Pearl Harbor line of communication.

Although Smith and Turner supported Spruance, Nimitz held firm. Armed with intelligence data indicating that the Japanese were strengthening the outer islands at the expense of Kwajalein, he decided that an attack on the latter would have a better chance of succeeding. Spruance feared, however that once Kwajalein was taken, the Japanese would use the surrounding air bases to mount attacks against the American lines of communication.

Nimitz met with Turner, Spruance, and Smith on December 14 in an effort to resolve the issue. After listening attentively to all the arguments, Nimitz stuck to his guns. Kwajalein would remain the primary target.

Resignedly, Spruance ordered his staff to plan for the seizure of Kwajalein and Roi-Namur, both of which sat in the large Kwajalein atoll. Moore offered a suggestion that made the plan more acceptable to Spruance. He recommended the simultaneous seizure of Majuro Atoll, approximately two hundred thirty miles to the southeast of the primary target. Majuro had an excellent lagoon which would make a splendid fleet anchorage. Spruance concurred and also proposed shifting D-Day from January 16th to the thirty-first. Nimitz gave his consent to the changes.

In planning for the assault on Kwajalein, Spruance called on the experience garnered at Tarawa. Overwhelming force was naturally a prerequisite. Thus he suggested three days of air and sea bombardment as compared to the three hours of the same at Betio.

Meanwhile, Spruance was also having problems with

Admiral Towers. The air commander at Pearl Harbor continued to resent the fact that Spruance, a battleship admiral, was commanding carriers. He disagreed with Spruance's strategy of harnessing the offensive power of the carriers and restricting it to support of amphibious assaults. Towers strongly criticized their use during Galvanic and openly disapproved of their intended use during the forthcoming operation. He was relentless in his insistence that the carriers be more mobile and allowed to range over the ocean, attacking and destroying enemy air bases and shipping. Spruance, he felt, reduced the carriers to a supporting role, rather than using them to spearhead the fleet. Carrier air power, Towers claimed, could defeat the Japanese on its own—not the costly amphibious assaults. Therefore, he insisted that the carriers have the freedom to seek out and decisively defeat the Japanese Fleet once and for all.

Spruance refused to accept Towers' theory. He felt that Towers and the aviators were oblivious to the problem of logistics. Spruance believed in the concept of overwhelming superiority. That meant that every objective to be assaulted had to be isolated from reinforcements. Only by use of sea and air power simultaneously could the target be isolated and systematically reduced. For that the carriers were essential and could not be allowed to roam free.

As was the case with Galvanic, Flintlock would have a northern and southern attack force. Rear Admiral Richard L. Conolly commanded the Northern Attack Force whose objective was Roi-Namur. The southern force, under Turner, had the capture of Kwajalein as its primary mission. Admiral Hill was to seize Majuro. Rear Admiral Marc Mitscher, who had succeeded Pownall, commanded Task Force 58, comprising six fleet carriers, six light carriers, eight battleships, six cruisers, and thirty-six destroyers. The Central Pacific Force now contained three hundred seventy-five ships, eighty-five thousand troops, and over one thousand aircraft.

Before leaving to command Flintlock, Spruance pored over the most recent reconnaissance photos of Eniwetok Atoll. They revealed that the atoll was not heavily defended, but they also indicated increased activity. If the enemy were allowed enough time, the defenses would be intensified. An attack on Eniwetok was scheduled for May 1. Spruance wished to move the assault up, but there was one problem with this, the carriers were scheduled to join Halsey in the south immediately after the capture of Kwajalein. By delaying until May 1, however, the Americans ran the risk of having Eniwetok become another Tarawa.

Spruance left Pearl on January 19, 1944, without any alteration to the plan. Apparently the capture of Eniwetok would have to wait for the already-agreed-upon date.

On the twenty-fourth Spruance arrived at Tarawa. He was amazed at the changes wrought on the atoll which only two months previously had been the scene of so much desolation.

By the evening of January 26, he was en route to Kwajalein. Three days later Mitscher sent the carrier planes of Task Force 58 over the Marshall Islands, hitting every Japanese air base in the area. That same evening battleships lobbed their heavy-caliber projectiles into the Japanese defenses. Kwajalein Atoll was completely isolated from Japanese planes and ships.

On D-Day, January 31, the remaining enemy strong points on Kwajalein and Roi Namur were bombarded. Majuro was captured by Hill with little trouble and its excellent anchorage was made ready to receive American ships. At Roi-Namur the marines poured ashore and moved quickly across the island. Within twenty-four hours they had secured their objective.

At Kwajalein, forty-five miles to the south, the Seventh Infantry Division, veterans of the fighting at Attu, were finding progress slower, but were no less successful. The Marshalls, supposedly the more difficult target, resulted in casualties much lower than at Tarawa. One hundred marines were killed on Roi-Namur, compared to over one thousand in the former battle.

The rapid seizure of Roi-Namur was gratifying. Admiral Hill had a reserve of nine thousand three hundred assault troops for use, but thanks to the swift victory these were no longer needed. King, Nimitz, Spruance, Turner, and Smith all conceived the idea of using this reserve against Eniwetok. Approval from the Joint Chiefs was forthcoming on February 3. The chiefs also gave their approval for a carrier strike against the Japanese naval bastion at Truk.

On February 3 the *Indianapolis* weighed anchor at Roi-Namur and sailed to Kwajalein to observe the continued fighting there. As usual, army tactics proved slower than those of the marines. Though the Seventh Division fought well it took four days to capture their objective compared to the one-day battle for Roi-Namur.

It is difficult to judge which tactic proved better. Obviously the marines were more than capable of producing a quick victory, but many times the casualty rate was high. The army, on the other hand, usually advanced slowly and methodically behind intensive artillery preparation, all the while protecting its flanks and keeping the line of advance intact. In contrast, the marines swarmed forward, overrunning enemy positions, and saving the mopping up of isolated pockets of resistance for later. The difference between the U.S. Army and Marine Corps doctrine resulted in an explosive climax in the Marianas.

D-Day for Eniwetok was set for February 17. To prevent Japanese interference, Task Force 58 was ordered to raid Truk again.

On the eighth, the *Indianapolis* steamed into Majuro harbor where the Central Pacific Forces had assembled. The next day Spruance transferred his flag to the battleship

New Jersey. On the tenth he received word that he had been promoted to full admiral, making him, at age fifty-seven, the youngest naval officer to hold that rank. The same day he issued orders for the seizure of Eniwetok and the raid on Truk. The latter was considered essential to the success of the Eniwetok assault.

Aboard his new flagship, Spruance left Majuro on the fourteenth in order to rendezvous with Mitscher. He then assumed tactical command from Mitscher, a departure from the normal method of operation. Not until Task Force 58 was near Truk did Spruance hand the reins back to Mitscher.

At 8:00 on February 16, the American carrier planes arrived over Truk. The Japanese were caught totally by surprise. As a result targets were plentiful. Spruance formed a battle squadron of capital ships and with himself in command moved to within twelve miles of the northern entrance to Truk Lagoon. At his insistence, the squadron engaged a damaged Japanese destroyer, to the chagrin of Moore whose staff was not prepared to direct ships in actual combat. Moore attempted to convince Spruance to turn tactical command over to one of the battleship captains whose staff was more experienced in dealing with the fluid battle situation of combat. Spruance refused. Perhaps this act of bravado was his symbolic way of impugning Japan's empire. Then again, it may have been the culmination of a lifelong dream, to lead a battleship division in combat. The opportunity to use the old battle line might never come again.

Early in the evening, however, he finally passed tactical command to Rear Admiral Robert Griffin of the *Minneapolis*. The results of the raid were satisfying. Almost forty enemy ships had been destroyed along with approximately two hundred enemy planes. Cost to the Americans was seventeen planes.

On the way back Nimitz suggested that the Task Force

raid the Marianas Islands airfields. He discussed the prospect with Mitscher and finally gave the go-ahead. Mitscher's superb handling of the Truk raid had renewed Spruance's confidence in the former's ability. Spruance ordered the *New Jersey* to return to Kwajalein.

While the *New Jersey* was en route, Hill's attack at Eniwetok occurred precisely on schedule. The operation proved highly successful. By the twenty-second, Mitscher's raid on the Marianas had also culminated in a triumph. Over one hundred Japanese aircraft and more than a dozen ships were destroyed. In addition the carrier pilots strafed and bombed shore installations. The Americans lost six aircraft.

The capture of the Marshalls represented a strategic and tactical victory. The U.S. forces could now use the islands as a staging area for amphibious assaults against the Carolines or Marianas. Incorporating the lessons of Tarawa, the tactics used in the Marshalls established a pattern that would be utilized for the rest of the war. The campaign also was a morale victory thanks to the relatively low rate of casualties; less than six hundred Americans had died. The entire Marshalls chain was in American hands.

In addition, confidence, which had waned after the disastrous Gilberts attack, was restored. For Spruance it was a personal victory. He had handled the fleet masterfully over the vast open expanses and brilliantly coordinated the many aspects of the campaign. His star was on the rise.

As stated in the King and Nimitz chapters, General MacArthur attempted to derail the central Pacific drive in deference to his own advance along the north coast of New Guinea into the Philippines. Admiral King, however, in defiance of MacArthur and Nimitz, who wanted to attack Truk, convinced the Joints Chiefs and later the Combined Chiefs, that the next objective should be the Marianas. King argued that the Americans could sever the Japanese lifeline from southeast Asia with the capture of the Marianas.

Using General "Hap" Arnold of the Army Air Force as an ally, King doggedly pushed his arguments until they were accepted. The Combined Chiefs of Staff accepted both a central Pacific thrust and MacArthur's southwest Pacific offensive. The two-pronged strategy had become official.

Nimitz continued to covet Truk and wanted it seized forthwith. Moore was against the idea, feeling that Truk could be bypassed. He also opposed the seizure of the Marianas, as did Nimitz. Moore felt that the best strategy was the one that placed American forces in China from where an attack on Japan could take place. He was of the opinion that an advance through New Guinea and the Philippines would put the U.S. forces in China faster than by any other route. Inadvertently, he advocated the same strategy urged by MacArthur and one totally anathema to King.

Moore placed his recommendations in a memorandum and gave it to Spruance on February 20. Spruance read them without comment. Moore also gave a copy of the memo to Admiral Pownall, the man scheduled to relieve Towers. The latter was about to become deputy CinCPac. Pownall showed the memo to Nimitz who expressed his approval. Spruance remained neutral.

The entire episode was academic. King turned thumbs-down on Moore's proposal, and pushed through the Marianas plan.

Meanwhile, MacArthur continued his efforts to derail the central Pacific offensive. Another Washington conference was held in early March. At this meeting the Joint Chiefs upheld the two-pronged attack and officially issued orders for the seizure of the Marianas in mid-June. When Nimitz returned from the Washington conference he informed Spruance of the decisions derived and ordered him to begin planning a carrier raid against Japanese air and naval bases in the Palau Islands in support of a MacArthur offensive on the north coast of New Guinea.

Spruance's staff completed the paperwork for the Palau raid by March 21. Task Force 58 would have eleven carriers, six battleships, thirteen cruisers, and forty-eight destroyers to complete the task. Two days later, aboard the *New Jersey*, Spruance ordered the fleet from Majuro lagoon for the two thousand-mile transit through Japanese-infested waters.

Unfortunately, Japanese aircraft soon spotted the American armada. Forewarned, the Japanese Fleet left the Palau anchorage. On the day of the American attack, March 20, the planes roared from the carriers toward the target. For the next three days the planes came and went with impunity, but Spruance was unable to form an exact estimate of what had been accomplished. He refused to break radio silence to report the results of the raid as long as he had no accurate information. Secretary of the Navy Knox wanted to know what was going on and pressed for information. Even Nimitz ordered Spruance to break radio silence, but to no avail. Finally, on April 6, when the *New Jersey* dropped anchor at Majuro, Mitscher reported to Spruance. Twenty-nine minor auxiliary ships sunk, seventeen more damaged, two hundred fourteen aircraft damaged or destroyed, and many shore installations damaged, some of them beyond repair. The Japanese Fleet, however, had escaped.

After the raid Spruance got down to the business of planning for the invasion of the Marianas, Operation Forager. In the midst of this planning, Spruance learned that he would have to relinquish Moore as his Chief of Staff after the operation. Thanks to a new policy, all nonaviators were to have aviators as their Chiefs of Staff and vice versa.

By mid-May the designs for the attack on the Marianas were complete. Spruance took advantage of the lull to visit California and spend time with his family before the demands of the war required his presence in the Pacific.

The Marianas would present the attackers with an

entirely different type of objective. Whereas the Gilberts and Marshalls were low-lying coral atolls, the Marianas were large, rugged islands, covered with thick vegetation, and contained towns with large civilian populations, many of whom were Japanese.

The Japanese felt that the Marianas had to be held at all costs. These islands represented the main bastion of their inner defensive ring. If they fell, the home islands would be placed in jeopardy. Consequently, the Japanese were determined to hold on to the Marianas at whatever the cost.

The Fifth Fleet's first objective was Saipan. Turner, along with Holland Smith, would direct the Northern Attack Force, made up of the Second and Fourth Marine Divisions with the Twenty-seventh Infantry Division in reserve. D-Day was scheduled for June 15, 1944. After Saipan was secured, Tinian, just to the south, would be assaulted.

A Southern Attack Force under Rear Admiral Richard L. Conolly and Marine Gen. Roy S. Geiger, consisted of the Third Marine Division, and the First Marine Brigade. In reserve was the Seventy-seventh Infantry Division. Their target was Guam. The date for the attack was tentatively set for June 18.

One major question that haunted the American planners was whether the Japanese Fleet, which had remained quiescent since late in 1942, would come out to fight for the Marianas. Spruance doubted that they would. Nevertheless, he prepared for the eventuality.

On May 26, Spruance left Pearl Harbor aboard his flagship and headed for the Marshalls where the Fifth Fleet had assembled for the operation. Task Force 58 had the responsibility for eliminating any Japanese air threat in the Marianas. Mitscher's force was to hit the islands from June 11 onward.

Meanwhile, the Japanese Fleet was making its own preparations. Since the beginning of the war it had been the desire of the Japanese Navy to destroy the American Fleet in a major naval engagement. In preparation for an American move toward the Marianas, the Japanese planned just such an engagement, Operation A-Go. The basic concept of A-Go was to lure the American Fleet to an area south of the Palau-Yap-Wolei line and bring it to battle with all their air, surface, and undersea forces.

Spruance's flagship crept to within eyesight of Saipan. Submarines kept him informed of the Japanese movements. Late in the evening of June 13, the submarine *Bowfish* reported that four enemy battleships, six cruisers and six destroyers were moving into the Sulu Sea north of Borneo. Was the Japanese Fleet on the move?

When Spruance received the report from the *Bowfish* he did not react immediately since the report was inconclusive. He decided to go ahead with the landings on Saipan as scheduled. However, he continued to press for further information on the movement of the Japanese Fleet.

As more information came in, it appeared as if the enemy was indeed intending to seek battle. In order to track the Japanese movements, Spruance ordered extensive searches by both seaplanes and whatever submarines were available in the area.

While the Americans prepared to take on the Japanese Fleet, the Marines landed on Saipan on June 15. By evening the D-Day objectives had been reached, albeit at a heavy cost. Nevertheless, Turner recommended that the Guam assault, scheduled for June 18, go ahead as planned.

On the evening of the same day, however, the submarine *Flying Fish* reported that a large Japanese naval force, including carriers and battleships, had entered the Philippine Sea via San Bernardino Strait, north of the Philippine island of Samar. At its current rate of speed the Japanese Fleet could be expected to reach Saipan in three days.

Spruance's initial reaction was to order the scattered

carrier groups of Task Force 58 to assemble near Saipan by June 17. For efficiency of command, the Task Force had been broken into four carrier Task Groups and a support group of battleships. Two of these groups, however, were en route to a mission against the airfields on Bonin and Volcano islands. Spruance did not order them to return immediately to Saipan, but he did direct them to limit their strike to one day. This would allow them to return to the vicinity of Saipan by the seventeenth.

On the morning of the sixteenth the submarine *Sea Horse* made contact with another enemy Task Force two hundred miles north of Mindanao. This force was also sailing into the Philippine Sea. A frightening specter now stared Spruance in the face. The western Philippine Sea seemed to crawl with Japanese ships. Obviously the Japanese were ready to risk their fleet in the long-sought-after major engagement. Spruance's first reaction was to postpone the Guam landings and to call for an immediate conference with Turner and Smith. What he did not know, however, was that the two Japanese formations were headed for a rendezvous with each other.

At the conference with his subordinate commanders Spruance told them of the Japanese advance. His immediate concern was for the vulnerable transports. He asked Turner if they could be moved to the east, out of harm's way. Turner answered that this was impossible in light of the fierce fighting ashore. The transports, he said, with their vital supplies, could not be spared from the beachhead. Mitscher would have to keep the Japanese at bay with his carriers.

On the seventeenth, Spruance's scout planes began to search for the Japanese Fleet. No contact was made. He wrongly assumed that the enemy's primary target was the transports. Since the Japanese were advancing from two different directions, or so he thought, Spruance feared that they might attempt to turn his flank and descend on the helpless transports. He was thus wary of any move that would draw him out and allow the Japanese to sideslip him. He would not deviate from his position that his primary objective was the protection of the transports. The destruction of the Japanese Fleet, though desirable, was secondary to the primary objective. The transports could not be jeopardized.

Spruance composed his battle plan.

> Our air will knock out enemy carriers as operating carriers . . . then will attack enemy battleships and cruisers to slow or disable them.[15]

This plan was based on the assumption that the Japanese would approach close enough for a fleet engagement. But what if the Japanese limited their attack to long-range carrier air strikes? Their carrier planes outranged the Americans'. Since Spruance was obsessed with protecting the transports would he allow the carriers to move westward within range of the Japanese Fleet and leave the transports without air cover? Those questions were left unanswered in the battle plan.

Thus his plan was ambiguous. What was Mitscher's primary objective? To sink the Japanese Fleet or to protect the transports? The vagueness of the plan would raise controversy later on. On June 17, the two objectives did not seem incompatible. Nevertheless, when battle finally did ensure, their incompatibility became obvious.

> The two missions seemingly would become impossible to achieve simultaneously.[16]

A battle line of battleships under Admiral Lee was positioned twenty miles to the west. Behind this line were the carriers with the four Task Groups operating independently on a north/south axis. The rationale for this

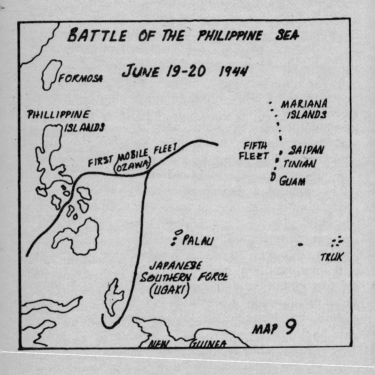

BATTLE OF THE PHILIPPINE SEA

JUNE 19-20 1944

FORMOSA

PHILLIPPINE ISLANDS

FIRST MOBILE FLEET (OZAWA)

MARIANA ISLANDS

FIFTH FLEET

SAIPAN

TINIAN

Guam

PALAU

TRUK

JAPANESE SOUTHERN FORCE (UGAKI)

MAP 9

NEW GUINEA

formation was threefold. First of all, the battle line could blast the Japanese planes with antiaircraft fire as they passed overhead en route to their main target. Secondly, the enemy planes, seeing the battleships, might be tempted to hit the expendable surface ships instead of the valuable carriers. Finally, if the en:my surface ships approached the American battle line, an old-fashioned broadside battle could take place with the heavily armored surface vessels able to protect the thin-skinned carriers.

Meanwhile, on land the fighting raged savagely and the casualties mounted steadily. Over fifteen hundred Americans were killed during the first three days alone.

The Japanese Fleet continued to baffle Spruance. During the night of the seventeenth he received reports of its whereabouts, but dared not move his own fleet. Thus he passed the initiative to his opposite number, the Japanese Admiral Ozawa. They would have to make the first moves—to the disgust of the American aviators.

On the eighteenth, search planes scouting to the west continued to send back negative reports. The Japanese were still beyond range. Spruance decided to allow Mitscher's carriers to move westward until midnight, but not a minute longer. If no contact was made by then, they were to reverse course and head back to Saipan. Mitscher radioed the Fifth Fleet commander that he would like to continue the advance beyond midnight, but Spruance reaffirmed his original order. His fear for the transports continued to dominate strategy and would cost the Americans an overwhelming victory.

On the morning of the nineteenth, Mitscher launched his search planes once more. Again nothing was found. Then, a few minutes before 9:00 A.M, Spruance received a delayed sighting report from a long-range seaplane based at Saipan. It had made contact with a large enemy force at the exact spot to which Mitscher had asked permission to advance. Still Spruance refused to give Mitscher the go-ahead. The other Japanese force was still unaccounted for. Spruance had no way of knowing that the two had actually merged into one large formation before splitting once more, but to be mutually supportive of each other, not to act independently. Unless he could account for every enemy naval force within range of Saipan, Spruance would not risk exposing the beachheads by sending the carriers away.

At 10:00 A.M. radar detected the approach of hundreds of Japanese aircraft. The American carriers quickly turned into the wind and launched their own planes. As envisioned, the Japanese planes concentrated first on Admiral Lee's battle line of surface ships, the first targets they ran across. Lee's ships were like magnets as the enemy planes swarmed all around. The sky became black with flak. Into this melee dived the American planes. A series of spectacular aerial duels ensued. Like autumn leaves, hundreds of flaming Japanese aircraft splashed into the sea. Throughout the day the battle raged as wave after wave of Japanese planes was intercepted and turned back, but the source of the enemy planes, the carriers, remained undetected. Though search planes continued their efforts, no contact was made.

By mid-afternoon Spruance's fear of an end run had abated. The great loss of enemy planes convinced him that the transports were relatively safe. He thus ordered Mitscher to search aggressively and attack westward.

By early evening, after the last American plane had landed, Task Force 58 was moving at high speed westward toward the anticipated location of the Japanese Fleet. Reports from a submarine indicated that Ozawa's force was approximately three hundred seventy-five miles to the west of Mitscher.

Spruance added up the day's total. In the spectacular air duel the Japanese had lost three hundred eighty-three planes to only twenty-five for the Americans. The U.S. pilots had appropriately given the battle a nickname, "The

Great Marianas Turkey Shoot."

With the offensive sting removed from the enemy, the belated advance on the unscathed carriers was on. Reports came in stating that one Japanese carrier had been struck by a torpedo from an American submarine, but other than that, the fleet remained intact.

By mid-morning of the twentieth, the exact whereabouts of the Japanese force was still a mystery. Spruance gave orders to continue searching all day and if no contact was made by evening, then the fleet would have to return to Saipan. In the middle of the afternoon, however, the Japanese ships were finally located.

According to the sighting reports the enemy formation was at the extreme range of attack aircraft, and with darkness approaching, recovering the planes would be a risky matter since most of them would be low on fuel. In the darkness, the pilots would be unable to locate their own ships easily. Despite the obstacles, Mitscher wanted to proceed with the attack.

Admiral Ozawa, upset over having his flagship, the carrier *Taiho,* sunk from under him by a submarine, put eighty planes in the air to act as a combat air patrol. Mitscher's mighty air arm headed directly for them.

By the time darkness forced the American planes to break off the attack, the carrier *Hiyo* had been blasted to the bottom of the ocean, *Zuikaku* and *Junyo* were battling raging fires, three tankers had been sunk, and two heavy cruisers were fighting to stay afloat. Sixty-five planes of the combat air patrol were also splashed by the skillful American pilots. The Japanese wisely broke off the action and retreated. Ozawa left the Philippine Sea with but thirty-five planes remaining on the decks of his surviving carriers. Though the bulk of the Japanese force made good its escape, its offensive punch had been destroyed. Never again would the proud Japanese carrier force be a factor in battle.

The returning American planes arrived over Task Force 58 in the darkness. Despite the potential threat of Japanese submarines, Mitscher ordered all carriers to turn on their lights to aid the pilots. Flashing different-colored beacons to designate individual ships, Mitscher's carriers guided their pilots home. For many it was too late. But for the majority of the American pilots the sight of that huge force glowing like a Christmas tree was the most welcome sight they had ever seen. Seventy-three planes ran out of fuel and never made it back, but most of their pilots were fished out of the water by destroyers or patrolling submarines. Thanks to the decision to illuminate the fleet, however, the vast majority of the American planes landed safely.

Throughout the next day Task Force 58 continued westward in vain. The Japanese were gone. At 8:00 that evening, Spruance ordered the force back to Saipan. The Battle of the Philippine Sea was over.

"The enemy fleet had escaped," Mitscher disappointedly wrote in his battle report. Before the ink had even dried, criticism from the aviators of the fleet abounded. Towers went so far as to demand that Spruance be fired for his inept handling of the fleet.

Despite the criticism, Spruance had accomplished his goal of protecting the transports. The aviators, however, countered this by insisting that he had placed the carriers in jeopardy by holding them back until the Japanese made the first move.

Fortunately, the Japanese planes were destroyed during the air battles of the nineteenth without harm to the carriers. The story might have been a very different one indeed if the enemy had broken through and hit Task Force 58. The aviators lambasted Spruance for not having given Mitscher the go-ahead to search out and destroy the Japanese carriers early in the battle before they could launch their planes. Fortunately, the Japanese pilots were not of the same caliber as those of the early months of the war.

Actually, Spruance could have ordered the transports out of harm's way as early as the eighteenth. When he had first asked Turner on the sixteenth if the transports could be moved, Turner had said no, because their presence was urgently required at Saipan thanks to the intensity of the battle. However, though the fighting remained fierce, the presence of the transports was not nearly as critical on the eighteenth as it had been two days previously. They could easily have been moved eastward. Then, with them safe, Mitscher's carriers could have been allowed freedom of action. Acting on the premise that the transports were still needed offshore, Spruance never broached the question during his later meeting with Turner.

Spruance also misread Ozawa's intentions. He thought the Japanese admiral would split his forces, using one as a decoy while the other sideslipped and attacked the American beachhead. But Ozawa did just the opposite. He concentrated his fleet and never had any intention of doing otherwise. Unhappily for him, the Japanese pilots were so ill-trained that they were devastated before they could accomplish their primary mission, the destruction of the American carriers, not the transports.

In all, the Japanese lost four hundred sixty-seven planes and four hundred forty-five pilots. On the other hand, the Americans lost one hundred thirty planes, but only forty-three pilots. U.S. submarines sank two carriers, while Mitscher's pilots destroyed one more and damaged two others. Six Japanese carriers did survive, however.

Although the surviving enemy carriers made good their escape, they were empty shells. There were few planes or pilots left. Nevertheless, Spruance continued to be criticized. To his dying day he maintained that his actions at the Philippine Sea were the best policy. At the beginning of such a large and important amphibious operation, Spruance felt he could not afford to gamble and place the entire operation in jeopardy. When Admiral King met with

Spruance during a visit to Saipan, he told the latter point-blank that his conduct during the battle was above reproach. Perhaps King was just being polite.

While the controversy swirled, the land battle continued unabated. The Twenty-seventh Infantry Division landed to support the marines. On June 24, Holland Smith told Spruance that he wished to fire Maj. Gen. Ralph Smith, the Twenty-seventh's commander. According to Holland Smith the division was demonstrating the same lack of aggressiveness as it had at Makin. He placed the blame on the division's commander, Ralph Smith, and wanted him relieved. Thus Spruance found himself in the unenviable position of a naval officer being advised by a marine officer to fire an army general. Interservice cooperation was bound to suffer.

Ralph Smith was replaced by Major General Jarman. The performance of the Twenty-seventh did not change radically so on June 28, Major General George W. Griner replaced Jarman.

In a letter to Nimitz, Spruance told his boss that the relief of Ralph Smith was regrettable but necessary. Luckily for Spruance, the Army did not focus its odium on him, but rather on Holland Smith. In his postwar book, *Coral and Brass*, Smith vented his anger at the army and its tactics, an anger he rarely hid during the campaign.

While the fighting on Saipan continued, Spruance frequently went ashore to see firsthand how the battle was proceeding. In his book, Holland Smith commented on a Spruance visit.

Another visitor to my Saipan headquarters was Spruance who was always eager to learn firsthand what was happening. The admiral caused me many anxious moments. He refused to wear a steel helmet or green dungarees. Instead he came ashore in conspicuous khaki uniform which made him a first-class target for a Japanese sniper. He coolly disregarded measures for his safety by exposing himself in the forward areas, which he generally visited unarmed, accompanied only by an aide. I finally had to call him down for his recklessness. "Admiral", I said, "you are in command of this entire operation, but I am in command ashore. I cannot let you come onto the beach unless you follow the route I prescribe and let me send an armed escort with you!" Being above all a reasonable man, Spruance agreed.[17]

On July 3 with the Saipan campaign winding down, Spruance was ready to select a date for the invasion of Guam. He recommended July 25. That date would allow the Seventy-seventh Infantry Division time to arrive off Guam. Nimitz pressed for an earlier date since June 18 had originally been proposed for the invasion date, but Spruance, counseled by his marine advisors, was told that the full weight of the Seventy-seventh was vital for success. A compromise was reached when Nimitz offered to provide more transports. This would allow the Seventy-seventh to arrive at Guam as a complete unit. Therefore, the date was advanced to July 21. As for Tinian, D-Day depended on the completion of the Saipan operation since the same forces would be involved.

Saipan was finally secured on July 9, although months of mopping up remained. Turner recommended that the assault on Tinian take place on July 24. A conflict arose as to which beaches on the island to assault. In the chapter on Kelly Turner this conflict will be examined in depth.

In the interim, various notable visitors arrived at Saipan to view the battlefield. One of these was Lt. Gen. Robert Richardson, the senior army general in the central Pacific. He wished to inspect personally the fitness of the Twenty-seventh Division in order to refute Holland Smith's accusations. Spruance ordered Smith not to argue no matter how provoked he became. Smith complied, but not Turner, who was quite rude to Richardson. The army general, insulted by Turner's behavior, denounced him to Spruance who made light of the incident by saying that it was simply Kelly Turner's way. Richardson was not pacified. Interservice squabbling could have destroyed any future operations if it weren't for Nimitz, who managed to soothe everyone's ill feelings.

On July 17, King and Nimitz arrived on Saipan.

> King's first act on stepping ashore was to tell Spruance that he had done exactly the correct thing with the Fifth Fleet in the Battle of the Philippine Sea, no matter what anyone else might say . . . King repeated to Spruance that his decision had been entirely correct.[18]

During one of the meetings, King asked Spruance what the next objective should be. Spruance responded, Okinawa. King, however, had designs on Formosa, but he kept his ears attuned to the proposals of the Fifth Fleet commander.

As D-Day for Tinian and Guam approached, the bombing of targets on the islands intensified. A new type of jellied gasoline, napalm, was used for the first time. Its effects, Admiral Hill commented, were "awe-inspiring."

The landing on Tinian went like clockwork and the island was quickly overrun. At Guam, weeks of difficult fighting lay ahead, but another island fortress eventually fell to the American attackers.

With the operation all but over, the Fifth Fleet was turned over to Halsey and its numerical designation became the Third Fleet. Spruance returned to Pearl Harbor to plan for the next operation which at the time was still un-specified.

In mid-August, Rear Admiral Art Davis arrived at

Saipan and reported to Spruance with orders to relieve Moore as the admiral's Chief of Staff. Spruance lost an old friend.

By the fall of 1944, the noose was being tightened around Japan. From the newly acquired bases in the Marianas, B-29s attacked the Japanese homeland. Halsey invaded Peleliu on September 15, and MacArthur made his dramatic return to the Philippines in October.

Spruance, however, wondered about his next assignment. Early in September, Nimitz told him that the next attack would be made against Formosa, a target coveted by King but not particularly to the liking of Spruance. Instead, he preferred to concentrate on Iwo Jima and Okinawa.

Spruance wanted Iwo Jima primarily for use as an air base because of its strategic location astride the Marianas-Japan line. It would supplement reliance upon the carriers in addition to providing an emergency airfield for damaged bombers returning to the Marianas from Japan. As for Okinawa, Spruance knew that possession of this island would give the Americans control of the East China Sea from where they could blockade Japan. Deep down, he hoped that an invasion of the Japanese homeland would not be necessary.

Nevertheless, Formosa remained the designated target. Undaunted, Spruance flew to California for a brief vacation with his family. While there he was summoned by Nimitz to meet with him and King in San Francisco on September 29. Nimitz's staff was going to attempt to persuade King to abandon Formosa. The staff report recommended Iwo Jima and Okinawa as alternatives. The debate was furious, but King finally relented, albeit reluctantly.

Planning for an attack on Iwo Jima began as soon as Spruance returned to Pearl Harbor. Holland Smith commented that Iwo could be hard to take and would cost many lives. The pessimistic assessment of his marine general disturbed Spruance. Nevertheless, planning continued.

Iwo Jima is an island five miles long and a little over two and one-half miles wide. Its southern end is dominated by a five hundred fifty-foot-high extinct volcano, Mount Suribachi. This pork-chop-shaped island lacks vegetation. Instead, it is covered by a black volcanic ash. It promised to be a difficult operation.

The Japanese correctly guessed that Iwo Jima would be one of the next American objectives and began to turn it into a fortress. Caves and tunnels were quickly dug. Every inch of the island was made into a killing zone filled with twenty thousand determined, fanatical Japanese under a highly skilled commander, General Kuribayashi.

Though the island was subjected to repeated bombing by American aircraft based in the Marianas, the defenses were so heavy that most were impervious to anything but a direct hit. In six months of repeated bombing, little was achieved. Because of this, Holland Smith advocated a ten-day pre-invasion bombardment in hopes that the heavy-caliber guns of the capital ships might make a difference. Turner, however, said that only a three-day bombardment was possible. He and Smith compromised on four days, but were overruled by Spruance who was concerned with Japanese air attacks from Japan. Three days was all the bombardment that would be allowed.

Spruance planned to send Task Force 58 on a potentially dangerous mission against enemy air bases in Japan itself. If Iwo was assaulted before Mitscher began his attack on the Japanese airfields, it would alert the enemy and jeopardize the carriers. Spruance wanted the initial surface bombardment to coincide with the carrier attacks. The Marines later blamed the lack of sufficient preinvasion bombardment for the high number of casualties.

Spruance was still bothered by the skepticism of his marine commanders. Would Iwo Jima be worth the prospective cost? On January 28, Maj. Gen. Curtis LeMay, the commander of the Twenty-first Bomber Command in the Marianas discussed the forthcoming operation with Spruance. LeMay convinced the admiral of the importance of Iwo Jima. The bombing of Japan, the general said, would be significantly increased with fewer casualties to the airmen if the island was in American hands. Spruance was reassured.

For Iwo Jima three marine divisions were scheduled to make the assault. They were under the overall command of Maj. Gen. Harry Schmidt. On February 11, the invasion fleet comprising nine hundred ships assembled off Saipan. Unhappily, Turner picked this time to become ill and there was a question whether he would be well enough to take part in the attack on Iwo. Spruance felt great anxiety. Not only was Turner his best friend, the latter's expertise was considered indispensable to the operation. Fortunately, Turner recovered in time.

As previously noted, to help cover the Iwo Jima attack the carriers of Mitscher's Task Force 58 were to raid Japan, the first raid of the home islands since Doolittle's attack in April, 1942. Spruance was apprehensive about taking his carriers so close to Japan, but he felt that the operation was a vital corollary to success at Iwo.

In heavy rain, the planes of Task Force 58 lifted from the decks of their carriers, formed up, and sped off toward their designated targets. Aboard his flagship, *Indianapolis*, Spruance monitored the results. The attacks came as a complete surprise to the enemy. By evening, the American planes had destroyed three hundred fifty aircraft, blasted airfield installations, and sunk or damaged thirty-three ships at the cost of thirty-two planes of their own. The next day the planes were up again searching for more targets. The weather was just as bad, but the pilots were not discouraged. Spruance, however, felt that the deteriorating weather mitigated against a continuation of the operation.

A little after noon, he directed Mitscher to cease launching planes. After recovering his aircraft, Mitscher retired toward Iwo Jima.

Hoping that the prelanding bombardment had done its job, Spruance gave the order for the landing to begin as scheduled on February 19, 1945, thus initiating a month-long battle, the bloodiest in Marine Corps history. The twenty thousand Japanese on the island were determined to hold on. Before the battle was over, thirty thousand Americans became casualties. From the deck of his flagship, Spruance watched as Old Glory was unfurled atop Mount Suribachi on the fifth day of the battle. Despite initial successes, the fighting continued unabated deep into March. Meanwhile, Task Force 58 left for another raid on Japan.

Early in March as the battle raged, Spruance and Turner returned to Ulithi to begin making preparations for the invasion of Okinawa. Eventually, the bloody fighting on Iwo Jima ground down to its inevitable conclusion. The heavy toll of lives weighed heavy on the Fifth Fleet commander's heart, but he was soon to take consolation from the fact that strategically, Iwo Jima would play an important part in winning the war.

For the invasion of Okinawa, Spruance would command fifteen hundred ships, the largest fleet in history. Aboard the ships were one hundred eighty-two thousand assault troops of Lt. Gen. Simon Bolivar Buckner's Tenth Army.

Spruance was primarily concerned with enemy air attacks against the fleet. Okinawa's proximity to enemy airfields in the home islands, Formosa, and the remaining Ruyuku Islands made the task of achieving air superiority rather difficult.

To diminish the threat, Spruance directed Mitscher to hit Kyushu again on March 18 and 19. Once more Spruance emphasized the importance of surprise. On the fourteenth, he set sail on the *Indianapolis* for Ulithi to rendezvous with Mitscher. Unfortunately, the Fifth Fleet was spotted before it reached its launching point. Consequently, during the raid the Japanese retaliated, causing moderate damage to a few of the carriers. One carrier, the *Franklin*, sustained heavy damage. In all, four of Mitscher's eleven carriers had to depart for repairs. This was the first significant damage suffered by Spruance's carriers since the beginning of the central Pacific drive.

Though it was estimated that five hundred fifty enemy planes were destroyed during the raid, many more remained hidden away waiting for the opportunity to pounce on the American Fleet when it arrived off Okinawa.

During the final days of March the heaviest preinvasion bombardment to date took place against Okinawa. Then, on March 31, D-1, a Kamikaze hit the *Indianapolis*. The resulting fires were quickly extinguished, but the ship was forced to head for the recently occupied Kerama Retto, a small island off Okinawa which the Seventy-seventh Division had captured five days earlier for the express purpose of providing a haven for damaged ships. The services of the *Indianapolis* were lost.

The landing at Okinawa was unopposed. The ominous quiet of the landing, unfortunately, did not dispel the impending bitterness of the battle. The Japanese deliberately forfeited the beachhead. Their previous experiences had taught them that they could not turn back the invasion. Instead, what they did was to establish themselves in tunnels and caves deep within the bowels of the island. Over one hundred forty thousand determined defenders were prepared to sell their lives dearly.

With the *Indianapolis* disabled, Spruance shifted his flag to the battleship *New Mexico* on April 5. The next day the first of nine massive air attacks hit the American Fleet. Over seven hundred Japanese planes, half of which were the dreaded Kamikaze, flung themselves headlong at the American ships.

In Japanese, Kamikaze means "divine wind." The pilots believed that by crashing themselves and their aircraft into Allied ships they would achieve godhood. Some had even attended their own funerals before taking off. Then they climbed into their aircraft and were airborne.

"I am determined to destroy with my own body the enemy ships that menace our holy soil. I shall strike without returning."[19]

This was their sacred vow.

The Kamikazes came by the droves. Combat air patrols and antiaircraft fire were the only weapons available for use against the deadly foe. By the time the Kamikazes were through, over thirty Allied ships were sunk and three hundred sixty-eight others damaged. It was the worst damage suffered by the navy throughout the entire war.

The Japanese were intent on pulling out all the stops. They also sent the remainder of their surface fleet in one final attack. There was only enough fuel available for a one-way journey. Among the suicide craft was the super battleship, *Yamato*, formerly the flagship of the great Admiral Yamamoto. The *Yamato* was intercepted by Mitscher's carrier planes and sunk along with her escorts.

On land the campaign was savage with the dead on both sides mounting rapidly. Spruance lamented the length of the campaign and wondered if the Marines could have taken the island faster, though he never openly expressed his feelings. He knew, however, that the longer the campaign took, the longer his fleet would remain exposed to Japanese air attack.

On May 12, the *New Mexico* was hit by a Kamikaze. Spruance pitched in and helped extinguish the raging fires. Realizing that the lengthy battle was exacting a heavy toll on the commanders, Nimitz ordered Halsey, Hill, and McCain to relieve Spruance, Turner, and Mitscher respectively. On midnight, May 27, Spruance left bloody Okinawa aboard his flagship bound for Guam where he would begin planning for the final assault: Japan.

On June 1, Spruance shifted his flag to a shore headquarters at Guam. Debate ensued as to what approach to take next. After his experience of fighting the Japanese across the Pacific, Spruance was not anxious to invade Japan. Rather, he wanted to blockade the home islands. He also advocated reinforcing the Chinese Army and using it to smash the Japanese Army in China. However, he failed to take into consideration America's impatience with continuing the war via an indefinite blockade. He assumed that the blockade would cause the Japanese to do something they had never before done, surrender voluntarily. He also erred in thinking that reinforcing China's Chiang Kai-shek would make the Chinese leader fight the Japanese in a more spirited and determined manner. Chiang's performance to date had been less than satisfactory.* Thus, when it came down to the bottom line, invasion was the only option. Or was it?

Early in August Spruance assembled his staff in his office and read a top-secret dispatch stating that within a few days' time, a new type of bomb, an atomic bomb, would be dropped on two Japanese cities. He hoped that the bomb would convince the Japanese to surrender without having to resort to an invasion. Gratefully, the atomic bomb achieved its purpose. Following the dropping of the bombs on Hiroshima and Nagasaki, and after having been insured of the inviolability of the emperor, Japan capitulated on August 14, 1945.

Spruance's first assignment after the cessation of hostilities was to land General Kruger's Sixth Army on western Honshu, Kyushu, and Shikaku to carry out occupation

*See *The Great Commanders of World War II, The Americans,* Chapter IV, Stilwell.

duty. Spruance himself was not present for the September 2 peace-signing ceremony in Tokyo Bay. Instead, he was aboard the *New Jersey* at Okinawa.

Spruance viewed the occupation of Japan not as a punitive measure taken by a conquering nation, but rather as a means of rebuilding and reestablishing a strong ally in the western Pacific. He wanted it to be an enlightened and forward-looking occupation. Spruance arrived in Japan on September 15, and immediately set to work repatriating the thousands of Allied prisoners of war held in Japan.

In early November, Towers relieved Spruance as commander of the Fifth Fleet. Later in the month, Spruance replaced Nimitz as CinCPac. He remained in this position until February, 1946, when he was again relieved by Towers. Spruance returned to the United States to become president of the Naval War College.

The new Chief of Naval Operations, Fleet Admiral Nimitz, gave Spruance a directive to revitalize and modernize the curriculum at the war college. Spruance emphasized interdependence of strategy, tactics, and logistics, and incorporated those lessons learned during combat and fit them into the studies. Under his leadership, the college grew in size. Its revitalized curriculum fit the navy of the future.

When he reached the age of sixty-two in July, 1948, Spruance retired and settled down in California to what he hoped would be a quiet retirement. He quickly acquired a great liking for horticulture and became an avid gardener.

In January, 1952, Admiral Spruance was nominated to be ambassador to the Philippines. Because of the threat of Communism in that country, it was felt that the situation demanded a military man who could think for himself, one of integrity, wisdom, and who was knowledgeable in foreign affairs, government, and economics.

Spruance's years as ambassador coincided with a stormy presidential election in the Philippines which saw him back the pro-American candidate, Ramon Magsaysay. As Philippines Ambassador he occasionally intervened in the nation's internal affairs, which was more than was allowed by protocol. After three stormy years in office, he retired once more in the spring of 1955.

At the age of sixty-nine Spruance returned to his gardening, but by the late 1960s his health started to deteriorate. Arteriosclerosis began to dim his once-sharp memory. In 1969, a fatal accident took the life of Spruance's only son, Edward. After the tragedy his own health went rapidly downhill. On December 13, 1969, he passed away. Spruance was buried with full naval honors next to Chester Nimitz and Richmond Kelly Turner.

Raymond Spruance was America's steadiest admiral. He was a brilliant strategist, a leader of men, and a fearless fighter. He earned the full respect of his subordinates and superiors. Spruance knew how to select good subordinates and trusted their judgments. He refused to stand in the limelight and knew how to share acclaim. Though he was denied a fifth star, it was not because he had not earned it; there simply was no authorization to create another fleet admiral.

Though Spruance had his critics, time has justified his moves at Midway. Perhaps he might have been over-cautious at the Philippine Sea, but he did accomplish the main objective. After that battle the Japanese striking force ceased to exist. Though not as well known as Nimitz, King, and Halsey, Raymond Spruance's name will nevertheless always shine as one of America's greatest naval commanders.

Chapter Four

"If you want something tough done, call on Turner."[1] So spoke Adm. William "Bull" Halsey. Richmond Kelly Turner can be described in many terms: hard working, best strategist in the navy, an intellectual, a man without fear, a man with a computer brain. It is the name "Terrible Turner," however, that is probably remembered most. He made little or no effort to make people like him, he worked his men to the limit, and believed in kicking people when necessary. Turner drove people to the breaking point, including himself.

Holland Smith, who commanded the expeditionary troops in the Fifth Amphibious Force said this of Turner:

> Kelly Turner is aggressive, a mass of energy, and a relentless taskmaster. The punctilious exterior hides a terrific determination. He can be plain ornery. He wasn't called 'Terrible Turner' without reason.[2]

"Terrible Turner" probably did more than any one man to help bring about the defeat of the Japanese. It was his genius, his drive, and his enthusiasm which drove the amphibious forces of the United States Navy from the jungles of Guadalcanal through the sands of Iwo Jima to the doorstep of Japan. Turner won the Navy Cross and four Distinguished Service Medals, yet he suffered from a serious drinking problem.

During his long naval career, Kelly Turner had his ups and downs, and he had the remarkable ability to bounce back whenever he was down. The two low points in his career occurred while he was a member of the Navy War Plans Division and during the disaster at Savo Island in the Solomons. Despite all, he rebounded and became America's greatest amphibious expert.

In sketching Turner's career, the authors will presume that the reader has already digested the previous chapters in this volume. The political decisions as to why a particular island was selected for assault as opposed to others will not be rehashed here since that subject has already been detailed in both the King and Nimitz chapters. Instead, Turner and his command decisions are the major focus of this chapter.

The Turner family emigrated from England in the early eighteenth century and settled into colonial Maryland. In the early nineteenth century the Turners became part of the westward movement, making the hazardous cross-country journey to California in 1850. Following the Civil War, Enoch Turner, Richmond's father, moved to Oregon. In 1867 he married Laura Francis Kelly and on May 27, 1885, Richmond Kelly Turner was born in East Portland, the seventh child of Enoch and Laura.

The Turners raised their children in the traditional manner, believing that if you spare the rod you spoil the child. Enoch was a firm believer in education and stressed its importance to all his children. Five of the Turner children eventually became teachers. Thus, from his father, Kelly gained a healthy respect for discipline and a love for learning. From his mother he learned steadfastness.

Richmond Kelly Turner was a mixture of English and Irish stock. The name Richmond was derived from Laura Kelly's youngest brother, Richmond Kelly. The Kelly family, like the Turner's, had also migrated across America and suffered the many hardships of frontier life. The experience of battling raw nature produced a hardy stock, Richmond Kelly Turner being a product.

He attended grammar school and high school in Stockton, California. When he was thirteen the Spanish-American War began. Young Richmond listened to many inspiring speeches exhorting young men to enlist in the ranks. He was impressed with the prospect. In 1904, his father brought his son's attention to a local newspaper article announcing that a competitive exam would be given by the local congressman for appointments to the naval academy and the military academy at West Point.

Young Richmond studied diligently for the examination despite his mother's opposition to the prospect of having her son participate in the military. Nevertheless, he took the exam and earned the coveted appointment. On June 13, 1904, Richmond Kelly Turner entered the naval academy as a member of the class of 1908.

The naval academy of that era was in the midst of a renaissance. The United States, blossoming as a world power, urgently required a modern school to produce naval officers of high caliber to man its rapidly expanding fleet.

Midshipman Turner easily made the transition from civilian life to that of a naval cadet. After surviving the rigors of plebe year, on his first summer cruise he served aboard the cruiser *Atlanta,* commanded by William F. Halsey, father of the future admiral. The four years at the academy wove Turner into a naval officer. His overall academic rank was fifth, but during his final year he ranked fourth.

His first assignment as a passed midshipman was on the small cruiser, *Milwaukee.* During the next year he served on four different warships before being posted to the cruiser *West Virginia* in July, 1909. On the *West Virginia* he earned the first of many outstanding fitness reports. As a member of that ship's company, in September, 1909, Turner made his first Pacific cruise. The voyage gave the young officer an invaluable lesson in geography as the ship called at most of the exotic ports of the South Pacific.

During the voyage he saw the Philippines and his future enemy, Japan.

In June, 1910, Passed Midshipman Turner became Ensign Turner. That August he married Harriet Sterling, a young woman he had loved since high school.

Turner remained with the *West Virginia* until June, 1912, when he was assigned to duty on a torpedo boat destroyer. His fitness reports continued to be excellent and were sprinkled with such adjectives as forceful, active, and painstaking.

In June, 1913, Turner was promoted to lieutenant, junior grade. Three months later he was ordered to report for postgraduate instruction in ordnance study. After six months of learning he was detached from his studies and ordered to the gunboat *Marietta*. This vessel was part of the Cruiser Squadron, U.S. Atlantic Fleet. With trouble brewing in the Dominican Republic, the lives of American citizens and their property were endangered. The *Marietta* was dispatched to the Caribbean nation to protect the rights of the Americans.

The *Marietta*'s landing party was commanded by Lieutenant Turner. In August, 1914, he landed his small force on the island and through force of arms, enforced respect from the rebels for a neutral zone. Heretofore, these rebels had refused to honor such a zone. For the first time in his naval career, Turner found himself under fire. Though the action was but a war in miniature, he had nevertheless proven himself and his fitness report spoke in glowing terms.

> *Marietta* landing force under command of Lieutenant Turner was landed to enforce respect for a neutral zone by the government forces and the rebels. . . . This duty continuing on the second and third of August was performed by Lieutenant Turner in a highly credible manner and was entirely successful in its purpose.[3]

When the trouble abated at the end of the year, Turner returned to his course of instruction. As a student he excelled and developed a great interest in naval theory.

Upon completion of his postgraduate studies in mid-1916, Turner was assigned to the battleship *Pennsylvania* as turret officer. The following year he was made assistant gunnery officer. Late in the same year he was transferred to the *Michigan* as gunnery officer.

After America's entrance into the First World War, both the *Pennsylvania* and the *Michigan* were used as training vessels. Turner found himself rapidly advancing in rank, first to lieutenant and then to lieutenant commander before the end of 1917.

Through official channels, Turner proposed a new idea on how to improve the fire-control apparatus for the big guns of the fleet. The Bureau of Ordnance appreciated the suggestions and before the end of 1918 they rewarded Turner with a transfer to the new battleship, *Mississippi*. His fitness reports continued to be excellent. One report described him as:

> exceedingly able and thoroughly conscientious in the performance of duty . . . self-reliant, with excellent judgment . . . valuable whenever scientific reasoning is required . . . hard-working, conscientious and loyal.[4]

At war's end the chief of the Bureau of Ordance wisely decided to utilize Lieutenant Commander Turner's talents and nominated him to the Bureau of Navigation for duty at the Naval Gun Factory, Navy Yard, Washington, D.C. While at the factory Turner took a correspondence course in strategy and tactics. He also found time to author two articles which were published in the navy's *Proceedings*.

On July 17, 1922, Turner was sent to the new battleship, *California*, as gunnery officer. The following May he received a telegram asking him if he would consider the position of gunnery officer in the scouting fleet. Turner accepted the position and reported for duty on June 29. Though he excelled at his job, Turner did not get along with his superior officer, Vice Admiral Newton McCully. His fitness reports began to contain negative comments.

Individual ability too strong to make a good subordinate. With increased rank and experience this defect will undoubtedly disappear.[5]

Fortunately for him, the selection board for commander had already met and recommended him for promotion. The negative fitness report was filed away and subsequently forgotten.

In June, 1924, Turner's promotion to commander came through. At that time he was also given a new command, the destroyer *Mervine*. He commanded the *Mervine* for eight months. Opinion among his subordinates varied as to the manner in which he ran the ship. Some praised his excellent leadership and determination. Others remembered his intolerance. There was only one way to do things when aboard a ship commanded by Turner, the Turner way! In his fitness report, his divisional commander did not rate Turner highly, stating that he had average ability except in ordnance in which he was superior. Obviously, Turner did not get along with his superiors. If anything, he was not average.

In March, 1925, Turner was ordered to the Bureau of Ordnance as the new head of the Design and Turret Mount and Machinery Section. While serving in this department he sought to qualify as an aviator. Convinced that aviation was the wave of the future and would be a vital factor in warfare, Turner reported for instruction at the naval air station in Pensacola, Florida on January 3, 1927. He completed the course eight months later.

Upon qualifying as a pilot he was sent to command the aircraft squadron in the Asiatic Fleet. Commander Turner arrived in Manila on January 19, 1928, and immediately set to work. One of his immediate concerns was the problem of China. That country was in a state of political turmoil. The new Nationalist leader of China, Chiang Kai-shek was desirous of uniting all of China under his control. He was also out to destroy the Communists and foreign influence. The lives of all foreigners were in peril in the politically turbulent nation.

When he arrived in Manila, Turner found he had much to do. First, the air squadron was undermanned. In the process of trying to increase the size of the naval air station, he ran into fiscal problems since the United States was reluctant to increase military expenditures.

Working with a tight budget, therefore, Turner nevertheless pushed his small force to the limit. One positive contribution made by his squadron was an extensive aerial reconnaissance of the Philippine Islands and the China coast. Never one to shun his responsibility, Commander Turner flew his share of the reconnaissance flights. He drove his squadron hard through the wearisome task, but by the time his tour of duty was over, he could report the completion of all operations in connection with airway chart preparation. He also participated in joint maneuvers with the Army Air Corps pilots. These exercises paved the way for future combined operations.

On April 20, 1929, Turner left the Asiatic station and headed for home. His tour in the Orient was marked by his hard work. However, he had not been universally liked. In fact, at times, his demands seemed unreasonable. He was not one to accept a half-done job. It either had to be done to his standards or he would get someone else to do it. Some felt he lacked consideration and was deliberately uncooperative. On the whole, however, Turner proved highly competent as an administrator. He was aggressive, worked hard, and usually accomplished what he set out to do. The Kelly Turner of World War II, the tough, exacting commander, began to develop.

Arriving back in the States, Turner reported to the Plans Division of the Bureau of Aeronautics. Two years later, in March, 1931, he was directed to join the General Board of the Navy Department for temporary duty in drawing up recommendations for still another of the many disarmament conferences held between the wars. This one was to be held in Geneva in 1932. Turner worked both day and night preparing for the conference. During the day he worked for the Bureau of Aeronautics developing naval air operations at a time when the economic depression was holding back expenditures. At night he studied the recommendations or positions taken by the various participating nations in the disarmament talks.

On November 27, 1931, Turner set out for Geneva, Switzerland, to participate in the conference. He remained there until the following July when the talks stalled, although Turner's efforts were commendable. In a letter to the Secretary of State written by the chief delegate, Turner's technical knowledge and skill in handling all matters pertaining to air questions was praised.

The day after Christmas, 1932, Commander Turner returned to sea as executive officer of the aircraft carrier *Saratoga*. In this position he demanded that the aviators participate in ship duties along with their flying duties. Previously, the flyers simply flew, with a minimum of shipboard duties assigned to them. Turner wanted his aviators to develop into complete naval officers and be familiar with all the responsibilities of that position. He did not endear himself to his subordinates, but dividends were reaped during the Second World War when many of these aviators found themselves in positions of great responsibility.

In 1934, Turner was made Chief of Staff to Commander, Aircraft, Battle Force, Rear Admiral Alfred W. Johnson.

This command consisted of three carriers, the *Lexington*, *Saratoga*, and the *Langley*. A fourth carrier, the *Ranger*, was added in 1935. Turner initiated a change when he convinced Johnson to begin night-flying training instead of sticking to daylight training exclusively. This skill would also pay dividends during the war with Japan.

In June, 1935, Turner was again ordered back to the Naval War College, first as a student and then as a member of the staff. This coincided with his promotion to the rank of captain. During this period, the newly promoted captain began to develop his advanced theories. The days of the battleship were over. Future wars would be centered on air operations and amphibious campaigns. He taught these theories and developed these ideas in his position as head of the strategic section at the war college.

Anxious for flag rank, Turner knew the one thing he lacked was command of a man-of-war. As an aviator, however, the competition was stiff for the few commands available. Therefore, Turner had to seek a nonaviation assignment for his next tour at sea, either aboard a battleship or heavy cruiser. This decision did not reflect any doubt on his part regarding the future of aviation. Hardly! It was but an expedient for his own personal advancement. At the time, rumor said that Turner was actually let go as an aviator. That was preposterous, however. He left aviation of his own volition.

Captain Turner was given command of the cruiser *Astoria*. As skipper of the cruiser he ran a tight ship. In the various fleet exercises and competitions the ship fared exceedingly well. Personally, however, Turner made a number of enemies. He was intolerant of delay, inefficiency and laxness on the part of his officers. His impatience usually expressed itself in a violent public attack on the culprit, regardless of rank or rating. This type of embarrassment went against the naval tradition of publically commending but censuring in private. No doubt Turner was a man who wanted the job done, and done right the first time. Nevertheless, the *Astoria* was efficiently run regardless of the seething discontent among the officers regarding "Terrible Turner." In contrast to his handling of his officers, to the enlisted men on his ship Turner was most solicitous. He was kind, almost fatherly to his crew although he was always firm and consistent.

Turner's assumption of command of the *Astoria* coincided with a dangerous period in U.S.–Japanese relations. The war in China had strained the relations between the two nations to the breaking point. War clouds began to gather on the horizon.

Abruptly, Turner was assigned an important good-will mission, one designed to smooth over the deteriorating Japanese-American relations. On February 26, 1939, the former Japanese Ambassador to the United States, Hiroshi Saito, died suddenly in Washington. The State Department decided to have the *Astoria* return the ashes of Saito to Japan with full honors.

Departing the east coast, the *Astoria* sailed through the Panama Canal and arrived at Pearl Harbor on April 4. From there the ship began the final leg of the journey, arriving at Yokohama on April 17. The American gesture was intended to be just that, a gesture of peace.

While in Japan, Captain Turner played the role of diplomat. Nonmilitant Japanese went out of their way to impress upon him their nonbelligerence. At various receptions Turner met Admirals Yamamoto, Koga, and numerous other dignitaries. For nine whirlwind days Turner was wined and dined. The good-will gesture was accepted wholeheartedly by his hosts. Unfortunately, its effects were not long-standing. The war in China continued, along with Japanese expansion into Indochina.

On September 14, 1940, Turner was detached from the *Astoria* after a two-year tour of duty. His next assignment was one ideally suited for his analytical mind, Director of

War Plans in the office of the Chief of Naval Operations. The new position was followed in January, 1941 with a new rank, that of rear admiral.

As Director of War Plans, Turner automatically became a member of the Joint Planning Committee of the Joint Board. The Joint Planning Committee was responsible for coordinating and controlling joint Army and Navy operations. The greatest problem facing the board in the fall of 1940, according to Turner, was the lack of any clear line of national policy to guide the direction of military efforts in preparing for a war situation. Along with Col. Joseph McNarney, Turner produced a study on the problem and called it "Study of the Immediate Problems Concerning Involvement in War." Uncannily, the report forecast the precise course of events.

> With respect to Germany and Italy, it appears reasonably certain that neither will initiate open hostilities with the United States, until they have succeeded in inflicting a major reverse on Great Britian in the British Isles or in the Mediterranean.
>
> With respect to Japan, hostilities prior to the United States's entry into the European war or to the defeat of Britain may depend upon the consequences of steps taken by the United States to oppose Japanese aggression. If these steps seriously threaten her economic welfare or military adventures, there can be no assurance that Japan will not suddenly attack United States armed forces.[6]

The paper went on to emphasize the danger of imposing economic sanctions on Japan and discussed the prospect of a two-ocean war. It also placed emphasis on a Europe-first strategy. The study was an important one for it later provided a basis from which the war planners would develop their strategy when war finally did come to America.

With France and Britain under the Nazi blitz and the possibility of the United States's involvement, answers were needed for some very important questions regarding what the attitude of America should be. Once more Turner and McNarney went to work and drafted another study: "Joint Instructions for Army and Navy Representatives for Holding Staff Conversations with the British."

Meanwhile, the situation in the Pacific reached the boiling point. In July, 1941, Japan occupied southern Indochina. The United States reacted by freezing Japanese assets and imposing an oil embargo. Turner opposed this stiff line. He had already met with Japanese Ambassador Nomura prior to the Japanese occupation and did so again afterward. Turner appreciated the difficulty Nomura faced and respected the latter's good intentions and his desire for peace.

Turner was also involved in preparing a memorandum regarding the undeclared war in the Atlantic and the role of the U.S. Navy, particularly the possibility of having to escort convoys to Scotland, an eventuality that became a reality in the late summer of 1941.

In August, Turner accompanied the CNO (Chief of Naval Operations), Admiral Stark, to the Atlantic Conference where Churchill and Roosevelt laid down the basis for an agreement known as the Atlantic Charter. The conference was important to both the War and Navy Departments in planning future moves. It also broke the ice regarding combined planning with the British.

On the morning of December 7, Turner was shown the decoded Japanese intercept stating that the fourteen-part dispatch severing negotiations was to be submitted by 1:00 P.M. He recognized the importance of the message and asked Stark if anything had been done about it. Stark replied that General Marshall was already sending a dispatch to all Pacific commands. In John Toland's latest book, *Infamy,* the author presents convincing evidence that the President, the Chief of Staff, Chief of Naval Operations, and the Secretary of War all knew of the approach of the Japanese Task Force toward Hawaii. Underestimating the Japanese ability, these leaders viewed this as an opportunity to get America involved in the war with the people totally behind such a just cause. Whether Turner knew about the attack in advance is unclear. Though he did feel that an air attack on Pearl Harbor was a distinct possibility, there is no proof that he in fact knew that Pearl Harbor was going to be attacked on December 7, 1941.

There are, however, some unanswered questions. All decoded messages had to be cleared through Turner's office, he was the ultimate censor. From this office the information was sent out to the appropriate commands. Turner later claimed that Admiral Kimmel in Pearl Harbor was sufficiently warned. The evidence does not agree with this. Thus, for now it can only be stated that although he was rude, gruff, and disliked by many, Turner was not one to allow the navy, which he loved, to be humiliated if there was any way to avoid it.

With war coming to America, Turner, as Chief of Naval War Plans, found himself faced with monumental tasks to perform. Though he was later interrogated during the many investigations into the Pearl Harbor disaster, there was a more urgent task to perform. America was engulfed in war and the War Plans Division had to prepare for a lengthy one, particularly after Germany and Italy followed their Axis partner and declared war on America on December 11. The United States was embroiled in a two-ocean war.

On January 28, 1942, the Joint Board of Army and Navy War Planners discussed the creation of a Super Joint General Staff. As head of the Navy War Plans Division, Rear Admiral Turner was one of the two members of the Joint Planning Committee. His counterpart in the Army was Brig. Gen. Dwight D. Eisenhower. Turner and Eisenhower were given the responsibility for determining the structure of a new military command organization that would provide direction for the war. Both officers submitted their own separate plans. It was Turner's that recommended a Joint Chiefs of Staff committee consisting of the CNO, Chief of Staff, Commander in Chief of the U.S. Fleet, and the Commanding General, Army Air Forces. The President endorsed Turner's proposal.

Thus, Richmond Kelly Turner became the father of the Joint Chiefs of Staff.[7]

It was apparent to Turner that a department should be established within the Commander in Chief's headquarters that would specialize in amphibious warfare. In April he formally proposed this to Admiral King, stating that a joint army, navy, and marine section be established with specific responsibility to develop material and methods for amphibious warfare.

Since these matters were then handled by various agencies, Turner urged that they be combined under one person. His recommendation for coordination was endorsed by others. Though the department was not established along the lines he had originally envisioned, the new section was formed on June 4. It was called the F-26 Section and its purpose was to handle amphibious warfare.

Even before that date, however, on April 29, King had issued orders for the establishment of the South Pacific Amphibious Force. In these orders the South Pacific Amphibious Commander would be under the command of the Commander, South Pacific Force.

The decision to initiate an offensive in the Solomon Islands is covered in both the King and Nimitz chapters and need not be repeated. In this chapter we intend to review the role Turner played in America's first offensive in World War II.

As one of the Joint Staff planners it was Turner who advanced Admiral King's South Pacific plan. The struggle with Europe-firsters was heated and furious. Most of the Army planners were dead set against any diversion of resources into the Pacific. The official position taken by the Army is stated in the Army's official history.

> To emphasize the need for economy of effort in subsidiary theaters. They classified as subsidiary theaters not only the Far East, but also Africa, the Middle East, the Iberian Peninsula, and the Scandinavian Peninsula. . . . To consider all other operations as strictly holding operations, and to regard with disfavor any proposal to establish and maintain in a 'subsidiary' theater the favorable ratio of Allied to enemy forces that would be necessary in order to take the offensive there.[8]

In the officially accepted plan, "Rainbow Five," however, although it advocated the preeminence of Europe, the plan also called for amphibious assaults on the Japanese-held islands in the Pacific. This is what Admiral King and his chief planner, Turner, had been fighting for.

King and Turner placed great emphasis on securing the lines of communication between Australia and Hawaii. It was their position that strong, mutually supportive defensive positions should be established in Samoa, Fiji, and New Caledonia in order to insure the sea and air lines of communication. The way the Japanese juggernaut was gobbling up one island after another made the danger of their severing that line more acute. Turner had to convince the army planners that it was necessary to send forces to those islands in order to insure their safety.

King's scheme, however, was not merely the protection of the lines of communication with Australia, but also the preparation of a step-by-step general advance through the

New Hebrides, Solomons, and Bismarck Archipelago.

The Army and Navy planners disagreed as to whether the holding of Australia was vital to the United States war effort. Eisenhower, representing the Army point of view, stated:

> The United States interest in maintaining contact with Australia and in preventing further Japanese expansion to the southeastward is apparent. . . . But . . . they are not immediately vital to the successful outcome of the war. The problem is one of determining what we can spare for the effort in that region without seriously impairing performance of our mandatory tasks.[9]

Turner, however, felt that because of the critical position caused by the deteriorating situation in southeast Asia and the southwest Pacific, the necessity of maintaining contact with Australia was vital. Luckily for the navy planners, President Roosevelt felt the same way.

In April, Turner presented King with a memorandum on his concept of how the war against Japan should be waged. It included four stages, the first being the assembly and training of the amphibious naval, and air forces needed for an assault. The second stage, Turner said, would be an assault in the Solomon Islands and New Guinea and included the capture of the Bismarck Archipelago and the Admiralty Islands. The third stage was the seizure of the Caroline and Marshalls Islands where the fleet could be established along with advanced air bases. The fourth stage would entail either an advance into the Netherlands East Indies or the Philippines. King approved the memorandum and it became the basis for all future planning.

What finally tipped the scales into a joint agreement for action in the South Pacific was the Japanese invasion of Tulagi and their subsequent occupation of Guadalcanal in early May, 1942—that and pressure from General MacArthur in Australia.

After the amazing American victory at Midway, King and Turner both felt that immediate action was necessary in order to seize the initiative. By early July, King finally had received official permission for an offensive. It was code-named Operation Watchtower.

Meanwhile, back in April, Turner had learned that he was going to be relieved from his current assignment. In June, doubts regarding his next posting were lifted when he was named Commander Amphibious Force, South Pacific, under Admiral Ghormley, Commander, South Pacific. Turner assumed command on July 18, two weeks before the projected date of the first American amphibious landing in the war.

The first problem facing Turner was the assembling of a staff. Hardly anyone selected by the Bureau of Navigation had any amphibious training. Therefore, Turner would have to rely on the amphibious-oriented Marines. In all, he formed a staff of eleven men.

Turner's offensive plan called for the capture of Tulagi and Guadalcanal. The importance of capturing the latter increased daily when it was discovered that the Japanese were constructing an airfield on the jungle-clad island. The original date for the assault was August 1, but that was later changed to the seventh. Turner prepared and ordered last-minute training in the short time allotted. For his flagship he commandeered the merchant ship, *McCawley*. Though this ship was deemed adequate for his needs, the experience later proved that the *McCawley* lacked the many essentials for the successful conduct of an amphibious operation. It even lacked voice radio.

Turner's force was officially termed Task Force 62. Leaving Auckland, New Zealand, the force advanced to Fiji where they were to undergo a dress rehearsal. Turner and his staff composed an eighty-seven-page operation plan by which the first amphibious operation would be governed.

On Sunday, July 26, Vice Admiral Frank J. Fletcher, the commander of the American carriers, held a conference aboard his flagship, *Saratoga*. Fletcher announced that the carriers would remain in the area for only two days in support of the Tulagi-Guadalcanal landings. After that, the landing forces would be on their own. Fear of Japanese attacks against the carriers dominated Fletcher's planning.

Turner's Chief of Staff, Captain Peyton, remembers the conference as a very stormy one. Fletcher, he said, criticized the operation plan saying that it was put together too hastily and therefore not thoroughly planned. Turner shot back criticizing Fletcher's decision to pull the carriers out after only two days. Admiral Ghormley was not present at this conference. Instead, he was represented by his Chief of Staff, Rear Admiral Daniel Callaghan. If Ghormley had been present, Turner felt that he would have sided with him and ordered Fletcher to remain in the vicinity longer. Turner had no one to turn to. Years later, when asked why he did not appeal the decision, he said:

> Whom to, and who was I to do so? Fletcher was my old boss, and at that moment the most battle-experienced commander in our navy. It was his judgment, and it was my job to live with it.[10]

As far as Turner was concerned, then, the conference was less than satisfactory. Fletcher was immovable. Turner turned to the all-important rehearsal scheduled for July 28 thru 31.

The dress rehearsal proved inadequate. Koro Island in the Fijis lacked proper beach conditions and proved hazardous to boats, the same craft that Turner could ill afford to risk because of the shortage of the same. As a result, only one third of the marines who were to have the benefit of a rehearsal for the forthcoming amphibious operation, actually partook of the vital practice session. The rehearsal, however, was not totally without value. The gunfire-support ships and the support aircraft did function adequately and derived needed experience. Major General Vandergrift, Commander of the First Marine Division, the force designated to invade Guadalcanal, complained that the rehearsal was unsatisfactory because of the poor beach conditions.

After the dress rehearsal, Task Force 62 headed for its destination, eleven hundred miles away. On the night preceding the operation, Turner drafted a message stating the significance of the operation and the confidence he felt in the skill and courage of all the forces. The message was transmitted around the fleet.

Careful to maintain radio silence, Task Force 62 approached its target. Moving silently through the Coral Sea, the force glided around the western end of Guadalcanal through the twelve-mile-wide channel separating that island from the Russell Islands. On August 7, the first American amphibious attack of the war hit the beaches of Guadalcanal and Tulagi.

The weather that morning was all that an attacker would hope for. After passing Cape Esperance on the northwest corner of Guadalcanal, the Task Force had split up. The lead transports, Group Yoke, moved north of Savo Island toward Florida Island. The larger of the two groups, Group X-ray, headed for Lunga Point on Guadalcanal.

The first sight of Guadalcanal inspired Marine correspondent H. L. Merillant to say:

Guadalcanal is an island of striking beauty. Blue-green mountains, towering into a brilliant tropical sky or crowned with cloud masses, dominate the island. The dark green of jungle growth blends into the softer greens and browns of coconut groves and grassy plains and ridges.[11]

The assault beach on Guadalcanal was just east of the mouth of the Tenaru River and five miles east of Lunga Point. With nine transports and six cargo ships, Group X-ray achieved complete surprise.

The three transports, four destroyer transports, and one cargo ship of Group Yoke made for the west central sector of the south coast of Tulagi. They were also under orders to land on tiny Gavutu Island and at two small points on Florida Island.

At 6:15 A.M. that morning, the order went out to "land the landing force." Zero hour was 8:00 at Tulagi and an hour later at Guadalcanal. On the latter, the landings were unopposed. The marines quickly moved inland to occupy the airfield which was later named Henderson Field in honor of a pilot who had died during the battle of Midway. In contrast, at Tulagi and Gavutu, the Japanese put up a determined struggle.

Turner's amphibians immediately went to work providing logistical support. It did not take the admiral long to see that drastic improvements were needed. There was an obvious need for more officers to staff the amphibious ships. The unloading was taking much too long. More officers could have provided more direction. Not only were more officers needed, the need for more hands to do the actual unloading was evident. During the first few days at Guadalcanal, confusion reigned supreme. Too few men had been assigned to the unloading. While these few were attempting to off-load the mounds of supplies, truck drivers, tank crews, and combat marines lounged nearby, went swimming, or played cards while waiting for their equipment to come ashore. The frustrated crews involved in the actual unloading became rather careless. Many of the vital supplies were simply dumped from the boats only to be destroyed when the tide came in. Nevertheless, within twenty-six hours the amphibians had manhandled a large percentage of the marines' supplies out of the holds and onto the beaches in spite of three Japanese air raids and numerous false alarms.

Meanwhile, the troops were establishing their positions on Guadalcanal and Tulagi. News of the landings reached Japanese Admiral Mikawa at Rabaul. His immediate reaction was to dispatch reinforcements to Guadalcanal and a squadron of ships to attack the American transports.

With a force of cruisers and a destroyer, Mikawa headed down the Slot (the body of water separating the twin chain of the Solomons) for Guadalcanal. His battle plan called for the Japanese force to enter the waters north of Guadalcanal (an area subsequently dubbed Ironbottom Sound because of the great number of ships that rested on its bottom) in the early morning of August 9 and strike the American ships protecting the expeditionary force. Then, after the destruction of these ships, Mikawa would attack the defenseless transports before retiring north to Rabaul.

A combination of Japanese luck and American mistakes allowed Mikawa's force to approach undetected. The Japanese force had been sighted by an Australian pilot, but the report of the sighting did not reach Turner until eight hours later. When he did receive the report it was misleading since the pilot had mistaken two of Mikawa's cruisers for seaplane tenders. Because of the tardy and inaccurate report, therefore, Turner felt that the Japanese would not attack that night but would first attempt to establish a seaplane base north of Guadalcanal and attack at a later date.

Guarding the transports that fateful night were three separate formations. Patrolling between Tulagi and Guadalcanal was a small force under Rear Admiral Norman Scott. Off the western coast of the island, on each side of the small island of Savo, were two groups of cruisers under Rear Admiral Crutchley of the Royal Navy. Crutchley had no established battle plan in the event of an enemy attack.

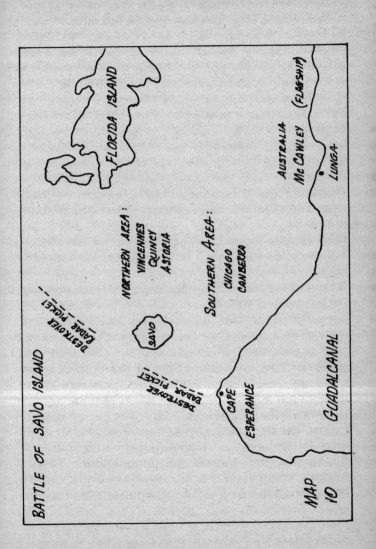

BATTLE OF SAVO ISLAND

FLORIDA ISLAND

NORTHERN AREA:
VINCENNES
QUINCY
ASTORIA

SOUTHERN AREA:
CHICAGO
CANBERRA

DESTROYER RADAR PICKET

SAVO

DESTROYER RADAR PICKET

CAPE ESPERANCE

GUADALCANAL

AUSTRALIA
McCAWLEY (FLAGSHIP)

LUNGA

MAP 10

Turner, not expecting an attack and worried over Fletcher's decision to leave with his carriers, summoned Crutchley to his flagship which was moored off the beach, twenty miles from Savo.

With Crutchley absent from the scene, all hell broke loose in the vicinity of Savo. After two days at general quarters and not anticipating any hostile action, the Allied naval forces were fatigued. At 11:45 on the evening of the eighth, three planes were reported by the picket destroyer *Ralph Talbot*. Turner did not receive this report. The cruiser captains erroneously assumed that the planes were friendly. In fact, the planes had been sent on ahead by Mikawa.

At 12:20 A.M. on the ninth, Mikawa, in view of Savo, ordered his force to battle stations. A few minutes later lookouts on the flagship, *Chokai*, sighted the picket destroyer, *Blue*. Mikawa slowed his formation and allowed the *Blue* to pass serenely by. The *Blue* had not noticed a thing.

At 1:36 the Japanese opened fire on the unsuspecting American ships. In the brief span of a few minutes the Australian cruiser *Canberra* was hit and mortally wounded and the U.S. cruiser, *Chicago*, was fighting for her life.

Having smashed the southern allied force, Mikawa maneuvered his formation north of Savo. Though the action had occurred only a few miles from the second group of American ships, a heavy rain squall had masked the action. Captain Bode of the *Chicago*, who was standing in for the absent Crutchley, failed to signal the northern group of ships about the Japanese attack.

At 1:48 the *Chokai* launched its deadly "long lance" torpedoes at the cruiser *Astoria*, formerly commanded by Capt. R. K. Turner. The torpedoes missed, but *Chokai*'s eight-inch shells were more accurate. Tons of deadly steel rained down on the decks of the *Astoria* and the American ship began to burn furiously. The *Quincy* was next.

A searchlight from the Japanese cruiser *Aoba* illuminated the hapless *Quincy* which was immediately shelled from both sides. At 2:35 the ship rolled over and sank. The first pieces of iron began to lay their carpet over Ironbottom Sound.

Next in line was the heavy cruiser *Vincennes*. She retaliated and hit the cruiser *Kinugasa*, but shortly thereafter, the unfortunate cruiser was overwhelmed by the entire might of Mikawa's squadron. Like her sister, the *Vincennes* plunged to the bottom of Ironbottom Sound.

At 2:20 Mikawa ordered his scattered formation to re-form northwest of Savo Island so that it could make an organized attack on the now-unprotected American transports. However, the Japanese admiral had second thoughts about continuing the attack for fear that by daylight his squadron might be raked by U.S. carrier planes. Fortunately for Turner, Mikawa had no way of knowing that Fletcher had already pulled his carriers out of range. Incredibly, Mikawa ordered his ships to set course for Rabaul, leaving the vulnerable transports unmolested.

Nevertheless, despite their missed opportunity, the Japanese had won a tremendous victory. In just over half an hour they had destroyed four heavy cruisers and a destroyer and damaged another cruiser. One thousand, two hundred and seventy American sailors were killed and seven hundred and nine wounded. Japanese losses were light: thirty-five killed and fifty-seven wounded.

Who was responsible for the debacle? Was Turner in any way to blame for the Savo Island fiasco? In an article written by the *Saturday Evening Post* in 1962, Samuel Eliot Morison said:

Turner made a bad guess that the Japanese were not coming through that night. He allowed his fighting ships to be divided into three separate groups to guard against three possible sea approaches by the enemy. . . . Turner was so certain that the enemy would not attack that night that he made the further mistake of summoning Crutchley in *Australia** to a conference on board his flagship *McCawley* to decide whether the partly unloaded transports should depart that night or risk repeated Japanese air attacks without air protection.[12]

Morison seems to place the blame squarely on Turner's shoulders. Yet, in the post-Savo investigations that lasted from December 23, 1942, to May 13, 1943, Turner was not criticized for his actions that fateful night. Admiral King, not one to cover up anyone's guilt, approved of Turner's conduct that night. Both Turner and Crutchley, he said, found themselves in an awkward position, and both did their best with the means at their disposal.

Then what had caused the fiasco at Savo? High on Turner's list was inadequate and faulty air reconnaissance. When he had first received word of the approach of the Japanese formation it was eight hours after the fact. At that point, the Japanese ships were forty miles east of Kieta on the island of Bougainville. The enemy ships had not even reached the Slot. To reach Guadalcanal by the night of August 8-9, their speed would have had to be between twenty-two and twenty-six knots, a speed at which the Japanese force was not reported to be traveling. Why had it taken over eight hours for the pilot's report to reach Turner? Morison offers an explanation.

Instead of breaking radio silence to report as he had orders to do in an urgent case, or returning to base which he could have done in two hours, the pilot spent most of the afternoon completing his search

*The heavy cruiser HMAS *Australia*, Crutchley's flagship

mission, came down at Milne Bay, had his tea, and then reported the contact.[13]

Then, when the pilot did finally report, he misidentified the enemy ships. In addition, he had failed to trail and track his contact. Added to this was another sighting of Mikawa's force by a plane from General MacArthur's command. This report took nine hours to reach Turner.

The two sighting reports caused confusion rather than clarifying the situation since the second sighting indicated that the Japanese formation had moved northward and westward. Turner thus concluded that the Japanese were heading for Rabaul.

Turner also blamed the lack of aerial reconnaissance by Fletcher's carriers. Proper reconnaissance might have alerted Crutchley to the approach of the Japanese. Lacking sightings other than those previously reported which had placed the enemy hundreds of miles to the north, it is understandable why Turner was reasonably certain that no enemy ships were in the vicinity on the fateful night.

In 1960, Turner admitted that failure was due to his assumption that the pilots were sending adequate information and that Fletcher's carriers would keep him completely informed. Little did he know that the carriers had limited their reconnaissance because of bad weather and impending orders to leave the area.

As already seen, Fletcher had decided not to risk the carriers. Since he had already suffered the loss of one carrier during the Battle of the Coral Sea and another one at Midway, he was fearful of Japanese torpedo-plane attacks. Allowing that fear to dominate his thinking, therefore, Fletcher justified his departure by saying that he was under orders not to risk his ships.

With the navy now on the defensive, the marines on Guadalcanal also went over to the defensive, entrenching themselves in a perimeter around the airfield.

In retrospect, the Battle of Savo Island was a major defeat. The causes of the disaster were many and Turner had to shoulder his share of the responsibility. Luckily, America's military leadership was wise enough not to call for Turner's relief and to use him as a scapegoat to cover up the debacle. What was important was that Turner learned from his mistakes and in turn became a better commander. The struggle for Guadalcanal was just beginning and Turner was one of America's greatest assets.

With the departure of the carriers on the eighth and the Battle of Savo behind him, Turner ordered the transports to depart at 1:30 P.M. on the ninth. He simply could not risk exposing them to another Japanese surface attack. The marines were effectively stranded. Turner was unhappy at having to leave them to their own devices with the supplies already landed. Originally, he had intended to remain at Guadalcanal and deal with the logistical problem, but when he realized that the island was inadequate to do a proper job, he left for Noumea where he was able to do a far more comprehensive job of providing logistical support for the marines. Though rumor was spread by some marines that Turner ran away, it was in fact a much sounder decision than remaining behind at the mercy of the Japanese Fleet.

For the next four months Turner was intimately involved in bringing men and supplies to the beleaguered island. During the Battle of the Eastern Solomons on August 24, 1942, Turner's cargo ships ferried in the first significant support since he had pulled up anchor on the ninth. On September 18, his ships brought in an additional four thousand marines and their supplies.

Turner concluded that the supply system was haphazard at best and vowed to do something about it. During Watchtower, logistical support was provided by large transports and cargo ships. This meant that supplies had to be lifted out of deep holds, loaded onto small landing craft, and brought ashore. Once near shore, the supplies would be hand-lifted off the smaller craft and piled onto the beaches by sailors or occasionally marines. There were no LST (Landing Ship Tank) or LCT (Landing Craft Tank) or DUKW (Amphibious Truck). In later assaults, these landing craft would go directly up onto the beaches, making it easier and more convenient to bring supplies ashore. Turner found that during the first four months of the Guadalcanal campaign, eighty percent of his time was spent concentrating on logistical support.

Turner concluded that an advance base was needed closer to Guadalcanal. Unhappy with having to rely on his supplies coming all the way from New Zealand, in late August he ordered the establishment of an advanced supply base at Noumea and another at Espiritu Santo. These supporting bases became operational by November and their effects were quickly felt on Guadalcanal. By December, with Noumea as the main fleet base and Espiritu Santo serving as an advanced depot, the problem of supporting operations on Guadalcanal was largely solved.

Turner was not only concerned with keeping the forces at Guadalcanal adequately supplied, he was also anxious to develop that island as a base for future operations into the northern and central Solomons. In addition, he also had to deal with the issue of the Army's relief of the marines on Guadalcanal. Not until October 6, 1942, did the Army commander in the South Pacific offer troops. These troops were not, however, offered as relief for the marines, but as reinforcements.

Beginning on October 13, Turner landed the One Hundred Sixty-fourth Infantry Regiment of the Americal Division. Additional Army troops followed early in November when the One Hundred Forty-seventh Regiment was landed. Finally, on December 9, command of the ground troops was formally transferred from the marine general, Vandergrift, to an army general, Alexander Patch. Two days prior to that, Turner himself was finally relieved of responsibility for defending Guadalcanal. However, he was still responsible for transporting reinforcements, relief units, supplies, and equipment.

During those months, Turner was a tireless worker. His Chief of Staff said of him:

> Kelly Turner was an officer with the highest mental capacity. He was a tireless worker and had tremendous drive. His mental capabilities were such that he did all the brainwork for the staff. The staff carried out the mechanics of operations and filled in all the details of the operation orders. He was a one-man staff.[14]

Once Guadalcanal was secured, what would the next step be? In late November, Turner began to give serious thought to that question. Much had been learned regarding amphibious landing and logistic support. By January, 1943, new techniques had been developed and new amphibious craft were becoming available. Guadalcanal had taught the amphibians much and they were anxious to try out their newly acquired expertise.

By February 8, the last of the Japanese had been evacuated from Guadalcanal, ending the six-month-long struggle. The next attack would be against the strategically important Russell Islands, northwest of Guadalcanal. They were considered important because one of the islands, Banika, had a jungleless plain that was perfect for construction of an airfield.

Turner, as amphibious commander, was also named commander of the joint force, designated Task Force 61. The commanding general of the Forty-third Infantry Division was appointed landing-force commander.

Aboard the *McCawley*, Turner sailed with the Forty-third

Division from its staging area at New Caladonia; destination Guadalcanal. On February 16, he moved his operational staff ashore. Turner then shifted his flag to the fast minesweeper, *Hopkins*.

Turner ordered three simultaneous landings to begin at dawn on February 21. The landings were accomplished with textbook precision. In the next four days, over seven thousand troops were landed. The movements of the American vessels took place at night so as not to alert the Japanese that the Americans were on the move. During the next few months, the Russells became a beehive of activity with over sixteen thousand men and nearly fifty thousand tons of supplies being landed. The islands were transformed into an advanced air and naval base ready to be used for the next target in the Solomons, New Georgia.

On March 3, Turner was relieved and he returned to Noumea to plan for the operation against New Georgia, Operation Toenails.

The seizure of New Georgia was merely part of the overall plan for eventually neutralizing the main Japanese air and naval base at Rabaul, on New Britain. In order to attack Rabaul with a reasonable chance of success, the United States required airfields within fighter range of the Japanese bastion. The seizure of the central and northern Solomons was therefore, a necessary step on the road to Rabaul. From these islands, Rabaul could be pounded from the air while troops came ashore.

The New Georgia group was considered by most planners to be a vital target. Munda airfield on New Georgia was a mandatory target both for supporting America's advance northward and eliminating the Japanese threat.

New Georgia was heavily jungled and rugged. The island was surrounded by coral reefs and coral-filled lagoons. The jungle was so thick that it came right down to the water's edge. Logistic support would be a nightmare.

While Turner planned for Toenails, the Joint Chiefs of

Staff debated. Initially, the central Solomons were under the Phase II task of the original July, 1942, directive. That meant this area fell within the area of the commander of the southwest Pacific, Gen. Douglas MacArthur. In March, 1943, however, a Pacific military conference was held in Washington. After ten days of deliberations, the Joint Chiefs reaffirmed the original directive, but with a modification. A new directive was issued for the neutralization of Rabaul, Operation Cartwheel. The chiefs directed that operations in the central Solomons would be commanded by the Commander, South Pacific, Admiral Halsey, but under the general strategic directives of MacArthur. Ships and aircraft from the Pacific Fleet would remain under the Commander of the Pacific Ocean Area, Admiral Nimitz.

Toenails was originally scheduled for April, but one delay after another caused it to be postponed until June 30. The first definitive planning directive for the central Solomons campaign was issued on May 17. The specific tasks were to seize, hold, and then develop: 1) the Wickham Anchorage area, 2) Viru Harbor, 3) a fighter airstrip at Segi, New Georgia, 4) Rendova Island, and 5) Munda airfield on New Georgia.

Turner was scheduled to depart for Koli Point on Guadalcanal on June 7, where he would have his headquarters ashore. Before his departure, however, he came down with malaria and was sent to the hospital ship, *Solace*, where he remained for a week.

As we have seen, the overall objective of Toenails was the capture of airfields and anchorages. The waters near Munda were inhospitable for landing craft because of the sharp coral reefs in what was known as the Munda Bar. Because of this obstacle, a frontal assault against Munda airfield was not possible. Thus Turner had to come up with an alternate plan. One was developed that called for a major assault east of Munda airfield with a simultaneous landing on the southern coast. Japanese support lines to the

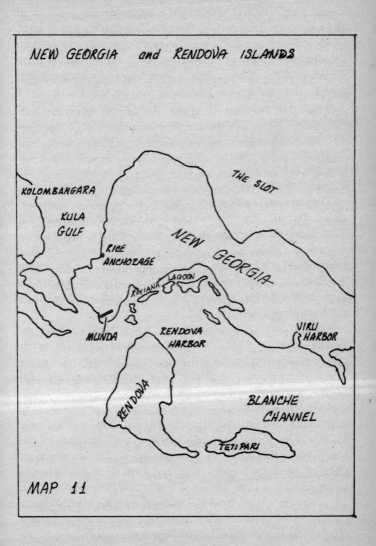

NEW GEORGIA and RENDOVA ISLANDS

THE SLOT

KOLOMBANGARA

KULA GULF

RICE ANCHORAGE

NEW GEORGIA

ROVIANA LAGOON

MUNDA

RENDOVA HARBOR

VIRU HARBOR

RENDOVA

BLANCHE CHANNEL

TETIPARI

MAP 11

north would be severed by landing a small group on Kula Gulf.

Meanwhile, on June 20, a coastwatcher reported that three barges loaded with Japanese troops had landed at Segi Point on New Georgia. Aware that D-Day was only nine days away, Turner decided to land marines the next day to insure that the enemy would not have an opportunity to dig in. The marines landed with very little opposition.

D-Day for Toenails was June 30. The weather dawned rainy and windy, but the landing proceeded. Bad weather continued to hamper the Americans for the next four days with some relief coming on July 4. The first major task on D-Day was the landing of sixty-three hundred troops on Rendova Island. Another task was the landing of a force on Zamana Beach on New Georgia. As the Americans moved ashore on Rendova, they were immediately attacked by Japanese aircraft. The enemy reported the sinking of a cruiser, two destroyers, and eight transports along with the destruction of fifty planes. In reality, the American losses were one transport, the *McCawley*, Turner's former flagship, and seventeen aircraft. The Americans downed sixty-five enemy planes.

Once more logistical problems plagued the amphibians as rain and mud slowed the landing of supplies. Still, having learned much over the previous months, the transports did a superb job in spite of the terrible weather and enemy air attacks.

For the next two weeks, fighting was intense and furious in the central Solomons. Accurately guessing that Munda was the primary American target, the Japanese moved over three thousand troops from Kolombangara to the area. Additional troops were transferred from the northern Solomons.

On July 5, a battalion of the One Hundred Forty-fifth Infantry Regiment secured Rice Anchorage, fifteen miles north of Munda. American forces converged on Munda from all directions.

Meanwhile, Turner's days in the Solomons were numbered. Earlier he had been ordered to conclude the planning for Toenails and report to a new assignment as commander of the Amphibious Force, Central Pacific. Turner's presence was urgently required at Pearl Harbor to begin planning for future attacks in the central Pacific. After a year of almost total action in the South Pacific, Turner left one hot spot for one that was potentially hotter.

During his time in the South Pacific, Turner was under a heavy strain. There was no doubt that he was a fighter, and a hard one at that, but he was also human.

> It was after this . . . rough-and-tumble contest with a first-class fighting Japanese Navy was over and won, that Rear Admiral Turner started to find in a nip at the bottle the necessary uplift to willingly wrestle another four or five hours of work each day after completing a normal twelve hours.[15]

After being relieved of his South Pacific command on July 15, Turner reported to Admiral Nimitz at Pearl Harbor. Following his debriefing, Turner was sent to the west coast of the United States to begin training the amphibious forces for the central Pacific drive.

On August 25, the new commander of the Fifth Amphibious Force reported to his immediate superior, Vice Admiral Raymond A. Spruance. Along with Turner, Spruance received the services of Maj. Gen. Holland Smith. Spruance's biographer says:

> He knew both of these officers to be extremely able fighters. He recognized that each was a strong personality, stubborn in support of his own views, and foresaw that there would be conflicts of views between the two, but believed, correctly, that he could diplo-

matically reconcile any differences of opinion between them.[16]

Turner's first concern on his return to Pearl Harbor was the assembling of a new staff for the Fifth Amphibious Force. As Chief of Staff he selected Capt. Paul Theiss, a man he was acquainted with from the earlier South Pacific campaigns.

Based on the experience of the past year, Turner was aware that an adequate flagship was a necessity if the multiple jobs of the amphibious force were to be handled efficiently. The old battleship *Pennsylvania* was designated his flagship. Though the *Pennsylvania* did not meet all his needs, the battleship was the best that could be provided for the first operation against the Gilberts, Operation Galvanic.

It was vital that Turner learn all he could about the proposed target. The Gilberts were low, flat, and sandy ribbons of coral, strung out in the ocean like a string of pearls. Turner was specifically interested in the tides. According to an Australian who had lived in the Gilberts before the war, landing conditions would be best during November and December.

By October, most of the data was compiled and a plan of attack drafted. Turner would be assault force commander with responsibility for the overall operation. In addition, he would command the Northern Attack Force whose target was Makin. Rear Admiral Hill would be subordinate to Turner and lead the Southern Attack Force against Tarawa.

A full dress rehearsal for the operation was impossible since it was not possible for all the assault units to participate. They were too widely dispersed. The Second Marine Division, slated to assault Tarawa, was en route from New Zealand. The Makin assault force, the Twenty-seventh Infantry Division, was in Hawaii. Nevertheless, a practice run was made with those forces that were available. Turner said:

> Abbreviated final rehearsals of the assault echelons were held in Efate and Hawaii, though some of the combatant vessels and a large part of the carrier aircraft could not participate.[17]

Turner's plan called for the islet of Butaritari in Makin Atoll to be assaulted from both the seaward and lagoon beaches. As for Tarawa, it was decided to have the Marines assault Betio islet from the lagoon beaches. Intelligence sources indicated that Tarawa was far more heavily defended than Makin. The official Army history states:

> Tarawa was the most heavily defended atoll that would ever be invaded by Allied forces in the Pacific. With the possible exception of Iwo Jima, its beaches were better protected against a landing force than any encountered in any theater of war throughout World War II. Makin, by comparison, was lightly held. But any beach guns that are manned and ready to fire are formidable enough to the men of the first waves of an amphibious landing force.[18]

Naturally, surprise was considered essential. Japanese air raids from bases in the Marshalls were an ever-present threat. Because of this threat, the two or more days of pre-landing shore bombardment, though desired, was considered too dangerous. If the Japanese were alerted to the American target, they would be able to mass their aircraft over the Gilberts and attack the transports. Thus, bombardment by the heavy ships and planes was limited to a few hours on the morning of D-Day itself.

Proceeding to their destination, the northern and southern attack forces rendezvoused six hundred miles southeast of the Gilberts on November 17. While the entire force moved toward its objective, the fast carrier units carried out a series of bombing raids against targets in the Marshalls.

Assembled off Makin Atoll on the morning of November 20 were four attack transports, three LSTs, and a landing dock. Altogether, sixty-five hundred assault troops were prepared to descend onto the atoll. Supporting battleships, cruisers, destroyers, and other vessels were available for various tasks. Within range of Makin also, were three small and three large carriers.

Around 6:00 A.M., aerial attacks began to strike targets on Butaritari. These attacks were followed soon afterward by an intensive naval bombardment. While the prelanding bombardment continued, the attack forces aboard their assault vehicles waited in the rendezvous area for orders to move to the line of departure. A little after 8:30, the troops began landing. No mines or barbed wire hindered the landings on the seaward side, but ragged coral obstacles caused some landing craft to run aground and delay the landings. Because of these delays, the assault troops fell behind schedule. By the time the fifth wave landed it was over one hour behind schedule. Besides the delay in landing the troops, there was also a delay in bringing equipment ashore. A reporter on the scene said:

Hydrographic conditions on both beaches, Red-1 and Red-2, prevented boats from landing as organized waves, causing boats to land as best they could through the coral. . . . The beach was wholly rocks and coral.[19]

At 10:00 Turner sent the news that the troops had landed with no opposition. Up to that point Japanese resistance had been negligible.

Two hours after the seaward landings, the lagoon

landings commenced. As they moved ashore, the attackers were peppered by Japanese snipers. Once again beach conditions were poor, making it difficult to land men and supplies.

It took the Army troops three days to eliminate Japanese resistance on Butaritari. Though it aroused interservice strife, the relative slowness of the advance was as much indicative of the defenders' ability as the attackers cautious methods. Logistical support was a nightmare due to the unfavorable beach conditions. Tracked landing vehicles were found to be the only vehicles suitable for bringing supplies ashore.

Thanks to tireless efforts on everyone's part, the transports were unloaded completely by the afternoon of the twenty-third. By that time the island was secured. The assault forces reembarked on the morning of the twenty-fourth after turning the area over to garrison troops. By the twenty-ninth, all logistic support for the garrison was ashore.

Because of the length of time it took for the campaign and the unloading of the transports, there was danger of Japanese retaliation both from air and sea. The sea danger proved a reality when, on November 24, the Japanese submarine *I-175* torpedoed the escort carrier *Liscombe Bay*. The carrier went down with heavy loss of life. The destruction of the *Liscombe Bay* raised the point that the longer the amphibious assault phase, the greater the risk to the fleet. Had the capture of Makin been conducted in a more speedy manner, the *Liscombe Bay* probably would have been out of the danger area before the twenty-fourth.

One of the officers on Turner's staff made this assessment of his superior's conduct of the operation.

His exercise of command was personal and direct, as he extended it through every echelon down to all levels. He prepared his orders in minute detail. On

D-Day with ships and craft of every type and size in the transport area, he knew where each should be and when, and he did not hesitate to heap abuse on any skipper who was slow or timid moving into position.[20]

Since Turner was so deeply enmeshed in his own problems at Makin, Harry Hill conducted the operation at Tarawa pretty much on his own. The battle at Tarawa has been thoroughly covered elsewhere in this book and will not be repeated here. It should be noted, however, that although this battle was costly, many valuable lessons were learned.

Following the battle, much controversy developed as to whether the Gilberts should have been invaded at all. Turner felt that they were a natural and obvious road into the eastern part of the Japanese Empire and that possession of them would provide essential bases for the advance into the strategically important Marshalls.

A French naval historian has put the importance of Tarawa in proper perspective.

For Tarawa was the staging base to the Fiji and Samoan Islands, and although the need for its capture was not too apparent in November, 1943, its possession by the United States was the final link in the denial of the South Pacific to Japan.[21]

The seizure of the Gilberts was thus considered necessary despite the critics. The experience alone benefited all future operations. In addition, by the end of December, fighters from the newly acquired airfields in these islands began bombing and reconnaissance missions over the Marshalls. Dividends from the heavy investment were about to pay off.

Turner was determined to utilize all his expertise during the forthcoming Marshalls campaign, Operation Flintlock.

He wanted this operation to be as economical as possible.

While returning to Pearl Harbor in early December, Turner wrote a paper entitled "Lessons Learned at Tarawa." He also drafted an operational plan for the Marshalls calling for a preliminary landing at Wotje and Maleolap. After pausing, the Americans would then assault Kwajalein and Eniwetok. At that very moment, Nimitz's staff was embroiled in a heated debate over targets in the Marshalls. Nimitz had a proposal of his own which called for a direct advance to Kwajalein. Along with Spruance, Turner opposed Nimitz's suggestion. He wanted to start at the eastern edge of the island chain and work toward the middle. Nimitz, however, was in possession of reconnaissance photos taken of Kwajalein on December 4. These showed that the Japanese were building an airstrip on the island and were heavily reinforcing the atoll. Nevertheless, Turner was apprehensive of striking into the heart of the Marshalls initially for fear that from the fringe islands, the enemy would be able to use their land-based air power to decimate the support shipping assembled off Kwajalein. Spruance attempted to argue his case with support from both Turner and Holland Smith, but Nimitz would not be moved. In referring to Turner, Nimitz said:

When I made the decision we would take Kwajalein first, I was told by Kelly that it was dangerous and reckless. I finally told Kelly, "This is it." If you don't want to do it, the department will find someone else to do it. Do you want to do it, or not? He smiled and said, "Sure I want to do it." And he did it to a T. That was the only real difference of opinion between Kelly Turner and me.[22]

D-Day for Flintlock was slated for January 17, 1944. This meant that Turner had but seven weeks between the two operations for planning. Furiously he digested the lessons of

Tarawa and implemented changes and improvements in tactics and techniques.

Among the improvements he wanted to make were, first, an improved method of acquainting the attackers with the exact nature of the assault beaches, particularly the under-water geography. To aid in this phase he recognized the need for underwater demolition teams. Therefore he recommended the formation of such teams on a permanent basis. Second, a quicker method of loading and unloading was necessary. Better organization at the beachhead was the answer to this problem. Turner suggested that a beach-master with adequate rank be assigned to take charge of the beachhead and organize the flow of traffic. The beach-master would bring order out of the chaos and congestion usually found on an assault beach. Third, follow-up shipping must be improved and fourth, additional LVTs were needed. Finally, improved and more precise close-in gunfire support was necessary.

As D-Day approached, Turner decided that more preparation time was needed. He recommended to Nimitz and Spruance that the date be postponed for two weeks in order to allow for the arrival of additional amphibious tractors for the Seventh Infantry Division. January 31 became the new D-Day.

For Flintlock, Turner was the commander of both the joint expeditionary force and of the Southern Attack Force. He would personally supervise the landings on the southern half of the large atoll of Kwajalein. Rear Admiral Richard Conolly would command the Northern Attack Force. Conolly's objectives were the twin islets of Roi-Namur in the northern half of Kwajalein Atoll.

Along with Kwajalein, Majuro was also to be seized. However, that atoll was considered to be lightly held if in fact it was defended at all.

To facilitate the movement of ships into Kwajalein Lagoon, the small islands guarding the main entrances to the lagoon were to be seized first. Meanwhile, from the recently conquered Gilberts, land-based bombers began a systematic bombardment of the Marshalls.

On January 8, the *Rocky Mount,* flagship of Admiral Turner, left Pearl Harbor to conduct rehearsals. The main body of the Joint Expeditionary Force, Task Force 51, left on the twenty-second.

The initial landings on the small islets covering the sea passage into Kwajalein Lagoon took place right on schedule during the late night of January 30, and the early morning of the thirty-first. Little opposition was encountered.

The main assault on Kwajalein itself commenced on the morning of February 1. The day before, the UDT units went to work on the beach approaches, but found neither underwater obstacles nor antiboat mines off the assault beaches. The Japanese were caught completely by surprise.

The order went out at 6:01 to land the landing force. The landings went off without a hitch with the first wave touching firm ground at 9:30. Coral did hamper landings in the Red Beach area, but the logistical support was able to be brought ashore over the other beaches.

For the Seventh Infantry Division, progress was slow but steady. The Japanese opposed every step viciously just as they had in the Gilberts. Nevertheless, on the fourth, Turner announced the capture of Kwajalein. Three weeks later, he left Kwajalein satisfied with the performance of the amphibians. A member of his staff described Turner during the campaign.

I truly saw him in action night and day, afloat and ashore. Admiral Turner had an almost unbelievable capacity for work. He drove himself without mercy, and he expected and demanded the same of those around him. I never saw him relax or take his ease.[23]

While Turner was engaged at Kwajalein, Admiral

Conolly coordinated the Roi-Namur landings. This operation was expertly conducted and the Fourth Marine Division captured the twin islands in short order.

Before returning to Pearl Harbor, Turner participated in the decision to attack Eniwetok Atoll immediately. As we have already seen in the Spruance chapter, the target date for this attack was May 10. It was apparent to the Fifth Fleet Commander, however, that the longer he waited to move on Eniwetok the more time the Japanese would have to fortify the island. The only question was whether enough forces could be assembled for an immediate attack before the fleet left to support General MacArthur's drive across New Guinea.

Since the Kwajalein operation had gone well, the reserve of over ten thousand troops was not committed. Admiral King inquired if the capture of Eniwetok, Operation Catchpole, could be conducted using these troops. King recognized the opportunity, as did Nimitz. Turner meanwhile, had, even before King's inquiry, dispatched a message to Spruance stating that he and Holland Smith both agreed that the Eniwetok operation should be undertaken at once. He suggested a target date of February 10. After much deliberation, however, D-Day was set for February 17. Even though Turner did not eventually lead the attack at Eniwetok, his initiative and influence were behind the operation and his experience added to Admiral Hill's success.

Turner could reflect upon the Marshalls campaign with a sense of satisfaction. The lessons of Makin and Tarawa paid huge dividends. The beach parties and beach masters functioned magnificently. The technique for determining underwater depth and obstacles was a success. From that point forward, underwater demolition teams became an essential part of all preassault preparations. The landing craft, the LVTs and DUKWs, justified their value. All in all, the Marshalls set the stage for future success using proven techniques established by Richmond Kelly Turner.

While the Kwajalein attack was still in progress, Nimitz sent King a dispatch recommending Turner for promotion to vice admiral. After a month of congressional debate and hearings, the recommendation was finally approved. Later, it was discovered that the promotion was delayed because of the objections of one congressman whose son had been killed in the Battle of Savo Island. This politician had blamed Turner for America's loss in the battle ever since. There had also been some unflattering press coverage of Turner's personality. *Time* magazine, in its February 7, 1944 issue, called Turner a "mean son of a bitch."[24] The article went on to degrade Turner's character. Nevertheless, despite the bad press, Turner was finally promoted on March 14, 1944.

By that time, Turner had already returned to Pearl Harbor to begin planning for the next step in the central Pacific drive, the Marianas.

The Marianas were Japan's inner defensive ring. Admiral King felt that these islands were the key to the western Pacific and if held by the Americans, could be used to sever the Japanese line of communication between the homeland and their southern empire. In addition, possession of the Marianas would place Japan within bombing range.

The Marianas attack was code-named Forager. The islands themselves were different from the small, flat coral atolls found in the Gilberts and Marshalls. The Marianas were large islands containing mountains, tropical vegetation, and a sizable urban population. Saipan contained not only a large native population, but a Japanese civilian one as well.

Turner's command responsibility now increased. His new title was Commander Amphibious Forces, Pacific. Accordingly, his staff had also grown and now totaled thirty officers. With this new staff Turner planned for what possibly was the most difficult operation of the war.

The three islands designated for assault were Saipan, Tinian, and Guam. The first was an island twelve and three-quarters miles long and five and three-quarters miles wide. From March, 1944, forward, the Japanese had anticipated an American move against Saipan and had rapidly increased their defenses. Realizing the vital importance of the Marianas, the Japanese planned a do-or-die campaign both on land and at sea. Defending the island of Saipan was Vice Admiral Chuichi Nagumo of Pearl Harbor fame and now commander of the Central Pacific Area Fleet. He was aided by Lt. Gen. Hidiyoshi Obata, the commander of the Thirty-first Army.

During that spring of 1944, thousands of Japanese reinforcements poured into the Marianas despite harassing attacks by U.S. submarines. The Japanese were determined to stop the invaders on the beaches.

Turner, though commander of the joint expeditionary force, Task Force 51, was also commander of the Northern Attack Force. Admiral Conolly had the Southern Attack Force. Turner's attack order for his force was a whopping three hundred forty-one pages.

Rehearsals were held between March 15-19 in the Hawaiian Islands. As a firm believer in thorough rehearsals and preparation, Turner insisted on a lengthy one. Though it served its purpose, the rehearsal encountered bad weather which grounded a few of the LSTs.

After the rehearsal the ships returned to Pearl Harbor. Then disaster struck. Since only six ammunition ships were available in the entire Pacific Ocean area, sixteen LSTs were designated to carry necessary shells and powder while ten more were loaded with rockets and machine-gun ammunition. These ships rested side by side, ammunition and rockets in their holds and gasoline drums littering their topsides.

On May 21, a shell exploded during loading which started a huge chain reaction. Fires and explosions raged.

Even Turner pitched in to fight the fires. He boarded a tug and personally led the fight to salvage whatever could be saved. At great personal risk, the admiral supervised the operation until the fires were out. Six LSTs and three LCTs were destroyed with a loss of one hundred sixty-three lives. Three hundred ninety-six more were injured.

King blamed the disaster on the carelessness, training, and discipline of the amphibious forces. Understandably hurt by these negative comments, Turner, notwithstanding the tragedy, drove himself and his amphibians hard to overcome the stigma and meet the timetable.

D-Day was scheduled for June 15, with the target, Saipan. After careful study, the beaches close to the village of Charan Konoa were selected as the landing point. The plan was to use the divisional reserve to make a feint about four miles north of the actual landing point in the hope of deceiving the enemy as to the actual invasion site.

By the time the invasion date rolled around, control of the air had been achieved. The underwater demolition teams reported that the barrier reef before Charan Konoa was flat enough to permit DUKWs to cross. They had also found no mines or underwater obstacles at the selected beaches. Instead, the Japanese had heavily mined the beaches close to Aslito airfield since they considered this area to be the obvious invasion point.

Two Marine divisions were scheduled to land simultaneously across the reef on eight beaches covering a six thousand-yard front. Eight thousand troops were expected to land in the first hour alone. This represented the largest amphibious landing in the Pacific to date and necessitated enormous logistic support. To quote Turner, the landings were "on the button."[25]

In the face of heavy machine-gun and mortar fire, the marines drove across the beaches. Though Turner's reports were optimistic, the lower echelons experienced some mechanical breakdowns. An LST's ramp chains broke during the assault. Others were disabled by enemy fire. The heavy fighting near the beaches posed serious problems for the follow-up forces carrying supplies ashore.

At nightfall, the weather deteriorated, causing more problems in ferrying in supplies. In addition, Japanese aircraft from airfields on Iwo Jima slowed operations. From June 17 until July 7, daily air attacks caused the amphibians many anxious moments. The greatest threat, however, came between June 19–21 during the Battle of the Philippine Sea.

In the Spruance chapter the aforementioned battle is covered in detail. The most significant aspect of the Battle of the Philippine Sea was that Spruance considered the protection of Turner's transports the most important objective.

While the naval battle raged, Holland Smith assumed command of the land forces at 10:00 A.M. on June 20, allowing Turner to turn his attention to Guam. The admiral insisted on Guam's early capture, but despite his insistence, the attack was postponed until July.

The reason for the postponement was the Battle of the Philippine Sea and the stiff Japanese opposition on Saipan. The Japanese defense caused the Americans to commit their force reserve, the Twenty-seventh Infantry Division. The intense fighting continued until July 10, when Saipan was finally declared secure. The cost was heavy with over fifteen thousand American casualties. Though the toll was high, the amphibious techniques were superb and were a vital factor in ultimate victory. Commodore H. B. Knowles wrote:

The Saipan landing plan is a landmark in Pacific amphibious history. . . . Described in this plan for the first time are the duties and organization of a control and beach-master set-up to handle a landing of multiple troop divisions, an expanded communication network to cover this more complex structure; a system for the transfer of assault troops to LSTs in the final staging area and the dispatch at the line of departure with troops already embarked, the use of rocket and mortar ships in direct support of the assault waves, and the addition of hospital LSTs close in shore to speed casualty handling.[26]

One negative sidelight to the Saipan campaign was the Smith versus Smith controversy. As a result of Holland Smith's disatisfaction with the Twenty-seventh Division's fighting ability, he recommended the relief of Maj. Gen. Ralph Smith, the division's commander. Turner concurred with the recommendation having had firsthand experience with the division at Makin. Turner also resented the attitude of Lt. Gen. Robert Richardson, the army commander of the Central Pacific Area, who sought to diminish the marines' authority by highlighting the army position. Richardson used the controversy to strike out at Holland Smith and the Marine Corps.

Angrily, Turner wrote to Nimitz complaining of Richardson's unwarranted assumption of command authority. Nimitz chose to disregard the letter. This in turn infuriated Turner even more and probably accounted for his rudeness when Richardson arrived at Saipan to examine the situation firsthand. Needless to say, the controversy could have split the services apart had it not been for the cool hand of Nimitz.

During the Guam landings, Turner was present for only three of the twenty days required for the island's capture. The operation was primarily left in the capable hands of Admiral Conolly. For twenty grueling days the assault forces battled a determined foe before Guam was finally declared secure. Months of mopping-up activity, however, were required before opposition was eliminated entirely.

For the Tinian operation the biggest problem was the

disagreement over which beaches to assault. Adm. Harry Hill was appointed force commander. The troops were for the most part, the same ones who had fought on Saipan. So confident was Turner in Hill's ability that on the actual day of the attack, he was aboard the *Rocky Mount* at Guam. It was prior to the attack that Turner made his greatest input.

Tinian is flat and open when compared to the hilly Saipan and Guam. There were three possible landing areas on Tinian: Sunharon Bay on the southwest coast, Asiga Bay on the east central coast, and the northwest coast nearest to Saipan.

Though they did not have the greatest sea approaches, the beaches at Sunharon Bay had some distinct advantages. The beaches did not have extensive swampy and wide lowlands behind them as did those at Saipan. This would allow for quick exits from the beach. Secondly, once a beachhead had been established, there was an excellent small-craft harbor with a narrow entrance. Behind the entrance was a shallow protective reef that would permit unloading in all but the most violent weather. The lone drawback was the fact that the Japanese also recognized the potential of this area and had dug in accordingly, fully expecting the Americans to invade at this point. Obviously, alternatives had to be explored, but the problem with this was that there were no other beaches that had a suitable topography for aiding the amphibious effort.

The beaches closest to Saipan, southwest of Ushi Point, known as White Beach One and Two, were possible alternatives. Unfortunately, they were not ideal since one was narrow and fringed by coral, the jagged edges of which protruded at low tide. The other beach featured a narrow exit into hilly country littered with rocks and heavy brush. Though wider than White Beach One, White Beach Two also had its share of coral in the waters offshore. The beaches at Asiga Bay were totally eliminated.

Though the final choice would be Admiral Hill's, any

decision was still subject to Turner's approval. The latter preferred the beaches by Tinian Town. Hill, however, favored the White beaches. Their proximity to Saipan would allow for direct artillery support from that island. Though the White beaches had small frontage and narrow, steep exits, Hill and his staff were convinced that they were still the most suitable. When he approached Turner, Hill was given emphatic orders to cease all planning for a landing at the White beaches. A hot-and-heavy debate ensued with Hill stating that a deeper reconnaissance of the beaches should be made before totally eliminating them as landing points. In Hill's own words:

> Here I was charged with the sole responsibility of planning, but ordered to prepare a plan that neither I nor Harry Schmidt (Landing Force Commander for Tinian) liked. I could fully appreciate Turner's fear of trying to use these little handherchief-sized beaches, but realized that we had considered all angles of the problems much more fully than he had.[27]

Hill respected Turner's judgment, but wanted to explore the possibility of using the White beaches further. Therefore, he split his planners into two groups, with one concentrating on a Tinian Town plan while the other continued to explore the potential of the White beaches.

The underwater demolition teams conducted an exhaustive survey of the beaches in question. Though beach obstacles were found, the general consensus was that the White beaches were usable.

Armed with this information, Hill went to the *Rocky Mount* to confront Turner. The latter was adamant and refused to listen to Hill's arguments. Turner again ordered Hill to concentrate on planning for landings at Tinian Town.

Hill was not to be outdone. He found an ally in Holland Smith who favored the White beaches himself. From there, Hill went to the Fifth Fleet commander and outlined his plan. Spruance liked the boldness of the plan, particularly the surprise element, since the Japanese were not anticipating a landing at that point. Spruance told Hill that he would call a conference in which Turner would be present along with Smith, Harry Schmidt, Thomas Watson (commander of the Second Marine Division), and Hill.

After a lengthy and frank discussion of the subject, Spruance called for a vote. The tally was four-to-one in favor of the White beaches. Everyone expected Turner to explode, but to their relief, he accepted the decision in good spirit.

Turner's primary concern was the logistic problem presented by an invasion of the White beaches. However, a detailed report presented at the conference convinced him of the practicality of using these beaches. Therefore, Hill was given the green light for an attack on the White beaches.

The landings went well thanks to the tactical surprise achieved. The Japanese were expecting the landings near Tinian Town. Though the narrowness of the White beaches did hamper the assault, the quick action of the marines minimized the negative aspects and the landings worked like a well-oiled machine. The attackers quickly captured the nearby airfields. This allowed cargo planes to bring in emergency supplies. By August 1, Tinian was in American hands. During this battle, a deadly weapon made its debut, a new type of bomb: napalm.

When viewed as a whole, the Marianas operation, from a logistic standpoint, was a huge success, one Turner could justifiably be proud of. With Japan's inner defensive ring pierced, her war effort was doomed.

At the completion of the Marianas campaign, Turner and his staff returned once more to Pearl Harbor, there to begin planning for the next objective. But no one knew just what the next objective would be.

In the debate between King and MacArthur, Turner sided with the general by favoring the capture of Luzon in the Philippines. Turner wanted Luzon in order to obtain fleet bases which he considered necessary for an attack against either China or Formosa. His opinion became a matter of record when King arrived at Pearl Harbor in July, 1944.

After much debate and discussion, Iwo Jima and Okinawa became the next objectives of the central Pacific forces. The former was targeted for invasion on January 20, 1945, and the latter for March 1. These dates were later changed to February 19 and April 1, respectively.

Loading for detachment, the capture of Iwo Jima, began on December 27, 1944. On January 10, Turner shifted his flag from the *Rocky Mount* to a new amphibious command ship, the *Eldorado*.

Iwo Jima is a volcanic island four and one-half miles long and two and one-half miles at its widest point. Dominating the island's neck is Mount Suribachi, an extinct volcano rising to a height of five hundred forty-six feet. The northern half of the island is rocky and hilly, rising three hundred feet above sea level. This area features many cliffs, canyons, and caves, excellent for conducting a defense. Between Mount Suribachi and the northern plateau is a large layer of volcanic sand. All of Iwo's beaches are also covered with a thick layer of sand.

Besides the normal logistical problems involved in supporting an assault, Iwo gave the amphibians a new problem: the need to transport fresh water since the island had no fresh-water wells or clear-running streams.

Turner knew that the American forces would face adverse weather which would add to the difficulty of unloading ships. The Fourth and Fifth Marine divisions were assigned to land along the southeastern beaches of the island. Rehearsals were held in Hawaii from January 11 to the eighteenth. Turner missed them because of a virus infection. Admiral Hill commented on Turner's health:

Turner had a bad back which required him to wear a heavy brace, but primarily he had been driving himself so hard for the past two years that he had lost weight and looked badly.[28]

When the expeditionary force sailed from the Marianas, Turner again took sick with a high fever. For a while it appeared as if he would be too ill to participate in the Iwo Jima attack, but fortunately, he recovered in time.

The Japanese had turned Iwo Jima into a veritable fortress. Knowing that the island would eventually be a target they had prepared for the inevitable attack. The preliminary bombardment was extensive. Thirty percent more ammunition was expended than had been at Saipan. Aware that the island was only seven and one-half square miles, as opposed to Saipan's seventy square miles, one could easily see why it was possible to give Iwo Jima an enormous pasting. Yet, the Japanese skill in concealing their guns left many still operational to greet the marines on the nineteenth of February.

The first assault wave hit the beaches at 9:00 A.M. and moved inland for the first three hundred fifty yards quickly. By 9:20, when the later waves began to hit, Japanese gunfire was heavy and deadly accurate. The steep beaches and the volcanic sand made movement slow and difficult. Nevertheless, by the end of the first day, thirty thousand marines were ashore.

Logistic support was a headache due to the strong inshore current. As each succeeding wave moved shoreward, boats were literally picked up and thrown broadside onto the beach where the waves swamped them and drove them deep into the volcanic sand.

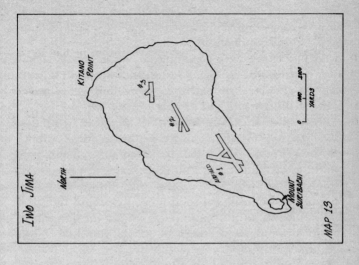

TINIAN

NORTH

USHI POINT

AIRFIELD

AIRFIELD

WHITE-1 BEACH

WHITE-2 BEACH

ASIGA BAY

GURGUAN POINT

TINIAN TOWN

AIRFIELD

MARDO POINT

MILES

0   1   2

MAP 12

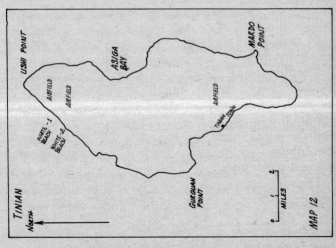

Iwo Jima

KITANO POINT

NORTH

#3

#2

AIRFIELD #1

MOUNT SURIBACHI

YARDS

0   1000   2000

MAP 13

During the next few days the weather deteriorated, further complicating the logistical difficulties. Added to that was the heavy Japanese resistance which created difficulty in enlarging the beachhead. This resulted in massive congestion. Supplies mixing with wreckage made the beaches resemble a huge junkyard.

Because of the dense concentration of assault shipping in a narrow sea area, collisions were also frequent. Thirty-six ships in all were involved in collisions during the period between February 16 and March 6.

Besides the natural difficulties and the bitter fighting on land, Japanese air attacks added to the American woes.

On February 23, the hard-working amphibians momentarily paused to view a thrill that each would remember for years: the historic flag-raising on Mount Suribachi. The thrill was short-lived, for a hard fight and difficult logistical problems lay ahead. On the very day of the momentous flag-raising, an article appeared in the Japanese *Domei News*:

According to reports issued by the enemy, the man who commands the American amphibious forces which effected landings on our Iwo Jima is Vice Admiral Richmond Turner. . . . He is the man who can be termed a devil man, being responsible for the killing of countless numbers of our own younger and elder brothers on the various islands throughout the central Pacific area.

This man Turner is called and known as the 'Alligator' in the American Navy. He is associated with this name because his work is very similar to that of an alligator, which lives both on land and in the water. . . . This man Turner, who has been responsible for the death of so many of our precious men shall not return home alive—he must not, and will not. This is one of the many things we can do to rest at ease the many souls of those who have paid the supreme sacrifice.[29]

And like an alligator, Turner's forces held on to Iwo Jima despite the Japanese boasts, and Turner himself continued to live. On March 9, he turned the amphibious forces over to Hill and returned to Guam in order to complete the planning phase for the Okinawan operation.

Iwo was declared secure on March 16, concluding a bloody battle. For the amphibians it had been their toughest challenge thus far. The unloading phase had been a nightmare, and was only accomplished because of their determination and resourcefulness. From Turner and Hill on down to the lowest seaman, the dangerous-but-necessary job helped make the Marine Corps' difficult task, which saw over six thousand of them killed and nearly twenty thousand wounded, a success.

Next came Okinawa, an island on the very doorstep of Japan. The operational name for the assault on the Ryukus, of which Okinawa was a part, was Iceburg. The plan featured an attack on Okinawa, initially scheduled for March 1, 1945, but later postponed to April 1. Planning for Iceburg was done in conjunction with the planning for Iwo Jima. This meant that initially, Turner's workload was doubled since there were two separate expeditionary troop commanders. For Iwo the troop commander was Holland Smith. For Okinawa, it was the Army's Lt. Gen. Simon Bolivar Buckner. Iceburg was the only operation in the central Pacific drive that involved the landing of an entire field army.

Okinawa is an island of four hundred sixty-five square miles. Sixty miles long, it is the largest island in the Ryukyu chain and is positioned a mere three hundred fifty miles from the Japanese island of Kyushu. Therefore, the attackers had to consider the added problem of air attacks from the Japanese home islands. The capture of Okinawa,

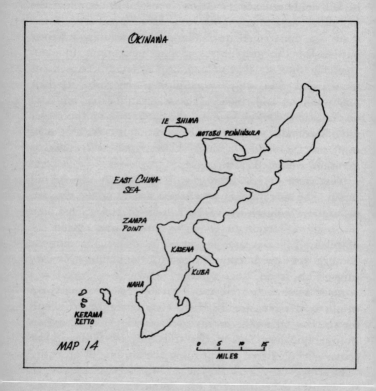

OKINAWA

IE SHIMA

MOTOBU PENINSULA

EAST CHINA
SEA

ZAMPA
POINT

KADENA

KUBA

NAHA

KERAMA
RETTO

MAP 14

0   5   10   15
MILES

however, was deemed essential by Allied staff planners, for the development of air bases and fleet anchorages to support a landing on Japan itself. (Map 14)

A necessary first step in the Iceburg plan was the seizure of Kerama Retto, a group of small islands twenty miles west of Okinawa. Containing an excellent anchorage, these islands would provide a sheltered haven where ammunition and other critical supply ships could be assembled. From there the ships could quickly reach Okinawa and deliver much-needed supplies to the fighting forces.

The beaches chosen for the assault were on the west coast of Okinawa about eleven miles north of the city of Naka. A bitter contest was anticipated now that Japan's back door was about to be blasted open. Buckner favored these west coast beaches because they were the only ones wide enough to permit the landing of two corps abreast of each other. In addition, two of Okinawa's main airfields were in that area.

The Japanese plan of battle called for the beachhead not to be defended. Instead, they would defend from prepared supporting positions in the interior. The Japanese had used this tactic in September of the previous year during the defense of Pelilieu and again at Iwo Jima with great success. Though they eventually lost these islands, the toll they exacted was high.

After leaving Iwo Jima on March 9, Turner stopped briefly at Guam en route to Leyte Gulf where the rehearsals for Iceburg were scheduled to take place. Joint rehearsals were out of the question, due to the fact that the assault forces were scattered throughout the Pacific.

Following the rehearsals, the various assault forces began their movement toward the Ryukyus. Kerama Retto was the first objective. It presented the amphibians with a complicated task because the attack would take place on eight small beaches on four different islands. The assault was swift and successful. Kerama Retto began operating as an American base on March 28.

Meanwhile, the underwater demolition teams were carrying out their dangerous chores off the assault beaches of Okinawa. The assault forces plodded steadily forward toward their April 1 rendezvous date, but bad weather dogged the armada.

The April 1 landings went like clockwork since, as already related, the Japanese elected not to defend the beaches. The attackers moved across the beaches with relative impunity. Objectives not counted on being captured until the tenth day fell during the first few days. The major problems during those initial days were created by high winds that caused high swells and choppy seas. On the fourth day, the weather deteriorated even further. From noon of April 5 to the morning of the seventh, all unloading ceased. Many ships were grounded. A few collided.

When the weather cleared, a new threat struck the fleet causing even worse delays. The dreaded Kamikazes arrived in force. Despite all, the amphibians did a magnificent job of supporting the fighting forces, bad weather and Kamikazes notwithstanding. Okinawa was a tremendous victory, but in the navy's view, the cost was high. Casualties were enormous. Three hundred sixty-eight ships were damaged, thirty-six were sunk—fifteen of the latter were amphibious ships. Forty-nine hundred and seven sailors lost their lives.

After a month and a half of violent activity at Okinawa, Turner, who by now commanded the largest amphibious force of the Pacific war, was relieved from duty along with Admirals Spruance and Mitscher. This respite was intended to give them a well-deserved rest while allowing them time to prepare for the next objective, Japan. Admiral Hill took over from Turner on May 17.

On May 28, while he was in Guam, word reached Turner that he had been promoted to full admiral. The only other classmate of the class of 1908 to reach that high rank was

Thomas Kinkaid.

Turner submitted his plans for Operation Olympic, the invasion of Kyushu. In his opinion, the main purpose of the landings was the neutralization of the southern part of Japan as an enemy base and the establishment of naval and air bases for further operations against the Japanese homeland.

The amphibious forces designated for Olympic were more than twice the number used at Okinawa. Turner arrived in Manila on June 14, to begin joint planning with General MacArthur. From the fourteenth until the atomic bomb was dropped on Hiroshima on August 6, Turner worked around the clock on the amphibious phase of Olympic. From August 6 forward he continued to monitor the situation until the Japanese emperor finally made his historic statement of surrender. The war was over. Turner left Manila for Guam on the twenty-fifth. From there he proceeded to Japan so that he could be present at the surrender ceremony on the deck of the USS *Missouri*.

After the surrender, Turner, along with two other naval officers, made a quick visit to Tokyo. The naval hierarchy, however, realized that Turner needed to get home and rest after three years of heavy burdens. The job had taken a heavy toll of his health. This was compounded by his problem of excessive indulgence in alcohol. Turner's biographer said:

The umph from the bottom of the bottle had kept Richmond Kelly Turner doing the work he relished so heartily.[30]

So the warrior returned from the war. By late October he was in California where he was ordered to report to the general board. There he was ordered to ready himself to testify before the congressional investigation on the disaster at Pearl Harbor.

As his first postwar assignment, Turner asked for the presidency of the Naval War College. However, Ray Spruance was appointed to that position. Instead, Turner was assigned as the United States representative on the military staff committee of the United Nations Organization.

In March, 1946, Turner took up his duties at the U.N. headquarters in New York City. He found himself engaged in many debates with the Russians. His work was both interesting and frustrating. The frustrations increased as the United States and the Soviet Union moved from being allies to antagonists. Turner also held the opinion that Germany and Japan should both be restored to productive nations. In the process of arguing his beliefs, more and more he became an ardent anticommunist.

On July 1,1947, Turner reached the mandatory retirement age. This did not come easy to a man so accustomed to an active life.

On October 26, 1953, Turner accepted an invitation to become an honorary member of the Pacific War Memorial Commission.

Mrs. Turner died in January, 1961. After her death the admiral became terribly depressed. A little over a month later, Kelly Turner himself was dead, having choked on a chicken bone. Six months later, his personal physician disclosed that the actual cause of the admiral's death had been a heart attack. It seems he suffered the attack while eating the chicken and, as he gasped for breath, sucked in a piece of chicken bone which became lodged in his windpipe.

Turner was buried in Golden Gate Memorial Cemetery.

"Terrible Turner" was truly an alligator, just as the Japanese had insisted. When he bit into something, he never let go of it. His contribution to eventual victory in the Pacific was enormous. One could disregard his hard disposition and even overlook his drinking problem, for when it came to the performance of his duty, Turner performed magnificently. Kelly Turner never missed a D-Day. His all-persuasive direction led the amphibians in the performance of their duty.

For four long and bitter years the United States Navy battled the naval forces of the rising sun of Japan across the vast expanses of the Pacific Ocean. During those years one man became one of the most beloved, respected, and famous naval leaders in American history. That officer was, of course, none other than Adm. William F. "Bull" Halsey. At times his fame rivaled or even eclipsed that of the publicity-conscious Gen. Douglas MacArthur. Incredibly, despite the latter's burning desire for headlines, he and Halsey got along famously and MacArthur did not begrudge the admiral his share of the glory.

The contribution to the war effort of Admirals Spruance, Nimitz, and King probably equaled, or in the opinion of some, surpassed that of Halsey. However, that is open to question and careful scrutiny. Halsey was a fighter whose sole purpose was the total destruction of Japan. Coupled with his affable manner, this attitude quite naturally endeared him to the press corps who were always looking for good copy. Accordingly, press releases heralded Halsey's exploits while those of his peers went relatively unnoticed by contrast. Nevertheless, Halsey was deserving of the praise heaped upon him.

William F. Halsey, Jr. was born on October 30, 1882, in Elizabeth, New Jersey. From the seventeenth century onward the Halseys were seafaring men. One forefather had been a pirate, others were whaling captains and merchant seamen. William's father had graduated from the naval academy in 1873 and rose to the rank of captain before retiring in 1907. He returned to active duty briefly during World War I, but soon afterward went back into retirement for good. Thus it was almost a foregone conclusion that young William would also seek a seafaring career.

William was two and one-half years old before he first saw his father, since the elder Halsey was at sea when his son was born and remained there for an extended period. The years that followed were typical for naval offspring. Each year William and his sister saw another naval base and another school. Not until he was thirteen years old did William, Jr. attend the same school for two consecutive years.

At the age of fifteen William began to entertain thoughts of entering Annapolis where his father was then serving as a physics and chemistry instructor. A letter written to President McKinley by the aspiring cadet requesting an appointment went to naught. So, too, did the efforts of his parents. Finally, after two exasperating years, the elder Halsey consented to his son entering the premedical school at the University of Virginia. After one semester, Halsey received his long-awaited appointment to Annapolis thanks to congressional authorization for an increase in the size of the brigade of midshipmen and his mother's machinations.

On July 7, 1900, William F. Halsey was sworn in as a member of the class of 1904. During his four years at the academy, Halsey was simply an average student with a penchant for mischief, despite the fact that his father was a member of the faculty. Halsey did excel at one thing, football. During his last two years he was the varsity fullback, but until the day he died Halsey downplayed his achievements on the gridiron.

Upon graduation in February, 1904 (President Theodore Roosevelt had shortened the academy course in order to staff his rapidly expanding navy), Halsey joined the battleship *Missouri*, forerunner of the famous "Mighty Mo" of

World War II fame. Near the end of 1905, Halsey was transferred to a former Spanish gunboat, the spoils of the Spanish-American War. The *Don Juan* was sent to Santo Domingo.

> For six solid months we never moved out of Samana Bay. Our only amusement was the comic-opera revolutions, and our only excitement the weekly mail steamer from the States.[1]

In February, 1906, Passed Midshipman Halsey received his long-awaited commission as an ensign in the U.S. Navy. A year later he was posted to the new battleship *Kansas* that was being prepared for President Roosevelt's ballyhooed dispatch of the American Fleet on an around-the-world flag-showing cruise. That fall, the "Great White Fleet," comprised of sixteen battleships, left the east coast on the first leg of its journey. The voyage took the fleet down the east coast of South America, around the tip of the continent, and north to California. From there the fleet moved on to Australia via Hawaii. Next came a stop at the Philippines before dropping anchor at Yokohama, Japan.

The Japanese rolled out the red carpet for their visitors. Officers and men alike were treated to a round of parties.

One particular party stood out in Halsey's mind. This gala took place on the *Mikasa*, flagship of the legendary Admiral Togo, victor of the Battle of Tsushima. Near the end of the festivities, some junior Japanese officers seized the commander of the American Fleet and tossed him into the air three times as a complimentary gesture. Naturally, the younger American officers reciprocated by doing likewise to Admiral Togo. One of these officers was Halsey who later commented on the ceremony:

> We were big, and he was a shrimp, so instead of tossing him gently, we gave him three real heaves. If

we had known what the future held, we wouldn't have caught him after the third one.²

Halsey returned home from the around-the-world cruise to a double jump in rank to lieutenant. Shortly after his return he married Francis Grandy, a Norfolk, Virginia, girl whom he had courted for a few years. Following their honeymoon, Halsey became executive officer of the destroyer *Lamson*. Then, in April, 1912, after a brief period of shore duty, he received his first independent command, that of the destroyer *Flusser*. Thus began a career in destroyers that would last for over twenty years. Unhappily, however, the *Flusser*'s division was ordered into reserve almost immediately.

In 1913, the new destroyer *Jarvis* was entrusted to Halsey's command. After two years at sea, he was once more assigned to shore duty at the naval academy as discipline officer. With the prospect of America being forced to enter the war then raging in Europe, Congress authorized an increase in the size of the navy. In the meantime, Halsey was rapidly becoming bored with life at Annapolis. America entered the war in April of 1917. The following December, Halsey was ordered to Ireland to take command of the destroyer *Benham*.

The destroyer division of which the *Benham* was a member was primarily responsible for escorting convoys safely to England. At war's end, Halsey was sent to join the Pacific Fleet as commander of a division of his own. In the fall of 1922, after a brief tour of duty in Washington, Halsey was appointed naval attaché in Germany. He remained in this post for two years before rejoining destroyers, a handful of which were on station in Europe at the time. Halsey was given command of one of these, the *Osborne*. For the next eighteen months the *Osborne* visited the various ports of call in Europe and saw extended duty in the Mediterranean. While on a visit to Malta, Halsey caught his first glimpse of an aircraft carrier, HMS *Hermes*.

In February, 1927, Commander Halsey became Captain Halsey. The new rank was accompanied by orders to return to duty at the naval academy. Shortly after arriving at Annapolis, Halsey received his initial exposure to naval aviation when he found himself responsible for a handful of pilots. Therefore, he set out to learn whatever he could about flying so that he could better understand the mentality and responsibilities of his subordinates.

Then, in 1930, the chief of the Naval Bureau of Navigation offered Halsey the opportunity to take the flying course at the naval air base at Pensacola. However, thanks to failing eyesight, a disability that he was unwilling to admit to, Halsey failed to pass the physical for pilot. Disappointed, he returned to sea as commander of Destroyer Squadron 14 in the Atlantic Fleet.

In June, 1932, Captain Halsey received a break. He was ordered to duty at the Naval War College at Newport, Rhode Island. From there he was given the opportunity to study at the Army War College. Obviously he was being considered for flag rank. The following year he was offered command of the carrier *Saratoga* by the chief of the Bureau of Aeronautics, Adm. Ernest King, providing, of course, that he earned his wings by taking the aviation observation course at Pensacola.

Halsey never had liked the fact that senior officers were able to earn their wings simply by flying as a passenger for a specified number of hours. To him it seemed like cheating. Therefore, upon his arrival at Pensacola in July, 1934, he used his influence to have his classification changed from student observer to student pilot. Later, he soloed for the first time despite his corrected vision. Within a year he had his wings and was ready to take command of the *Saratoga*. Halsey remained with the carrier for a year before returning to shore duty. Around the same time he was given his first star and promoted to rear admiral.

May, 1938, found the new admiral back at sea commanding Carrier Division 2, consisting of the two new carriers, *Yorktown* and *Enterprise*. Halsey selected the "Big E" as his flagship and thus began a relationship that was to last for four years. The following January, Halsey's division joined Carrier Division 1 for maneuvers in the Caribbean. The latter was made up of the carriers *Ranger* and *Lexington*. All were part of the battle force commanded by Admiral King. Among the carriers' captains were McCain, Pownall, and Hoover. Along with Halsey these men were pioneers in the use of aircraft carriers and all would eventually become household words in the halcyon days of the great carrier fleets of World War II.

Meanwhile, war clouds were forming over the Pacific. Halsey had never trusted Japanese motives and was convinced that war was inevitable. In his opinion it was only a matter of time before America would enter into a conflict with Japan in the Pacific. Europe had been at war for over a year.

After a change in commanders, Carrier Division 1 was ordered to Hawaii following the Caribbean maneuvers. The new commander of this force was Halsey. Upon arrival at Pearl Harbor, he was promoted to the temporary rank of vice admiral and given command of all carriers in the Pacific including his own division which he would continue to command directly.

That summer, Halsey had his first glimpse of an amazing new technical development, radar. So impressed was he with this invention that he made every effort to have it installed in as many of his ships as possible.

If I had to give credit to the instruments and machines that won us the war in the Pacific, I would rank them in this order: submarines first, radar second, planes third, bulldozers fourth.[3]

The next year and a half were spent with the Pacific Fleet on maneuvers and polishing the skills of the seamen and aviators alike. As the threat of war increased daily during the summer of 1941, the Pacific Fleet began to swell in size until it became a formidable force, although hardly capable of standing up to the powerful Japanese Fleet.

Despite their pride in the new carrier force, however, America's naval leaders, with few exceptions—such as King, Halsey, and Nimitz—continued to subscribe to the battleship theory. To them, the mighty battleships with their huge guns would ultimately decide the outcome of any battle. To think that aircraft carriers alone could win a struggle with the enemy was absurd.

By 1941, it was obvious to many that war with Japan was just a matter of time. Halsey shared this opinion. In February of that year Adm. Husband Kimmel was appointed Commander in Chief of the Pacific Fleet with headquarters at Pearl Harbor. Kimmel was an old friend of Halsey's and thus inclined to allow the latter a relatively free hand in the operation of the carrier force.

As November rolled around, few military men would admit that the threat of war did not exist. Accordingly, the Pacific Fleet command decided to bolster the defenses of Midway and Wake Islands with additional aircraft. Meanwhile, Kimmel realigned the fleet by creating separate Task Forces built around the carriers. Halsey became commander of Task Force 2, centered on the *Enterprise*.

On November 27, the Chief of Naval Operations, Admiral Harold Stark, sent a war warning to all commands. A war warning meant that the various commands should begin making preparations for war, as opposed to a war alert that would place all commands in a state of instant readiness. Stark's decision was based on information gathered, thanks to the breaking of the Japanese code.

The next day, the *Enterprise* and her escorts set sail for

Wake Island with a cargo of Marine fighter planes for Maj. James Deveraux, the garrison commander. Once at sea Halsey split his force, leaving the slow battleships behind to carry out maneuvers while the carrier force, redesignated Task Force 8, set a course for Wake. After making sure that the lumbering battleships were out of range, the admiral raised the eyebrows of his staff by issuing orders that stated that any Japanese shipping encountered, whether merchant or warship, was to be sunk immediately. The order went on to state that any Japanese aircraft were to be shot down.

Early in the morning of December 4, the *Enterprise* reached her launching position near Wake Island. The twelve Marine fighters were launched and Task Force 8 turned for home. The schedule called for the *Enterprise* and her consorts to reach Hawaii shortly after dawn on December 7. Fortunately, rough weather hindered refueling operations and the formation was delayed. At dawn it was still over two hundred miles from its destination.

At 6:00 A.M. Halsey ordered eighteen of *Enterprise*'s planes to take off and fly on ahead to Ford Island. Two hours later, the *Enterprise* received reports that there was an air raid taking place at Pearl Harbor. Halsey's original conclusion was that his own *Enterprise* planes were being fired upon so he quickly ordered a dispatch sent to Admiral Kimmel stating that the supposed attackers were in fact American planes. Before the message could be sent, however, other signals began being received in rapid succession, including "Air raid on Pearl Harbor. This is no drill. Japanese planes attacking Pearl and airfields on Oahu."

Kimmel immediately ordered all ships in the harbor to sortie and join up with Task Force 8. This meant that every ship at sea in the area of Hawaii was placed under Halsey's direct command. The only force not affected by this was the *Lexington*'s Task Force 12 which was en route to

Midway with a squadron of planes for that island's defense.

Halsey immediately split his force to search for the enemy fleet since there was no doubt that the attack on Pearl Harbor had been launched from the decks of aircraft carriers. Throughout the day and all through the night, Task Force 8 tracked down reported locations of the Japanese Fleet. Each report proved false. At mid-morning on the eighth, with fuel running low, Halsey ordered the Task Force to break off the search and head for Pearl.

That afternoon the *Enterprise* steamed slowly into the harbor. As the great ship moved majestically past the burning and sunken ships of the Pacific Fleet, Halsey surveyed the carnage from the bridge of his flagship.

The admiral was silent for a while; then we heard him mutter, "Before we're through with 'em, the Japanese language will be spoken only in hell."[4]

After a hasty refueling job, Task Force 8 sortied again the following morning to search for Japanese submarines and to defend against any possible Japanese landings. For six days the formation remained at sea before returning to base for fuel. As he stepped ashore, Halsey was informed that Kimmel had been relieved by Admiral Nimitz.

To his dying day Halsey defended Kimmel's actions at Pearl Harbor. As far as he was concerned the unfortunate Kimmel was simply a scapegoat for years of neglect, inadequate resources, and a complete lack of information regarding Japanese intentions even though Washington was relatively certain of the state of affairs and the possibility of a Japanese attack. However, no one thought that the attack would take place at Pearl Harbor.* Therefore, if Washington, with its up-to-date and accurate information

*John Toland's book *Infamy*, however, presents some interesting alternate views.

could not guess where the attack would fall, how could Kimmel?

The next month was spent escorting convoys from America and reinforcements to Wake and Midway. Near the end of the month Nimitz ordered Halsey to take Task Force 8 and raid the northern Marshall Islands. At the same time, Task Force 17 under Adm. Frank Fletcher in the *Yorktown* would hit the southernmost Marshalls and the Gilberts. On February 1, the *Enterprise* struck Japanese bases on Wotje, Kwajalein, Roi-Namur, Maloelap, and Taroa, while Fletcher carried out his raid farther south. The raid was a success in that it achieved complete surprise. Enemy installations were severely damaged and numerous aircraft were destroyed. American losses were light. Unfortunately, the *Enterprise* was damaged by a Japanese suicide plane that managed to sneak through the antiaircraft screen.

Three months after the attack on Pearl Harbor the situation in the Pacific was ominous. The Japanese had conquered the Bismarcks, Bougainville, and New Britain. From Rabaul on this latter island, Japanese forces struck southward into the heart of the Solomons. Singapore capitulated on February 15. The disastrous Allied defeat in the Battle of the Java Sea at the end of the month sealed the fate of the Dutch East Indies.

On March 30, the Joint Chiefs of Staff, unable to reach an agreement regarding one overall commander for the Pacific, split the theater in two, giving General MacArthur responsibility for the southwest Pacific and Nimitz command of the Pacific Ocean area. Nimitz and his chief, Admiral King, subsequently divided the Pacific Ocean area into three zones and appointed Adm. Robert Ghormley to act as commander for the South Pacific area.

Meanwhile, Task Force 8 had been active. Wake and Marcus islands were subjected to raids by *Enterprise* aircraft. Halsey remained at sea for most of the month before bringing the task force back to Pearl. There he was briefed by Nimitz about a special operation that Halsey was to command and of which only a handful of high-ranking officers were aware.

Halsey soon found himself on the way to San Francisco to meet with Army Air Force Col. James Doolittle. The colonel wished to discuss the possibility of attacking Japan itself with bombers. However, in order to accomplish this, the bombers would have to be ferried close enough to the target, since the United States did not possess a bomber with sufficient range to reach Japan. Halsey and Doolittle hit it off immediately. Halsey liked the spirit and determination of Doolittle. For his part, Doolittle was impressed by Halsey's aggressiveness. After reviewing the plan, Halsey stated that the operation could probably be carried off providing the planes were able to take off from the relatively short flight decks of the carriers. He emphasized that there was no way that the planes could land back aboard the ships. Doolittle had already reached the same conclusion and had made plans for the bombers to hit Japan and land at Chinese airfields. Halsey gave his approval to the daring plan. Anything that would bring the war to the enemy was all right with him providing it did not prove futile or wasteful.

Armed with Halsey's approval, Doolittle went ahead with plans for the operation. On April 1, sixteen B-25 medium bombers were loaded aboard the carrier *Hornet* at Alameda, California. The next day the *Hornet* weighed anchor and set sail for a predetermined rendezvous point.

On the thirteenth, the *Hornet* rendezvoused with Task Force 16, commanded by the newly appointed Commander, Carriers, Pacific, Admiral Halsey who continued to fly his flag at the masthead of the venerable "Big E." The mission called for the B-25s to be launched within range of the Japanese homeland.

During daylight hours on the seventeenth, the entire

Task Force refueled a thousand miles from Japan. The next day it headed at high speed toward the target. When it reached a position approximately six hundred fifty miles from Japan, a few Japanese fishing boats were encountered. Halsey ordered his escorting ships to sink these vessels. Then, although he was still two hundred fifty miles from the planned launching point, Halsey ordered Doolittle's planes launched. He could not run the risk of exposing his carriers to retaliation by the enemy. It was almost a certainty that the fishing vessels had sent off sighting reports before they could be sunk.

Before the B-25s took off, a number of medals were attached to the bombs carried by the raiders. These were medals and decorations that various American officers had received during tours of duty in Japan between the wars. Now they were being returned with a vengeance. Among the decorations were the ones received by Halsey during his cruise with the "Great White Fleet." Immediately after the final plane left the *Hornet*'s decks, Halsey reversed course and headed home at full speed.

Doolittle's raid accomplished little in the way of significant material damage. The Japanese, though, were totally confused as to how the Americans had developed such long-range bombers. Although Admiral Nagumo's carrier fleet set out to sea in an effort to locate any American carriers that might have been lurking about, the Japanese never suspected that the B-25s had successfully taken off from the decks of aircraft carriers. Instead, they felt that the planes could only have come from landing fields, probably at Midway. Therefore, Admiral Yamamoto had little trouble convincing the Japanese High Command of the necessity of conquering the American base at Midway.

While Task Force 16 was still at sea, the Americans intercepted and decoded a Japanese message indicating that an attack on Port Moresby, New Guinea was imminent. Nimitz quickly sent Admiral Fletcher with the carriers *Lexington* and *Yorktown* to intercept the Japanese force. Immediately upon his return to Pearl, Halsey with the *Enterprise* and *Hornet* was ordered to join forces with Fletcher. Task Force 16 sailed on April 30.

Unfortunately, the distance to the Coral Sea was too great to cover in the time available. While Halsey was still over a thousand miles away the Battle of the Coral Sea erupted. Fletcher's forces managed to sink the light carrier *Shoho* and damage the fleet carrier *Shokaku*. On the other hand, Fletcher lost the *Lexington,* and the *Yorktown* suffered heavy damage. Nevertheless, the Japanese invasion fleet turned back. A few days later, Task Force 16 was recalled to Pearl Harbor where Halsey was to face one of the greatest disappointments of his long career.

As far back as the meeting with Doolittle in San Francisco, an old nervous disorder, chronic dermatitis, had begun bothering Halsey. The itching was so bad that on many nights the best he could hope for were a few hours' sleep at best. During the following six weeks at sea the condition worsened until the itching became almost unbearable. Consequently, by the time the *Enterprise* dropped anchor at Pearl on May 26, Halsey was exhausted and obviously in need of treatment and a prolonged rest.

Before entering the hospital Halsey met with Nimitz. The latter briefed Halsey on the details for the forthcoming Midway operation and was anxious to have his recommendations for a replacement commander for Task Force 16. Halsey immediately forwarded the name of Adm. Raymond A. Spruance. Nimitz was reluctant to part with so valuable a staff officer, but nevertheless concurred with Halsey's recommendation. On May 28, Halsey watched from his hospital window as Spruance took the force to sea for its rendezvous with destiny: the great carrier Battle of Midway.

Halsey remained on the sick list for over two months with hospital stays at Pearl Harbor and Richmond, Virginia. Finally, late in August, the doctors certified him fit for duty once more. Early in September, he arrived back at Pearl Harbor to shouts of joy from the officers and men of the fleet. In his absence, much had transpired.

On August 7, the Americans had invaded Guadalcanal and Tulagi in the Solomons. Japanese were constructing an airfield on the former and with this was threatening to cut the lines of communication from Pearl Harbor to Australia. Originally the Solomons lay in MacArthur's southwest Pacific area. However, since any action against Guadalcanal would be primarily a naval show, and since Admiral King refused to allow MacArthur to command naval forces, the Joint Chiefs compromised and placed Guadalcanal in Nimitz's sphere. With the Pacific Ocean area split into three subcommands, responsibility for the Guadalcanal campaign fell to the Commander, South Pacific, Admiral Ghormley.

Ghormley was not the right man for the job, even though both King and Nimitz had recommended his appointment. He was unable to keep pace with the rapid sequence of events in the Solomons. On the night of August 8-9, at the Battle of Savo Island, the American cruisers *Quincy*, *Astoria*, and *Vincennes* were sunk along with the Australian cruiser *Canberra*. The cruiser *Chicago* was heavily damaged and two American destroyers were sunk. Only the failure of the Japanese Admiral Mikawa to follow up his spectacular victory saved the American beachhead on Guadalcanal from annihilation. Admiral Fletcher had not protected the beachhead with his carriers, fearing land-based enemy air attacks and the loss of yet another carrier.* Ghormley had concurred with Fletcher's decision to draw the carriers out of range. As a result of the Battle of Savo, Adm. Kelly Turner was forced to withdraw his amphibious

---

*Fletcher had lost the *Lexington* in the Coral Sea and the *Yorktown* at Midway.

forces from Guadalcanal leaving the marines there stranded.

On August 24, Fletcher mishandled his carriers at the Battle of the Eastern Solomons resulting in heavy damage to the *Enterprise*. The Americans did manage to sink the light carrier *Ryujo* during the battle, but failed to prevent the Japanese from reinforcing their forces on Guadalcanal.

On August 31, the *Saratoga* was torpedoed for the second time in the war and was laid up until the following November. Two weeks later, a Japanese submarine torpedoed and sank the carrier *Wasp* leaving Nimitz with the *Hornet* and the damaged *Enterprise* as the only two operational carriers in the Pacific. The Americans did manage a measure of revenge by sinking two Japanese destroyers and damaging two cruisers for the loss of one destroyer during the Battle of Cape Esperance on the night of October 10–11.

Ghormley, by this time, was becoming increasingly pessimistic over the events on Guadalcanal. The land battle was going nowhere and it seemed as if every time an American force entered the waters off the island — known as Ironbottom Sound in deference to the many ships that had already been sunk there — it was engaged by the enemy fleet.

Nimitz was unhappy with the way Ghormley was handling the situation. Early in September, General Arnold of the Army Air Forces and a member of the Joint Chiefs of Staff, met with Ghormley and was taken aback with the admiral's pessimistic attitude. Arnold immediately reported his findings to Nimitz who decided to see for himself.

On September 25, Nimitz arrived at Ghormley's headquarters in Noumea and was quickly convinced that there was no alternative but to relieve his unfortunate subordinate. Ghormley's pessimism was becoming infectious and was spreading throughout the South Pacific command. On October 16, after first obtaining King's permission,

Nimitz relieved Ghormley and replaced him with Halsey. The latter had repeatedly demonstrated that he was willing to fight and Nimitz was convinced that the South Pacific theater needed a fighter, one who could breathe some fire into the Guadalcanal campaign.

Unaware of the circumstances surrounding Ghormley, Halsey was awaiting his next command. While he marked time, he decided to make a fact-finding tour of the South Pacific. When his plane arrived at Canton Island on October 17, Halsey was handed a dispatch ordering him to proceed to Noumea immediately. As soon as his plane touched down at Noumea, Halsey was handed a letter marked "secret," ordering him to relieve Ghormley and to assume the position of Commander in Chief, South Pacific. His reaction was

"Jesus Christ and General Jackson! This is the hottest potato they ever handed me."[5]

Halsey spent the remainder of the day reviewing the theater situation with his predecessor. Ghormley graciously filled Halsey in on all pertinent information before heading for Pearl Harbor. Despite Ghormley's assessment, however, Halsey felt that a number of questions remained unanswered. Therefore, he scheduled a council of war with the key commanders on Guadalcanal.

The meeting took place at Noumea on the twentieth. Halsey asked the Marine commander, General Vandergrift, if he could hold on to his present position. The general replied yes, but he emphasized that in order to do anything more he would need reinforcements and supplies. Halsey promised to dig these up and kept his word. Support troops and additional marines were hastily dispatched to the island.

Meanwhile, American code breakers had discovered that the Japanese were planning a major attack against U.S.

positions on Guadalcanal. A large portion of their fleet had assembled at Truk. This could only mean one thing: a major offensive.

To meet the threat, Halsey combined Task Forces 16 and 17 containing the *Enterprise* and *Hornet* respectively and ordered them to patrol north of the New Hebrides. On the twenty-fifth, the Japanese force was sighted steaming south. The next day the carrier Battle of Santa Cruz was fought. Two enemy carriers were seriously damaged and over one hundred planes were destroyed along with their experienced pilots. On the American side, only twenty planes were lost, but, after a severe mauling, the *Hornet* was abandoned and sunk. Despite the loss of the *Hornet*, though, the battle was a strategic victory for the Americans. The Japanese force turned around and headed back to port.

On November 8, Halsey flew to Guadalcanal for a first-hand view of the situation. He toured the front lines, met with his commanders, and talked to the men in the field. Before leaving for Noumea the following day, the admiral held a press conference. When one of the correspondents asked what his intentions were, he replied "Kill Japs, kill Japs, and keep on killing Japs."[6]

Since Japanese transmissions were being read daily, it was discovered that the enemy was planning yet another major attack on the night of November 12. The Japanese Fleet would bombard U.S. positions on Guadalcanal to cover a major landing of reinforcements. At the time, Admiral Turner was planning a major delivery of supplies and reinforcements to the American troops. Turner stepped up the schedule and by the time the Japanese arrived, all his ships were unloaded and heading for home. But it had been a close call.

Halsey turned his attention to finding a force that could prevent the Japanese from carrying out their mission. A force of cruisers and destroyers under Adm. Norman Scott was patrolling south of Guadalcanal. Unfortunately, Scott's formation was much too small to engage the Japanese on its own. Therefore, Halsey ordered another similar but larger force under Adm. Dan Callaghan, that was escorting a convoy from Noumea, to leave his charges behind, head for Guadalcanal, and, as senior officer, assume tactical command of both his own and Scott's formations. Halsey also ordered Admiral Kinkaid, commander of Task Force 16 *(Enterprise)*, to make for the area at full speed. Unfortunately, this force was miles to the south and would need time to reach the area. This was also the case for a force of two new battleships, under Adm. Willis Lee. Nevertheless, Halsey was determined to spare no effort so he ordered Lee to take his battleships, *South Dakota* and *Washington,* and proceed to Guadalcanal at the highest possible speed.

Callaghan's and Scott's combined fleet contained five cruisers and eight destroyers. Shortly after midnight on the twelfth, Japanese Admiral Abe brought his force of two battleships, one cruiser, and fourteen destroyers into the waters near Guadalcanal. The Americans blundered headlong into Abe's formation. Callaghan maneuvered his formation between the twin columns of the enemy and quickly found himself under fire from both sides. The battle quickly became one of mass confusion with ships milling around, out of formation, and firing at each other at point-blank range.

Early in the battle the *Atlanta*'s bridge was hit, killing Admiral Scott. Callaghan lost his life a few minutes later when the bridge of the *San Francisco* was deluged by Japanese shells. The American battle line, leaderless and flanked by enemy warships, became a confused flotilla of harassed and burning ships. Only the grace of God spared the Americans from total annihilation. Nevertheless, in addition to the *Atlanta,* four destroyers were lost. They were joined at the bottom of Ironbottom Sound by two

Japanese destroyers. With few exceptions, all American ships suffered damage. To add to the American woes, the cruiser *Juneau*, carrying the five Sullivan brothers, was torpedoed by a Japanese submarine the next morning and disintegrated in a hail of fire and steel.

During the course of the battle, Admiral Abe's flagship, the battleship *Hiei*, was repeatedly hit by the small-caliber fire of American destroyers. Although the tin cans' guns had no hope of penetrating the armor-plating of the Japanese leviathan, they did manage to score some hits in vital areas. The battleship's upper works were riddled and fires broke out. Eventually, the fires reached the vital section of the ship. While Abe was retreating up the Slot, the *Hiei*'s controls failed her and, north of Savo Island, she began steaming in circles, unable to respond to her helm.

The next morning, American planes from Henderson Field and the *Enterprise*, the latter having been ordered on ahead by Kinkaid to aid in the defense of the island, pounded the *Hiei* unmercifully and sent her to the bottom. Small consolation for the loss of so many brave American lives. The deaths of Scott and Callaghan in particular distressed Halsey. However, the first Battle of Guadalcanal was just the beginning.

On the thirteenth, Admiral Tanaka set out from the Shortlands with his "Tokyo Express," carrying reinforcements and supplies for the Japanese troops on Guadalcanal. Tanaka's force was covered by Admiral Mikawa with a force of one battleship, four cruisers, and nine destroyers.

Meanwhile, Kinkaid was steaming at full speed for the area. When Tanaka's force was sighted by coastwatchers south of New Georgia, the *Enterprise* launched her planes and caught up with Tanaka in the Slot. Aided by planes from Henderson Field and B-17s from Espiritu Santo, the Big E's pilots managed to sink six transports and damage another extensively. The latter was forced to return to the Shortlands. Tanaka's remaining transports were beached on Guadalcanal where they were later destroyed by marauding American aircraft.

Meanwhile, Mikawa and Lee were racing toward Guadalcanal on opposite courses. Just before midnight on the forteenth, the two formations sighted each other east of Cape Esperance. The Japanese were under the impression that all American surface opposition had vanished with the destruction of Callaghan's force two nights earlier. Thus, Mikawa, anticipating a free hand in bombarding Guadalcanal, was totally unaware that another American formation had reached the area. The Japanese were even more surprised by the presence of the *South Dakota* and the *Washington*.

Soon after the battle began, the Japanese battleship *Kirishima* became the target of the American ships. Hit repeatedly, the *Kirishima* settled to the bottom of Ironbottom Sound. She was joined there by the destroyer *Ayanami*. The heavy-caliber guns of Lee's formation had turned the tide. Thanks, however, to their marvelous talent for night-fighting, the Japanese managed to sink three American destroyers. But the Japanese attack had been beaten off. The second naval Battle of Guadalcanal was a victory for the Americans and a morale builder for Marines and Navy alike. "Bull" Halsey had kept his word. He would stop at nothing to protect the American forces on the island, even though he was scraping the bottom of the barrel.

Halsey continued to pour reinforcements into Guadalcanal. Anxious over the exhausted condition of the marines, he demanded and eventually obtained, Army reinforcements. General Patch's Americal Division relieved the First Marine Division on December 9. Patch immediately went over to the offensive. Later, bolstered by the addition of General "Lightning Joe" Collins' Twenty-fifth Division, the Americans began to drive the Japanese into one small corner of the island.

Meanwhile, other naval battles were fought. One of these, the Battle of Tassafronga, resulted in a striking and decisive victory for the brilliant commander of the Tokyo Express, Admiral Tanaka. On the night of November 20, Tanaka's destroyer column was discovered running supplies into Guadalcanal. A force of American cruisers and destroyers under Rear Admiral Carleton Wright moved to attack. Tanaka immediately reacted. The Japanese destroyer *Takanami* came under fire from the combined guns of Wright's force. A few moments later, the American formation was a wreck.

The *Minneapolis* lost her bow, as did the *New Orleans*. The *Pensacola* had a hole blown in her side by the Japanese long-lance torpedoes. The same fate befell the *Northampton* which was hit twice and left burning and dead in the water to sink a few hours later.

Despite the debacle at Tassafronga, the American steam-roller on Guadalcanal rolled inexorably forward during the remaining weeks of December and on into January. Halsey decided to put a halt to the harassing enemy air attacks once and for all. The Japanese were in the process of building an airstrip on the island of Kolombongara, north of New Georgia. On the night of January 23–24, a formation of American cruisers and destroyers under Admiral Ainsworth bombarded this airstrip and put it out of commission temporarily.

As January drew to a close the end was in sight on Guadalcanal. The Americans were by this time simply too powerful and the momentum had swung their way for good. Nightly Tokyo Express runs and Japanese submarines were beginning to withdraw what remained of the Japanese forces on Guadalcanal. To protect against these forays, Halsey had a force of cruisers and destroyers patrolling up the Slot night and day.

Task Force 18 under Adm. Robert Griffin was on just such a patrol on the night of January 29, when it was jumped by a swarm of Japanese planes from Munda. The cruiser *Chicago* took two torpedoes in her side and stopped dead in the water. Griffin's force managed to beat off the rest of the attack with minimal damage to itself. The next day another flight of enemy planes located the helpless *Chicago*, which was under tow. Four more torpedoes sent the survivor of the battle of Savo to the bottom. This battle was the last sea engagement in the six-month-long struggle for Guadalcanal. By the end of the first week in February, the Tokyo Express had withdrawn all remaining Japanese troops from the island and deposited them on New Georgia and Kolombongara. On February 9, General Patch sent this message to Halsey at Noumea:

> Am happy to report this kind of compliance with your orders . . . Tokyo Express no longer has terminus on Guadalcanal. The sufferings have been tremendous, but they have brought a priceless reward.[7]

Halsey demonstrated his sense of humor by wiring back:

> When I sent a patch to act as a tailor for Guadalcanal, I did not expect him to remove the enemy's pants and sew it on so quickly. Thanks and congratulations.[8]

Halsey had justified Nimitz's and King's faith in him totally. Guadalcanal was securely in American hands and could now be used as a staging area for future operations in the Solomons. His reputation soared. Here was a man who actually led by getting involved in the day-to-day conduct of the battle instead of being an officer who merely commanded. He was respected by his subordinates as a man whose word could be counted on. Even more significant was the boost to American morale. The men in the field and at sea adored their fiery leader.

Now that Guadalcanal and, therefore, the southern Solomons were secure, the build-up for a drive up the Solomons chain began in earnest. The next target was the Russell Islands just north of Guadalcanal. From there the Americans would attack New Georgia where the Japanese had a major airfield at Munda. New Georgia would serve as a central Solomons base for future operations. The ultimate objective of the entire Solomons campaign was the great Japanese naval bastion of Rabaul on New Britain. The latter sat in the Bismarck Archipelago and was scheduled to be attacked by MacArthur's forces after they had secured New Guinea.

Originally, the Solomons were entirely in MacArthur's southwest Pacific command. However, since the campaign on Guadalcanal was primarily a naval show and Admiral King refused to allow MacArthur to command large naval forces, the Joint Chiefs of Staff compromised and placed Guadalcanal and Tulagi in Nimitz's Pacific Ocean command. No such compromise was forthcoming for the central Solomons drive. Thus Halsey now found himself in a confusing command setup. Tactically, he was responsible to MacArthur. But, since he had to draw his ships and men from Nimitz, he was also accountable to the latter.

During the second week in February, Halsey sent a small reconnaissance force to gather information about the terrain on the Russell Islands. The patrol returned on the eighteenth with word that no Japanese were present on the islands. Therefore, a full-scale invasion was unnecessary. Operation Cleanslate, the invasion of the Russell Islands was unopposed.

Once the Joint Chiefs settled the issue of command, MacArthur set his staff to drawing up plans for Elkton, the capture of New Britain and the elimination of the Japanese base at Rabaul. Elkton called for a drive up the east coast to New Guinea coupled with a drive up the Solomons, the latter to be known as Operation Cartwheel.

On April 15, Halsey flew to Brisbane for talks and his first meeting with General MacArthur. The admiral was seeking permission for an attack on New Georgia. Japanese aircraft from the airfield at Munda on New Georgia constantly harassed the American build-up on Guadalcanal. Munda had to be neutralized before any future operations in the Solomons could take place. In addition, New Georgia in American hands could serve as a jumping-off point for Bougainville, another island littered with Japanese airfields, the foremost being at Buin.

Each commander's staff looked forward to the meeting between Halsey and MacArthur with a sense of apprehension. The admiral was outgoing, aggressive, and eager to fight. The general on the other hand was haughty, arrogant, and inflexible. Both were the subject of much publicity and MacArthur did not relish sharing the spotlight.

The meeting went better than anyone dared hope. Halsey's proposal for an invasion of New Georgia was greeted with enthusiasm by MacArthur, who immediately ordered his staff to make the appropriate plans. The general was impressed by Halsey's aggressive manner. After the talks ended and Halsey was en route back to Noumea, MacArthur, never one to lavish praise, remarked:

> He was of the same aggressive type as John Paul Jones, David Farragut, and George Dewey. His one thought was to close with the enemy and fight him to the death. The bugaboo of many sailors, the fear of losing ships, was completely alien to his conception of sea action.[9]

For his part, Halsey was impressed with MacArthur. He was satisfied that he could work with the general, despite the latter's reputation as a difficult man to get along with. For the Solomons campaign, although Halsey would be primarily on his own, his drive would be mutually supportive of the New Guinea campaign that was preoccupying MacArthur.

Two days after Halsey's trip to Brisbane, an American listening post in the Aleutians intercepted a Japanese transmission detailing the itinerary of Admiral Yamamoto, Commander in Chief of the Combined Fleet, who was on a tour of Japan's South Pacific bases. The information was forwarded via Washington to Nimitz who passed it on to Halsey with this note:

> If forces in your command have capability intercept and shoot down Yamamoto and staff, you are hereby authorized to initiate preliminary planning.[10]

Since Halsey had not yet returned from his meeting with MacArthur, his executive officer, Adm. Theodore Wilkinson took the message to the commander of the air forces in the Solomons, Adm. Marc Mitscher. Both men were well-acquainted with Halsey's habit of allowing his subordinates a relatively free hand in his absence. Mitscher and Wilkinson felt that it was possible to intercept Yamamoto's plane as it was approaching Bougainville.

Halsey arrived back from Australia just in time to review the final plans for the operation. A new fighter plane had recently joined the American forces in the South Pacific. This rather odd-looking twin-engine plane, of course, was the P-38 or Lockheed Lightning. Fitted with additional fuel tanks, these planes had enough range to make the trip from Guadalcanal to Bougainville and back.

On April 18, as Yamamoto's plane flew over the jungles of Bougainville, it was jumped by a squadron of P-38s under the command of Maj. John Mitchell. In a few moments the admiral's plane was falling earthward in a column of smoke. Yamamoto's body was recovered a few days later. Next to the emperor, Yamamoto was the most revered figure in Japan at the time. His death was a severe blow to Japanese morale.

For his part, Halsey considered Yamamoto's death just revenge for Pearl Harbor. Mitscher's report of the attack said:

> Pop goes the weasel. P-38s led by Maj. John W. Mitchell, USA, visited Kahili about 0930. Shot down two bombers escorted by Zeros flying close formation. One shot down believed to be test flight. Three Zeros added to the score. Sum total six.[11]

Halsey was jubilant. He quickly informed his staff that Yamamoto was dead. Kelly Turner was estatic, but Halsey said to him:

> "Hold on, Kelly! What's so good about it? I'd hoped to lead that bastard up Pennsylvania Avenue in chains with the rest of you kicking him where it would do the most good."[12]

Nevertheless, Halsey ordered a congratulatory message sent to Mitscher.

> Congratulations to you and Major Mitchell and his hunters—sounds as though one of the ducks in the bag was a peacock.[13]

A year ago to the day, Halsey had escorted Mitscher's *Hornet* on its historic launching of Doolittle's raiders.

Attention now turned to the invasion of New Georgia. Before his death, Yamamoto had heavily reinforced Kavieng on New Ireland, Rabaul, and Buin on Bougainville in anticipation of an attack on Rabaul. If the latter fell, Truk, the great naval base in the Carolines would be isolated and the Americans would possess an ideal jumping-off position for an attack on the Philippines. Thus the Americans faced heavy opposition for a resumption of their drive up the Solomons.

On June 3, Halsey issued orders for Operation Toenails, the invasion of New Georgia. Munda airfield was the primary objective of the campaign. On the twenty-first, a battalion of marines landed at Segi Point on the southern tip of New Georgia. No Japanese defenders barred their way. Obviously the enemy were concentrating their forces for the defense of Munda. Even though the airfield there had been shelled by an American naval force under Admiral Ainsworth on May 15, it was completely operational a few days later. The only way to knock out Munda's airfield was by a land attack against the enemy.

After being reinforced, the marines set off overland through some of the world's thickest jungles. On the thirtieth, Admiral Turner's Task Force 51 landed a large force of American troops on Rendova Island. From there the troops jumped to New Georgia where both American bridgeheads were consolidated.

The Battle for New Georgia was one of the fiercest of the entire Solomons campaign. The terrain was horrendous. The troops had to hack their way through miles of thick tropical vegetation fighting Japanese all the way. After a month of heavy fighting, the American spearheads reached Munda on August 1. It took them another two weeks to capture the airfield. With defeat staring them in the face, the Japanese began to evacuate their troops to Bougainville and Kolombongara, the next target of Halsey's drive.

The struggle for New Georgia was not exclusively a land show. As they had at Guadalcanal, the Japanese used their Tokyo Express runs to reinforce the troops on the island. Halsey deployed his ships and planes in an effort to stop these forays. On the night of July 5-6, Admiral Ainsworth's force of cruisers clashed with a force of Japanese destroyers in the Battle of Kula Gulf. The Japanese lost two destroyers in the action, but their long lances sunk the cruiser *Helena*.

A week later Ainsworth and the Tokyo Express met head-on once more in the Battle of Kolombongara on the night of July 12-13. The Japanese cruiser *Jintsu*, Tanaka's old flagship, was quickly sent to the bottom before the Japanese found the range. Then a long lance smashed into the side of the New Zealand cruiser, *Leander*, putting the ship out of the war for months. After the engagement, the Japanese turned and fled up the Slot with Ainsworth in hot pursuit. A short while later the Japanese turned on their tormentors and unleashed their deadly long lances once more. The destroyer *Gwin* was sunk and the cruisers *St. Louis* and *Honolulu* damaged, but the Japanese reinforcement effort was thwarted for that night.

The next step on the central Solomons drive was intended to be Kolombongara. However, Halsey was beginning to have second thoughts. Why not attack Vella Lavella, the next island up the chain, bypass Kolombongara, and leave its garrison to wither on the vine? MacArthur endorsed the plan since he was always concerned with unnecessary casualties. The invasion of Vella Lavella, bypassing Kolombongara, became the first instance of island-hopping in the Pacific war. This tactic was later used throughout the Pacific with great success.

Meanwhile, the Japanese, convinced that Kolombongara was the next American target, continued to reinforce the island. Nightly Tokyo Express runs from the Shortlands and Rabaul brought in additional men and supplies. More troops crossed from New Georgia each night.

On the night of August 6-7, Commodore Frederick Moosebruger with a force of destroyers intercepted the Tokyo Express. The resulting naval battle of Vella Gulf cost the Japanese three destroyers. Moosebruger's destroyers chased the Japanese formation back up the Slot.

On August 15, U.S. Army troops landed on Vella

Lavella. Like the earlier Solomons landings, the assault forces were unopposed. In the South Pacific the Japanese preferred to fight from fixed positions inland rather than oppose the landings. In this way they avoided exposing their defensive positions to naval bombardment. This was a particularly astute decision since Halsey's commanders were roaming freely up and down the Slot.

It took the Americans a month to push the Japanese into the northwest corner of Vella Lavella. Halsey then pulled out the exhausted Army troops and replaced them with the fresh Third New Zealand Division which finished the job.

The Battle of Vella Lavella marked the end of the central Solomons campaign. Bougainville, the largest of the remaining islands left in the Solomons and close to Rabaul was the next target. Halsey sent reconnaissance teams to the island to determine the best point for a major landing. The teams reported back that Empress Augusta Bay, on the island's west coast seemed the best choice for an invasion point. D-Day was set for November 1.

The Bougainville operation was a complicated one with diversions designed to keep the enemy off balance. On October 26, the small islands of Mono and Stirling in the Treasuries were invaded and quickly overrun. The next day, a battalion of Marine paratroops landed on Choiseul, southeast of Bougainville. The Japanese rushed reinforcements to Choiseul, but by the time they arrived, the paratroops had been evacuated by a force of small American vessels. One of these was a PT boat, commanded by Lt. John F. Kennedy.

On November 1, the Third Marine Division splashed ashore at Empress Augusta Bay and met with little resistance. Opposition from Rabaul, though, was not long in coming. Japanese warplanes attacked the beachhead, but received more than they gave and were driven off without accomplishing much. A force of four Japanese cruisers and six destroyers headed for Bougainville.

Admiral "Tip" Merrill with four cruisers and six destroyers met the Japanese force in the Battle of Empress Augusta Bay early in the morning on November 2. Merrill's force sank the cruiser *Sendai* and a destroyer. Both sides had destroyers damaged, but the battle had been a decisive American victory. Over a hundred enemy planes attacked Merrill the next morning, but little additional damage was done.

The Japanese High Command were greatly concerned with the protection of Rabaul. If Bougainville fell, not only would this powerful base be open to attack, but Truk would be isolated. Therefore they decided to pull out all stops. A force of heavy and light cruisers under the command of Admiral Kurita was dispatched from the homeland to join the small fleet already at Rabaul. After refueling at Truk Kurita brought the heavy cruisers *Maya, Atago, Chokai, Takeo, Mogami, Suzuya, Chikuma,* and the light cruiser *Noshiro* and four destroyers into Rabaul's anchorage on the morning of November 5. The formation dropped anchor alongside the cruisers already in the harbor.

Halsey had been informed that Kurita was bringing his fleet to Rabaul. Since Merrill's force had been sent to the rear for rest and refit, Halsey had no surface force available to meet the threat; not that Merrill's light cruisers were a match for Kurita's powerful force anyway. Therefore, Halsey decided to gamble. Unlike Fletcher who had stood far to the south protecting his carriers while an American force was annihilated at the Battle of Savo, Halsey was willing to take a chance with his carriers.

Rear Admiral Frederick Sherman's Task Force 38 was refueling at that time in the southern Solomons. Halsey directed Sherman to take his force, which included the carriers *Saratoga* and *Princeton,* close to Rabaul and get in the first punch. Although Sherman would be exposing his ships to attack by the large Japanese land-based air force on Rabaul, Halsey felt the operation could be a success if total surprise were achieved.

Poor Kurita never had a chance. Around 10:00 A.M., less than three hours after the Japanese ships arrived at Rabaul, American planes showed up, too. Less than half an hour later, the Japanese Fleet lay smoking in the harbor.

The *Atago*'s hull was staved in by three near misses. The *Maya* raised steam and made for the harbor entrance at the height of the attack. There she was pounced on by a flight of dive bombers that ripped out her innards. Unable to navigate and with seventy dead and sixty wounded littering her decks, the *Maya* went dead in the water. The *Mogami* was struck in the side by a torpedo that started heavy fires. *Takeo*'s number two turret was destroyed by a bomb. The *Chikuma* was lucky; the only damage she incurred was a few splinter holes from near misses. The light cruisers *Noshiro* and *Agano* were also hit heavily. Before sunset, Kurita's smashed fleet was on the way back to Truk. The *Takeo* and *Maya* were in such bad shape they were left behind. The mighty force that the Japanese were relying on to smash the American invasion of Bougainville was a total wreck without having fired a gun. Halsey's gamble had paid off.

The old adage that lightning does not strike the same place twice did not hold true for Rabaul. On November 11, Task Force 38 was back, this time supported by Task Force 50.3, consisting of the new fleet carriers *Essex, Bunker Hill,* and the light carrier *Independence.* The damaged *Agano* was blasted to the bottom along with two destroyers. The Japanese counterattacked with every plane at their disposal. This attack was broken up as the skillful American pilots shot down almost half of the attackers. A few days later, the Japanese evacuated their few remaining ships and what was left of their air fleet. Rabaul had become too hot a spot. The fall of Bougainville, an inevitability, would make it even more so.

By December, it was obvious that the conquest of

Bougainville would be a long, drawn out, and painful affair. The Japanese kept pouring in reinforcements. Nevertheless, the Americans made steady progress, but it was measured in terms of yards rather than miles. Bougainville would not be completely secured for another four months. Halsey could not afford to wait that long.

In December, he stopped off to see MacArthur en route to a meeting with Nimitz in Hawaii. MacArthur, hoping to have his drive through the South Pacific given priority over Nimitz's central Pacific drive, told Halsey that the southwest Pacific was due to be reinforced with many warships. The British, he said, would also supply a large fleet. MacArthur offered Halsey command of this force.

"If you come with me, I'll make you a greater man than Nelson ever dreamed of being."[14]

Halsey was not interested in relegating Admiral Nelson to a back page in the history books. All he wanted to do was win the war and kill Japs. He was also acutely conscious of King's attitude about sending major naval forces to MacArthur. Therefore, Halsey replied that although the offer was a tempting and gracious one, he could not accept until after he had checked with King and Nimitz. The subject was dropped.

At the meeting with Nimitz, Halsey was informed that the Joint Chiefs had decided to bypass Rabaul. There were almost one hundred thousand Japanese troops there and it would be better to leave this strong point to wither on the vine by capturing other islands astride the line of communication between Japan and New Britain. The decision was not without a touch of irony since the capture of Rabaul was the objective of the entire Solomons campaign with the exception of Guadalcanal. The invasion of the latter was precipitated by construction of the Japanese airfield. During that campaign, the Japanese had sailed down from Rabaul, reinforced Guadalcanal and attacked American shipping by air and sea. Therefore it was determined that Rabaul had to be eliminated. Now the great naval base was neutralized without one American troop ever having stepped ashore.

As a substitute for Rabaul, Nimitz told Halsey that Kavieng on New Ireland and Manus in the Admiralties would be attacked.

Halsey felt that like Rabaul, Kavieng had outlived its usefulness. Since it was heavily defended Halsey proposed that Green Island, southeast of Rabaul, be assaulted instead. Then American aircraft from Manus and Green Island could totally isolate Rabaul and Kavieng. The plan was later approved by the Joint Chiefs.

Green Island was attacked on February 15. On the twenty-ninth of the month, it was the turn of Manus. To insure their isolation of Kavieng and Rabaul, the Americans also attacked Emirau in the St. Matthew's Group.

All organized resistance ended on Bougainville in the last few days of March. A few months earlier, on December 26, MacArthur's forces had jumped from New Guinea, across Dampier Strait to Cape Gloucester on New Britain. The Americans quickly established a strong defensive perimeter and patrolled inland, but MacArthur had no intention of incurring heavy casualties via a long, drawn out battle in the jungles. He was content to simply hold on to the eastern portion of New Britain to prevent the Japanese from using their large concentration of troops there against his flanks on New Guinea. Thus, by the end of March, 1944, Rabaul and Kavieng were completely ringed in and neutralized.

Early in May, Halsey accompanied Nimitz to San Francisco for a meeting with Admiral King. The previous fall, King had directed that the Pacific Fleet be designated Third Fleet when under Halsey and Fifth Fleet when operating with Spruance in the central Pacific. The latter had used the fleet in November to assault the Gilberts and in March to capture the Marshalls. The large new *Essex*-class carriers were joining the fleet in volume and a huge American carrier force now roamed the ocean. At the meeting in San Francisco, Halsey was told that he would return to sea in command of the Third Fleet since there was no further need for a separate theater commander in the South Pacific now that the Solomons campaign was over. The Third Fleet would be responsible for supporting MacArthur's southwest Pacific drive. Spruance would handle the central Pacific. With this decision King insured that MacArthur's drive would have adequate naval support, but the general would not have control over a major portion of the fleet. Because of MacArthur's respect for Halsey, he did not object to the arrangement.

After a final tour of the South Pacific theater, during which he was greeted with cheers at every stop, Halsey turned his command over to Vice Admiral John Newton on June 15. Two days later he arrived at Pearl Harbor and began planning for the capture of the Palaus and the western Carolines which included Yap and Ulithi. Peleliu and Anguar were the targets selected in the Palaus.

At the very moment Halsey was turning over his South Pacific command, Spruance was invading the Marianas supported by the might of the Fifth Fleet. The resulting Battle of the Philippine Sea ended in controversy. Spruance's pilots had all but wiped out what remained of the Japanese Naval Air Fleet, but the enemy carriers had escaped. Spruance was criticized for his lack of aggressiveness in not going after the Japanese Fleet. Nevertheless, thanks to the huge loss of aircraft and pilots, never again would the Japanese carrier fleet be a viable force in battle.

On August 24, Halsey sailed from Pearl Harbor with his flag in the powerful new battleship, *New Jersey*. Once at sea he officially assumed command of the Fifth Fleet which then became the Third Fleet. This fleet contained seventeen carriers under the tactical command of Adm. Marc Mitscher. The carrier force was broken down into four Task Groups. In addition, the Third Fleet contained five new battleships, thirteen cruisers and fifty-eight destroyers along with a fleet train of countless support ships. It was the most powerful naval formation the world had ever seen.

Halsey did not wait long to demonstrate the power of his fleet to the Japanese. On August 31 and September 1, Task Force 38, the carrier force, blasted Iwo Jima and Chichi Jima. On the third the fleet raided Wake. Then it was the turn of the Palaus. For three days Halsey's planes softened up the Palaus in anticipation of the forthcoming offensive. The fleet then made its presence known to the Japanese on Mindanao between the ninth and tenth. MacArthur was scheduled to attack this island in the Philippines in mid-October.

On September 12, the Third Fleet pounded the central Philippines. Over two hundred Japanese planes were destroyed in a two-day attack. Mindanao came in for more attention on the fourteenth. For the next ten days, Halsey roamed up and down the Philippines hitting Japanese targets at will. Eventually, his pilots began noticing that enemy opposition was either light or nonexistent. Halsey reviewed the pilots' reports and reached a dramatic conclusion.

MacArthur was scheduled to invade Mindanao on October 20 and Leyte the following month. In view of the relatively light opposition encountered, Halsey suggested canceling the invasion of Mindanao and advancing the invasion of Leyte to October 20. He also urged Nimitz to cancel the Peleliu and Morotai operations so that the troops designated for these attacks could be diverted to MacArthur's use.

Nimitz agreed with the Leyte proposal and forwarded the recommendations to King who also agreed. The latter in turn urged the Joint Chiefs to do likewise. However, Nimitz would not agree to the cancellation of the Palaus operation, stating that it was too late to cancel the attack. This was unfortunate because the Palaus battle became one of the bloodiest of the entire Pacific war.

The Joint Chiefs added their endorsement to Halsey's proposal. The invasion of Leyte was officially moved up to October 20, 1944.

To deceive the Japanese regarding the true intentions of the Americans, Halsey began a ten-day raid against Formosa on October 6. The Third Fleet then made a high-speed run back to the Philippines where it began to soften up enemy positions on Leyte and attack Japanese air bases throughout the islands. On the twentieth, Gen. Walter Krueger's Sixth Army, one hundred twenty thousand strong, began to wade ashore at Leyte. A beachhead was quickly established and the Americans began their advance inland. Admiral Kinkaid's Seventh Fleet, a force assigned to MacArthur finally by King, softened up the beachhead prior to the invasion and stood offshore to protect the landings.

The Japanese were determined to hold on to the Philippines whatever the cost. They knew that if the Americans were successful in their efforts to wrest those islands from the Japanese grasp, total defeat would be simply a matter of time. Therefore, the Japanese High Command felt that they had little choice but to commit all available resources to the defense of the Philippines.

The Japanese Sho-Go plan was an elaborate one. Like many of their previous operations, most notably Midway and the campaign in the Dutch East Indies, the plan was complicated and repeated a commonly used tactic, splitting the fleet. Throughout the war the Japanese repeated this mistake, often with disastrous results. They never got over their fondness for elaborate operations that relied on the precise timing of widely dispersed forces.

A striking force under Admiral Shima would sail down from the north, link up with a second force under Admiral Nishimura coming up from Brunei in Borneo, and move into Leyte Gulf from the west to attack the American transports and beachhead. This combined force was but one arm of a gigantic pincer. The second arm of the pincer was another more powerful force under Admiral Kurita, also based at Brunei. Kurita's force would move through the Sibuyan Sea, pass through San Bernardino Strait, make its way down the east coast of Samar, and attack the Americans in Surigao Strait in conjunction with the other two striking forces. Meanwhile, Admiral Ozawa would bring the remaining Japanese carriers down from the north, trail his coat about two-hundred miles east of Luzon, and lure the American carriers north. If this decoy role was successful, there would be no American force left to bar Kurita's way.

The Third Fleet was standing off the east coast of Samar and Luzon providing aerial support for MacArthur's troops. Throughout the islands Japanese targets were hit and hit again. Mitscher had split the four Task Groups. Adm. Frederick Sherman's TG 38.3 was off Luzon attacking Japanese air bases and positions in and around Manila. Off the south coast of Luzon was Adm. Gerald Bogan's TG 38.2, hitting other Japanese positions. Farther south was Adm. Ralph Davison's TG 38.4 hitting targets on Samar and Leyte.

By the twenty-second of October the Third Fleet had been at sea continuously for months. Accordingly, in light of their relatively weak opposition, Halsey felt it was time to begin resting his units. Adm. John McCain's TG 38.1 was therefore ordered to Ulithi for rest and replenishment. If events continued as they had, Halsey planned to dispatch Davison to Ulithi a few days later.

Halsey was operating under instructions from Nimitz to support and cover the forces of General MacArthur in their

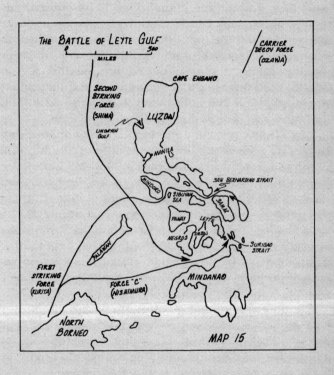

The Battle of Leyte Gulf

MILES
0   300

CARRIER DECOY FORCE (OZAWA)

SECOND STRIKING FORCE (SHIMA)

CAPE ENGANO

LUZON

LINGAYEN GULF

MANILA

SAN BERNARDINO STRAIT

MINDORO

SIBUYAN SEA

SAMAR

PANAY

LEYTE

NEGROS   CEBU

SURIGAO STRAIT

PALAWAN

FIRST STRIKING FORCE (KURITA)

FORCE "C" (NISHIMURA)

MINDANAO

NORTH BORNEO

MAP 15

seizure of the Philippines. However, the orders were conflicting in that Nimitz also directed Halsey to attack and destroy enemy shipping whenever and wherever it was found.

Just before dawn on the twenty-third, the U.S. submarines *Darter* and *Dace* sighted Kurita's force of five battleships, including the world's largest men-of-war, the battleships *Yamato* and *Musashi,* ten heavy cruisers, two light cruisers, and fifteen destroyers, moving up from Brunei via the Palawan Passage. The two American submarines slipped beneath the waves, sent off their sighting reports, and maneuvered into position for an attack. The *Darter* and *Dace* managed to sink the cruisers *Atago* and *Maya* and inflict heavy damage on the *Takeo.* The latter was ordered back to Borneo by Kurita.

When Halsey received word that Kurita was approaching he quickly guessed the Japanese intention. Davison's Task Group which had been dispatched in McCain's wake a few hours earlier, was hastily recalled. Orders went out from the *New Jersey* to the remaining groups to move closer to shore and be prepared to launch air strikes against Kurita the following day. A Task Group (34) of battleships was formed under Adm. Willis Lee and ordered to guard the exit from San Bernardino Strait. This latter message was misinterpreted by Kinkaid who concluded that no matter what, Lee would be guarding the strait.

The following morning American planes located a Japanese force. However, it was Nishimura's and not Kurita's. The American attacks against Nishimura failed to damage the force significantly. One battleship was hit, but its thick armor protected it. In the meantime, other American planes had located Kurita's force making its way through the Sibuyan Sea. It was obvious that this larger and more powerful force constituted the more serious threat so the Americans shifted their total attention to Kurita.

The first American wave of planes attained hits on the

Musashi and the cruiser *Myoko*. The latter was damaged so badly that Kurita ordered it detached and sent back to Borneo. Wave after wave of American planes battered the Japanese formation. The *Musashi* was like a magnet drawing the American pilots to her. The more she was hit, it seemed, the more the huge ship was attacked. Soon the *Musashi* had taken fourteen torpedoes and countless numbers of bomb hits. Down by the bows, Kurita ordered the leviathan beached. Before her captain could carry out these orders, the *Musashi* took three more torpedoes and plunged to the bottom of the sea.

There was still plenty of daylight left. The American planes were shuttling between their carriers and Kurita's force. The Japanese admiral felt he was steaming into the lion's den. Therefore, around 3:30 in the afternoon, he ordered his fleet to reverse course. Kurita's intentions were not to retreat, however, only to draw out of range of the American carrier planes until darkness could cover his run through San Bernardino Strait.

Halsey misinterpreted Kurita's move. American pilots returning to their ships exaggerated their claims, leading Halsey to believe that Kurita had turned back and was heading for home because of the battering he had taken.

While the Americans were concentrating on Kurita, Japanese aircraft on Luzon took advantage of the respite to attack Sherman's Task Group. The carrier *Princeton* was heavily hit and the ship began to burn furiously. The cruiser *Birmingham* moved alongside to aid in the fire-fighting efforts. Suddenly, the carrier's fires reached the ship's magazines. Explosions blew the flight deck apart. Steel splinters raked the *Birmingham*'s crowded deck, causing heavy casualties. By now it was obvious that the *Princeton* was doomed. Sherman ordered the carrier scuttled and the *Birmingham* back to Ulithi with its cargo of dead and wounded.

Meanwhile, Ozawa's decoy carrier force was steaming

leisurely east of Cape Engano hoping to be discovered. Thus far his mission had been a failure. The Japanese admiral had gone so far as to send seventy-five of his one hundred planes to Luzon to aid in the attacks against the American ships. Ozawa hoped that the arrival of his planes on Luzon would make the Americans aware of his presence in the vicinity. The ruse failed to work and Ozawa was left with two dozen planes on the decks of his carriers.

Consequently, Ozawa decided to send a small portion of his fleet even farther south in hopes that it would lead to the discovery of his formation. This maneuver finally proved successful.

On the bridge of the *New Jersey*, Halsey could not understand why the Japanese carriers had not made an appearance. Obviously the enemy was committing his entire fleet to the battle so where were the carriers? Around 5:30 on the afternoon of the twenty-fourth, the question was answered. One of Sherman's scout planes located Ozawa's force.

Halsey found himself on the horns of a dilemma. Should he remain on station guarding San Bernardino Strait and allow Ozawa to strike first? He could take on both Kurita and Ozawa simultaneously, but this meant splitting his attention and his fleet between two diametrically opposite forces. The remaining option was to ignore San Bernardino Strait and meet Ozawa with the entire might of the Third Fleet.

Halsey was confident that the Seventh Fleet could handle the combined force of Shima and Nishimura. Too overly optimistic reports of the American pilots regarding their attacks on Kurita indicated that the latter had suffered more heavily than he actually had. Kurita did nothing to dispel this myth when he had turned back temporarily to take his fleet out of range of the American carriers. This maneuver caused Halsey to draw but one conclusion. The reports of his pilots were correct.

On the other hand, Ozawa's force was fresh and unbloodied. When he had left Japan, however, his carriers could count only one hundred planes. Seventy-five of these had already left to join the forces on Luzon. Unfortunately, Halsey had no way of knowing that Ozawa's carriers could count on putting only twenty-five planes in the air.

After mulling over all the options and the latest information, Halsey made the only decision any fighting admiral would have done in his place. He ordered McCain's Task Group to return from Ulithi at full speed and directed his three remaining groups, along with Lee's battleships, to join up and head at full speed on an interception course with Ozawa. Unfortunately, he failed to notify the Seventh Fleet that he was leaving. The latter continued to operate under the impression that Lee's fast battleships were still guarding the exit to San Bernardino Strait.

Shortly after Halsey sailed north in pursuit of Ozawa, Kurita reversed course once more and made for San Bernardino Strait. All that stood between him and the American beachhead was a pitifully weak force of small escort carriers.

That night the Seventh Fleet easily disposed of Nishimura's and Shima's forces in the Battle of Surigao Strait. A little after midnight, Kurita exited from San Bernardino Strait and began to move down the east coast of Samar.

Halsey was excited. At long last the Americans had the opportunity to destroy the Japanese carrier fleet. All night long the Third Fleet drove north at high speed. Two hours after midnight scout planes located Ozawa's fleet. Shadowers followed it throughout the night reporting its exact course and speed. On board Task Force 38's carriers, pilots breakfasted, were briefed, and climbed aboard their planes awaiting the word to take off.

At 7:10, one hundred eighty American planes roared off the decks of their carriers. In less than an hour they were over Ozawa's helpless ships. The carriers *Zuiho*, *Chitose*, and *Zuikaku* were hit in the first attack. The destroyer *Akitsuki* was sunk.

At 9:45, the second American wave arrived. The carrier *Chiyoda* was left burning to sink later on. The cruiser *Tama* was hit.

Mitscher's third wave concentrated on the carriers *Zuiho* and *Zuikaku*, the last remaining veteran of the Pearl Harbor attack. Both carriers were hit repeatedly. Shortly after 2:30, the *Zuikaku* slipped beneath the waves. The fourth wave polished off the *Zuiho* and hit the hybrid battleship *Ise*. This ship and her sister, *Hyuga*, were actually battleships whose rear turrets had been removed and a flight deck added. Although they could launch planes via catapult, their flight decks were too short to allow for landings. Therefore, they were only capable of carrying seaplanes that could land in the sea nearby and be plucked out of the water and placed on the flight decks. These two ships held a peculiar fascination for Halsey who went out of his way to destroy them.

While Halsey was far to the north chasing Ozawa, Kurita moved unhindered toward Leyte Gulf. The resulting action will be thoroughly reviewed in the chapter on Kinkaid. However, Kurita's appearance on the scene caused a panic in the American camp. With victory in his grasp, the Japanese admiral suddenly broke off the action and retreated back from whence he had come. Nevertheless, Kurita had precipitated a controversy that has not abated to this day.

Kurita's arrival took the Americans completely by surprise. Kinkaid and Sprague, whose force of escort carriers suddenly found itself under attack by the powerful Japanese Fleet, were both under the impression that Halsey, with Lee's battleships, was guarding the exit from San Bernardino Strait.

At Pearl Harbor Nimitz was following the progress of the

great battle closely. He, too, was puzzled by Halsey's absence.

Far to the north, Halsey, on the bridge of the *New Jersey* found himself besieged by frantic messages from the Seventh Fleet. Just before 7:00 A.M. Seventh Fleet asked if Task Force 34 (Lee) was guarding San Bernardino Strait. An hour and a half later word came that a force of cruisers and battleships was attacking Sprague's escort carriers. This message was followed by one a few minutes later calling for help from Lee's battleships.

Halsey knew that this was impossible. Lee was with the rest of his fleet. Nevertheless, he sent a message off to McCain ordering him to attack the Japanese formation as quickly as possible. But McCain was still not within range.

The frantic calls for assistance continued to arrive. Halsey was torn between two storms. He was too far to offer immediate assistance and Ozawa's fleet was teetering on the brink of total annihilation. What to do?

Finally, a message was received from the Seventh Fleet requesting immediate assistance from Lee. Since the message had been sent in the clear, Halsey knew the situation at Leyte was critical. Shortly thereafter Halsey was handed one of the most electric messages of the entire war and one that made his blood boil.

In order to deceive enemy cryptographers, American messages were usually padded at the beginning and end with nonsensical phrases. It was the duty of the receiving radio operator to strike out this gibberish before giving it to the addressee. In this case, however, the padding seemed to be a part of the message and was left in. Therefore, when Halsey was handed the urgent message from Nimitz it read:

Where is Task Force 34. The world wonders.[15]

The last three words were actually the padding. Innocently, the radio operator at Pearl Harbor had added them to the message. It is easy to see though how the operator on the *New Jersey* could have misconstrued them to be a part of the message.

Halsey was incensed. How dare Nimitz insult him in this manner. More out of spite than common sense he ordered Lee's Task Group 34 and Task Group 38.2 (Bogan) to reverse course and head at full speed back to Leyte. Halsey knew that they would not reach the area before the next morning and could therefore be of little assistance. Mitscher, with Sherman's and Davison's groups, were left behind to finish off Ozawa. Nimitz later apologized for the misunderstanding.

Late in the afternoon what remained of Ozawa's fleet headed back to Japan. Mitscher dispatched a squadron of cruisers, *Sante Fe, Mobile, Wichita,* and *New Orleans* to pursue and polish off any stragglers and cripples. Then he turned his ships around and followed Halsey back to Leyte.

Ozawa's decoy operation was almost a total success. He had been unable to keep the American ships from harassing Kurita in the Sibuyan Sea, but eventually he gave Kurita a free run to the Leyte beachhead. Only the failure of the latter's nerve saved the American Navy from a disastrous defeat.

As he raced south, Halsey received word that Kurita had broken off the action and was now retiring. Halsey knew that there was no way that he could win the race for San Bernardino Strait, but he was determined to try anyway. His two fastest battleships, *New Jersey* and *Iowa,* were sent on ahead. The only Japanese ship they managed to catch, however, was the destroyer *Nowake,* crammed with survivors from the cruiser *Chikuma* that had been sunk by American aircraft in the battle off Samar. The hapless destroyer was quickly disposed of by the large guns of the American battleships.

The following morning Bogan and McCain rendezvoused off the coast of Samar. Throughout the day their planes harassed Kurita as he retired through San Bernardino Strait and across the Sibuyan Sea. The Americans managed to score hits on Kurita's already-battered ships, but failed to achieve anything significant. Late in the day the weather deteriorated, forcing a halt to further air strikes.

The Battle for Leyte Gulf marked the death knell of the Japanese Fleet. Never again would this once-powerful armada roam the Pacific in a combined operation. The survivors were eventually hunted down one by one and sunk by American aircraft or submarines.

The greatest naval battle in history was divided into four distinct phases. First was the Battle of the Sibuyan Sea where Halsey's aircraft pounded Kurita as he made his way toward San Bernardino Strait. This was followed by the annihilation of Shima and Nishimura in the Battle of Surigao Strait. Third was the near destruction of the American escort carriers in the action off Samar. Last came the Battle of Cape Engano where Halsey's chance to destroy the Japanese carriers was denied by the frantic calls for his return to Leyte. The Third Fleet did manage to sink four carriers, one cruiser, two destroyers, and damaged two battleship/carriers, two light cruisers and four destroyers during the Battle off Cape Engano.

Halsey had planned to rest his entire fleet at Ulithi after the battle and before taking it on a raid against Japan itself. But the Japanese air forces in the Philippines still constituted a significant threat to MacArthur. Therefore, the Third Fleet's presence was still required in the area.

Halsey's fleet stood off the east coast of the Philippines, attacking Japanese installations and providing air cover for the American troops ashore. Nevertheless, he did halve his force by sending McCain and Sherman to Ulithi. Once they returned, Halsey planned to relieve Bogan's and Davison's formations.

During this phase of the battle Halsey was introduced to what he considered one of the most diabolical and frightening weapons of the war: the Kamikaze. Admiral Fukodome had formed a fleet of volunteer suicide pilots who were eager to die for their emperor by smashing their planes into American ships. First to feel the effects of the Kamikazes was Bogan's flagship, the carrier *Intrepid*.

> Like the *Saratoga,* she could hardly poke her nose out of port without it getting rapped. She spent so much time in drydock that the fleet called her the 'Decrepid' and 'the Dry I.'[16]

The *Intrepid* was hit on October 29, but remained in action having suffered the loss of six men. The next day it was Davison's turn to witness the fearsome weapon. The carriers *Franklin* and *Belleau Wood* were hit so badly that they had to be dispatched to Ulithi for repairs.

Sherman returned from Ulithi on November 4, just in time to get his share of attention from the Kamikazes. The next day the (new) *Lexington*'s bridge was hit with the loss of forty-seven men.

Halsey had had enough. Instead of merely supporting MacArthur's advance and protecting his supply lines, he decided to hit the Kamikazes at their source, on the ground. In the next twenty days over seven hundred fifty Japanese planes were destroyed by the Third Fleet while they sat parked on their runways.

On November 25, however, the Kamikazes retaliated with a fury. The *Essex* was hit, then the *Cabot*. Both ships were able to repair their damage and remain on station. Not so the *Intrepid*. The luckless carrier was set ablaze as her aviation gasoline stocks were hit. After the fires were extinguished, the *Intrepid* also limped off to Ulithi.

With his force reduced by three carriers and his crews exhausted, Halsey made a plea to MacArthur to postpone his invasion of Mindoro, scheduled for December 5. Halsey could not ask his men and ships to do more until they were rested.

On November 27, the Third Fleet dropped anchor at Ulithi. There it was replenished while the crews relaxed. December 11 saw the fleet back at sea supporting the invasion of Mindoro. MacArthur's troops went ashore on the fifteenth. Halsey's fleet provided support until late the next day when it moved off to refuel before returning to continue its aerial blanket over MacArthur's forces. Then disaster struck.

As the Third Fleet was refueling, a storm came up. The fleet's meteorologist, Com. George Kosco, reported that a storm center was five hundred miles east of the fleet's current position and moving northwest. Accordingly, Halsey ordered the refueling operations suspended and told his ships to rendezvous the next day two hundred miles farther northwest. Kosco felt that the tropical disturbance would meet a cold front moving down from the north and slide off to the northeast. However, the cold front never arrived and the tropical disturbance became a full-scale typhoon, Cobra.

Later in the day Halsey received information that the storm center was less than two hundred miles to the southeast. This placed his rendezvous position directly in the path of the storm. He therefore canceled the rendezvous and set another for a point southwest of his current position. The next day fueling operations began once more. The fleet's destroyers were dangerously low on fuel and could not operate much longer without replenishment. In addition, MacArthur was depending on support from the Third Fleet's carriers. Shortly after the fueling operation began, the weather started to deteriorate. Instead of curving northeast as expected, Cobra had turned west. Directly in its path was the Third Fleet.

Around 8:30 the storm began to pound the fleet. Winds were reported at sixty-two knots. Even the heaviest ships felt the fury of the storm. Ships lost steering, fires were started, plates were staved in by the pounding waves, men were washed overboard, and superstructures were smashed. The smaller ships were picked up and tossed about the sea like matchsticks. By early evening the storm began to subside, but the Third Fleet was in bad shape. The destroyers *Spence, Hull,* and *Monoghan* had capsized and sunk at the height of the storm. Only a handful of survivors were picked up. Many of the small escort carriers and some of the larger ones had suffered some degree of damage. The remaining destroyers were a shambles. One storm had caused more damage in eight hours than the Japanese Fleet had caused in eight months. The crippled ships were sent to Ulithi for repairs.

After a hasty repair job the fleet set out once more to support MacArthur. It passed the New Year, 1945, off the Philippines. Then Halsey took it north to strike at Japanese air bases on Formosa on January third and fourth. During this raid over one hundred enemy aircraft were destroyed and sixteen merchant ships sunk.

Then it was back to the Philippines where the fleet covered MacArthur's landings at Lingayen Gulf on Luzon. The Third Fleet battered Japanese positions on the island until the eighth when it moved off again for Formosa which was hit on the ninth.

Halsey next took the fleet into the China Sea. It marauded up and down the China Sea for eleven days, sinking numerous ships and blasting enemy positions. There were reports that the *Ise* and *Hyuga* were in the area, but the Americans failed to locate them. Then the fleet's luck ran out.

En route via Okinawa where it was to carry out a photo-reconnaissance in anticipation of an invasion in the spring, the fleet became the focus of attention of the Kamikazes as it made one last attack against Formosa. The carrier *Langley* was hit and suffered slight damage as did the destroyer *Maddox*. The *Ticonderoga* was not as fortunate. Two Kamikazes smashed into the ship killing one hundred forty men and causing heavy damage to the island structure, hangar deck, and flight deck. The cruiser *Houston* was also damaged heavily. On January 25, the fleet dropped anchor at Ulithi where it once more became the Fifth Fleet as Spruance relieved Halsey.

Halsey returned to the United States for a period of well-earned rest and relaxation. After completing a few special assignments on behalf of Admiral King, he returned to Pearl Harbor on April 7. Halsey and his staff immediately began preparing plans for future operations, most of them aimed at an eventual invasion of the China coast.

At the end of April, Halsey went to Nimitz's new head-quarters on Guam where he was informed that he would relieve Spruance at the end of May. Spruance was at that time engaged in supporting the struggle for Okinawa.

On May 27, the Fifth Fleet officially became the Third Fleet once more. The dreaded Kamikazes were making a shambles of the fleet's destroyer picket line off Okinawa. Fourteen destroyers and destroyer escorts were lost and numerous others damaged. Halsey was unhappy at having to sit still and watch his ships being destroyed and his sailors killed. Unhappily he had little choice since the troops on the island itself needed the fleet's support.

To help alleviate the need for his carriers to stand off Okinawa, subjected to incessant Japanese attacks, Halsey had Marine Air Group 14 transferred to Okinawa from the Philippines. Halsey was fond of this group and called them MacArthur's flying artillery. Their presence on Okinawa would free the fleet for offensive action. Once more it was the theory of the aviator, Halsey, who felt that the carriers should be free to roam, versus the tactics of the nonaviator, Spruance, who felt that the fleet should be used to support landings.

On June 1, Commander Kosco was informed of another tropical storm brewing north of the Palaus. Despite this information, Halsey took Admiral Radford's TG 38.4 off on a raid against the Japanese island of Kyushu on the second and third. Admiral "Jocko" Clark's TG 38.1 was left behind to continue supporting the Okinawan operation.

On the way back from Kyushu, Halsey was made aware that another typhoon was stalking the fleet. Once again he took what he considered to be effective evasive action. Unfortunately, in the vast expanses of the Pacific there were no weather planes to track and monitor the progress of storms. Therefore, the Third Fleet was in the dark about the location of the storm until just before it struck. Neither could Halsey have anticipated an unusual weather phenomenon. The original storm split in two with one portion following the track that Halsey's weathermen had predicted and the same one that the fleet had successfully maneuvered away from. The second part of the storm smacked into the fleet in the early-morning hours of June 5.

Typhoon Viper was even more fierce than its predecessor, Cobra. Even the heavy battleships, relatively immune during the previous storm, felt the fury of Viper. Once more ships were picked up and tossed about like matchsticks. Decks and superstructures were battered. Fortunately, no ships were lost during the storm, but the heavy cruiser *Pittsburg*'s bow was wrenched off.

The Navy ordered a court of inquiry to investigate and place blame for the damage. Vice Admiral John Hoover was named president of the board. Other members were Vice Admiral G.N. Murray and Vice Admiral C.A. Lockwood, commander of the Pacific Submarine Force. The board found that Halsey and McCain, Mitscher's successor, were to blame for the near disaster. Hoover, however, was an ambitious man who was frustrated ashore and had designs on a seagoing command. Therefore, the board recommended that Halsey and McCain be relieved.

When he received the board's recommendations, Admiral King refused to honor them. McCain was eventually relieved, but not until after Japan surrendered. As for Halsey, King thought it was madness to relieve

America's most popular naval hero simply because he had been caught in a storm. The very thought of it was absurd. Consequently, Halsey got off with a mere reprimand.

At the beginning of July, Halsey took the fleet to sea for the final time. For the next month it ranged up and down the Japanese coast, attacking factories, hitting installations, and polishing off what remained of the Imperial Japanese Navy, including the *Ise* and *Hyuga*. The Japanese ships were restricted to home waters because of a lack of fuel and had sought refuge at Kure. There they were located by the American pilots and brought to bay.

During these final few weeks of the war, Task Force 37, the British carrier formation in the Pacific joined the Third Fleet in its attacks against the Japanese homeland. A few months earlier Admiral King had caused a diplomatic furor when he had refused the British offer of ships for use in the final push against Japan. The proud British Fleet was insulted. King eventually was forced to change his mind. Admiral Rawlings' formation held their own and earned the respect of their American comrades. Halsey never did share King's distaste for the British. He and Rawlings quickly became close friends. Halsey was happy to have the British Task Force serving alongside his own forces. The British assessment of Halsey was:

He was a fine sea commander, and a lovable man, much loved by those who served under him. Admiral Halsey's leadership could be described as inspirational rather than intellectual.[17]

On the morning of August 15, while he was eating breakfast on board his flagship, the battleship *Missouri*, Halsey's flag secretary burst into his cabin and interrupted the admiral with the news that Japan had surrendered. The two atomic bombs dropped the previous week had sealed the enemy's fate. The war was over. There would be no need to invade the Japanese homeland, something every senior Allied commander dreaded.

The *Missouri* was designated to be the site of the formal surrender ceremony. This was appropriate since the new American President, Harry S Truman was from that state. Another coincidence was that Halsey had begun his naval career as a passed midshipman on the old USS *Missouri*. On August 27, the "Mighty Mo" sailed majestically into Tokyo Bay and dropped anchor in a branch of that body of water. Halsey set the crew to polishing and painting the ship so that she was immaculately groomed when the actual ceremony took place.

On September 2, the formal Japanese surrender took place on the deck of the *Missouri*. Halsey had shifted his flag to the battleship *South Dakota* out of respect for Nimitz whose flag now flew at the Mighty Mo's masthead. Halsey stood behind Nimitz as the latter signed the surrender document on behalf of the United States. (MacArthur signed on behalf of the Allied powers.)

The following day, Nimitz informed Halsey that Spruance would relieve him on the twentieth. Since Halsey had already expressed his intention to retire immediately after the war was over, he took the news in stride. For the next few weeks he occupied himself by liberating POWs, assessing the war damage in and around Tokyo, and aiding in MacArthur's efforts to establish an occupation force.

On September 19, Halsey sailed on the *South Dakota* for Pearl Harbor. In Hawaii the Third Fleet was reconstituted from ships slated to return to the United States. This fleet arrived in San Francisco on October 15 to a tumultuous welcome. In December, Halsey was given his fifth star and promoted to fleet admiral, joining King and Nimitz in that illustrious rank. He remained on active duty until April 1, 1947, when he officially joined the retired list.

Halsey always liked to claim that the nickname "Bull" was actually a mistake. He insisted that the name stemmed from a correspondent's error when, during a press conference, the admiral had told reporters that he liked to be called Bill. Supposedly, one of the reporters misspelled Bill and the nickname stuck. Whatever the cause, the admiral's bulldoglike tenacity and ferocious looks made the nickname seem appropriate. However, no one dared call him "Bull" to his face. To his friends he was simply Bill.

For the next ten years Halsey's illustrious name was associated with a number of major corporations as a member of their board of directors. But the admiral took only a passing interest in the day-to-day operations of these corporations.

On August 15, 1959, Fleet Admiral William F. Halsey passed away quietly at the age of seventy-seven. He was buried at Arlington Cemetery five days later during an elaborate ceremony, the likes of which were usually reserved for heads of state.

Mrs. Mary Ann Davis, whose husband was a marine stationed in Washington at the time, watched as the funeral procession passed and was overwhelmed by the spectacle.

I had only heard of Halsey through the newspapers and television. As I stood there I could not help but be awed by the entire thing. There were so many high-ranking bemedaled officers that I soon lost count. Rows upon rows of marines and sailors marched behind the coffin. Old and young men alike stood on the sidelines and wept openly as the funeral cortège passed. I could not help but think that surely this was a deeply loved and a great man.[18]

Without question, Bull Halsey was one of America's greatest commanders of the war. He certainly was without peer as a fighting admiral. His aggressiveness and conduct of carrier operations left an indelible print on the history of warfare.

Thomas Cassin Kinkaid's career in World War II was overshadowed by those of his fellow fleet commanders, Halsey of the Third Fleet and Spruance of the Fifth. Nevertheless, Tom Kinkaid

> probably has been in more shooting scrapes with the Japanese than any other senior naval officer and is known to be absolutely fearless.[1]

Kinkaid was born in Hanover, New Hampshire, on April 3, 1888. Thomas's father was a career naval officer and ultimately reached flag rank before his retirement. The elder Kinkaid's occupation took the family to numerous naval bases and cities during young Kinkaid's early years. In this atmosphere the young man was regaled by tales of the sea and the magnificent freewheeling and carefree life of a sailor. Therefore, even before he entered his teens, Thomas had made up his mind. A naval career was for him.

After passing the appropriate examinations, Thomas Kinkaid was appointed to the U.S. Naval Academy at Annapolis as a member of the class of 1908. Entering the academy also in 1904 were Marc Mitscher and a fiery young officer named Richmond Kelly Turner. During his four years at Annapolis, Kinkaid was no more than an average student, but was popular with his fellow cadets. The academy yearbook bears witness to that fact.

> Kink (is a) black-eyed rosy-cheeked noisy Irishman,

who loves a roughhouse and the training-table grub. . . . He has a corking good disposition and is in every way a man of the first order.[2]

In the spring of 1908, Cadet Kinkaid became Passed Midshipman Kinkaid whose specialty was gunnery and ordnance. There followed a series of assignments aboard the smaller ships of the fleet as gunnery officer. Tours of duty at sea were interspersed with brief spells at naval ordnance schools and desk positions.

When America entered World War I, Kinkaid was serving as gunnery officer on the new battleship, *Pennsylvania*. Later in the war he was transferred to a similar position aboard the *Pennsylvania*'s sister ship, *Arizona*. The American Fleet saw little action in the war so Kinkaid had no opportunity to practice his skills as a gunner.

After the war he was appointed Assistant Chief of Staff to Rear Admiral Bristol whose squadron spent the next two years in the Mediterranean, most of that time in and around Turkey. Kinkaid was then given his first independent command, captain of the destroyer *Isherwood*. He remained with this ship for two years and proved as popular with his crew and subordinate officers as he had been at Annapolis. Although an exacting taskmaster, Kinkaid was nevertheless fair, treated everyone equally and with respect, and was a jovial commander. Every man on board the Isherwood was sorry to see him leave when his tour of duty was over. The next stop was the Naval Gun Factory in Washington.

Kinkaid spent a year as an advisor at the gun factory. Having learned his craft well and having been recognized as somewhat of an authority on guns in the years following his graduation from Annapolis, he was made gunnery officer of the U.S. Fleet following his year at the gun factory. In this capacity he was expected to serve in a dual capacity as aide to the Commander in Chief.

Two more years passed before Kinkaid was ordered to participate in the course of study at the Naval War College. By that time he had risen to the rank of commander. Attendance at the war college virtually assured that he would eventually reach flag rank.

In 1932 the nations of the world met in conference at Geneva, Switzerland, to discuss a halt to the arms race. As an expert in gunnery, Kinkaid was appointed naval advisor to the American delegation. In Geneva, Kinkaid's genial and gracious manner coupled with his obvious expertise, made an impression on all present.

At the conclusion of the conference, Kinkaid returned home to a seagoing assignment, executive officer of the battleship *Colorado*. Kinkaid remained with the heavy ships of the fleet until late in 1938, when he was named naval attaché in Rome. By that time he had risen in rank to captain. The following year he went to Belgrade, Yugoslavia, and served for a year as U.S. Naval Attaché in that city.

In March, 1941, Kinkaid returned to sea as captain of the *Colorado*. In November of the same year, he was promoted to rear admiral and given command of a squadron of cruisers. This new assignment took him to Pearl Harbor where his brother-in-law, Adm. Husband Kimmel, was commanding the Pacific Fleet.

Kinkaid was at sea on the fateful morning of December 7, 1941, and thus missed the notorious Japanese attack on the American Fleet. For the next few months he was busy with his cruisers escorting Admiral Fletcher's carriers in a series of raids against Japanese positions in the Pacific.

In April, Nimitz's intelligence team discovered that the Japanese were planning an attack against Port Moresby, New Guinea. Adm. Aubrey Fitch's Task Force 11, centered on the carrier *Lexington,* was quickly dispatched from Pearl Harbor to the Coral Sea. Rear Admiral J.C. Crace of the Royal Australian Navy, with the cruisers *Australia*, *Hobart*, and *USS Chicago* commanded Fitch's support group.

At that point in the war it was American policy to form separate Task Forces around each of their carriers. Fitch's Task Force 11 was at Pearl Harbor. Halsey's Task Force 16 was escorting Doolittle's fliers on their raid against Japan. At Noumea in the New Hebrides was Task Force 17 under Fletcher. This force contained the carrier *Yorktown*. Kinkaid, with the cruisers *New Orleans*, *Chester*, *Portland*, *Minneapolis*, and *Astoria* commanded Fletcher's support group. Fletcher was ordered to take his force into the Coral Sea where as senior admiral he would assume tactical command of his and Fitch's Task Forces.

En route to the Coral Sea, on May 4, Fletcher detoured to the southern Solomons and attacked the recently established Japanese positions on the island of Tulagi. Then he headed south where he linked up with Fitch the next day.

Just after dawn on May 7, Crace took his three cruisers westward to intercept the Japanese invasion fleet. Fletcher's carriers hovered southeast of New Guinea waiting for the Japanese carriers to make an appearance.

In mid-morning an American patrol plane sighted a portion of the enemy fleet moving south. Fletcher immediately launched a heavy air strike. The American pilots located the Japanese light carrier *Shoho* an hour later and quickly wrote *finis* to that ship's brief career. Meanwhile, the Japanese were searching for the American carriers.

Throughout the day Fletcher continued to search for the remaining Japanese carriers, but all efforts proved futile. The Japanese, however, located the fleet oiler *Neosho* and the destroyer *Sims* approximately one hundred miles south of Fletcher's position. The Japanese planes attacked with fury, sank the *Sims* and left the *Neosho* a blazing wreck. The unfortunate oiler remained afloat for four days before succumbing to her wounds.

At 9:00 A.M. on May 8, Fletcher launched a full strike against the supposed enemy location. Around the same time Admiral Takagi, by this time reasonably certain of the whereabouts of the American force, launched a seventy-plane attack from the *Shokaku* and *Zuikaku*. Both formations arrived over their targets at approximately the same time.

The American planes screamed down on the *Shokaku* and planted three bombs on her flight deck, causing heavy fires and leaving the ship in no condition to recover her aircraft, many of whom were eventually lost for want of a place to land. The *Zuikaku* escaped harm by hiding beneath a nearby rain squall.

One hundred and fifty miles to the south, the Japanese pilots proved more effective than their Japanese counterparts. Three bombs and two torpedoes struck the *Lexington,* despite the heavy antiaircraft fire of Kinkaid's cruisers. Two more bombs were dropped on the *Yorktown.*

The *Lexington* was in deep trouble. Fires raged from stem to stern, setting off explosions that ripped out the insides of the great ship. Fletcher limped off with the stricken *Yorktown* and ordered Kinkaid to take charge of salvage operations. Kinkaid ordered the *New Orleans* and *Minneapolis* to close with the *Lexington* and assist in efforts to save the ship, but it was too late. The "Lady Lex" was mortally wounded. Explosion after explosion triggered off additional fires. Her skipper, Captain Sherman, finally bowed to the inevitable and gave the order to abandon ship. Kinkaid's cruisers and destroyers stood by to pick up survivors. Many of the *Lexington*'s officers later stated that Kinkaid's deft maneuvering of his rescue force was one of the finest demonstrations of seamanship they had ever witnessed. The cruisers and destroyers steamed slowly back and forth expertly plucking the *Lexington*'s crew from the water. Not one man was lost after leaving the sinking carrier. Finally, just before 6:30, but only after he was satisfied that all hands were safely off the ship, Kinkaid ordered the destroyer *Phelps* to sink the blazing carrier with torpedoes. After the gallant *Lexington* slipped beneath the waves, Kinkaid made one more sweep to look for survivors before setting a course for home.

The Battle of the Coral Sea was a strategic victory for the Americans, but a tactical loss. The Japanese invasion force heading for Port Moresby turned back. This marked the first time in the war that a Japanese invasion attempt was thwarted. In addition, the *Shokaku* was heavily damaged and the *Zuikaku* had lost a large percentage of her air crew. Neither ship would be able to participate in the forthcoming operation at Midway. On the other hand, the *Lexington* was gone forever.

The *Yorktown* and her escorts arrived back at Pearl Harbor on the afternoon of May 27. The next morning, Admiral Spruance, having relieved the ill Halsey, took the *Hornet* and *Enterprise* north to Midway. Like the majority of the *Yorktown* force, Kinkaid anticipated a brief respite after the great battle in the Coral Sea. It was estimated that repairs to the *Yorktown* would consume the greater part of three months. As soon as the ship docked, however, dockyard workers began to swarm over the ship. For three days, welders' torches burned around the clock in a frantic effort to make the carrier seaworthy. On May 30 the *Yorktown*, escorted by Kinkaid's support group, steamed out of Pearl Harbor for a rendezvous with Spruance north of Midway.

The Battle of Midway is considered the turning point of the war, but it was strictly a carrier battle. For the most part, Kinkaid was simply a spectator as the Japanese lost four of their fleet carriers. Kinkaid's escorting force did, however, find themselves in another disappointing rescue operation. The *Yorktown* was damaged by Japanese planes, torpedoed by an enemy submarine, and sunk. Thus the high spirits of the Americans were slightly dampened with the loss of yet another carrier. Nevertheless, Midway had been a great victory.

Nimitz was reluctant to part with his Chief of Staff, Spruance, prior to Midway and had emphasized at that time that Spruance's seagoing command was only temporary. Thus, when the fleet dropped anchor at Pearl Harbor, Spruance returned to his former duties ashore.

With Spruance grounded and Halsey ill, Fletcher automatically became the senior carrier admiral in the Pacific. The fact that Nimitz wanted Spruance's services so desperately probably saved Fletcher's command for the time being even though the latter was considered a nonaviator. The fleet reverted to its former make-up with separate Task Forces centered on the carriers. Kinkaid was elevated to command of the famous Task Force 16, Halsey's old command built around the *Enterprise*.

Kinkaid's selection to command the *Enterprise* force caused a stir of controversy. The Navy was divided in theory along two schools of thought. There were the aviators like Halsey and King who advocated the striking power of carriers and enthusiastically promoted the increased use of naval aviation. On the other side were the big gun theorists who clung to the belief that battleships were the queens of the fleet. Kinkaid came from the latter school, although following the Japanese attack on Pearl Harbor and the battles of Midway and the Coral Sea, he was rapidly swinging around to the aviators' way of thinking. Unfortunately, since senior experienced officers were in short supply and could not be spared to take the aviator's course, Kinkaid remained in the classification of nonaviator. Consequently, his assignment to command the *Enterprise* group was met with objections from the aviators of the fleet.

As already seen, late in May the Japanese had landed in the lower Solomons at Tulagi. Fletcher had paused to attack this island en route to the Coral Sea. The following month, the Japanese jumped to the neighboring island of

Guadalcanal and began construction of an airfield. From this field their planes could harass the Allied lines of communication between Australia and Hawaii. The Americans knew that the Japanese had to be stopped. Therefore, an invasion of Guadalcanal was scheduled.

During the first week in August a large armada of warships set out for the Solomons. Aboard were the First Marine Division of Gen. Archer Vandergrift. The marines formed the assault force for the invasion of the lower Solomons. Adm. Richmond Kelly Turner was in tactical command of the beachhead with responsibility for delivering the marines and their logistical support. Turner had a force of cruisers and destroyers to provide close escort. Covering the entire force were the carriers *Wasp*, *Saratoga*, and *Enterprise* under the overall command of Admiral Fletcher. Kinkaid was in the *Enterprise*.

Fletcher's assignment was to provide aerial protection for the assault and beachhead. Just after dawn on August 7, aircraft from the three American carriers began launching strikes against enemy positions on Guadalcanal, Tulagi and Gavutu. Two hours later the marines began landing.

The Japanese were taken by surprise, but quickly recovered and struck back. Planes from Rabaul flew down the channel between the twin chain of the Solomons known as the Slot. They were intercepted by the American carrier planes and driven off. An American destroyer was hit by a bomb, but with that exception the Japanese attack was relatively unsuccessful. However, the American pilots quickly discovered that the Japanese pilots were far from amateurs.

The next day it was much the same. Another American destroyer was damaged along with a transport. Fletcher's pilots waded into the Japanese bomber formations and drove them back. By the end of the second day the enemy had lost almost one hundred planes. The *Enterprise* pilots were the most active of the three carriers and had acquitted themselves well. Nevertheless, by evening of August 8,

Fletcher's force had lost twenty-one planes.

At a pre-invasion conference of all the key commanders of the attack, Fletcher stunned everyone by announcing that he would protect the American beachhead for two days only. Having lost two carriers in the war already he was not about to expose his precious ships to land-based air attacks. Kinkaid, like Fletcher a nonaviator, had also been present at the Coral Sea and Midway and wavered between supporting Fletcher and protecting the beachhead. The loss of the *Lexington* and *Yorktown* were still fresh in his mind. Finally, torn between two sides, he cast his lot with Fletcher. Kelly Turner ranted and raved to no avail. The Commander in Chief, South Pacific, Admiral Ghormley, was also in Fletcher's corner. Thus, just after dusk on the eighth, Fletcher ordered his force to draw out of range.

The American carriers were still conducting operations when a Japanese force of cruisers and destroyers sailed from Rabaul. When the American carriers moved off, Turner was left with a handful of cruisers and destroyers as his only protection against an enemy surface attack. Late that evening the Japanese reached Guadalcanal. At the resulting Battle of Savo Island Turner lost virtually his entire screening force. Three American and one Australian cruiser were blasted to the bottom of the sea along with two destroyers. Another American cruiser was damaged and Turner's transports lay wide open to attack. Fortunately, the Japanese commander, Admiral Mikawa, satisfied that he had won a great victory, retired up the Slot without following up the victory by attacking Turner's vulnerable transports and beachhead. Nevertheless, the next day Turner was obliged to pull his transports out leaving the marines stranded with only half of their supplies having been brought ashore. Had Fletcher remained in position, his scout planes might have discovered the Japanese formation heading toward Guadalcanal. The carrier planes could have attacked Mikawa's formation and even if they had not inflicted any damage, at least Turner would have been aware of the enemy approach. As it was, the American ships were taken completely by surprise.

When word of the disastrous defeat at Savo was received aboard the American carriers, Kinkaid quickly urged Fletcher to turn the carriers around and head back to Guadalcanal. If they hurried, they could catch the Japanese force retiring up the Slot and perhaps sink or damage some of their ships. Furthermore, Kinkaid went on, the carriers could resume their combat air patrol and allow Turner's transports to remain in the vicinity. Fletcher refused. Under no circumstances would he expose the carriers to the hazards of attacks by Japanese land-based aircraft.

The Japanese now began to pour reinforcements into Guadalcanal. On the night of August 21 the marines grimly beat off a heavy counterattack with huge losses to the attackers. Meanwhile, at sea, the Japanese were preparing for a major operation.

The Japanese plan called for a large convoy of troops and supplies to land at Guadalcanal. The convoy would be preceded by a carrier attack against American positions. Both the strike carrier and the convoy would be covered by a larger force of carriers and battleships commanded by Admiral Nagumo. The Japanese had put the first team into the game.

Through their ability to read the Japanese code, the Americans were aware that the Japanese were planning something. Fletcher was ordered to take his carriers east of the Solomons and prevent the Japanese from carrying out their plans. This time, however, Fletcher would find himself up against a skilled and formidable opponent in Nagumo.

Throughout the day of August 23, Fletcher's scout planes searched in vain for the Japanese Fleet. At the end of the day he reported to Pearl Harbor that he had been unable to make contact with the enemy force. A message came back containing an intelligence assessment that the Japanese Fleet must still be near Truk. Feeling that there would be no battle for a few days, Fletcher detached the *Wasp* for refueling. But the intelligence estimate had been wrong.

The next morning American patrol planes from Espiritu Santo located the carrier *Ryujo* which had been sent on ahead to cover Tanaka's reinforcement group and to lure the American Fleet into attacking. The *Ryujo* was over sixty miles from the main body of the Japanese Fleet. Two hours after noon, Fletcher ordered both of his remaining carriers to launch a strike against the only target available, the *Ryujo*.

Shortly before the American planes reached their target, scout planes located Nagumo's main formation. Fletcher immediately ordered his strike to alter course, but the message never reached the pilots. The *Ryujo* was pounded to the bottom of the ocean.

While the American planes were battering the *Ryujo*, Nagumo launched a heavy strike from the *Zuikaku* and *Shokaku*. The *Enterprise* had a combat air patrol of some fifty planes in the air over the American Fleet. Around 4:30 the Japanese planes arrived. The *Saratoga*, ten miles away from Kinkaid's *Enterprise*, was spared as the Japanese pilots concentrated on the "Big E."

Kinkaid was on the bridge with Capt. Arthur Davis when the Japanese strike arrived overhead. He watched as his fighter planes beat off an attack by torpedo planes aided by heavy antiaircraft fire from the battleship *North Carolina*.

Before the Americans could catch their breath, however, a flight of enemy dive bombers arrived over the fleet. Once more it appeared as if the legendary luck of the *Enterprise* would hold. The first Japanese attackers were destroyed by the combat air patrol and the combined antiaircraft fire of the escorts. But there were too many Japanese planes. At 5:14 a bomb plunged through three decks and exploded.

Thirty seconds later another bomb plunged into the carrier's innards. A third bomb tore a gaping hole in the ship's flight deck. Badly damaged, the *Enterprise* limped out of the battle.

Brilliant efforts by her damage control teams stemmed the blazing forces and saved the ship. Hasty repairs to the flight deck allowed Kinkaid to recover planes, but half an hour after the first bomb struck, the ship's rudder jammed and she went dead in the water with another Japanese strike headed her way.

Fortunately, the Japanese flight was unable to locate either American carrier. That night, her rudder repaired, Kinkaid took the *Enterprise* back to Noumea.

Following the Battle of the Eastern Solomons the unfortunate Fletcher was relieved of command of the carriers. Admiral Halsey replaced Ghormley as Commander in Chief, South Pacific. Halsey was a fighter and determined to defeat the Japanese on Guadalcanal.

Bolstered by reinforcements delivered by the Tokyo Express, the Japanese were preparing another major offensive against the marines on Guadalcanal. Halsey was determined to prevent the Japanese Fleet from taking part in this attack. He ordered Kinkaid to take Task Force 16 northeast of Guadalcanal, link up with Adm. George Murray's Task Force 17 containing the carrier *Hornet*, and intercept the enemy fleet if it ventured into the area. Once the two forces combined, Kinkaid, the senior admiral, would assume command.

Admiral Yamamoto was disturbed by the lack of results on Guadalcanal. Unless the Army accomplished something, he said, he would take the Japanese Fleet out of the area. Accordingly, the Sendai division began an all-out attack on October 25, and quickly announced that Henderson Field had been captured. This report was completely false. For two days the Sendai battered itself against the well-dug-in Marine positions. The bulk of their troops were left dead on the battlefield without having made any significant progress. Nevertheless, the premature announcement of the fall of Henderson Field stirred the Japanese Fleet to action.

It was a typical Japanese operation with the fleet divided into two distant sections. Admiral Kondo's advance force contained the light carrier *Junyo*, two battleships, five cruisers, and fourteen destroyers. Nagumo's striking force was made up of the carriers *Zuiho*, *Shokaku*, and *Zuikaku*, escorted by two battleships, five cruisers and fifteen destroyers.

Around noon on October 25, an American patrol plane from Espiritu Santo sighted Nagumo's force moving south. The American carriers were far to the south, but as soon as he drew within range, Kinkaid launched search planes of his own. An hour later a full strike from the *Enterprise* was in the air and headed toward the reported enemy position even though Kinkaid's force was at extreme range.

Meanwhile, Nagumo had reversed course. Consequently, when the *Enterprise* pilots arrived over the spot where the Japanese Fleet was reported, they found nothing but empty ocean. Throughout the rest of the day the two fleets probed for each other without success.

Half an hour after midnight another American patrol plane reported that the Japanese fleet was approximately three hundred miles north of Kinkaid's position. Another sighting was made three hours later, but was reported via Noumea. As a result, this report, placing the Japanese one hundred miles closer to the Americans, never reached Kinkaid until after 5:00. By that time he had already launched his own patrol planes. Accompanying the delayed sighting report from Noumea was one from Halsey, blunt and to the point:

"ATTACK—REPEAT—ATTACK."

The later report confused the issue by reporting the

presence of one enemy carrier whereas the earlier report confirmed the presence of two or more carriers. The one hundred mile difference in the reported enemy position muddied the picture even further. Therefore, Kinkaid decided to wait for verification from his own patrol planes before acting.

Around 6:30 two *Enterprise* scout planes located the Japanese force containing the *Junyo*. Twenty minutes later Nagumo's main force of three carriers was sighted. In the interim, however, the Japanese had also located Kinkaid's force.

Kinkaid had had the foresight to arm his scout planes with bombs. The two that located Nagumo's force, after getting off their sighting report, planted their bombs squarely on the deck of the carrier *Zuiho*. With a large hole in her deck and fires blazing below, the *Zuiho* was soon ordered back to Truk.

Half an hour after receiving the report of the American Fleet, Nagumo launched a large strike from his carriers. Kinkaid countered with one from the *Hornet* a short time later. The *Enterprise* then launched her strike. The opposing planes passed each other en route to their targets.

A few minutes after 9:00 the Japanese located Kinkaid's fleet. At that moment the *Enterprise* was engulfed by a rainstorm, so the Japanese pilots concentrated on the only target in sight, the *Hornet*. There were simply too many enemy planes for the combat air patrol and antiaircraft fire to contend with. The unfortunate *Hornet* was hit by four bombs and two torpedoes. In addition, two dying Japanese pilots plunged their burning aircraft into the stricken carrier. Burning from stem to stern, the *Hornet* went dead in the water and took on an immediate list.

While the *Hornet* was undergoing her ordeal, the ship's own dive bombers were forming up to attack Nagumo's force. The *Shokaku*'s flight deck was blasted open by four hits. Unfortunately, the *Hornet*'s torpedo planes failed to locate the enemy.

Meanwhile, *Hornet*'s crew was struggling desperately to keep the ship afloat. Fires raged out of control and the carrier was unable to maneuver. A second Japanese strike bypassed the stricken *Hornet* and concentrated on the undamaged *Enterprise*.

Hatless and helmetless, Kinkaid was pacing the bridge in his shirt sleeves when the enemy planes arrived overhead. Disdaining efforts to make him seek shelter, the admiral directed the battleship *South Dakota* and the antiaircraft cruiser *San Juan* to form a tight circle around the *Enterprise*. For the past few hours Kinkaid had been busy monitoring reports, directing the battle, and issuing orders for the salvation of the *Hornet*. Now he could only stare in awe as the Japanese pilots peeled off for the attack.

The combined firepower of the *San Juan* and *South Dakota* accounted for more than half of the attackers. The *Enterprise*'s combat air patrol shot down some more. But there were simply too many of the enemy. Two determined Japanese pilots managed to sneak through the hail of fire and steel to plant their bombs on the flagship. The forward elevator was jammed in the down position and fires broke out beneath decks.

Hard on the heels of the dive bombers came a formation of torpedo bombers. Fortunately the two bomb hits had not affected the *Enterprise*'s mobility. Her skipper, Capt. Osborne Hardison skillfully maneuvered his ship and successfully eluded the oncoming torpedoes. Thanks to his brilliant efforts, the ship was spared further harm.

Kinkaid was now faced with a dilemma. The *Hornet* was in dire straits and the *Enterprise* was damaged. He ordered the cruiser *Northampton* to take the *Hornet* in tow, but these efforts ultimately proved unsuccessful as did all efforts to put out the raging fires. Even if the ship could be saved, she would obviously be out of the war for many months. Then there were also the *Hornet*'s planes to consider. With the ship unable to recover planes and a mile-high cloud of smoke hanging over her, Kinkaid directed *Hornet*'s planes to land on the *Enterprise*.

Despite the gaping hole in her deck caused by the elevator being jammed, Kinkaid ordered the "Big E" to begin recovering planes. As soon as the first group was landed, he ordered them refueled and flown to Espiritu Santo. In this way he made additional room for returning planes. Although some of the American planes were forced to ditch at sea, Kinkaid's decision undoubtedly saved a number of their lives. After the recovery operation was complete, Kinkaid ordered the *Enterprise* to leave her present position so that additional enemy attacks would not be able to locate her. Then he turned his attention to the fate of the *Hornet* once more.

The Japanese advance force was rapidly approaching the American position from the north. Two additional air strikes, after failing to locate the still seaworthy *Enterprise*, took their wrath out on the hapless *Hornet*. By early evening it was obvious that there would be no saving the ship that had delivered Doolittle's raiders to Japan. The *Hornet* was doomed. Kinkaid therefore ordered her screening destroyers to sink the carrier with gunfire and torpedoes. Despite their best efforts, however, the *Hornet* refused to sink. Then reports of an enemy surface force approaching caused Kinkaid to order the American ships to leave the area.

The *Enterprise* was the only remaining carrier left in the Pacific at that point. And her operational effectiveness was limited by the huge hole in the flight deck. Wisely, he refused to become involved in a night action. Accordingly, he turned his fleet toward Noumea.

When the Japanese formation arrived on the scene the *Hornet* was almost white hot from the intense fires raging throughout the ship. There were no signs of life anywhere. Japanese destroyers finished off the carrier with torpedoes.

Kinkaid was criticized for abandoning the *Hornet*. Halsey never forgave him for it, but the latter's mind was clouded by his fierce fighting spirit that demanded a fight to the finish. Kinkaid had a cooler head. He was able to look ahead to the consequences. The *Wasp* had been sunk a few weeks earlier and the *Saratoga* was laid up repairing torpedo damage. The *Enterprise*, damaged elevator and all, was the only American carrier left in the Pacific. Kinkaid had no other choice but to take her out of harm's way and hope that she could be speedily repaired. Events ultimately proved his decision correct for the Big E's presence was felt a few weeks later at Guadalcanal.

At the beginning of November, the marines on Guadalcanal went on the offensive. In a two-week battle they pushed the Japanese steadily back. But the Japanese had been pouring reinforcements into the island via the Tokyo Express in anticipation of a major offensive of their own. General Vandergrift expected the enemy offensive. Accordingly, he called a halt to his own and began to dig in.

Meanwhile, at Truk, Admiral Yamamoto was putting the finishing touches on yet another of his grandiose schemes for driving the marines from Guadalcanal and the U.S. Navy from the waters of the Solomons. The plan would take a strong surface force into Ironbottom Sound, destroy all naval opposition, and bombard Henderson Field until it was out of commission. Then the Tokyo Express would deliver a large contingent of troops and adequate supplies to their forces on the island. With Henderson Field out of commission and unable to launch aircraft, the supply run could be carried out with relative impunity. After all, after the Battle of Santa Cruz, no American carriers were left in the area. When the reinforcements landed they would immediately go on the offensive aided by another naval bombardment of Henderson Field and American defensive positions.

Meanwhile, the Americans were also building up their

forces on Guadalcanal. Admiral Halsey suggested that the enemy were preparing for an all-out attack. All their activity of the previous weeks pointed to it. Therefore he ordered Kinkaid up from Noumea where the *Enterprise* was still repairing the damage suffered at Santa Cruz. Task Force 16 set out with repair crews still aboard. This time Kinkaid had a surprise for the Japanese. Accompanying him were Adm. Willis Lee's two new and recently arrived battleships, *South Dakota* and *Washington.*

On November 11, a convoy of American supply ships began unloading at Guadalcanal. These ships had arrived escorted by a force of cruisers and destroyers under the command of Adm. Norman Scott. The next day Adm. Daniel Callaghan's cruisers and destroyers escorted a second convoy safely to Guadalcanal. All the transports were unloaded by early evening and Admiral Turner, commander of the amphibious forces, ordered the transports to retire. Scott's squadron was placed under Callaghan's command. Callaghan took the combined force into Ironbottom Sound to intercept the enemy formation reportedly moving down the Slot.

Dan Callaghan knew that his opponent's force contained at least two battleships. However, Kinkaid and Lee were still too far away to take a hand in the battle so he felt that he had no choice but to take on the enemy fleet and place his trust in providence.

Providence was not enough on the night of November 12-13. Callaghan's force was overwhelmed. He and Scott were both killed in a confusing fight during which commanders on both sides lost control of the battle. The Americans lost two cruisers and four destroyers while the Japanese cost was two destroyers. Virtually every other American ship with the exception of the destroyer *Fletcher,* was damaged to some extent.

One additional casualty of the battle was the Japanese battleship *Hiei.* Damaged during the battle, the *Hiei* had begun to withdraw up the Slot when the many fires raging in the ship destroyed her controls. The battleship went dead in the water a few miles north of Savo Island and lay helpless awaiting aid.

Coming up from the south was the *Enterprise*, two battleships, and their escorting destroyers. Kinkaid knew that he had no chance of reaching Guadalcanal in time to aid Callaghan and Scott. But at first light he decided to send whatever help he could. Fifteen of the Big E's planes were dispatched to aid the Marine pilots on Guadalcanal. Nearing their destination, the *Enterprise* air group spotted the disabled *Hiei*, which by this time had recovered power but was steaming in circles unable to steer. The opportunistic carrier pilots planted two torpedoes in the battleship's side. They landed at Henderson Field, refueled, rearmed, and joined the Marine pilots in another attack on the crippled giant. Late in the afternoon, the *Hiei* plunged beneath the waves. The *Hiei* was the first Japanese battleship sunk in the war.

Later that night, two Japanese cruisers snuck into Iron-bottom Sound and carried out a brief bombardment of American positions. Kinkaid made them pay for their audacity. The next day the *Enterprise*'s pilots caught the two cruisers retreating up the Slot. The heavy cruiser *Kunugasa* was blasted beneath the waves and her accompanying light cruiser heavily damaged.

The same day, the Tokyo Express, four destroyers and eleven transports, attempted to make a run into Guadalcanal. Kinkaid was aware of the approach of the Japanese ships. The *Enterprise* launched continuous strikes against the Japanese flotilla. Six transports were sunk and one more was damaged so badly that it was forced to turn back. The remaining four beached themselves on Guadalcanal. Although the latter's cargo of troops managed to scamper ashore, well over half of the Japanese reinforcements and most of the supplies failed to reach the island. The beached transports never went to sea again. The *Enterprise* pilots saw to that. The hapless transports were pounded where they lay and damaged beyond repair.

Meanwhile, the follow-up Japanese bombardment fleet was making its way down the Slot. But Kinkaid had another surprise up his sleeve. He detached Lee's battleships with orders to proceed to Ironbottom Sound at full speed and intercept the enemy force. The Japanese commander, Admiral Kondo, had no inkling that the Americans had any battleships in the area. As far as he knew all surface opposition had been eliminated two nights earlier.

Lee and Kondo collided in the waters off Guadalcanal half an hour before midnight on the fourteenth. Lee's luck did not hold, but his courage never wavered. Early in the battle three of his four destroyers were hit and damaged beyond repair. The fourth suffered a crippling hit that put it out of action. Then the *South Dakota* suffered a power failure. The enemy force concentrated on the helpless battleship which was unable to retaliate. This left the *Washington* to continue the struggle alone.

Fight she did. Her accuracy that night was deadly. *Washington*'s sixteen-inch guns overwhelmed the Japanese battleship *Kirishima* which was so badly battered that Kondo ordered her scuttled. *Washington* also blew the destroyer *Ayanami* out of the water. Kondo turned and fled up the Slot. From that moment on, the initiative in the naval struggle for the Solomons swung over to the Americans. There would be other battles and more tragic American losses, but never again would the Japanese sail unmolested into Ironbottom Sound. Kinkaid's forces had sunk two battleships in three nights, obliterated a Tokyo Express run, and harassed the enemy until they drew out of range.

With the major surface threat neutralized, Nimitz decided that the Americans needed to pay more attention to the Tokyo Express. His staff proposed the formation of a cruiser/destroyer squadron to patrol the waters north of Guadalcanal constantly. This fleet would intercept the nightly Tokyo Express run and prevent it from delivering supplies and reinforcements to the Japanese troops on Guadalcanal. Nimitz approved of the proposal and decided that the new force needed a skilled surface commander, one familiar with surface tactics and willing to fight. He therefore ordered Kinkaid to relinquish command of Task Force 16 and take command of this new Task Force.

Kinkaid officially assumed command of the new Task Force on November 24. Throughout the naval struggle for Guadalcanal the Japanese had utilized superior tactics. The evidence of Savo and the first Battle of Guadalcanal bore grim witness to that fact. Kinkaid immediately scrapped the American tactic of parading their forces in a single line with destroyers at the head and tail of the formation. Instead, he grouped the destroyers together at the head of twin columns of cruisers. Each group would contain at least one ship with the most up-to-date radar. Under no circumstances were searchlights to be used during battle. Finally, the cruisers would hold their fire until the van destroyers had delivered a torpedo attack against the column of enemy ships.

All well and good, but Kinkaid never had a chance to prove his theories in battle. Four days later, he was once more given a new assignment and had to relinquish command of the newly created squadron. Adm. Carleton Wright succeeded him, reverted to the old tactics, and led the formation to disaster at the Battle of Tassafronga on November 30.

On November 27, Admiral Kinkaid left Noumea and flew to Hawaii. Upon arrival he went immediately to Nimitz's headquarters where he was greeted cordially by the commander of the Pacific Fleet. After the amenities were over Nimitz turned to Kinkaid and stated that the latter would be leaving the South Pacific. At first Kinkaid thought that he was being relieved, but could not fathom why. To his immense relief Nimitz went on to say that Kinkaid was to be commander of his own theater, the north Pacific. Nimitz's Pacific Ocean command was divided into three subtheaters; South Pacific under Halsey, central Pacific under his own command, and the north Pacific. The Commander in Chief emphasized that Kinkaid's first task would be to drive the Japanese out of the Aleutian Islands. The Joint Chiefs had issued a directive calling for the recapture of enemy-held positions in these islands.

The Aleutians are a chain of islands originating off the southwest coast of Alaska and stretching in a great arc for over a thousand miles into the Bering Sea. Few of the islands are fit for habitation. The weather in the Aleutians is probably among the worst in the world. Frequent storms known as williwaws sweep in from the Pacific. Cold and dampness dominate. The clash of cold artic air and warm air moving up from the south creates a layer of fog that blankets the Aleutians almost constantly. Sunny days are an exception. Why then were these islands so strategically important?

The westernmost Aleutians are only six hundred and fifty miles from Japan's northern outpost, the Kuriles. It was from the Kuriles that Nagumo had set out on his historic voyage to Pearl Harbor. The Japanese used these islands for air bases and fleet anchorages. In the spring of 1942, Admiral Yamamoto decided to eliminate this threat to Japan's northern flank by capturing the two westernmost islands suitable for the creation of air bases, Kiska and Attu. The attack on the Aleutians was scheduled to take place just prior to the operation against Midway and would serve a dual purpose. Besides securing Japan's northern flank, it was hoped that the Aleutians attack would draw the American Fleet north to meet the threat thereby allowing Yamamoto a free run into Midway. With both Midway and the Aleutians in Japanese hands, any threat of air attack against the home islands would be eliminated.

Admiral Nimitz refused to take the bait. Despite the fact that the Aleutians attack marked the only Japanese offensive against U.S. territory in North America, Nimitz kept his carriers by Midway. Admiral Nagumo's carrier force suffered a disastrous defeat at Midway.

On June 3, 1942, a two-carrier Japanese Task Force launched an attack against the U.S. Naval Base at Dutch Harbor, halfway down the Aleutian chain. The handful of American forces managed to hold off the enemy at Dutch Harbor, but Kiska and Attu were occupied without opposition. Fortunately for the Americans, as long as Dutch Harbor remained in their hands, the Japanese threat to Alaska was neutralized.

The Army commander in the Alaskan theater, under which the Aleutians fell, was Gen. Simon Bolivar Buckner. An aggressive, gruff officer, Buckner was nonetheless popular with his officers and men. His opposite number in the Navy was Adm. Robert "Fuzzy" Theobold. Buckner and Theobold did not get along at all.

> Theobold was cautious, brainy, inclined to be bitter because his pessimistic side always saw the possible perils of any undertaking.[3]

In the six months following the Japanese invasion, there had been no concerted American effort to drive them from Kiska and Attu. Other than sporadic bombing attacks by Buckner's pitifully small air force when weather permitted, offensive action against Kiska and Attu was virtually nonexistent. Theobold complained that the handful of ships in his command represented too small a force with which to launch a full-scale attack. He may have been correct, but he never had the opportunity to find out because he never tried.

Then again there was his relationship with Buckner.

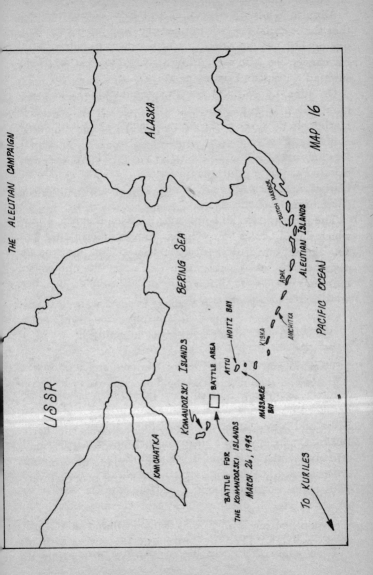

THE ALEUTIAN CAMPAIGN

USSR

KAMCHATKA

Komandozski Islands

BERING SEA

ALASKA

BATTLE AREA

HOITZ BAY

ATTU

MASSACRE BAY

KISKA

AMCHITKA

ADAK

DUTCH HARBOR

ALEUTIAN ISLANDS

PACIFIC OCEAN

BATTLE FOR
THE KOMANDORSKI ISLANDS
MARCH 26, 1943

TO KURILES

MAP 16

Intraservice rivalry resulted in the stagnation of the entire Aleutians campaign. The Joint Chiefs of Staff wanted the Japanese driven from American soil. Prodded by the Joint Chiefs' directive, Nimitz concluded that one of his first moves would have to be the replacement of Theobold. Nimitz needed an officer whose personality was compatible with Buckner's. But above all, the job called for a fighter, one who would not hesitate to utilize all the resources within his command, however small. In Nimitz's opinion, other than Halsey who could not be spared, the Pacific theater contained only one man who fit this description, Rear Admiral Tom Kinkaid.

After a brief period of rest, Kinkaid began familiarizing himself with his new command. For two weeks he attended intelligence briefings, made plans, and put together a staff. On January 2, 1943, Kinkaid set out for the Aleutians. Two days later he arrived at the Navy's Alaskan headquarters in Kodiak.

When I first arrived in Kodiak, I took a walk to look the place over, walked up through the town, and decided that I didn't want to do it again.[4]

Kinkaid and Buckner hit it off immediately. Both were fighters and shared the same opinions regarding the reconquest of the Aleutians.

From the moment of Kinkaid's arrival, neither commander was to make a single important decision without first consulting the other. It made for a tight relationship with almost awesome mutal cooperation which far exceeded Nimitz's wildest hopes.[5]

When he arrived in Kodiak Kinkaid found that Nimitz had been right. There was precious little to work with and there was no hope for significant reinforcements since the demands of the campaign in the Solomons rated priority. His fleet consisted of a handful of PT boats, a few destroyers, one heavy cruiser, the *Indianapolis*, and the light cruiser *Raleigh*, a twenty-year-old veteran. Undaunted, Kinkaid wasted little time in setting to work. Adm. Charles "Soc" McMorris was ordered to blockade Kiska and Attu with his small force of ships.

To everyone but Kinkaid the idea of a blockade sounded preposterous. Kiska and Attu were almost three hundred miles apart. How could McMorris' small force blockade both islands simultaneously? Easy, replied Kinkaid. Cut the Japanese supply line where it was the narrowest, at its base. Therefore McMorris positioned his force off the northern Kuriles. After the American ships sank a few Japanese transports, the enemy ceased dispatching unescorted freighters to their garrisons. McMorris broke the tedium of constant patrol duty by shelling Japanese positions on Kiska and Attu. The blockade worked. Not, however, before the Japanese made one final effort to reinforce their garrisons and destroy the American blockade.

On March 26, McMorris was patrolling south of the Kamandorski Islands with four destroyers, the *Raleigh* and the *Salt Lake City*, the latter having recently arrived as a replacement for the *Indianapolis*. McMorris flew his flag on the *Raleigh*. Over the horizon came a force of Japanese warships escorting a convoy of supply ships.

Admiral Hosogaya's force contained the heavy cruisers *Nachi* and *Maya*, light cruisers *Abukuma* and *Tama*, and four destroyers. McMorris was unquestionably outmatched. For the next three and a half hours the two fleets engaged each other as McMorris kept maneuvering for a chance to get at the Japanese transports. Midway through the battle the *Salt Lake City* was hit seriously. Nevertheless, through skillful use of his destroyers and brilliant maneuvering, McMorris kept the vastly superior enemy formation at bay. Frustrated, low on ammunition, and unable to finish off the Americans' force, Hosogaya reversed course and headed back to Japan. The Battle of the Komandorskis marked the final Japanese attempt to reinforce their garrisons on Kiska and Attu with surface ships. From that point on they resorted to using submarines whose cargo space was so limited that it almost seemed a waste of time. Only a few submarines successfully made the run to Kiska and Attu.

Meanwhile, Kinkaid had drawn up a plan for the reconquest of the Aleutians. He and Buckner put their heads together and decided to occupy Amchitka Island where an airfield would be constructed. From this field American planes could attack Japanese positions of Kiska and Attu whenever the weather permitted.

A force of American troops under Gen. Lloyd Jones landed on Amchitka on January 12. Construction was immediately begun on the airfield. Two weeks later, the airstrip received its first contingent of fighter planes.

Kinkaid was used to being in the thick of action. He was unhappy with directing against the extreme western end of the island chain from a headquarters at the opposite end. Therefore he suggested to Buckner that the theater headquarters be moved forward to Adak, midway down the chain. At the end of March, Kinkaid, Buckner, and their air force commanders set up headquarters in a Quonset hut on Adak.

Now that Kinkaid's command was firmly established, his headquarters moved forward, and the effects of the blockade being felt by the Japanese garrisons, it was time for the final push. Buckner requested reinforcements and received the Seventh Division, a unit that had spent the previous year training for combat in the desert of north Africa. There were no deserts in the Aleutians, only cold, damp, mountainous islands.

Despite the arrival of the Seventh Division, Kinkaid felt that he still lacked adequate forces to assault both enemy-held islands simultaneously. Landing on a hostile shore in the horrendous and unreliable Aleutian weather would be a perilous undertaking to say the least without biting off more than one could chew. Because his intelligence staff had reported that the defenders of Kiska were more numerous than those on Attu, Kinkaid decided to bypass the former until such time as enough reinforcements reached the theater. Attu would be the preliminary stroke for the total recapture of the Aleutians. In addition, it would provide the assault forces with badly needed experience.

Beginning in April, aircraft from Amchitka began to plaster both islands daily. Most of the attacks were directed at Kiska in hopes that it would deceive Attu's defenders into thinking that Kiska was the actual target. A week before the invasion date, the weight of the Aleutians air forces was shifted exclusively to Attu.

In the previous few weeks, Kinkaid had been reinforced by the addition of three old battleships, two more cruisers, and a squadron of destroyers. All-important amphibious ships were also sent by Admiral Nimitz. To command the amphibious forces, Kinkaid chose Rear Admiral Francis Rockwell. Kinkaid himself had been promoted to vice admiral shortly after his arrival in the Aleutians.

On May 4, the invasion convoy carrying the Seventh Division set out from Alaskan bases. Unfortunately, the weather turned sour and the force was forced to turn back. On the Eighth, even though the bad weather had not totally abated, the force set out again.

Because of the prevailing bad weather, Attu's garrison relaxed their vigil. On May 11, American battleships began to soften up the two landing beaches. Late in the morning, the Seventh Division initiated Operation Landcrab by landing at Holtz Bay and Massacre Bay in high seas and dense fog.

Colonel Yamakazi's garrison consisted of just over two thousand six-hundred men. With this small force Yamakazi knew that he would be unable to effectively oppose a strong

American landing. Therefore, he withdrew most of his force to a valley between the two beaches and elected to make a stand there in the hills overlooking the valley and both beaches. In these hills he positioned strong rear-guards.

Gen. Albert Brown, the Seventh Division's commander, went ashore with his troops at Massacre Bay. On the first day of the invasion, Brown concentrated on building up the beachhead. The next day, when he attempted to move inland, Brown's force was stopped dead in their tracks by Japanese troops positioned on the heights overlooking Massacre Bay. There was no support from the air force because a heavy blanket of fog had settled in over the island. All efforts to dislodge the enemy proved futile.

Brown was stuck. Every effort to move inland resulted in a bloody repulse. Back at his headquarters, Kinkaid was unhappy with Brown's lack of progress. The force at Holz Bay was moving steadily forward, but enemy opposition on that front was not nearly as heavy as it was at Massacre Bay. All Brown could do was send for reinforcements and build up his beachhead.

Kinkaid's aggressive nature took exception to Brown's lack of progress. Admiral Rockwell continued to pour troops and supplies into the beachhead, but the Seventh Division remained confined to a few square miles around Massacre Bay. Finally, Rockwell informed Brown that because the beachhead was becoming crowded, he would not send anything more ashore. Brown protested. However, even though as an Army officer Brown was technically responsible to Buckner, Kinkaid was the theater commander and Brown's appeals were in vain. Kinkaid sent Admiral Rockwell a directive.

No more troops should be put ashore until the congestion there is relieved. Obtain from General Brown information as to why more troops are needed.[6]

Brown met with Rockwell and managed to convince the admiral that if additional reinforcements were landed, he would be able to move inland. Rockwell passed the information along to Kinkaid who replied, "If Brown lacks aggressiveness, he should be relieved.[7]"

Kinkaid's patience was wearing thin. He met with Buckner and asked that Brown be relieved. Buckner hesitated. Perhaps Brown's lack of aggressiveness stemmed from his lack of experience in the Aleutians theater. But there were not many commanders with such experience. There was one, however — Gen. Eugene Landrum who had commanded the landing on Adak. Buckner deferred to Kinkaid who was left alone to make the decision. On May 16, he radioed Nimitz.

In view of the unsatisfactory situation ashore at Attu . . . it is with regret that the Task Force commander has decided that the commanding general, landing force, must be superseded. Therefore, General Landrum will proceed today by plane and relieve General Brown.[8]

By that time the Americans had incurred over one thousand casualties, many of them caused by exposure. But they had twelve thousand troops on the island.

Unfortunately for Brown, his relief had come a few days too early. On the seventeenth, patrols at Massacre Bay discovered that the enemy had fled. Faced with the threat to his rear from the force at Holtz Bay, Colonel Yamakazi elected to make his last stand at Chichagof Harbor in the northeast part of the island. Skillful rear-guard action prevented the Americans from pursuing zealously.

Landrum made sure that the Japanese continued to retreat. Whenever the enemy paused, the pursuing Americans brought up heavy artillery and blasted and levered the enemy out of their positions. Finally, as May was drawing to a close, Landrum had driven the Japanese into a small pocket at Chichagof Harbor. On the twenty-ninth, the desperate Yamakazi launched a full-scale suicide attack. A few American positions were overrun, but the Seventh Division stood its ground. Over fifteen hundred Japanese troops perished in the attack. Late in the day, Yamakazi and five hundred surviving Japanese troops committed suicide.

Kinkaid now turned his attention to Kiska. The Japanese garrison there was reputedly much stronger than that at Attu. If that fact was indeed true, then the attacking force would have to be significantly larger than the one that had assaulted Attu. Nimitz felt the same way and began to send a steady stream of reinforcements to the Aleutians. Through June and into July, Kinkaid made plans for the invasion of Kiska and concentrated on training the newly arrived troops.

Meanwhile, the Japanese were reassessing their priorities. The demands of the war in the South Pacific were proving a huge drain on their resources. Accordingly, Admiral Koga, Yamamoto's successor, decided that the Aleutians were a luxury he could not afford. Even before Attu was secured, Japanese submarines began evacuating wounded from Kiska.

Bolstered by the success of the submarine evacuation, Koga decided to use this method to evacuate the entire Kiska garrison. The attempt was a failure. Some of the submarines were forced to turn back because of the weather. Others were sunk by Kinkaid's antisubmarine patrols. With the limited space available on the submarines, Koga realized that it would require a huge force of these ships if anticipated losses were taken into consideration. In addition, Koga was in a hurry. Only July 28, a small force of destroyers, using the fog as an ally, successfully eluded the American patrols, dashed into Kiska, and in less than an hour evacuated over five thousand Japanese troops.

By mid-August, Kinkaid's invasion force had swelled to over thirty-four thousand troops. He was now ready to put an end to the Aleutians campaign via an invasion of Kiska. But the Admiral had been receiving disturbing reports for the past few weeks. Aircraft flying over Kiska reported no signs of enemy activity. There was no anti-aircraft fire, and smoke from cooking fires was nonexistent. Nevertheless, Kinkaid decided to launch the invasion.

On August 16, the first American troops began landing on Kiska. There were no Japanese anywhere. For three days patrols combed the island, but found absolutely no signs of life except for a few stray dogs. The Aleutians were secured.

Samuel Morrison called the Aleutians "the Theater of Military Frustration."[9]

But for Kinkaid the Aleutians were the theater of opportunity. In every sense he had justified Nimitz's faith in him. Kinkaid proved that he was a team player, one who possessed the ability to get along with his opposite numbers in the Army and Air Forces. His aggressiveness was clearly evident. Kinkaid operated under the theory that any decision was better than no decision at all. Therefore, unlike many theaters of the war, the Aleutians did not suffer from indecisiveness. Nimitz was convinced that the war could not do without "Fighting" Tom Kinkaid.

With the Aleutians no longer an active theater, Nimitz began to cast about for another assignment for Kinkaid. Despite Admiral King's aversion to allowing General MacArthur to command naval forces, the Joint Chiefs recognized that the southwest Pacific Command needed its own naval force to enable it to complete the capture of New Guinea, the isolation of Rabaul, and the eventual jump to the Philippines. Even though this force initially consisted of amphibious forces and a handful of light warships, it was designated the Seventh Fleet. Kinkaid would take the Seventh Fleet soaring to new heights of glory.

In November, 1943, Kinkaid reported to MacArthur's

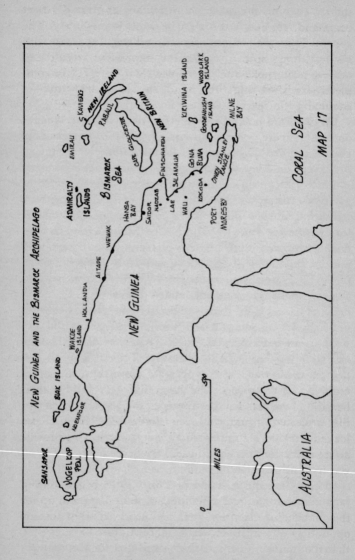

NEW GUINEA AND THE BISMARCK ARCHIPELAGO

SANSAPOR

BIAK ISLAND

ABENDAUR

VOGELKOP PEN.

WAKDE ISLAND

HOLLANDIA

AITAPE

WEWAK

NEW GUINEA

ADMIRALTY ISLANDS

HANSA BAY

SAIDOR

EMIRAU

BISMARCK SEA

S. KAVIENG

NEW IRELAND

RABAUL

CAPE GLOUCESTER

NEW BRITAIN

NADZAB

FINSCHHAFEN

LAE

SALAMAUA

WAU

KOKODA

BUNA

GONA

OWEN STANLEY RANGE

PORT MORESBY

KIRIWINA ISLAND

WOODLARK ISLAND

GOODENOUGH ISLAND

MILNE BAY

CORAL SEA

MILES

0   500

AUSTRALIA

MAP 17

headquarters. He had been promoted to vice admiral shortly after his arrival in the Aleutians and rated a fleet command. He and MacArthur hit it off immediately. The general liked the genial Irishman and was impressed with his fighting spirit. Kinkaid's impressive record of achievement spoke for itself. Yes, MacArthur was completely satisfied with the man the navy had sent to command the Seventh Fleet.

By 1944, the Japanese were being thrown back throughout the Pacific. The isolation of Rabaul was virtually complete; the Solomons were for the most part firmly in American hands and MacArthur's forces were advancing steadily along the coast of New Guinea. The Seventh Fleet was responsible for all naval activity in the southwest Pacific. As such, Kinkaid successfully directed MacArthur's leapfrog operations in New Guinea. At one point he conducted an invasion over four hundred miles in the enemy's rear at Hollandia. Along the way Kinkaid's fleet successfully participated in the capture of the Admiralties and Cape Gloucester on New Britain. By mid-summer, 1944, plans were being made for MacArthur's triumphant return to the Philippines. The first target was Mindanao.

The Seventh Fleet had by this time expanded to include many amphibious ships. Battleships, although not the new fast ones, were assigned to Kinkaid along with numerous cruisers and destroyers. The Australian Navy added their handful of cruisers and destroyers to the Seventh Fleet. For the projected invasion of the Philippines, Nimitz also loaned Kinkaid a force of small escort carriers to provide aerial cover for the beachheads. By September, 1944, all was in readiness.

In mid-September, Halsey's Third Fleet began hitting Japanese positions in the Philippines, softening them up for the impending invasion. Halsey observed that enemy opposition was relatively light. Accordingly, he suggested that the invasion of Mindanao, scheduled for October 20, be scrapped, and in its place the invasion of Leyte be pushed ahead a month.

MacArthur and Nimitz agreed to Halsey's proposal. When confronted with the suggestion, Kinkaid initially had reservations. After reviewing the entire picture, however, he gave his consent.

As Commander in Chief, Seventh Fleet, Kinkaid had overall responsibility for the landings. He borrowed a force of small escort carriers from Nimitz. These ships were to be used in direct support of the assault forces. Halsey's fleet carriers would lay off the east coast of the Philippines, add their weight to that of the escort carriers, keep the enemy air forces in the Philippines pinned down, and protect MacArthur's forces from intervention by the Japanese Fleet.

On October 18, Kinkaid sent his battleships and cruisers under Adm. Jesse Oldendorf into Leyte Gulf. For two days this force bombarded enemy positions near the landing beaches. Three groups of escort carriers sat off the east coast of Samar and Leyte. Planes from the carriers flew hundreds of sorties against Japanese installations on Leyte.

On the morning of October 20, Kinkaid's amphibious forces, commanded by Adm. Daniel Barbey, began landing MacArthur's troops at two beaches on Leyte; one near Tacloban and the other farther south near Dulag.

On the first day it was a matter of getting the troops ashore, about seventy thousand or eighty thousand that first day. Then two days later about thirty thousand or so more went ashore.[10]

Kinkaid was to exercise overall command until the beachhead was firmly secure. Then he would turn command over to the Sixth Army commander, General Walter Krueger. Initial Japanese opposition was light, but a few enemy planes managed to get through. One put a torpedo into the light cruiser *Honolulu* and another crashed aboard the cruiser HMAS *Australia*. Kinkaid had to order both ships to the rear for repairs.

The Japanese were ready to strike back. Loss of the Philippines meant that Japan's southern empire would be completely cut off. From the Philippines the Americans could jump to Luzon or the coast of China. Therefore, the Japanese High Command decided to commit everything they had in an effort to hurl the Americans back.

An elaborate naval operation, Sho-Go, was prepared. On October 17, when Kinkaid's fleet was sighted approaching Leyte, the Japanese put their plan into motion. (See Map 15)

Down from the north came Admiral Shima's force of two cruisers and four destroyers. Shima planned to rendezvous with a force of two battleships, one cruiser, and four destroyers moving up from Brunei, Borneo, commanded by Admiral Nishimura. The combined force would move into Leyte Gulf from the south and attack the American beachhead and transports. At the same time, Admiral Kurita with a powerful striking force of thirteen cruisers, four battleships, and fifteen destroyers, also based at Brunei, would move up the west coast of Palawan Island, across the Sibuyan Sea, and down the east coast of Samar. Kurita would then enter Leyte Gulf from the east in conjunction with the forces of Shima and Nishimura.

At the same time, the few remaining Japanese carriers under Admiral Ozawa, would hover off the northeast coast of Luzon, and lure Halsey's carriers north, thereby allowing Kurita a free passage through San Bernadino Strait. It was a grandiose scheme that relied on precise timing, something that the Japanese had thus far proved inept at.

On October 23, the U.S. submarines *Darter* and *Dace* sighted Kurita's force off the west coast of Palawan. The two submarines got off a sighting report before submerging for an attack. They managed to sink two of Kurita's cruisers and damage a third so badly that it had to return to

Brunei. The word was out about the approach of the Japanese.

At first light Halsey had his planes in the air looking for the enemy fleet. In mid-morning the American pilots located a Japanese force moving through the Sulu Sea. This was of course, not Kurita, but Nishimura. The American aviators attacked, but caused little damage. A few hours later Kurita's fleet was sighted in the Sibuyan Sea. Halsey, feeling that Nishimura was the lesser of the two evils turned his attention to Kurita.

Kinkaid was in his command post on the transport *Wasatch* when word came of the approach of Nishimura's force. Although his mind was preoccupied with the landings and fighting ashore, Kinkaid had little trouble guessing Nishimura's intentions. He quickly ordered General Kruger to go ashore and assume command of the ground troops. Then he passed the word for all noncombat ships to haul off and be prepared to sail at a moment's notice. If the Japanese broke through, Kinkaid would not have the vulnerable transports exposed.

Tom Kinkaid prepared a hot reception for Nishimura and Shima. It was one of the most brilliant ambushes in naval history, worthy of a Drake, Nelson, or Dewey. Every type of warship in his command was pressed into service.

In the mouth of and at the approaches to Surigao Strait, Kinkaid positioned thirteen squadrons of PT boats strung out so that the approaching Japanese Fleet would have to pass each one in turn. Lining both sides of the upper portion of the narrow body of water were four squadrons of destroyers. At the head of the strait steaming back and forth was a battle line under Oldendorf. Six old battleships, *Mississippi, West Virginia, Tennessee, California, Pennsylvania,* and *Maryland,* the latter five salvaged from the mud of Pearl Harbor, were the heart of this force. Slightly forward and at each end of the battle line were two groups of cruisers, *Phoenix, Boise,* and the Australian *Shropshire* on the right; *Portland, Minneapolis, Denver, Columbia,* and Oldendorf's flagship *Louisville* on the left. MacArthur had asked permission to join the battle line in his flagship, the cruiser *Nashville,* but a flabbergasted Kinkaid would not hear of it. Nishimura missed his rendezvous with Shima. The latter deliberately slowed his speed so that he would not have to operate under Nishimura. There was an intense jealousy between the two. Consequently, Shima's force was a good two hours behind the more powerful force of his fellow admiral.

Three-quarters of an hour after midnight the first PT boats sighted the leading Japanese formation and raced in for the attack. The enemy ships successfully avoided the American torpedoes, but they were entering the gauntlet. For the next two hours the story was the same. A squadron of PT boats would suddenly dart out of the darkness. Japanese fire drove the small boats off without suffering any damage, but it was an unnerving experience. The Japanese crews had to be constantly on the alert, peering out into the darkness. As the fleet passed each successive PT squadron, their advance was reported to Kinkaid.

Around 3:00, the Japanese force was in the heart of the strait when the destroyer attacks began. The American ships, hidden against the darker background of the land, had the advantage of surprise. First it was three destroyers of Desron 54. A torpedo slammed into the side of the battleship *Fuso*. The giant swerved out of line, burning and listing.

The second destroyer attack cut Nishimura's force in half. His own destroyers were leading the formation in line abreast. Suddenly the *Yamagumo* exploded in a fiery tower of smoke and flame. The *Michishio* was hit and left in a sinking condition. The *Asagumo's* bow was blown completely off. Only the *Shigure* escaped damage. A torpedo also plowed into the side of Nishimura's flagship, the battleship *Yamashiro*, but the resulting damage failed to slow the battleship and she steamed on.

The next attack scored another hit on the *Yamashiro*. Nishimura's flagship slowed momentarily, but was soon able to resume speed. The floundering *Mishishio* was finished off in the attack. Despite seeing his force halved, Nishimura continued on, the *Shigure* and cruiser *Mogami* leading the damaged flagship. But the worst was yet to come.

Just before 4:00, another powerful destroyer attack, nine ships strong, raced in for the kill. At the same time the battle line opened up. A hail of fire and steel rained down on the hapless Japanese formation. *Mogami* staggered under countless hits, her upper decks a wreck and fires raging throughout her length. Accompanied by the *Shigure*, *Mogami* turned out of the battle. The *Yamashiro*, too, was pounded by numerous heavy-caliber hits. No one knows at what point in the battle Nishimura perished, but at 4:20 his blazing flagship slipped beneath the waves. Ten minutes later the burning *Fuso* blew up, broke in half, and sank.

Mogami and *Shigure* headed down the strait away from the hell they had just experienced. *Portland, Denver,* and *Louisville* set out in pursuit. Then the lumbering American battleships joined the chase. Oldendorf was anxious to finish the job.

Meanwhile, Shima was just entering Surigao Strait. Suddenly his flagship, *Nachi,* collided with the retiring *Mogami.* The latter's speed was reduced even further. *Shigure* signaled an account of the battle to Shima who decided that Nishimura's fate was not for him. He turned his force around and fled.

The pursuing American cruisers quickly caught up with the bowless *Asagumo* and finished her off. Then they came across the hapless *Mogami.* The Japanese cruiser was subjected to a withering fire, but refused to sink. Eventually, the American ships altered course and continued the chase. *Mogami* was sunk by American torpedo planes a few hours later.

The Battle of Surigao Strait was but one segment of the Battle for Leyte Gulf. It was, however, the most decisive. Nishimura lost six of his seven ships, including two battleships and a heavy cruiser. Another heavy cruiser, Shima's *Nachi* had been damaged. Other than some damage to one destroyer and a few PT boats, Kinkaid's force remained totally intact. His positioning of Oldendorf at the head of the strait had resulted in the latter being able to execute the time-honored naval maneuver, "capping the T."

There would be no resting on laurels, however. While Oldendorf was pursuing the retreating Japanese with his cruisers and battleships, events took a dramatic turn for the worse north of the Leyte beachhead.

The strongest of the four Japanese formations was Kurita's striking force of battleships and cruisers. The previous day Halsey's Third Fleet, standing off the coast of the Philippines, had caught this force as it was crossing the Sibuyan Sea and punished it severely. Wave after wave of American planes from Halsey's ships sank the battleship *Musashi,* and battered the rest of the fleet. Late in the afternoon the Japanese admiral reversed course and appeared to be retreating.

Meanwhile, Halsey was beginning to wonder why the Japanese carriers had not yet taken part in the battle. Shortly after Kurita reversed course, this question was answered. Ozawa's force was discovered northeast of Cape Engano on Luzon. Earlier that day Halsey had sent a signal to Pearl Harbor stating that he was forming a Task Group of battleships and would position them off the exit to San Bernardino Strait to hit Kurita's force as it came through. The message was not addressed to Kinkaid, but was intercepted by a radio operator at the latter's headquarters and passed on to Kinkaid.

Halsey's failure to communicate with Kinkaid directly

was not unusual in that the Seventh Fleet was directly subordinate to MacArthur while Halsey's Third Fleet reported to Admiral Nimitz at Pearl Harbor. Therefore, only those messages directly concerning Kinkaid were forwarded to Seventh Fleet. Nevertheless, Kinkaid had managed to intercept the transmission regarding the formation of Task Group 34, the Third Fleet's fast battleships. Accordingly, Kinkaid concluded that come what may, his rear was protected.

When Halsey learned of the presence of Ozawa's carriers, he was caught in a dilemma. Should he pursue Ozawa or continue to guard against a Japanese movement through San Bernardino Strait? Since Kurita appeared to be retreating, Halsey correctly chose to take on Ozawa. He ordered his entire fleet, including Admiral Lee's battleships, to head north in pursuit of Ozawa. Unfortunately, he failed to notify anyone of his decision. Therefore, while the Battle of Surigao Strait was in full swing, Kinkaid directed operations under the assumption that a powerful force of battleships was guarding the exit from San Bernardino Strait.

Soon after Halsey began the chase, under cover of darkness, Kurita reversed course again and headed for his scheduled rendezvous in Leyte Gulf with Nishimura and Shima. If the American communications were bad, the Japanese communications were even worse. Throughout the night Kurita attempted to contact Nishimura. Every effort went to naught. Kurita sailed blindly on unaware of the fate that had befallen Nishimura and Shima. The last transmission from the southern force was shortly after midnight when Nishimura announced that he was entering Surigao Strait. After that there was nothing.

Supporting the fighting ashore were three groups of small escort carriers. These formations were called Taffys. Adm. Thomas Sprague's Taffy 1 was off Mindanao. Taffy 2 (Adm. Felix Stump) was the closest to Leyte Gulf. North of

Stump was Adm. Clifton Sprague's Taffy 3.

At first light all three Taffys had their antisubmarine scouts in the air and were busily readying their first strikes against Japanese positions on Leyte. Lulled into a false sense of security brought about by Halsey's presence on their northern flank, Sprague's force had ignored a message from Kinkaid.

> The night before (24th) I had directed Sprague to have attack groups ready on deck (of the jeep carriers), looking forward to what might be the morning situation. I'd directed him to send one attack group down to Mindanao to get any stragglers or escapees from the night action, which he did. I'd also directed him at daylight to send a search northward along the San Bernardino Strait. I did that mostly out of curiosity to know what had gone on up there, because I thought that Lee was there with Task Force 34, and I didn't expect to find anything that we had not planned. I was quite wrong in that.
>
> Unfortunately, that search did not get off. Sprague, got off his antisubmarine patrols, and he got off an attack group against stragglers from the night action. . . .[11]

Sprague had passed the message on to Stump who was unable to get planes in the air on time.

At 6:45 a message was received on Sprague's flagship, *Fanshaw Bay*.

> Enemy surface force of four battleships, seven cruisers, and eleven destroyers sighted twenty miles northwest of your Task Group and closing on you at thirty knots.[12]

Sprague requested verification. The reply was not long in coming.

Sprague knew he was in trouble. He radioed Kinkaid that a Japanese Fleet was approaching his position and requested permission to move closer to Leyte Gulf. Kinkaid was dumfounded. Where had this enemy force come from? Was this the force that had been attacked in the Sibuyan Sea the previous day? If so, where was Lee? Why wasn't he guarding San Bernardino Strait?

Kinkaid denied Sprague's request. He preferred to risk the escort carriers rather than the helpless transports and the beachhead itself. Nevertheless, he swung into action and radioed Halsey that his force was under attack, inquiring as to the whereabouts of Lee's battleships. He also recalled Oldendorf who was far down Surigao Strait.

Far to the north, Halsey, on the *New Jersey,* was handed one frantic transmission after another. Kinkaid was asking for help. "Where is Lee?" "Send Lee." As he read the urgent messages Halsey became more and more disturbed. He was on the verge of destroying Ozawa's entire force and would not be dissuaded. Kinkaid's forces should be able to take care of any enemy fleet. Then he was handed what he considered an insulting message from Pearl Harbor.*

Incensed, Halsey ordered Lee's battleships and one Task Group of carriers to return to Leyte Gulf at full speed. But it was too late. Kinkaid's Seventh Fleet rose to the challenge.

When he was refused permission to close on Leyte Gulf, Sprague made off at his best possible speed away from the beachhead. Unfortunately, his best speed was only half that of which the enemy was capable. In a short time heavy caliber shells began to straddle Taffy 3.

The Americans fought back with everything they had.

*See Halsey—Chapter 5.

Sprague ordered his aircraft to abort their missions against Leyte and instead turn their attention to the advancing enemy fleet. Stump's planes from Taffy 2 were given the same directive. The American pilots harassed Kurita unmercifully. Those planes that were unable to land aboard their own fleeing or damaged carriers shuttled back and forth between the Japanese Fleet and a hastily prepared airfield at Tacloban. This was particularly true of Stump's planes whose round trip to their own ships would consume precious time.

Sprague also ordered his escorts, three destroyers and four little destroyer escorts, to attack the enemy with their torpedoes. Bravely the small ships raced in for the attack. Some scored hits, but three of the small boys were overwhelmed by the heavy fire of the enemy ships.

The combined counterattack managed to sink the cruisers *Suzuya*, *Chokai*, and *Chikuma*. The *Kumano* was badly damaged. Meanwhile, the heavy Japanese guns had sent the *Gambier Bay* to the bottom and inflicted heavy damage on the *Kalinin Bay, Fanshaw Bay,* and *Kitkun Bay*.

Harassed by a seemingly never-ending swarm of American planes, attacked by a force of destroyers, his proud cruisers smoking and sinking, Kurita turned tail and fled. He had been under constant attack for two days and had had enough.

Halsey caught the Japanese force moving through the Sibuyan Sea again the next day, but his attacks failed to accomplish much before bad weather put an end to air attacks. Kinkaid had been lucky. With the battle at an end, it was time for fixing the blame for the almost disaster at Samar. Was the blame Halsey's or Kinkaid's?

Actually, it was neither's. Kinkaid had rightly assumed that Halsey was protecting his rear. He had no reason to believe otherwise. As for Halsey, he had erred in not notifying anyone that he was moving north, but even had he done so, the dual command picture did not necessarily mean that he would have notified Kinkaid of his decision anyway. Halsey was operating under a conflicting set of orders to protect the American beachhead but to seize every opportunity to destroy the Japanese Fleet. The latter was just what Halsey had done when Ozawa was discovered.

Admiral King, a friend and admirer of Halsey, attempted to shift the blame to Kinkaid for whom he did not care. He attributed

> the element of surprise in the Battle of Samar not only to Halsey's absence in the north, but also to Kinkaid's failure to use his own air squadrons for search at a crucial moment.[14]

But as already stated, Kinkaid had issued orders for an air search to be carried out, the orders were simply not followed.

Following the Battle of Leyte Gulf the emphasis on fighting shifted ashore. Seventh Fleet's escort carriers continued to provide aerial cover since the Army Air Forces still lacked sufficient strength to do the job alone. The Japanese struck back viciously with their fearful Kamikazes. The Amphibious forces carrying supplies to Leyte were the prime victims. Daily, Kinkaid was handed reports of the sinking of yet another ship or two. Gamely, the Seventh Fleet maintained its constant flow of supplies to the beachhead.

The advance on Leyte was slow and threatened to upset MacArthur's timetable for the capture of the rest of the Philippines. The general therefore suggested landing a division behind enemy lines at Ormoc. Despite his reservations and the threat of enemy air attacks, Kinkaid's amphibious forces executed the maneuver in brilliant fashion on December 5. From that point forward Japanese resistance on Leyte began to collapse.

Before invading Luzon, the next major objective, MacArthur wanted to secure the central Philippines. There was an urgent need for additional air bases to cover the invasion on Luzon. Leyte was too far away and its soil and heavy rains made that island unsuitable for air bases. Consequently, MacArthur wanted to invade the island of Mindoro prior to making an all-effort assault on Luzon. At first Kinkaid objected, stating that en route to Mindoro his fleet would have to pass through the Sulu Sea where it would be an easy target for the Kamikazes. The fleet's losses had already been far too heavy. However, after considering the prospect at length, Kinkaid was able to recognize the strategic importance of having strong air cover over the beachhead on Luzon. But it was a moot point. Nimitz refused to risk the needed shipping.

MacArthur went into a tirade. He took his wrath out on Kinkaid while the admiral stood quietly by. The general railed against the navy's unwillingness to risk ships while daily the Army was risking men and tanks. For over an hour he carried on before turning to Kinkaid and saying, "But Tommy, I love you just the same. Let's go to dinner."[15]

Kinkaid was able to convince Nimitz that the capture of Mindoro was absolutely essential to the invasion of Luzon. Eventually Nimitz relented and agreed to provide the necessary shipping.

Mindoro was invaded on December 15, and was found to be lightly defended. The Americans quickly overran the handful of defenders and immediately began refurbishing the abandoned Japanese airfields. But the enemy suicide pilots operating from bases on Luzon exacted a terrible toll of the ships supporting the construction battalions.

In the first week in January, the largest naval force the Pacific war had seen to date moved northward through the Sulu Sea: destination, Lingayan Gulf on Luzon. The Japanese detected the approach of the American Fleet and struck back with a vengeance. Over fifty American ships were hit by Kamikazes during the voyage, but Kinkaid's huge fleet of over one thousand ships pressed on. On January 10, 1945, after a preliminary two-day bombardment by the fleet battleships, the huge naval force dropped anchor in Lingayan Gulf. General Krueger's Sixth Army splashed ashore and began to move inland.

In Lingayan Gulf the Kamikaze attacks reached their height of ferocity in the Philippines. Fortunately for the Americans, the Japanese pilots preferred to concentrate on warships rather than the amphibious forces. Battleships were attacked with little effect, cruisers and destroyers were hit and sent to the rear, but for the most part the amphibians' losses in relation to the vast amount of shipping were relatively light. Eventually, the efforts of Halsey's Third Fleet carriers and General Kenney's land-based Army Air Forces neutralized the Kamikaze threat until the dreadful attacks became more and more sporadic.

The invasion of Luzon was Kinkaid's last major operation of the war. After that enormous undertaking the rest seemed anticlimactic. For the next five months he was occupied moving reinforcements to Luzon and conducting landing operations on the remaining smaller islands in the Philippines. By mid-June, virtually the entire Philippine Island chain was securely in American hands.

With the final fall of the Philippines and the capture of Okinawa, the Joint Chiefs of Staff turned their attention to an invasion of Japan itself. As a compromise General MacArthur was to have overall command of the land forces while Nimitz would take charge of all naval forces including responsibility for the invasion itself. Nimitz's forces would be comprised of three powerful fleets: Halsey's Third, Spruance's Fifth, and Kinkaid's Seventh. Thus Kinkaid was placed on an equal footing with his illustrious peers of the central Pacific force. The dropping of the atomic bombs in August eliminated the necessity of invading

Japan, much to Kinkaid's relief. He was just as happy because he knew that in any invasion of the Japanese homeland both naval and land forces were likely to suffer heavy casualties.

Kinkaid returned to the States in October to a well-deserved hero's welcome. Unlike Halsey, King, and Spruance, however, he elected to remain on active duty. In January, 1946, he was commander of the Atlantic Sea Frontier. He remained in the post until 1950, when he decided to end his forty-six year naval career. On May 1, 1950, he retired.

Retirement agreed with Kinkaid. He used his leisure time to pursue his major interests (other than navy), bridge, tennis, and golf. In 1972, at the age of eight-four, Admiral Kinkaid's heart finally gave out and he passed away at his home.

Thomas Kinkaid was truly a remarkable naval commander. But his accomplishments were overshadowed either by events or other commanders. Early in the war he was subordinate to Halsey while the latter was making headlines in the Solomons. From there, Kinkaid went to an almost forgotten theater, the Aleutians, where in less than nine months he drove the Japanese from the entire area. He then moved on to the Philippines to serve under a commander who encouraged the glorification of his exploits, but was reluctant to share the spotlight. Nevertheless, despite MacArthur's frequent tirades against the Navy, the difficult general liked Kinkaid and the two got along famously. In fact, Kinkaid was one of the few subordinates who could get away with disagreeing with and talking back to MacArthur.

Kinkaid's bravery was legendary. At Santa Cruz and the eastern Solomons he refused to seek cover while swarms of Japanese planes were attacking the *Enterprise*. His eagerness to fight was demonstrated at the Battles of Guadalcanal and later in the Aleutians where his "shoot from the hip" style got things done in a hurry.

Perhaps the words of Thomas Parrish best sum up the general feeling for Fighting Tom Kinkaid.

No American naval commander in World War II was more highly respected in his own service.[16]

Notes

Introduction

1. Ronald Lewin, *The American Magic*, p. 8.
2. *Ibid.*, p. 92.
3. W. J. Holmes, *Double Edged Secrets*, p. 107.
4. *Ibid.*, p. 110.
5. Lewin, *op. cit.*, p. 188.
6. Holmes, *op. cit.*, p. 128.

Chapter 1 Footnotes

1. Thomas Buell, *Master of Sea Power*, p. x.
2. *Ibid.*, p. x.
3. Ernest King and Walter Whitehill, *Fleet Admiral King: A Naval Record*, p. 23.
4. *Ibid.*, p. 121.
5. Buell, *op. cit.*, p. 47.
6. *Ibid.*, p. 71.
7. *Ibid.*, p. 78.
8. J.J. Clark, *Carrier Admiral*, p. 45.
9. *Ibid.*, p. 64.
10. Buell, *op. cit.*, p. 114.
11. King, *op. cit.*, p. 345.
12. Buell, *op. cit.*, p. 150.
13. M. Matloff and E. Snell, *Strategic Planning for Coalition Warfare*, p. 156.
14. Robert Ferrell, ed., *The Eisenhower Diaries*, pp. 50–51.
15. Arthur Bryant, *The Turn of the Tide*, p. 279.
16. Buell, *op. cit.*, p. 190.
17. H. Stimson and M. Bundy, *On Active Service in Peace and War*, pp. 425–426.
18. Buell, *op. cit.*, p. 206.
19. Bryant, *op. cit.*, p. 445.
20. General Lord Ismay, *The Memoirs of General Lord Ismay*, p. 253.
21. M. Matloff, *Strategic Planning for Coalition Warfare 1943–1944*, p. 36.
22. William D. Leahy, *I Was There*, pp. 160–161.
23. Buell, *op. cit.*, p. 575.
24. Bryant, *op. cit.*, p. 575.
25. Leahy, *op. cit.*, p. 175.
26. King, *op. cit.*, p. 501.
27. Joseph W. Stilwell, *The Stilwell Papers*, p. 245.
28. Buell, *op. cit.*, p. 420.
29. William F. Halsey, *Admiral Halsey's Story*, p. 227.

Chapter 2 Footnotes

1. E. B. Potter, *Nimitz*, p. 175.
2. Edwin P. Hoyt, *How They Won the War in the Pacific*, p. 43.
3. Potter, *op. cit.*, p. 198.
4. Hoyt, *op. cit.*, p. 28.
5. Potter, *op. cit.*, pp. 49-50.
6. Samuel Eliot Morison, *History of United States Naval Operations in World War II, Vol. IV: Coral Sea, Midway and Submarine Actions*, p. 27.
7. Potter, *op. cit.*, p. 107.
8. John Costello, *The Pacific War*, p. 329.
9. Potter, *op. cit.*, p. 242.
10. Michael Carver, ed., *The War Lords*, p. 410.
11. Potter, *op. cit.*, p. 322.
12. *Ibid.*, pp. 368-69.
13. *Ibid.*, p. 374.
14. William Manchester, *American Caesar*, p. 381.
15. *Ibid.*, p. 374.
16. Potter, *op. cit.*, p. 395.
17. *Ibid.*, p. 395.
18. William F. Halsey, *Admiral Halsey's Story*, pp. 202-208.
19. Samuel E. Morison, *History of United States Naval Operations in World War II, Vol. XII: Leyte*, p. 109.
20. Potter, *op. cit.*, p. 406.
21. Carver, *op. cit.*, p. 417.
22. Potter, *op. cit.*, p. 445.
23. Carver, *op. cit.*, p. 418.
24. Samuel Eliot Morison, *History of United States Naval Operations in World War II, Volume XIV: Victory in the Pacific 1945*, p. 367.

Chapter 3 Footnotes

1. Michael Carver, ed., *The War Lords*, p. 452.
2. *Ibid.*, p. 460.
3. Thomas B. Buell, *The Quiet Warrior*, p. XIII.
4. *Ibid.*, p. 32.
5. *Ibid.*, p. 70.
6. *Ibid.*, p. 107.
7. F. P. Forrestal, *Admiral Raymond A. Spruance, USN, A Study in Command*, p. 26.
8. Buell, *op. cit.*, p. 122.
9. Forrestal, *op. cit.*, pp. 38-39.
10. *Ibid.*, p. 56.
11. Buell, *op. cit.*, p. 149.

12. Samuel Eliot Morison, *History of United States Naval Operations in World War II, Volume IV: Coral Sea, Midway, Submarine Actions*, p. 158.

13. Buell, *op. cit.*, p. 198.

14. Holland M. Smith, *Coral and Brass*, p. 129.

15. Buell, *op. cit.*, p. 264.

16. *Ibid.*, p. 266.

17. Smith, *op. cit.*, p. 191.

18. Ernest J. King and Walter M. Whitehill, *Fleet Admiral King*, p. 563.

19. Henry Salomon, *Victory at Sea*, p. 237.

Chapter 4 Footnotes

1. George C. Dyer, *The Amphibians Came to Conquer*, p. 1153.

2. Holland M. Smith, *Coral and Brass*, p. 110.

3. Dyer, *op. cit.*, p. 48.

4. *Ibid.*, p. 56.

5. *Ibid.*, p. 66.

6. *Ibid.*, p. 158.

7. *Ibid.*, p. 199.

8. M. Matloff and E. Snell, *Strategic Planning for Coalition Warfare, 1941–1942*, pp. 101–102.

9. *Ibid.*, p. 157.

10. Dyer, *op. cit.*, p. 302.

11. Herbert L. Merillat, *The Island*, p. 20.

12. Dyer, *op. cit.*, p. 358–359.

13. Samuel Eliot Morison, *The Struggle for Guadalcanal*, p. 25.

14. Dyer, *op. cit.*, p. 453.

15. *Ibid.*, p. 593.

16. E.P. Forrestal, *Admiral Raymond A. Spruance, USN*, p. 69.

17. Dyer, *op. cit.*, p. 627.

18. P. Crowl and E. Love, *Seizure of the Gilberts and Marshalls*, p. 74.

19. Dyer, *op. cit.*, p. 665.

20. *Ibid.*, p. 681.

21. Andrieu d'Albas, *Death of a Navy*, p. 277.

22. Dyer, *op. cit.*, p. 741.

23. *Ibid.*, p. 799.

24. *Ibid.*, p. 849.

25. *Ibid.*, p. 906.

26. *Ibid.*, p. 923.

27. *Ibid.*, p. 955.

28. *Ibid.*, p. 1008.

29. Samuel E. Morison, *History of United States Naval Operations in World War II: Vol. XIV–Victory in the Pacific, 1945*, pp. 51–52.

30. Dyer, *op. cit.*, p. 1111.

Chapter 5 Footnotes

1. William Halsey and J. Bryann, *Admiral Halsey's Story*, p. 10.
2. *Ibid.*, p. 13.
3. *Ibid.*, p. 69.
4. *Ibid.*, p. 81.
5. *Ibid.*, p. 109.
6. Benis Frank, *Halsey*, p. 55.
7. C. Salmaggi and A. Pallavisini, *2194 Days Of War*, p. 351.
8. C. Pfannes and V. Salamone, *The Great Commanders of World War II, Vol. III: The Americans*, p. 42.
9. William Manchester, *American Caesar*, pp. 332–333.
10. Burke Davis, *Get Yamamoto*, p. 9.
11. *Ibid.*, p. 196.
12. *Ibid.*, p. 196.
13. *Ibid.*, p. 196.
14. Manchester, *op. cit.*, p. 332.
15. Donald MacIntyre, *Leyte Gulf—Armada in the Pacific*, p. 135.
16. Halsey, *op. cit.*, p. 229.
17. John Winton, *The Forgotten Fleet*, p. 314.
18. Author's interview, August, 1982.

Chapter 6 Footnotes

1. Chet Shaw, ed., *The Generals and the Admirals*, p. 50.
2. *Ibid.*, p. 50.
3. Brian Garfield, *The Thousand-Mile War*, p. 161.
4. *Ibid.*, p. 184.
5. *Ibid.*, p. 184.
6. *Ibid.*, p. 224.
7. *Ibid.*, p. 231.
8. *Ibid.*, p. 232.
9. Samuel Eliot Morison, *The Two-Ocean War*, p. 265.
10. Edwin Hoyt, *The Battle of Leyte Gulf*, p. 33.
11. *Ibid.*, p. 206.
12. S.E. Smith, ed., *The U.S. Navy in World War II*, p. 864.
13. *Ibid.*, p. 864.
14. Thomas Buell, *Master of Sea Power*, p. 580.
15. William Manchester, *American Caesar*, p. 397.
16. Thomas Parrish, ed., *The Encyclopedia of World War II*, p. 339.

Bibliography

Introduction

Clark, Ronald, *The Man Who Broke Purple*, Little, Brown & Co., Boston, 1977.

Holmes, W. J., *Doubled Edged Secrets*, Naval Institute Press, Annapolis, 1979.

Kahn, David, *The Code-Breakers*, Weidenfeld and Nicolson, London, 1967.

Lewin, Ronald, *Ultra Goes to War*, McGraw-Hill, New York, 1978.

Lewin, Ronald, *The American Magic*, Farrar Straus & Giroux, New York, 1982.

Pfannes, Charles, and Salamone, Victor, *The Great Commanders of World War II, Volume II: The British*, Zebra Books, New York, 1981.

Toland, John, *Infamy*, Doubleday & Co., New York, 1982.

Van der Thoer, Edward, *Deadly Magic*, Charles Scribner's Sons, New York, 1978.

Chapter 1 Bibliography

Bryant, Arthur, *The Turn of the Tide*, Doubleday & Co., Garden City, 1957.

Buell, Thomas B., *The Quiet Warrior*, Little, Brown & Co., Boston, 1974.

Buell, Thomas, *Master of Sea Power*, Little, Brown & Co., Boston, 1980.

Churchill, Winston, *The Grand Alliance*, Houghton Mifflin Co., Boston, 1950.

Churchill, *The Hinge of Fate*, Houghton Mifflin Co., Boston, 1950.

Clark, J. J. (Jocko), *Carrier Admiral*, David McKay Co., New York, 1967.

Grigg, John, *1943—The Victory That Never Was*, Hill and Wang, New York, 1980.

Halsey, William, and Bryann, J., *Admiral Halsey's Story*, McGraw-Hill, New York, 1947.

Harriman, Averell, and Abel, Elie, *Special Envoy to Churchill and Stalin, 1941–1946*, Random House, New York, 1975.

Ismay, General Lord, *The Memoirs of General Lord Ismay*, Viking Press, New York, 1960.

King, Ernest J., *U.S. Navy at War, 1941–1945*, U.S. Navy Dept., Washington, 1946.

King, Ernest, and Whitehill, Walter, *Fleet Admiral King: A*

Naval Record, W. W. Norton & Co., New York, 1952.

Leahy, William D., *I Was There,* Whittlesey House, New York, 1950.

Matloff, M., and Snell, E., *Strategic Planning for Coalition Warfare, 1941–1942,* Office of Chief of Military History, Washington, 1953.

Matloff, M., and Snell, E., *Strategic Planning for Coalition Warfare, 1943–1944,* Office of Chief of Military History, Washington, 1959.

Morison, Samuel E., *The Two-Ocean War,* Little, Brown & Co., Boston, 1963.

Pfannes, C., and Salamone, V., *The Great Commanders of World War II, Volume II: The British,* Zebra Books, New York, 1981.

Pfannes, C., and Salamone, V., *The Great Commanders of World War II, Volume III: The Americans,* Zebra Books, New York, 1981.

Pfannes, C., and Salamone, V., *The Great Commanders of World War II, Volume IV: The Japanese,* Zebra Books, New York, 1982.

Potter, E. B., *Nimitz,* Naval Institute Press, Annapolis, 1976.

Sherwood, Robert E., *Roosevelt and Hopkins, An Intimate History,* Harper & Bros., New York, 1948.

Stimson, H. and Bundy, M., *On Active Service in Peace and War,* Harper & Bros., New York, 1947.

White, Theodore, ed., *The Stilwell Papers,* William Sloane Associates, New York, 1948.

Winton, John, *The Forgotten Fleet,* Coward-McCann, New York, 1969.

Chapter 2 Bibliography

Carver, Michael, *The War Lords,* Little, Brown & Co., Boston, 1976.

Costello, John, *The Pacific War,* Rawson Wade Publishers, New York, 1981.

Dull, Paul S., *A Battle History of the Imperial Japanese Navy,* Naval Institute Press, Annapolis, 1978.

Halsey, William F., and Bryann, J., *Admiral Halsey's Story,* McGraw-Hill Book Co., New York, 1947.

Hoyt, Edwin F., *How They Won the War in the Pacific,* Weybright and Talley, New York, 1970.

King, Ernest, and Whitehill, Walter, *Fleet Admiral King—A Naval Record,* W. W. Norton & Co., New York, 1952.

Lundstrum, John B., *The First South Pacific Campaign,* Naval Institute Press, Annapolis, 1976.

Manchester, William, *American Caesar,* Little, Brown & Co.,

Boston, 1978.

Millot, Bernard, *The Battle of the Coral Sea*, Naval Institute Press, Annapolis, 1974.

Morison, Samuel E., *History of United States Naval Operations in World War II, Volume III: The Rising Sun in the Pacific*, Little, Brown & Co., Boston, 1948.

Morison, Samuel E., *History of United States Naval Operations in World War II, Volume IV: Coral Sea, Midway and Submarine Actions*, Little, Brown & Co., Boston, 1949.

Morison, Samuel E., *History of United States Naval Operations in World War II, Volume XII: Leyte*, Little, Brown & Co., Boston, 1958.

Morison, Samuel E., *History of United States Naval Operations in World War II, Volume XIV: Victory in the Pacific*, Little, Brown & Co., Boston, 1960.

Morton, Louis, *Strategy and Command: The First Two Years*, Office of Chief of Military History, Wash., D.C., 1962.

Pfannes, Charles, and Salamone, Victor, *The Great Commanders of World War II, Vol. IV: The Japanese*, Zebra Books, New York, 1982.

Pfannes, Charles, and Salamone, Victor, *The Great Commanders of World War II, Vol. III: The Americans*, Zebra Books, New York, 1981.

Potter, E. B., and Nimitz, Chester W., *The Great Sea War*, Prentice Hall, New York, 1960.

Potter, E. B., *Nimitz*, Naval Institute Press, Annapolis, 1976.

Russell, Michael, *Iwo Jima*, Ballantine Books, New York, 1974.

Salamon, Henry, *Victory at Sea*, Doubleday & Co., New York, 1959.

Smith, Holland M., *Coral and Brass*, Charles Scribner's Sons, New York, 1949.

Toland, John, *The Rising Sun*, Random House, New York, 1970.

Chapter 3 Bibliography

Buell, Thomas, *The Quiet Warrior*, Little, Brown & Co., Boston, 1974.

Buell, Thomas, *Master of Sea Power*, Little, Brown & Co., Boston, 1980.

Carver, Michael, *The War Lords*, Little, Brown & Co., Boston, 1976.

Cortesi, Lawrence, *Pacific Breakthrough*, Zebra Books, New York, 1981.

Costello, John, *The Pacific War*, Rawson Wade Publishers, New York, 1981.

Crowl, Philip, *Campaign in the Marianas,* Office of the Chief of Military History, Washington, D.C., 1960.

D'Albas, Andrieu, *Death of a Navy,* The Devin-Adair Co., New York, 1957.

Dull, Paul, *A Battle History of the Imperial Japanese Navy, 1941–1945,* Naval Institute Press, Annapolis, 1978.

Forrestal, E. P., *Admiral Raymond A. Spruance, USN,* U.S. Govt. Printing Office, Washington, D.C., 1966.

Fuchida, Mitsuo, and Okumiya, Masatake, *Midway—The Battle That Doomed Japan,* Naval Institute Press, Annapolis, 1955.

Garand, George, and Strobridge, *Western Pacific Operations,* Historical Division, U.S. Marine Corps, 1971.

Halsey, William, and Bryann, J., *Admiral Halsey's Story,* McGraw-Hill, New York, 1947.

Hough, Frank, *The Island War,* J. P. Lippincott Co., Philadelphia, 1947.

Hoyt, Edwin, *Storm Over the Gilberts,* Mason/Charter, New York, 1978.

Hoyt, Edwin, *To the Marianas,* Van Nostrand Reinhold Co., New York, 1980.

Ito, Masanori, *The End of the Imperial Japanese Navy,* W. W. Norton & Co., New York, 1956.

King, Ernest J., and Whitehill, Walter M., *Fleet Admiral King,* W. W. Norton & Co., New York, 1952.

Lord, Walter, *Incredible Victory,* Harper & Row, New York, 1967.

Morison, Samuel E., *History of United States Naval Operations in World War II, Volume IV: Coral Sea, Midway, and Submarine Operations,* Little, Brown & Co., Boston, 1949.

Morison, Samuel E., *History of United States Naval Operations in World War II, Volume VIII: New Guinea and the Marianas,* Little, Brown & Co., Boston.

Morison, Samuel E., *History of United States Naval Operations in World War II, Volume VII: Aleutians, Gilberts, and Marshalls,* Little, Brown & Co., Boston, 1953.

Pfannes, Charles, and Salamone, Victor, *The Great Commanders of World War II, Volume IV: The Japanese,* Zebra Books, New York, 1982.

Potter, E.B., *Nimitz,* Naval Institute Press, Annapolis, 1976.

Salomon, Henry, *Victory At Sea,* Doubleday & Co., Garden City, 1959.

Shaw, Henry; Nalty, Bernard, and Turnbladh, Edwin, *Central Pacific Drive,* Historical Branch, U.S. Marine Corps, Washington, D.C., 1966.

Smith, Holland, M., *Coral and Brass*, Charles Scribner's Sons, New York, 1949.

Y'Blood, William, *Red Sun Setting*, Naval Institute Press, Annapolis, 1981.

Chapter 4 Bibliography

Bartley, Whitman, *Iwo Jima: Amphibious Epic*, Historical Branch, Govt. Printing Office, Washington, 1954.

Conner, Howard, *The Spearhead: The WWII History of the 5th Marine Div.*, Infantry Journal Press, Washington, 1950.

Costello, John, *The Pacific War*, Rawson Wade Publishers, New York, 1981.

Crowl, P., and Love, E., *Seizure of the Gilberts and Marshalls*, Office of Chief of Military History, Washington, 1955.

D'Albas, Andrieu, *Death of a Navy*, The Devin-Adair Co., New York, 1957.

Dyer, George C., *The Amphibians Came To Conquer, Vols. I and II*, Government Printing Office, Washington, 1969.

Forrestal, E.P., *Admiral Raymond A. Spruance, USN*, Director of Naval History, Washington, 1966.

Frank, Benis, and Shaw, Henry, *Victory and Occupation*, Historical Branch, U.S. Marine Corps, Washington, 1968.

Garand, G., and Strobridge, *Western Pacific Operations*, Historical Branch, U.S. Marine Corps, 1971.

Heine, Robert, and Crown, John, *The Marshalls: Increasing the Tempo*, Historical Branch, U.S. Marine Corps, Washington, 1954.

Hough, F., Ludwig, V., and Shaw, H., *Pearl Harbor to Guadalcanal*, Historical Branch, U.S. Marine Corps, Washington, 1958.

Isely, Jeter, and Crowl, P., *The US Marines & Amphibious War*, Princeton University Press, Princeton, 1951.

Matloff, M., and Snell, E., *Strategic Planning for Coalition Warfare*, Office of Chief of Military Hist., Washington, 1953.

McMillan, George, *The Old Breed*, Infantry Journal Press, Washington, 1949.

Merillat, Herbert L., *The Island*, Houghton Mifflin Co., Boston, 1944.

Miller, John, Jr., *Guadalcanal: The First Offensive*, Historical Division, Govt. Printing Office, Washington, 1949.

Morison, Samuel, *History of United States Naval Operations in WW II, Volume V: The Struggle for Guadalcanal*, Little, Brown & Co., Boston, 1975.

Morison, Samuel, *History of United States Naval Operations in WW II, Volume XIV: Victory in the Pacific, 1945*, Little, Brown & Co., Boston, 1975.

Morison, Samuel, *The Two-Ocean War*, Little, Brown & Co., Boston, 1963.

Pfannes, C., and Salamone, V., *The Great Commanders of World War II, Volume III: The Americans*, Zebra Books, New York, 1981.

Pfannes, C., and Salamone, V., *The Great Commanders of World War II, Volume IV: The Japanese*, Zebra Books, New York, 1982.

Shaw, H., Nalty, B., and Turnbladh, E., *Central Pacific Drive*, Historical Branch, U.S. Marine Corps, Washington, 1966.

Sherwood, Robert E., *Roosevelt and Hopkins: An Intimate History*, Harper & Bros., New York, 1948.

Smith, Holland M., *Coral and Brass*, Charles Scribner's Sons, New York, 1949.

Toland, John, *The Rising Sun*, Random House, New York, 1970.

Toland, John, *Infamy*, Doubleday & Co., Garden City, 1982.

Chapter 5 Bibliography

Adamson, Hans, and Kosco, George, *Halsey's Typhoons*, Crown Publishers, New York, 1967.

Buell, Thomas, *Master of Sea Power*, Little, Brown & Co., Boston, 1980.

Buell, Thomas, *The Quiet Warrior*, Little, Brown & Co., Boston, 1972.

Clark, J.J., and Reynolds, Clark, *Carrier Admiral*, David McKay Co., New York, 1967.

Coggins, Jack, *The Campaign for Guadalcanal*, Doubleday & Co., New York, 1972.

Davis, Burke, *Get Yamamoto*, Random House, New York, 1969.

Falk, Stanley, *Palaus*, Ballantine Books, New York, 1974.

Frank, Benis, *Halsey*, Random House, New York, 1974.

Halsey, William, and Bryann, J., *Admiral Halsey's Story*, Zenger Publishing, Wash., D.C., 1947.

Horton, D.C., *New Georgia*, Ballantine Books, New York, 1971.

Hoyt, Edwin, *Guadalcanal*, Stein & Day, New York, 1981.

Hoyt, Edwin, *How They Won the War in the Pacific*, Weybright & Talley, New York, 1970.

Hoyt, Edwin, *The Battle of Leyte Gulf*, Weybright & Talley, New York, 1972.

Hoyt, Edwin, *Closing the Circle*, Van Nostrand Reinhold, New York, 1982.

Jones, Ken, and Kelley, Hubert, *Admiral Arleigh (31 Knot)*

Burke, Chilton Books, New York, 1962.

King, Ernest, and Whitehill, Walter, *Fleet Admiral King*, W. W. Norton & Co., New York, 1952.

MacIntyre, Donald, *Leyte Gulf—Armada in the Pacific*, Ballantine Books, New York, 1969.

Manchester, William, *American Caesar*, Little, Brown & Co., Boston, 1978.

Morison, Samuel, *The Two-Ocean War*, Little, Brown & Co., Boston, 1963.

Pfannes, C., and Salamone, V., *The Great Commanders of World War II, Volume III: The Americans*, Zebra Books, New York, 1982.

Pfannes, C., and Salamone, V., *The Great Commanders of World War II, Volume IV: The Japanese*, Zebra Books, New York, 1982.

Potter, E.B., *Nimitz*, Naval Institute Press, Annapolis, 1976.

Rowher, J., and Hummelchen, G., *Chronology of the War at Sea, Vol. II*, Arco Publishing, New York, 1974.

Salmaggi, C., and Pallavisini, A., *2194 Days of War*, Windward, London, 1977.

Smith, S.E., ed., *The U.S. Navy in World War II*, William Morrow & Co., New York, 1966.

Winton, John, *The Forgotten Fleet*, Coward-McCann, New York, 1969.

Chapter 6 Bibliography

Buell, Thomas, *Master of Sea Power*, Little, Brown, & Co., Boston, 1980.

Coggins, Jack, *The Campaign for Guadalcanal*, Doubleday & Co., Garden City, 1972.

Cortesi, Lawrence, *Valor at Samar*, Zebra Books, New York, 1980.

Garfield, Brian, *The Thousand-Mile War*, Doubleday & Co., Garden City, 1969.

Hoyt, Edwin, *Blue Skies and Blood*, Paul S. Eriksson, Inc., New York, 1975.

Hoyt, Edwin, *The Battle of Leyte Gulf*, Weybright & Talley, New York, 1972.

Hoyt, Edwin, *Guadalcanal*, Stein & Day, New York, 1982.

Hoyt, Edwin, *How They Won the War in the Pacific*, Weybright & Talley, New York, 1970.

King, Ernest, and Whitehill, Walter, *Fleet Admiral King—A Naval Record*, W. W. Norton & Co., New York, 1952.

Leckie, Robert, *Challenge for the Pacific*, Doubleday & Co., Garden City, 1965.

MacIntyre, Donald, *Leyte Gulf—Armada in the Pacific*, Ballantine Books, New York, 1969.

Manchester, William, *American Caesar*, Little, Brown & Co., Boston, 1978.

Millot, Bernard, *The Battle of the Coral Sea*, Naval Institute Press, Annapolis, 1974.

Morison, Samuel E., *The Two-Ocean War*, Little, Brown & Co., Boston, 1963.

Palavisini, A., and Salmaggi, C., *2194 Days of War*, Windward, London, 1977.

Parrish, Thomas, ed., *Encyclopedia of World War II*, Simon and Schuster, New York, 1978.

Pfannes, C., and Salamone, V., *The Great Commanders of World War II, Volume III: The Americans*, Zebra Books, New York, 1982.

Pfannes, C., and Salamone, V., *The Great Commanders of World War II, Volume IV: The Japanese*, Zebra Books, New York, 1982.

Potter, E.B., *Nimitz*, Naval Institute Press, Annapolis, 1976.

Reynolds, Clark, *The Fast Carriers*, McGraw-Hill, New York, 1968.

Rohwer, J., and Hummelchen, G., *Chronology of the War at Sea*, Arco, New York, 1972.

Shaw, Chet, ed., *The Generals and the Admirals*, Devin Adair Co., New York, 1945.

Smith, S.E., ed., *The U.S. Navy in World War II*, William Morrow & Co., New York, 1966.

Stafford, Edward, *The Big E*, Random House, New York, 1962.

Winton, John, *War in the Pacific*, Mayflower Books, New York, 1978.